Psychological Issues in Adoption

Psychological Issues in Adoption

Research and Practice

EDITED BY DAVID M. BRODZINSKY AND JESÚS PALACIOS

Advances in Applied Developmental Psychology, Number 24
Irving E. Sigel, Series Editor

PRAEGER

Westport, Connecticut
London

Library of Congress Cataloging-in-Publication Data

Psychological issues in adoption : research and practice / edited by
    David M. Brodzinsky and Jesús Palacios.
        p.   cm. — (Advances in applied developmental psychology ; no. 24)
    Includes bibliographical references and index.
    ISBN 0-275-97970-9 (alk. paper)
        1. Adoption—Psychological aspects. 2. Adopted children—Psychology.
    3. Adjustment (Psychology) in children. I. Brodzinsky, David. II. Palacios, Jesús.
    III. Series.
    HV875.P796 2005
    362.734'01'9—dc22   2005004053

British Library Cataloguing in Publication Data is available.

Library of Congress Catalog Card Number: 2005004053
ISBN: 0-275-97970-9

First published in 2005

Praeger Publishers, 88 Post Road West, Westport, CT 06881
An imprint of Greenwood Publishing Group, Inc.
www.praeger.com

Printed in the United States of America

The paper used in this book complies with the
Permanent Paper Standard issued by the National
Information Standards Organization (Z39.48-1984).

10   9   8   7   6   5   4   3   2

Contents

Series Foreword   *vii*

Preface   *ix*

1. Contemporary Adoption in the United States: Implications for the Next Wave of Adoption Theory, Research, and Practice
Devon Brooks, Cassandra Simmel, Leslie Wind, and Richard P. Barth   1

2. Changing Attitudes of Adoptive Parents in Northern European Countries
René Hoksbergen and Jan ter Laak   27

3. Prenatal and Postnatal Risks to Neurobiological Development in Internationally Adopted Children
Megan R. Gunnar and Darlene A. Kertes   47

4. Adverse Preadoption Experiences and Psychological Outcomes
Michael Rutter   67

5. Change and Continuity in Mental Representations of Attachment after Adoption
Jill Hodges, Miriam Steele, Saul Hillman, Kay Henderson, and Jeanne Kaniuk   93

6. Beyond Adopted/Nonadopted Comparisons
Jesús Palacios and Yolanda Sánchez-Sandoval   117

7. Reconceptualizing Openness in Adoption: Implications for Theory, Research, and Practice
David M. Brodzinsky   145

8. Openness in Adoption: Outcomes for Adolescents within Their Adoptive Kinship Networks
Harold D. Grotevant, Yvette V. Perry, and Ruth G. McRoy   167

9. The Construction of Adoptive Parenthood and Filiation in Italian
    Families with Adolescents: A Family Perspective
    Rosa Rosnati   187

10. International Adoptions in Scandinavia: Research Focus and Main
    Results
    Monica Dalen   211

11. Methodological Issues in Using Large-Scale Survey Data for
    Adoption Research
    Brent C. Miller, Xitao Fan, and Harold D. Grotevant   233

12. Recent Changes and Future Directions for Adoption Research
    Jesús Palacios and David M. Brodzinsky   257

References   269

Author Index   307

Subject Index   317

About the Contributors   321

Series Foreword

It is with great pleasure that I introduce David Brodzinsky and Jesús Palacios, who have edited a major compendium of research in the field of child adoption. The editors invited an international array of authors who were asked to report on the state of the art in his or her particular specialty. The authors, major figures from the United States and western Europe, each address one of the many topics that constitute the burgeoning literature of this complex social phenomenon of adoption.

The uniqueness of this volume rests not only on the diversity of subject matter addressed in detail but also on the clarity of the exposition. The reader, whether graduate student or experienced researcher, will find the material in each chapter informative because of the care with which the chapters were written and edited. In addition, the reader will discover the various controversies that exist among the researchers and policymakers working in this field.

Brodzinsky and Palacios have made a significant contribution to the field of adoption research, providing an in-depth overview of the field, and an invaluable resource in one volume.

Irving Sigel
Series Editor

Preface

As a social service field, the practice of adoption has changed dramatically over the past few decades not only in North America but in Europe as well. In most Western countries, fewer domestically born infants are being placed for adoption than in the past. In contrast, there has been a substantial rise in international adoptions. Many of these adoptions involve children of color who have been placed transracially with Caucasian parents. In other cases, they involve children who have lived in orphanages and experienced early social deprivation. In addition, there has been an increase in foster care adoptions and special needs adoptions in many countries. Typically, these children are older at the time of placement and often have histories of prenatal exposure to alcohol and drugs, maltreatment by birth parents, and/or multiple foster care placements. Changes in adoption agency policy and recruitment practices also have resulted in a more diverse group of individuals being approved for adoptive parenthood than in the past. In fact, the goal of current social casework practice for most North American and European adoption professionals is to screen in as many different types of adoption applicants as possible rather than restricting adoption to a select group of individuals, as was the case just a few decades ago. There also has been a discernible shift in many countries toward increased openness in adoption, with agencies offering adoptive parents and birth parents the option of meeting one another, sharing identifying information, and perhaps developing a plan for ongoing contact following the adoption finalization. Taken together, these changes and others have dramatically altered the profile of the adoptive family. Adoption practice today is so complex and the structure of adoptive families so diverse that it is virtually impossible to talk about the "typical adopted child" or "typical adoptive family."

Paralleling these changes in adoption practice and adoptive family life has been a growing interest among academic researchers in studying adopted children and their parents. Some researchers have focused on this group of individuals in an effort to understand the relative contribution of heredity and environment in human development. Others have been more interested in using this population to study the role of early experience on later patterns of adaptation. The majority of social science researchers, however, have been interested primarily in adoption outcomes. Typically, these researchers have adopted a "risk" perspective, viewing adoption as a nonnormative type of family and exploring the relative adjustment of adopted children compared to their nonadopted peers. Although most of the research in this area has supported the view that adoptees are more likely than nonadoptees to manifest academic and psychological problems, a growing body of empirical data has suggested that the differences between the groups are relatively small and that the vast majority of adopted children are well within the normal range of adjustment. As a result, we have begun to see a shift in theoretical models guiding adoption research from those emphasizing risk and psychopathology to those emphasizing resilience and positive adaptation.

It was in the context of these many changes in the adoption field that we decided to organize an edited book on adoption research. Nearly 15 years ago, one of us (DB), along with another colleague (Marshall Schechter), published an edited volume, *The Psychology of Adoption*, which was one of the first efforts to organize existing theory and research on adjustment patterns in adoption triad members. Although the book was very well received in the field, the substantial changes in adoption practice and adoptive family life since that time have rendered the findings and conclusions of the contributors somewhat out of date. Because adoption policy and practice needs to be well informed by sound empirical research, we decided to invite a number of leading scholars in the adoption field to provide an overview of selected areas of contemporary adoption research. Several goals were identified. First, we wanted to update readers on current trends in adoption practice and the relationship of these trends to children's adjustment to adoption. Second, we wanted to point out new directions in adoption research, including new methodological approaches being used to explore adoption adjustment. Third, we wanted our contributors to focus not only on issues of risk in adoption but also on resilience, that is, those individual difference and contextual factors preventing, minimizing, and/or ameliorating the impact of adverse biological and social experiences on the developing child. Fourth, we wanted to represent adoption research from a variety of national perspectives. Consequently, we invited contributions from both North American and European scholars. It is our hope that this effort will foster more interest in cross-national adoption research. Finally, we were interested in exploring the connection between research and practice. As a result, the contributors were asked to include sections dealing with the practice implications of their work.

In addition to the editors, 23 other adoption scholars joined us in this project, contributing 12 chapters on adoption research. Devon Brooks and his colleagues provide an overview of contemporary adoption practice in the United States, highlighting the changes that have taken place over the past few decades and discussing the implications of these changes for the next wave of adoption theory, research, and practice. This is followed by a chapter by René A. C. Hoksbergen and Jan ter Laak examining the emergence of different generations of adoptive parents in northern European countries over the past half century and how changes in societal attitudes, beliefs, values, and practices have impacted on adoptive family life and outcomes for adopted children. Megan Gunnar and Darlene Kertes then explore an underresearched area in adoption—prenatal and postnatal risks to neurobiological development in adopted children. Following this contribution, Michael Rutter presents an overview of research on early adverse preadoption experiences and their impact on later patterns of adjustment in adopted children. Research on change and continuity in mental representations of attachment in adopted children then is discussed by Jill Hodges and her colleagues, followed by an overview of research on various individual difference and family factors in the adjustment of Spanish adopted children by Jesús Palacios and Yolanda Sánchez-Sandoval. Next, two chapters on issues related to openness in adoption are presented. The first, by David Brodzinsky, discusses the distinction between family structural openness versus communicative openness as factors in children's adoption adjustment. The second, by Harold Grotevant and his colleagues, provides an overview of findings from the Minnesota/Texas Adoption Research Project, with particular attention to outcomes for adolescents within their adoptive kinship networks. Rosa Rosnati then presents research findings on the construction of adoptive parenthood and filiation in Italian families with adolescents, followed by a chapter focusing on psychological outcomes in international adoptions in Scandinavia by Monica Dalen. Next, Brent Miller and colleagues provide a thoughtful analysis of methodological issues in using large-scale survey data in adoption research. Finally, a concluding chapter, by the editors, Jesús Palacios and David Brodzinsky, summarizes the changes that have occurred in adoption research over the past few decades and highlight directions for future research.

It is our hope that this volume will stimulate discussion and new collaboration among adoption researchers and will provide the social service field, clinicians, and other adoption professionals with the necessary current information on adoption outcomes so as to formulate sound adoption policy and develop more effective and ethical adoption practices.

Along with our contributors, we wish to thank all the adoption agencies, adoptive parent groups, adoptive parents, and adopted children who have so willingly worked with us over the years as we labored in our research to understand the psychology of adoption.

This book is dedicated to Marshall D. Schechter, MD (1921–1999), a dear friend and colleague of the first editor (DB), and a pioneering clinician, researcher, and scholar in the adoption field. It is also dedicated to Irving E. Sigel, PhD, who has been a valued friend and respected colleague to both of us for many years.

Chapter 1

Contemporary Adoption in the United States: Implications for the Next Wave of Adoption Theory, Research, and Practice

Devon Brooks, Cassandra Simmel, Leslie Wind, and Richard P. Barth

As a result of numerous societal changes over the past few decades, adoption in the United States has become an increasingly common and accepted means of family formation. It is estimated that about 1.5 million children in the United States live with adoptive parents and that between 2 and 4 percent of American families include an adopted child (Fields & Casper, 2001; Stolley, 1993). Roughly 60 percent of Americans know someone who has adopted, been adopted, or placed a child for adoption (Evan B. Donaldson Adoption Institute, 1997). Further, about two-thirds of all Americans express favorable opinions about adoption and adoptive families (Evan B. Donaldson Adoption Institute, 2002b). Over the past decade, the number of international adoptions in the United States has more than tripled, from 6,472 in 1992 to 20,099 in 2002. Though U.S. families adopted children from approximately 106 different countries in 2002, nearly three-quarters of these children came from only five sending countries, including China (25%), Russia (24%), Guatemala (11%), South Korea (8%), and the Ukraine (6%) (http://www.travel.state.gov/orphan_numbers.html). While the exact number is neither current nor reliably reported, adoption experts estimated a decade ago that about 500 U.S. children were adopted in other countries. Most of these adoptions involved black or biracial children placed in Australia, Canada, and western Europe. Adoption of American children by families in other countries is legal in the United States and occurs primarily because adoption professionals find it easier and less time consuming to place black and biracial children overseas and because some birth parents want their infants placed abroad (Smolowe, 1994). Worldwide, a recent UNICEF report describes increases in the past decade in the number of countries placing children for adoption internationally. Additionally, in many countries, international adoptions have increased as a proportion of total adoptions (Evan B. Donaldson Adoption Institute, 2002a).

In the United States, agency adoptive placements are made by public social services departments or by private agencies, both of which may also offer intercountry adoption services. In most states, independent adoptions can also be made; these are made without agency involvement—directly between the parties with the aid of a lawyer, doctor, or other intermediary— and then reviewed and approved by a judge (Brooks, Allen, & Barth, 2002). Public agency adoptions typically involve foster children with special needs, whereas independent adoptions tend to involve non–special needs children (Barth, Brooks, & Iyer, 1995). Private agency adoptions fall somewhere in between, placing children of various backgrounds and types, depending on their agency mission (Brooks et al., 2002).

Greater acceptance of "alternative" families, including single-parent, interracial, step or blended, gay and lesbian, and older-parent families, has shaped contemporary adoption across all these adoption sectors (Stacey, 2002; Sykes, 2001). In some instances, American child welfare policy has responded to societal changes and trends in both child welfare and adoption practice with new initiatives. Conversely, policy has also shaped adoption practice. In so doing, the face of not only adoptive families but of *American* families more generally has been altered.

Recently, the Adoption and Safe Families Act of 1997 (ASFA) reinforced the long-standing policy position that adoption is the preferred exit from foster care when reunification cannot be achieved. It did this by placing greater emphasis on time limits to permanency (and, under extreme circumstances, eliminating the absolute requirement to make efforts to reunify children with their biological parents) and prohibiting states from impeding interstate adoptions. Prior to ASFA, the U.S. Congress passed the Howard M. Metzenbaum Multiethnic Placement Act (MEPA) and the Interethnic Adoption Provisions (IEPA), which prohibit federally funded agencies from delaying or denying adoptive placement on the basis of race, color, or national origin of the prospective adoptive parent or child. In essence, adoption agencies are now prohibited from the presumptive and categorical consideration of race, color, or national origin when making decisions about which children to place with which families. These legislative changes, along with other adoption initiatives and efforts by private and not-for-profit agencies and organizations (e.g., the Dave

Thomas Foundation for Adoption, the Annie E. Casey Foundation, and the Evan B. Donaldson Adoption Institute), should make adoption an even more prevalent and accepted permanency option for children, particularly those who come to the attention of the public child welfare system.

At the international level, the Hague Convention on Protection of Children and Cooperation in Respect of Intercountry Adoption was an effort to reform intercountry adoption practice (Varnis, 2001). This 1993 resolution establishes minimum norms and procedures for international adoption in order to "prevent the abduction, the sale of, or traffic in children" (cited in Varnis, 2001, p. 40). The American Intercountry Adoption Act of 2000 ratified the Hague Convention. The act requires that the U.S. government or its designee monitor requests for intercountry adoption from other countries also implementing the Hague Convention. This limits some of the autonomy of independent adoption operators but is not likely to substantially alter international adoption practices within the United States.

The previously described efforts were intended to improve adoption and child welfare outcomes, including those related to child placement, adoption stability, adoptee psychosocial development, and parental satisfaction with adoption. Adoption practice historically has aimed to enhance these outcomes and therefore attempted to address the unique needs that adopted children (not exclusively those adopted through the public child welfare system) were believed to have above and beyond those of children born to their families. The view that adopted children are more vulnerable to emotional, behavioral, and academic difficulties than nonadopted children has been widely held since the early days of formal adoption practice and research and provides a rationale for the efforts to find supportive and therapeutic services that will assist adoptive families. Child welfare professionals have expressed concern that adoptive families are challenged by characteristics and experiences that disadvantage the development of their children (Barth, 2002) and are faced with such complexity that some level of stress is almost inevitable (Sykes, 2001). This stress presumably results in or contributes to poorer outcomes overall for adoptees. Because of their characteristics, particularly those related to histories of maltreatment and out-of-home placement, poor outcomes appear to be especially pronounced for public agency adoptions. Similarly, among international adoptees in both the United States and abroad, studies indicate an association between poorer outcomes and older age at the time of adoption, poor prenatal and perinatal care, a variety of health problems, and physical disabilities (Hjern, Lindblad, & Vinnerljung, 2002 [Swedish international adoptions]; Collishaw, Maughan, & Pickles, 1998 [U.K. domestic adoptions]; Triseliotis, Shireman, & Hundleby, 1997 [U.S. international adoptions]; Verhulst, Althaus, & Versluis-den Bieman, 1992

[Dutch international adoptions]). A recent metanalysis (Bimmel, Juffer, van Ijzendoorn, & Bakermans-Kranenburg, 2003) of studies of internationally adopted adolescents indicates that they exhibit more behavior problems than nonadopted adolescents do but that all differences were small. According to the researchers who conducted the analysis, "The majority of the adopted adolescents [reviewed] are well adjusted and do not display significantly more problem behaviors than do their nonadopted peers" (Bimmel et al., 2003, p. 64).

Current perspectives on adoption practice need to be reexamined on account of adoption trends, increased diversity in family forms, and advances in adoption theory and research. As a first step toward such a reexamination, this chapter describes the predominant characteristics of contemporary U.S. adoptions. In some instances, we present empirical findings in order to enrich the descriptions of characteristics, particularly when findings are from recent studies. The chapter then offers implications for adoption theory and research. We close by considering practice-related issues and implications. Given the complexity and poorer outcomes of public agency adoptions and their centrality in U.S. adoption practice, a focus of this chapter is on adoptions involving children placed through the public child welfare system. Despite this focus, we still attend to and are informed by the literature on other types of adoptions, including international, independent, private agency, and stepparent adoptions. In most cases, we believe that the issues we discuss and the implications for theory, research, and practice we consider have relevance for all adoption types as well as for adoption practice in other countries.

CONTEMPORARY U.S. ADOPTIONS

Contemporary adoption practice in the United States allows for many different kinds of adoption, which increasingly recognizes the diverse and complex characteristics and needs of adoptive children and families. In large part, three decades of adoption research reveal that adoptive children and families routinely encounter considerable challenges. The results of twin studies, national probability studies of the general population, and studies on adopted children provide evidence that adopted children have more difficulties than children raised in households with two biological parents (Barth, 2002; Hjern et al., 2002; Slap, Goodman, & Huang, 2001). These difficulties appear so far to be associated primarily with a handful of factors related to the characteristics of adoptive children and families as well as some adoption processes. Yet empirical research also reveals that poor outcomes and adoption are not inexorably linked; adoptees and adoptive families can and *do* experience positive outcomes (Brooks, 2004).

Recent attempts by researchers (e.g., Haugaard, 1998; Hjern et al., 2002; Miller, Fan, Christensen, Grotevant, & van Dulmen, 2000) to explain inconsistent and negative findings of adoption studies suggest several possible explanations, including problems resulting from the wide range of methodologies used in past adoption research, biases in referral for mental health treatment among adoptive children and parents, and the influence of the shape of the distribution of adjustment problems in adopted and nonadopted populations. Building on Haugaard's (1998) examination of research relevant to adoption and risk for adjustment problems, Miller, Fan, Christensen, et al. (2000) compared adopted and nonadopted adolescents in a large, nationally representative sample. They also examined distributions of adopted and nonadopted adolescents across a range of outcomes. Findings show that the magnitude of group differences varies by the kind of outcomes considered and that group differences are moderated by numerous demographic and background variables. Age, race, gender, family structure, and parental education are among the variables. It is unclear in this study and others, however, *why* these variables would moderate adoptee outcomes.

Also unclear is whether difficulties are more common during particular stages in the adoptive family life cycle, whether difficulties dissipate over time, and the precise role that adoption services and supports play in deterring or alleviating difficulties. Brodzinsky (1987) has proposed a model whereby adoption presents a unique set of psychosocial tasks for families. According to the model, families' abilities to master these tasks successfully predict positive outcomes for adopted children (Miller, Fan, Christensen, et al., 2000). Clearly, both adoption theory and empirical research suggest that adoption professionals would be well served by a better understanding of how particular characteristics of adoptive children and families interact with each other (as well as with formal services and social supports) to affect adoption and family processes and outcomes. As a foundation for such an understanding, we offer a description of the characteristics of contemporary adoptive children and families as they relate primarily to public agency adoptions.

Adopted Children

Accurate and current statistics on the prevalence of adoption are not available (Maza, 1999). The best available statistics and empirical research suggests that about 3 percent of U.S. children are adopted (Stolley, 1993). In part because of the passage of the ASFA, the number of public agency adoptions of children who were in foster care (also referred to as "foster care adoptions") has increased in recent years. Data from the U.S. Department of Health and Human Services (DHHS) (U.S. DHHS, 2003) indicate that 542,000 children were placed in foster care in 2001, the most recent year for which national foster care data are available. About 18 percent (50,000) of the 263,000 children exiting foster care in 2001 did so through adoption. This figure is nearly double the number of adoptions (24,000) completed in 1996. In addition to the children who were adopted, there were approximately 116,653 foster children identified as having a goal of adoption or whose parental rights had been terminated. In 2001, 35 percent of all adopted foster youth were African American, 38 percent were Caucasian, and 16 percent were Hispanic. In that same year, 45 percent of waiting children were African American, 34 percent were Caucasian, and 12 percent were Hispanic. Nearly half the children adopted from foster care who exit to adoption entered as very young children (U.S. DHHS, 2003). Among newborns who enter foster care, about one-third will exit to adoption (Wulczyn, 2002). The gender distribution of children adopted from the public child welfare system is equally divided. Slightly more than two-thirds of adoptions completed in 2001 were by married couples, 30 percent by single females, 2 percent by single males, and about 1 percent by unmarried couples. Children waited a mean of about 16 months after termination of their parental rights to be adopted (U.S. DHHS, 2003).

International adoptions in the United States have also grown over the past several decades, with significant increases following both the Korean War and the Vietnam War. In 2002, approximately 20,099 international adoptions occurred (http://www.travel.state.gov/orphan_numbers.html), more than quadrupling the number of children adopted from overseas in 1973. At that time, most international adoptions were from South America, Vietnam, and Korea (National Adoption Information Clearinghouse, 2001). Now, adoptions from China, Russia, Guatemala, South Korea, and Ukraine account for the majority of international adoptions into the United States (http://www.travel.state.gov/orphan_numbers.html). Most internationally adopted children are infants or very young children. Among those adopted in 1998, 46 percent were less than a year old at the time of adoption, 43 percent were between one and four years old, 8 percent were between five and nine years old, and 3 percent were nine years old or older (Evan B. Donaldson Adoption Institute, 2002a). Unlike international adoptions, public agency adoptions in the United States typically involve older children as well as children with other "special needs conditions," such as having a history of maltreatment and out-of-home placement; being prenatally exposed to drugs; having emotional, behavioral, and/or physical problems; belonging to a racial or ethnic minority group; and being part of a sibling group (Brooks, Wind, & Barth, 2005). In central and eastern Europe and the Commonwealth of Independent States, an estimated 1.5 million children are in out-of-home—primarily institutional—care (Evan B. Donaldson Adoption Institute, 2002a). Many of these children who are available for adoption have characteristics similar to those of U.S. adopted children with special needs.

Not every special needs adoption, however, is of a child who was placed in out-of-home care. Special needs children can also be placed for adoption independently or through private adoption agencies, domestically or internationally. Thus, it is important to distinguish between public agency adoptions, which may involve special needs children, and special needs adoptions that do not necessarily involve foster children. These two types of adoptions can be strikingly different because of the histories of maltreatment and subsequent placement in out-of-home care experienced by children adopted from the public foster care system. Further, "special needs" may also refer to nonbehavioral factors, such as membership in a sibling group or being a male, which are commonly associated with impeding the location of adoptive homes. At the same time, families who adopt independently and through private agencies do not all adopt newborns or children who have had uncomplicated early years (Barth et al., 1995). Many of the children from other countries who are placed in the United States independently or through private agencies also have special needs, preplacement experiences, and health conditions that may not be readily identified in the United States (Staat, 2002). For these reasons, a growing number of clinics specializing in international adoptions are opening across the United States.

As mentioned previously, usually associated with foster care placement is the experience for children of abuse and/or neglect, multiple and chaotic placements in out-of-home care (e.g., foster care, emergency shelters, and group homes), and older age at adoption (Barth & Berry, 1988; Pagliaro & Pagliaro, 1997; Rosenfeld et al., 1997). Prenatal exposure to alcohol or other illicit drugs and significant stress due to domestic violence or relationship instability are other characteristics commonly associated with foster care placement (Mulder et al., 2002). In her study of children in the California Long Range Adoption Study (CLAS) adopted from public and private agencies and independently, Wind (2003) found that approximately 55 percent of the entire sample had at least one special needs condition, 35 percent had one to three conditions, 11 percent had four or five conditions, and 9 percent had six conditions or more. Not surprisingly, special needs conditions were consistently more common for public agency adoptions than private agency or independent adoptions for all special needs conditions, including preadoptive foster care placement, older age at placement, prenatal drug exposure, physical abuse, sexual abuse, neglect, emotional-behavioral problems, and physical/medical disability.

While data on the outcomes of earlier generations of foster children are available (e.g., Bohman & Sigvardsson, 1990; Lahti, 1982; Nelson, 1985), understanding the development and well-being of recent populations of youth adopted through public agencies is more elusive. Researchers have surmised that foster children currently available for adoption have experienced maltreatment and instability for a longer period of time and have more problematic and complex backgrounds and needs than foster children from previous decades (Rosenfeld et al., 1997; Simmons, Allphin, & Barth, 2000). New research is emerging on the impact of placement in foster care on the well-being and later functioning of recent generations of children adopted through the public child welfare system. With longitudinal data from CLAS, for instance, Simmel, Brooks, Barth, and Hinshaw (2001) analyzed children eight years after adoption and found significant associations between rates of attention-deficit/hyperactivity disorder and oppositional defiant disorder and history of being in foster care prior to adoption. To get a more refined picture of the foster care cohort, Simmel (2001) investigated the influence of preadoptive factors in conjunction with postadoptive familial factors on adoptees' psychosocial adjustment. She found markedly disproportionate rates of internalizing (e.g., anxiety-depression) and externalizing (e.g., hyperactive and antisocial) behavior problems in the foster care adoptees compared to the non–foster care adoptees. The rates of impairment appeared early on in the adoptive placement, in the first wave of the study (two years postadoption), and persisted throughout the second and third waves of the study (four and eight years postadoption). This finding was especially striking with regard to antisocial behavior. At each wave of measurement, approximately 40 percent of the foster care adoptees displayed antisocial conduct. This percentage is far higher than what is observed in the general population of age-comparable peers. Moreover, the rate of internalizing and externalizing behavior symptomatology in this adoptive cohort exceeds the rate in the general population of latency-age children by several times.

Findings from adoption studies not focusing specifically on foster care adoptions typically indicate that adopted males are more likely to be the object of concern of adoptive parents and agencies than are adopted females. In their study of domestic and international adoptions, Barth and Brooks (1997) found gender to be the most significant predictor of the adjustment of adopted children—girls were far more likely than boys to have positive adult outcomes. In fact, gender was a stronger predictor of outcome than whether the children were adopted internationally or domestically. Among families in a study by Smith and Howard (1999), being male was strongly associated with higher problem behavior scores. The trend of poorer outcomes for adopted males is consistent with the general nonadoptive population (Andrews, Goldberg, Wellen, Pittman, & Struening, 1995). The literature, however, is inconsistent with regard to whether being male or female is associated with *increased* risk for problem behavior for adopted children. Some studies find increased risk for adopted males (Collishaw et al., 1998), while others find increased risk for adopted females (Bimmel et al., 2003; Slap et al., 2001). Still other studies find no broad difference in the relative risk for boys and girls (Feigelman, 1997). Most recently, the male foster care adoptees in Simmel's (2001) study evidenced higher *risk* for manifesting problem behaviors, though their female counterparts also displayed troubling rates of problem behaviors at every time point measured.

Other preadoptive child characteristics appear to be more consistently associated with poor adoption outcomes for foster children. Both Simmel (2001) and James (2002) found that history of neglect, sexual abuse, and multiple foster placements were critical influences on later maladaptive behavior of children from public agency adoptions. Postadoptive environmental factors, however, appear to have the capacity to moderate adoptees' behavior. For example, in Simmel's analysis, adoptive parents were asked about their sense of readiness for their adoptive placement, their knowledge of the child's background, and their interactive and discipline style with their children. Lack of parental readiness and subsequent ineffective parent–child interaction style were significantly linked to poor outcomes. The lack of parental readiness, even as early as the first wave of the longitudinal study, suggests that the less prepared the family felt for the type of child they adopted, the less able they were to regulate the child's behavior problems. In other words, despite their verbalized desire to adopt a foster child, in hindsight as well as quite early in the adoptive arrangement, many of the parents admitted that they were quite ill prepared for handling behavior problems they might encounter (and indeed *did* encounter). Anecdotal evidence from child welfare workers supports the pattern that unrealistic or unmet expectations by adoptive parents of their adopted children portend family instability (Rosenthal, 1993). Such idealized expectations have been instrumental in the disruption of adoptions as adoptive parents disclose that they never imagined the potential behavior problems could be as difficult as they end up being (Barth, 2002; Brodzinsky & Pinderhughes, 2002; Rosenthal, 1993).

Age at Adoption

Empirical findings unfailingly demonstrate that probably the most predominant child factor influencing adoption outcomes is the child's age at adoption (e.g., Hjern et al., 2002; Smith & Howard, 1999). Statistical data from the U.S. DHHS (2003) reveal that the average age of the children adopted from foster care in 2000 was 6.9 years. About 2 percent of children were less than one year old, 45 percent were between the ages of one and five, 35 percent were between the ages of six and 10, and the remaining 18 percent were 11 years or older. Studies of special needs adoption populations have supported the notion that the older the child at adoption, the more likely the chance of adoption disruption. Perhaps the first of these studies was Kadushin and Seidl's (1971), but there have been many more (Barth & Berry, 1991; Festinger, 1986; Goerge, Howard, Yu, & Radomsky, 1997; Groze & Rosenthal, 1991; Partridge, Hornby, & McDonald, 1986).

Other studies on adoption indicate that age at adoption also influences the psychosocial outcomes of adoptees. Zill's (1990) analysis of data from the National Health Interview Survey of Child Health finds that "teens adopted in infancy showed somewhat more problems, on average, than those living with both biological parents, but nowhere near as many as teens adopted after infancy nor teens who lived with unmarried mothers" (p. 110). Older children, who are also more likely to have been older when separating from their biological families, have had time to experience the deleterious effects of abuse and neglect. In addition, they may have developed closer ties to biological parents, which in turn could make integration into a new family more difficult. Older children are also more likely to have spent time in foster care and to have had previous adoptive placements (Barth & Berry, 1988), adding difficulty to the developmental task of integrating into a new family. Pinderhughes (1996) provides a model of adoptive family adjustment for special needs adoptions, particularly families adopting older children, in which there is a multilevel process occurring at the individual, dyadic, and family systems levels. The four-stage model of family readjustment and relationship formation includes anticipation, accommodation, resistance, and restabilization. The initial stage, *anticipation*, relates to both child and parent expectations and fantasies of future events and appraisal of past events. Expectations refer to adoptive family members' perception of potential benefits and problems based on preplacement assessment and preparation experiences that lead to parent perception of what the adoptee will be like and the beginnings of self-perceptions as "parent." Older adoptees will also formulate their ideas regarding their new family, home, and neighborhood. Expectations between adoptive parents and adoptees may vary widely. Perceptions of both new relationships and changes in existing relationships are anticipated. During the second stage, *accommodation*, there is a testing of expectations developed in the previous phase with adjustment in perceptions. In the third stage, *resistance*, adoptees and their families must assess personal commitment, including what compromises are acceptable. This process leads to the *restabilization* stage, in which a new equilibrium occurs with one of three resolutions—healthy integration, unhealthy integration, or adoption disruption. Healthy integration creates a balance of autonomy and dependence on relationships and the family with resolution of ambivalence. Unhealthy integration occurs with minimal changes and compromises: adjustment is expected to occur within the adoptee rather than the family system, and accordingly the adoptee may present behavior symptomatic of the unhealthy organization. Adoption disruption can occur when the conflict of integration is overwhelming and intolerable.

Prenatal Drug Exposure

Substance abuse has received considerable attention as one of the major challenges facing the American child welfare system (U.S. DHHS, 2000). It is widely believed that the dramatic increase in foster care placements in the mid- to late 1980s resulted in part from the crack cocaine epidemic. Children prenatally exposed to cocaine and other illicit drugs are often placed in foster care shortly after birth either because of their own medical problems or because of abuse or neglect by their parents (Barth & Brooks, 2000). Reliable data on the number of foster care agency adoptions involving prenatally drug-exposed children are unavailable. However, some estimates place the percentage of children in foster care with parents having substance abuse problems as high as 80 percent (McNichol & Tash, 2001; Murphy et al., 1991). In many of these instances, prenatal drug exposure coexists along with severe early and chronic maltreatment. In addition, issues such as exposure to family and neighborhood violence and suffering from serious health impairments (e.g., HIV infections) are increasingly evident in foster children (General Accounting Office, 1994). Severe predisposing backgrounds therefore may necessitate the delivery of psychiatric, medical, and specialized educational services to address the problematic behaviors of prenatally drug-exposed foster and adopted children (see Rosenfeld et al., 1997). Although research on the characteristics and outcomes of prenatally drug-exposed adopted children is sparse, findings from relevant studies indicate that drug-exposed children are indeed prone to a variety of physical, behavioral, emotional, and educational problems (Barth & Needell, 1996) and that their outcomes can be mediated by postnatal environmental influences (Brooks & Barth, 1998).

Adoptive Families

In addition to the changing characteristics of adopted children, the characteristics of adoptive families and the way they adopt has evolved over the past few decades. In general, there has been an increase in the incidence or acceptance of several types of adoption that were formerly considered nontraditional adoptions, including international, transracial, open, gay and lesbian, and kinship adoptions.

International Adoptions

Studies of internationally adopted children in the United States and worldwide have addressed various aspects of children's psychosocial well-being and outcomes. Many of these studies find that children who are older at the time of adoption (and arrival in receiving countries) frequently exhibit a variety of health problems, such as malnutrition, skin problems, intestinal parasites, hearing difficulties, and physical disabilities (see Triseliotis et al., 1997). Studies on language development in international adoptees are inconclusive. Some researchers express concern over linguistic developmental problems that appear to be common among international adoptees (Dalen, 1988; Gardell, 1979; Hene, 1988). Researchers on a number of Dutch cross-sectional and longitudinal studies, however, indicate that they failed to detect any significant problems with language acquisition in their studies (Alstein & Simon, 1991; Schaerlakens & Dondeyne, 1985, cited in Triseliotis et al., 1997).

In light of the complexity of adjustment within a newly formed adoptive family and health- and language-related challenges, it is reasonable to expect international adoptees to experience difficulty with emotional and behavioral adjustment. Yet it appears that the majority of international adoptees overcome initial emotional and behavioral problems. Long-term problems are generally associated with older age at the time of arrival (Bagley, Young, & Scully, 1993; Gardell, 1980; Gunnarby, Hofander, Sjölin, & Sundelin, 1982; Hofvander, 1978, cited in Triseliotis et al., 1997; Simon, Altstein, & Melli, 1994). In the United States, Feigelman and Silverman (1983) studied adoptive parent perception of long-term adjustment of transracial adoptees from Colombia and Korea. They found that after six years in adoptive placement, transracial adoptees were as well adjusted as their in-racially adopted counterparts. Korean transracial adoptees demonstrated better adjustment than white in-racial adoptees. Additional research has found equal adjustment in peer relationships, self-concept, educational achievement, and self-esteem among Korean, Vietnamese, Latin American, and domestic transracial adoptees in Germany (Kuhl, 1985). A study of children from Thailand who averaged 10 months of age at arrival were reported to have positive parent–child relationships, positive school behavior, and a more positive attitude about school than nonadopted peers (see Triseliotis et al., 1997).

International transracially adopted children typically have closed adoptions; that is, they have no continuing contact with their biological parents. Nor do they have exposure to their countries of origin. At very early ages, then, they recognize physical differences between themselves and their adoptive families. Such differences can impact issues of attachment and sense of belonging within the family. As these children mature, they often struggle with a "double consciousness" (Stonequist, 1935, p. 96, cited in Friedlander, 1999) wherein two cultures are identified with simultaneously while at the same time experiencing some sense of alienation from both.

In some ways, the cultural experiences of children adopted internationally are similar to those who, within their countries of origin, are adopted transracially (i.e., by parents of a different racial or ethnic background). However, Friedlander (1999) identifies notable distinctions between the experiences of these two groups. First, children adopted internationally tend to be adopted in infancy and therefore have no direct memory of their cultures of origin. Because they are separated from their culture of origin, the formation of ethnic identity is likely more complex for international adoptees. They also may have little opportunity to engage in relationships with others from their culture of origin. Because of the absence of this reference group, the young child is likely to have difficulty understanding the meaning of being of a particular ethnic group. Second, international adoptees with Caucasian physical features are less likely to experience the same level of racism that those in racial or ethnic minority groups confront (Feigelman & Silverman, 1983).

Domestic Transracial Adoptions

Related in part to concerns about the exposure of children of color to racial and ethnic discrimination, transracial placements in the United States were historically regarded less favorably than in-racial placements and acceptable only when a child could not be placed in a racially matched home or in other special circumstances (Brooks, Barth, Bussiere, & Patterson, 1999). In nearly all instances, domestic transracial placement involves African American children and other children of color who are adopted by Caucasian parents (Barth et al., 1995). Because of the recent passage of MEPA and IEPA, the number of transracial adoptions is likely to grow. Available federal data do indicate an increase in the adoptions of African American and Hispanic children since the passage of MEPA and its provisions, but most of these increases have been attributed to kinship adoptions (Wulczyn, 2002). Success of MEPA and the IEPA relies on the availability of prospective adopters. Brooks, James, and Barth (2002) examined adoptive parents' preferences for certain characteristics in adopted children in order to determine whether current child welfare policies are sufficient for achieving permanency through adoption for available foster children. The researchers analyzed preferences by Caucasian parents (who constitute the largest pool of prospective adopters) for available foster children, including African American children, Latino children, older children, drug-exposed children, and children needing to be adopted along with a sibling. Based on their findings, Brooks et al. conclude that child welfare agencies will likely continue to have success locating adoptive families for infants and very young children as well as for Caucasian children. They have some concerns, however, about the ability of child welfare agencies to locate adoptive families for foster children of color and children with special needs.

Regardless of the impact of recent legislative changes, there will continue to be domestic transracial adoptions, and those adoptions will more than likely reflect some of the demographic changes already described. They may involve, for example, open adoptions or adoptions by gay men or lesbians. But little direction exists for understanding the complexities and needs of contemporary transracial adoptive families. Only a small number of empirical studies have adequately addressed issues relevant to the psychosocial development of prior generations of transracial adoptees.

Although there is considerable disagreement over the interpretation of the findings from these studies, most find that the experience of being adopted transracially does not harm children's psychological well-being per se (Bagley et al., 1993; Brooks, in 2004; Brooks & Barth, 1999; Fanshel, 1972; Feigelman & Silverman, 1983; Grow & Shapiro, 1974; Ladner, 1977; Shireman & Johnson, 1986; Simon et al., 1994; Vroegh, 1992). Findings do suggest, though, that transracial adoptees are highly acculturated to the majority, Anglo-American culture and have weak affiliations and identifications with others from their same racial, ethnic, and cultural group(s) (Andujo, 1988; Brooks, in press; McRoy, Zurcher, Lauderdale, & Anderson, 1982). Race, ethnicity, and gender appear at least to moderate the outcomes of transracial adoptees. In a 19-year follow-up study by Brooks and Barth (1999) of young- and middle-age adults who were adopted in the 1970s, females were found to have better social adjustment than males (as did individuals adopted from Asia) when compared to either African American or Caucasian domestically adopted individuals. Among domestic and international transracial adoptees, African American males appeared most prone to adjustment problems, but in-racially adopted Caucasian males were found to have the worst outcomes of adoptees overall.

Conceptual and methodological limitations typical of adoption studies in general also characterize studies on transracial adoption. Notwithstanding these limitations, there is little theoretical guidance for interpreting mixed findings of transracial adoption studies, particularly concerning the role of racial, ethnic, and/or cultural background and identification on the development and psychosocial adjustment of transracial and international adoptees. Steinberg and Hall's (2000) adoption awareness model is a notable exception. Their model proposes five stages through which transracially adoptive parents and adopted children progress individually and as a family. In the first stage, called *preconscious,* adoptees lack awareness of their adoption, and the adoptive parents believe that adoption and race do not matter. In the second stage, called *contact,* there is a realization of the ways in which transracially (domestic or international) adoptive families are treated and perceived differently and sometimes more negatively than either in-racially adoptive or biological families. Individuals may then move to the stage of *disintegration,* in which adoptees attempt to surround themselves with similar others and adoptive parents desire to change their communities. In the fourth stage, *internalization,* adopted children believe that transracially adoptive families are neither better nor worse than other families and make efforts not to stand out, while transracially adoptive parents accept that there are limits to what they can change. In the final stage of the model, *immersion/emersion,* transracial adoptees embrace themselves as both adopted people and people of color in an adoptive family, and transracially adoptive parents develop a sense of balance about what they can and cannot do about racism and "adoptism" and comfortably integrate aspects of their children's culture within the adoptive family. Empirical investigation of this model is under way.

Open Adoptions

Open adoption typically refers to the maintenance of contact between adoptive and biological families following the placement of adopted children. Contact can differ in terms of who initiates and is involved in the contact, including the adopted child, adoptive parents, biological parents, or other adoptive and biological relatives. Contact can also differ in form (e.g., information, pictures, gifts, letters, telephone calls, face-to-face visits), frequency, and duration. In short, open adoptions are unlike traditional, closed adoptions in that the latter generally involve the termination of *all* contact between adoptive and biological families and the former do not (Frasch, Brooks, & Barth, 2000). The practice of placing children in open adoptions has become standard in some agencies in the United States (Etter, 1993).

To date, most examinations of openness focus on infants and children adopted independently or through private agencies (e.g., Grotevant, McRoy, Elde, & Fravel, 1994). Only one significant study, the CLAS (see Frasch et al., 2000), has examined the use of open adoption with public agency adoptions. Findings from the third wave of CLAS (eight years postadoption) reveal that while the practice of openness is dynamic over time, there is remarkable stability in levels of contact and communication with the child's biological family. Almost 40 percent of families began with a closed adoption and reported no contact with the biological family during the eight years following adoption. About a quarter had contact with the biological family at or immediately after the placement and have continued to have some form of contact with them. The remaining one-third of families had significantly changed their arrangement, either starting contact when there was none or stopping contact altogether. Families in the study involved in open adoptions actually had very little contact with their children's biological family—only about one to three contacts per year by mail, by telephone, or in person. Some adoption professionals maintain that openness reduces the identity conflicts and confusion that adopted children in closed adoptions often experience, particularly during adolescence (Kirk, 1964). Other professionals (e.g., Kraft, Palumbo, Mitchell, Woods, & Schmidt, 1985b) suggest that continued contact with the biological parents interferes with the bonding process between the adoptive parents and child and that rather than easing the identity confusion that adoptees may experience, openness will only contribute to it (Blotcky, Looney, & Grace, 1982). While Frasch and her colleagues did not examine the impact of openness and contact on adopted children's psychosocial development, they suggest that given the limited contact observed in their study by families with open adoptions, it is unlikely that openness detrimentally affects adopted children's development.

Gay and Lesbian Adoptions

Increasingly, gay men and lesbians are exploring their parenting options by way of adoption (Brooks & Goldberg, 2001). Brodzinsky, Patterson, and Vaziri (2003) recently completed a nationwide study of the policies, practices, and attitudes of public and private adoption agencies with regard to gay and lesbian prospective adoptive parents. Based on findings from their study, the researchers concluded that about 2.9 percent of public and private adoptions involve children placed with self-identified gay and lesbian individuals and couples. This estimate, the researchers point out, is likely to underestimate the actual percentage of adoptions involving gay and lesbian individuals and couples because many individuals are unlikely to openly identify themselves as homosexual at the time that they submit an adoption application and because their study sample included only adoptions that were facilitated by licensed agencies. Other findings from the study reveal that about two-thirds of adoption agencies in the sample accepted applications from single gay men and lesbians. More than one-third of agencies were reported to have completed at least one adoption involving a gay or lesbian adult within the two-year period under study. Agencies that place special needs children for adoption were found to have more favorable attitudes about gay and lesbian individuals as prospective adoptive parents and were more likely to recruit these individuals and make placement of children into their homes. Despite the willingness of adoption workers to recruit gay men and lesbians as adoptive parents, several states have statutory bans on adoption of children by homosexual individuals, and adoption of children by gay and lesbian families remains controversial in the United States.

In addition to the study by Brodzinsky et al. (2003), only one other to date has addressed gay and lesbian adoptions. Brooks and Goldberg (2001) explored issues related to the placement of children with gay and lesbian adoptive and foster families. Their findings suggest that gay men and lesbians who adopt may have special strengths that make them particularly suited for adoptive parenting. These strengths include having extended networks of family and friends to assist them in caregiving activities, psychological stability, resourcefulness, sensitivity, educational accomplishments, and financial security. At the same time, Brooks and Goldberg found that subjects in their study—child welfare workers and gay and lesbian adoptive and foster parents—minimized and often dismissed the unique challenges of gay and lesbian placements. Subjects generally insisted that gay and lesbian adoptive families were no different than heterosexual adoptive families, though studies have shown that children raised in families in which a parent is gay or lesbian are often subjected to expressions of homophobia from others and discrimination because of their parents' sexual orientation. We know of no comprehensive review of international practices regarding adoption by gay and lesbian individuals and couples. Nevertheless, we are aware that such adoptions have been keenly debated in some countries (e.g., Sweden and the Netherlands) because of the concern that internationally adopted children have a disproportionate number of adverse outcomes (see Hjern et al., 2002), presumably from challenges resulting from negative preadoptive backgrounds and experiences—challenges that could be exacerbated by placement with gay or lesbian families.

Kinship Adoptions

As noted earlier, recent policy changes in the child welfare system have enhanced efforts toward securing permanent homes for children in the foster care system. At the same time, the number of children both reported to child welfare services and residing in the foster care system has grown dramatically (Pecora, Whittaker, Maluccio, & Barth, 2000; Schwartz, 2002). To contend with this burgeoning caseload and with the concomitant decline in traditional, family foster homes, many states have relied on kin caregivers. Although accurate data on the number of children living in kinship care are unavailable, there is evidence of a growing nationwide trend toward this practice. The U.S. Department of Health and Human Services (2002) reports that for 2000, about 21 percent of foster care adoptions were kinship adoptions compared with 15 percent in 1998. These adoptions involve the placement of children with their biological grandparents or other relatives. Some state statutes provide a preference for adoptive placement with kin, but these preferences do not create a general right for the relative to adopt. Rather, the statutes require only that the courts first consider whether adoption by a relative will be in the best interests of the child. In states with statutory preferences for kin, courts retain a considerable amount of discretion when determining what is in the best interests of the child. Moreover, though this discretion allows judges to make decisions based on the individual circumstances of the child, the statutes provide little guidance on how to evaluate the importance of biological relationships. This lack of clarity has resulted in substantial variation among states regarding the importance placed on familial relationships, even in states where the legislature has expressed a statutory preference for kinship adoptions (Oppenheim & Bussiere, 1996). While there is a substantial literature on kinship foster care (e.g., Brooks &

Barth, 1998; Mason & Gleeson, 1999; Schwartz, 2002) and a burgeoning literature on kin guardianships (Testa, 2002), no recent study has examined contemporary, formal kinship adoptions.

IMPLICATIONS FOR ADOPTION THEORY, RESEARCH, AND PRACTICE

Thus far, the primary focus of this chapter has been on the many changes that have taken place in adoption over the past few decades. We turn now to the implications of these changes for adoption theory, research, and practice.

Implications for Theory

Many perspectives on the adjustment of adoptees are offered in the adoption literature, including vulnerability due to object loss (Blum, 1983; Brodzinsky, 1987), failure of adoptive parents to successfully incorporate multiple roles (Brodzinsky, 1987), cognitive-developmental factors contributing to the child's understanding of the meaning of adoption (Brodzinsky, 1984, 1987), attachment-separation-loss processes (Bowlby, Ainsworth, Boston, & Rosenbluth, 1956), and biological processes (Deutsch et al., 1982; Loehlin, Willerman, & Horn, 1982). Most recently, however, the resilience paradigm, which focuses on positive adaptation despite adversity, has gained popularity and demonstrates strong applicability to adoptive family systems. In this context, adversity (or vulnerability) is often referred to as risk and is related to negative life circumstances or experiences (or risk factors) that research has demonstrated as being associated with problematic psychosocial adjustment. Conversely, positive life circumstances or experiences are referred to as protective factors. The eco-transactional model of resilience emphasizes the dynamic processes within and across physiological, psychological, environmental, and sociological domains wherein the impact of early experiences such as adoption, maltreatment, multiple placements, and prenatal assaults are viewed contextually, with consideration of both risk and protective factors, across different levels of the individual's ecological system (Cicchetti, 1996).

Central to understanding biopsychosocial development for adoptees from a resiliency perspective, then, is the interaction between individual vulnerability and environmental factors. That is, a single individual vulnerability may have some influence on development, but when combined with an environmental stressor such as family adversity, the probability of negative influence is far greater. In public agency adoptions, adoptees bring a level of individual vulnerability (e.g., gender and prenatal drug exposure) and postnatal/preadoptive vulnerability (e.g., history of maltreatment, multiple foster care placements, and out-of-home placements) that then interact with postadoptive factors (e.g., adoptive family characteristics and the adoptive family environment) to impact adoption and family processes and outcomes.

Interest in adoption as a mediating factor that improves child outcomes has led to consideration of issues specific to adoption and development within a life cycle framework. The adoption life cycle framework provides understanding of salient adoption issues over time. The adoptive family is and exists within an adoptive family network with specific developmental tasks associated with various systems within that network. The adoptive life cycle combines generalized phases and associated tasks of the life cycle framework (Carter & McGoldrick, 1980) as well as key tasks in each phase specific to the adoptive family network (Brodzinsky, 1987; Brodzinsky & Pinderhughes, 2002; Brodzinsky, Smith, & Brodzinsky, 1998; Hajal & Rosenberg, 1991; Rosenberg, 1992).

Clearly, both perspectives—resilience and adoptive family life cycle—can be applied to contemporary adoptive children and families. The eco-transactional model of resiliency offers general recognition of the interaction between pre- and postadoptive risk and protective factors at multiple levels of the ecological system and can easily be understood in relation to adoption adjustment. The adoptive family life cycle enhances that understanding by providing the contextual basis for adoption adjustment over time by specifying predictable developmental tasks that challenge adoptive families at different phases of the family life cycle. However, neither model explicitly incorporates the diverse structures present within contemporary adoptive families vis-à-vis contemporary nonadoptive families or considers differences in terms of adoption type, and only recently have the models been used to guide empirical investigations on adoption processes and outcomes.

Implications for Research

Before considering more fully the implications of adoption trends and characteristics of contemporary adoptive families for research, a brief overview of the status of adoption research is needed. Given its long history within child welfare, adoption research is not as well developed as it should be. Approximately a decade ago, in his review of adoption research, Barth (1994) wrote, "Recent years have witnessed a devastated infrastructure of adoption indicators, little basic adoption research, and the absence of rigorous adoption services research" (p. 625). Since then, despite considerable efforts among adoption and social science researchers, gains in adoption knowledge have been only modest. For the most part, adoption studies have been exploratory or descriptive and characterized by varied methodological limitations. For instance, although a number of longitudinal studies have been conducted (for a brief overview of these studies, see

Brodzinsky et al., 1998), most adoption studies rely on cross-sectional data. Use of cross-sectional studies limits application to the diversity of issues that emerge across the adoptive family life cycle. Further, simplistic or only partial conclusions result when data are from one point in time and are collected soon after the adoption. Development of the child and the family system that must accommodate the child are dynamic processes that take place over time. Adjustment to those processes may vary at different periods for all families, both birth and adoptive (Glidden & Johnson, 1999).

Further, heterogeneity in findings from previous studies may be due to the diversity within adoptive populations studied and samples that are not representative or adequate in some way. Studies including children in their samples or in which the unit of analysis is the child often fail to describe, examine, or control for characteristics of the adopted child (e.g., infant vs. older child, special needs vs. non–special needs) and of the adoption (e.g., transracial vs. in-racial, domestic vs. international, public vs. private or independent).

Measurement problems also abound in adoption research. Inadequate assessment of symptomatology due to nonstandardized assessment tools and nonblind diagnosticians are especially problematic (Haugaard, 1998; Wierzbicki, 1993). Warren (1992) cautions acceptance of findings based on tainted perceptions of adoptive parents and professionals who may be prone to overattribute slight behavior problems to adoption. Most adoption studies are based on parent report via survey. Exceptions include Brodzinsky, Schechter, Braff, and Singer (1984), who used a multi-informant approach with both parent and teacher reports of children's adjustment; Lightburne and Pine (1996), who utilized observation, audiotaping, and interviews combining qualitative and quantitative data; McDonald, Lieberman, Partridge, and Hornby (1991) and Daly and Sobol (1994), who surveyed agency personnel; and Phillips (1988) and Kramer and Houston (1998), who interviewed parents. In a study of psychosocial outcomes in in-racial and transracial adoptees, Brooks (2004) analyzed the agreement between adoptee adjustment data provided by both adoptive parents and the adult adoptees. Nonsignificant paired differences were found between the two reports. The evidence that parent reports are a reliable method of collecting data about adoptees, suggests Brooks, should encourage adoption researchers.

The literature almost unequivocally identifies the need for both pre- and postadoption support; however, little empirical data are available on the differences in provision of preparatory information and support or utilization of postadoption services based on differing adoptive family structures, type of adoption, or the child's type(s) of preadoptive risk history. In addition, adoption research has yet to examine the interaction between child and family characteristics, the child's preadoptive risk history, and the provision of preparatory information and support, utilization of postadoption services, and effectiveness of adoption services on adoptee outcomes. And although there is agreement that adoptive family needs change during the course of the life cycle, little is known about how these changes further complicate provision of effective services over the life cycle. Understanding the transactional influences of adoptive child and family characteristics, the child's preadoptive risk history, the provision of preparatory information and support, and adoption services utilization over time is therefore imperative to the effective support of successful adaptation of adoptive families, especially those with special needs children.

Despite considerable knowledge gaps and study limitations, social science researchers have acquired some important insights into adoption—just as the characteristics of adoption and the context in which it is practice began to change. Nevertheless, findings from some empirical studies suggest that adoption may be either a risk factor or a *proxy* for risk with regard to some psychosocial outcomes (Miller, Fan, Christensen, et al., 2000). At the same time, other studies show that adoptees are similar to non-adoptees (Brand & Brinich, 1999; Glidden, 1991). Recent efforts (e.g., Haugaard, 1998; Peters, Atkins & McKay, 1999) to explain negative and mixed findings often point to flawed and incomparable methodologies such as those discussed previously—characterizing adoptions studies. Aside from its inherent appeal, the resilience paradigm is almost certainly attractive to adoption researchers, who can use it to explain why certain characteristics are associated with poor outcomes in some studies and not in others. Yet the varied and inconsistent findings in the adoption literature are not necessarily problematic if they indicate the *range* of factors that may need considering. There are points—rather, areas—of convergence in the literature. For example, studies generally indicate that although genetic or heritable factors have been found to exert a major influence on individual differences in outcomes, environmental variations can enhance those outcomes.

But compared with some of the genetic and heritable characteristics of children, the impact of environmental factors (both postnatal/preadoptive and postadoptive) is less clear (Barth, 2002). Based on findings from their study of the potential links between early risk and problematic developmental outcomes in adopted children, Grotevant, Ross, Marchel, and McRoy (1999) promote the consideration of early risk factors (i.e., prenatal, perinatal, and preadoptive) and later, environment factors (e.g., postadoptive), independently and together. Indeed, the growing literature on resilience suggests that it is the *accumulation* of risk factors rather than the presence of one or two that affects children's development (Fraser, 2004; Garbarino, 1992; Seifer, Sameroff, Baldwin, & Baldwin, 1992). Findings from Wind's (2003) study examining the preadoptive risk histories of adoptees demonstrate that environmental risk factors account for 42 percent of the variance in service utilization and that genetic risk factors account for another 13 percent of the variance. Total cumulative risk was associated with greater utilization of adoption services. It is important to note, however, that Wind did not examine postadoptive, environmental factors, such as collaboration in relationships or family cohesion.

Given the characteristics of contemporary adoption, we turn now to implications for adoption research. As we see it, perhaps the most important challenge for the next wave of adoption research pertains to the *goal* of the research; it must be explanatory. While additional descriptive data are needed, it is essential that social science researchers aim to provide evidence-based data from studies that test interventions. Evidence-based, intervention research is the most direct route to knowledge about risk and protective factors for adoptive children and families, best practices, and effective preventive and rehabilitative services, including clinical interventions, programs, social supports, and policies. The characteristics of contemporary adoptive families make clear that adoption research can no longer rely on a "one size fits all" approach. Rather, research must acknowledge the complexities of adoption and family processes and adjustment within the context of widely diverse adoptive family structures and an increasingly diverse society.

As social scientists strive to test interventions designed essentially to ameliorate and prevent risk, they must be mindful of the methodological problems that have characterized past research on adoption. Advances in adoption knowledge will require a clear theoretical foundation and longitudinal study with large samples comprised of multiple informants and nonclinical adoptee subjects. The importance of using standardized measures to assess child, parent, and family outcomes appears to be fairly unanimous in the child welfare research literature. Such measures will allow valid and reliable comparison of intervention outcomes across programs, counties, states, and even countries. In short, we encourage social science researchers to aim toward the conduct of research more rigorous than past decades—highly controlled and generalizable *cross-cultural* research that captures the complex, multifaceted, and dynamic nature of contemporary adoption and family life.

Implications for Practice

Practice with adoptive families and services to prepare and support them for adoption vary widely. Preadoption services, for instance, range from extensive preplacement, multisession group educational and self-evaluative programs combined with individual and couple interviews to preplacement screening protocols designed to screen out criminals and others considered unsuitable as parents. Provision of comprehensive and accurate information to potential adoptive parents is highly desired by families during the preparatory phase. This aspect of adoption appears to be especially crucial for families adopting children with special needs (Sar, 2000). Several studies have found that families receiving thorough preparation (e.g., accurate child psychosocial history and discussion of separation and loss, attachment, family communication, behavior management, and importance of social support) demonstrate more realistic expectations for the adoption. Studies have further revealed that realistic expectations strongly reduce the likelihood of adoption disruption and enhance positive adoption adjustment (Barth & Berry, 1988; Brodzinsky & Pinderhughes, 2002; Partridge et al., 1986; Sar, 2000). Parental knowledge of children's special needs conditions or information about raising children with special needs may challenge prospective parents' perceptions about and expectations for adoption. For some prospective adoptive parents, this challenge will result in a decision not to accept particular children or children with particular special needs.

Wide variation also exists in the services offered to adoptive families after the child has been placed but before finalization of the adoption. Though preadoption and prelegalization adoption services historically have been readily available to adoptive families, postadoption services have been scarce (Berry, 1990). In recent years, however, there has been a steadily growing realization by child welfare professionals and social science researchers of the importance of postadoption services (Barth & Miller, 2001). Consequently, postadoption services are one of the fastest-growing sectors of American child welfare services. This growth has been spurred by the sharp increase in adoptions, by federal and state legislative mandates to provide postadoption services, and by incentives to states in the form of federal adoption bonuses and adoption preservation funds. Still, they continue to be minimally available through public child welfare agencies to large numbers of adoptive families except on an informal or occasional basis. To meet the need, private and not-for-profit adoption agencies and organizations have long offered educational programs and support groups for adoptive families. Some groups formed during the adoption process continue informally without professional agency assistance (Brooks et al., 2002).

Adoption service need, use, and helpfulness vary by the type of adoption—that is, whether it is a public agency, a private agency, or an independent adoption. Findings from a CLAS-derived study by Brooks et al. (2002) reveal that less than 30 percent of adoptive families used postadoption services. Considerably higher percentages of adopters read books and articles on adoption and attended lectures or seminars on adoption. Most adopters who received services found them helpful. Adopters of all types expressed a strong desire for material information about their adopted child's background and history as well as for ongoing informational resources to help them in raising their children. Brooks and his colleagues found that more public agency than private agency or independent adopters used child counseling, family therapy, and intensive crisis counseling. Compared with other adopters, fewer public agency adopters read books and articles on adoption, and of these, significantly fewer found the material helpful. Private agency adopters read books and articles and participated in support groups for both parents and children more often than public agency and independent adopters. Independent adopters generally made the least use of postadoption services of any kind. In discussing their findings, the researchers note that most of the public agency adopters in their study adopted children with special needs, including histories of maltreatment and multiple foster home placements. These children also were more likely to have been prenatally exposed to drugs and tended to be older than children adopted through other auspices. Further, respondents adopting children through public agencies were more likely than other adoptees to be single, had attained lower levels of formal education, and had lower incomes. The findings suggest that public agency adopters have a greater need for clinical services than do private agency and independent adopters (who appear to be more interested in informational services) because of differences in child and adoptive parent characteristics.

Although adoption, especially public agency and special needs adoption, may present multiple challenges for adoptive children and families, research indicates that these challenges have not negatively influenced the course of adoptive placements. Despite the surge in public adoptions, for example, there has been no parallel rise in adoption disruption (Barth, Gibbs, & Siebenaler, 2001). Moreover, difficult adoption experiences do not appear to discourage adoptive parents. Parents who adopted special needs children from public agencies reported high rates of satisfaction with their adoptions in studies by Brooks et al. (2002) and Howard and Smith (2000). Still, we would be remiss not to acknowledge the complexities of and potential challenges for public agency and special needs adoptions. Knowing that there are familial aspects that can be enhanced, such as parental knowledge and preparedness, to increase the probability of a positive adoptive placement and outcomes should fuel more targeted service provision toward these precarious arrangements.

In closing, successful adoption practice requires an understanding of the complex nature of risk and resilience as it relates specifically to adoptive families but also as it relates to families in general. Also required is knowledge about issues likely to be encountered by adoptive families during more or less predictable phases of adoption adjustment as well as the possible influence of multiple risk and protective factors that can interact with one another and result in a range of outcomes during the phases

(LeVine & Sallee, 1990). Further, how these factors interact similarly and differently with one another depending on other factors—related to adoption or not—and context must also be part of the equation for understanding family processes and outcomes for contemporary adoptive families both in the United States and abroad.

Chapter 2

Changing Attitudes of Adoptive Parents in Northern European Countries

René Hoksbergen and Jan ter Laak

In his book *Adoptive Kinship,* the Canadian sociologist David Kirk, a pioneering researcher in the adoption field, stressed that "adoptive kinship is a pattern of social relationships as well as a legally established social institution" (Kirk, 1981, p. xiv). He wrote about adoption in relation to the general views and opinions of society about social relationships and family life. In doing so, Kirk emphasized that the practice and meaning of starting a family by adoption must be understood in the context of the attitudes, values, beliefs, rules, and knowledge that govern a society and especially prospective adoptive parents. Because these basic societal phenomena change over time, it is assumed that the professional practice and meaning of adoption also is likely to change. Furthermore, it is our belief that these changes influence the attitudes and coping behavior of adoptive parents and, ultimately, the psychological adjustment of adopted children.

Changes in the attitudes of adoptive parents in the past half century form the core of our analysis in this chapter. Our goal is to highlight four generations of adoptive parents who have emerged over time. We describe societal dynamics that have shaped these different generations' views of adoption and the impact of these changes on the adjustment of adoption triad members (i.e., birth parents, adoptive parents, and the adoptee). We argue for a generational interpretation of changes in intercountry and intracountry adoptions and suggest that in northern European countries in the second half of the twentieth century (and perhaps elsewhere), a pattern of four generations of adoptive parents emerged.

Sociologists have discussed relationships between—and changes in—generations for a long time. Examples are Mannheim's (1928) article "The Problem of Generations" and Schelsky's (1957) "The Skeptic Generation." A generation is defined as "the grouping of an aggregate of individuals characterized by a specific historical setting and by common characteristics on an individual level (biographical characteristics, value orientations, motives) and on a system level (size, composition, culture, specific organizations, social networks)" (Becker & Hermkens, 1993, pp. 19–20). A generation of adoptive parents, then, is an aggregate of individuals who adopted at least one nonrelated child during the same historical time frame and who share a number of adoption-related experiences, ideas, attitudes, and behaviors. We view the construct of "adoptive parent generations" as a helpful framework to interpret changes in the motivation and value orientations of adoptive parents, their decision to adopt a child, the type of child they adopt, their attitudes and behavior regarding adoption related issues, and, ultimately, the outcomes for adoptive family members.

One important theoretical dimension for differentiating between generations of adoptive parents is Kirk's (1964) concept of rejection or acknowledgment of differences in relation to biological versus adoptive family life. In his writings, Kirk emphasized that in raising their children, adoptive parents are confronted with unique challenges that are not experienced by biological parents (e.g., accepting the reality that their children are not biologically connected to them, sharing this information with the children, supporting the children's reactions to this information, and coping with the children's search for their origins). He described these challenges as "role handicaps" and emphasized that they often create stress for adoptive parents. Based on his research, Kirk identified two coping patterns that parents utilized in managing the stress associated with these role handicaps—either a rejection-of-difference (RD) attitude or an acknowledgment-of-difference (AD) attitude. Both attitudes involve complex patterns of motivations and evaluations of adoptive parenthood and emerge from the strains of the adoptive kinship. Parents who adopt an RD attitude tend to minimize or deny the inherent differences in adoptive family life and try to simulate the biological family as much as possible. Consequently, they are likely to avoid discussions about the child's origins and the circumstances surrounding the relinquishment. Kirk also found they were likely to be less empathic about birth parents and to engage in fewer discussions with their children about their connection to them. In contrast, other parents adopt an AD attitude, which involves accepting the reality that adoption is inherently a different way of forming a family and is characterized by different types of experiences for both parents and children. Kirk reported that this type of parents more readily acknowledged and respected the child's dual connection to two families and were more empathic about the birth parents' circumstances and their children's feelings about their origins. Overall, Kirk emphasized that the AD pattern of coping was more likely to lead to better adjustment among members of the adoptive family.

Although Kirk's work originally was published in the early 1960s, the distinction between RD and AD attitudes of adoptive parents continues to have relevance today because some parents of domestic and intercountry adopted children still attempt to minimize the differences inherent in the upbringing of their adopted children. Although these parents may acknowledge that integrating an adopted child into their family could pose some problems in the first months after the placement, they also believe that with love and attention, they will be able to overcome these problems and raise the child "as if it were their own." As long as the adopted child is very young, this RD attitude can easily be maintained. However, by the time the child enters school and certainly by the stage of preadolescence, most parents find that the challenges of adoptive family life put a strain on their RD attitude. Psychological problems sometimes emerge for school-age children because of the unanswered questions about their background as well as the emotional pain and feelings of loss about being separated from birth family. In addition, as the adoptee gets older, consanguinity becomes an important criterion for defining parents and family. "The adopted child must then reconcile adoptive parents felt to be real parents with biological parents who are increasingly defined as the real parents" (Leon, 2002, p. 653). Thus, adoptive parents often find that parenting their older adopted child becomes more complex and their original RD attitude more difficult to maintain.

As patterns of coping, RD and AD attitudes are part of our analysis of generations of adoptive parents, but we consider other elements as well. The wider cultural and social context, the growing availability of research information about adoption, the changing attitudes of adoption professionals and changing practices of adoption agencies, and the type of children who are available for adoption (e.g., domestic or intercountry) are other variables we take into account when defining the time limits and content characteristics of each generation. Based on all these factors, we suggest the existence of four generations of adoptive parents: the traditional-closed generation (adoptions between 1950 and 1970), the open-idealistic generation (adoptions between 1971 and 1981), the materialistic-realistic generation (adoptions between 1982 and 1992), and the optimistic-demanding generation (adoptions since 1993).

Our analysis suggests that the emergence of these generations has not occurred by chance but is linked to critical historical circumstances that formed the basis for the reasons and direction for the observed change. Some of these circumstances refer to the society as a whole (e.g., the impact of the "cultural revolution" of the late 1960s on all aspects of social life, including family issues), while others refer to changes more specific to the adoption community (e.g., greater availability of empirically based knowledge about adoption outcomes and changes in adoption agency practice).

Our conceptualization of four adoptive parent generations is not meant to imply that the experiences, attitudes, beliefs, and behavior of these groups of parents are completely distinct from one another. In the population of adoptive parents at any one time period, there are characteristics of all four generations. However, our analysis leads us to believe that during the time periods specified, the majority of adoptive parents have been characterized by the critical experiences and dominant characteristics and attitudes outlined here. Moreover, these experiences, beliefs, and attitudes correspond closely to changes in the broader societal context related to family life in general and to adoption in particular.

Our analysis of adoptive parent generations is based on our knowledge of adoption in the Netherlands and other northern European countries. It is possible that this analysis is also valid for other countries and cultures, although the time frame we propose for each generation is bound to the circumstances of the countries on which our analysis is founded. Some of the changes we describe may be "universal" at least in Western countries—for example, the now generally accepted belief that adoptive and nonadoptive family life are characterized by some important differences as well as the recognition that the impact of adoption on adoption triad members has long-term, if not lasting, effects (Brodzinsky, Schechter, & Henig, 1992; Sorosky, Baran, & Pannor, 1978). Research evidence also has supported the greater psychological vulnerability in adopted children and the significance of loss of biological parents for these individuals (Brodzinsky et al., 1992; Verrier, 1993). Whether all the generational characteristics we describe and the societal changes that underlie them are generalizable to adoptive parents in other parts of Europe, North America, and around the world will need to be determined by future cross-cultural research.

THE TRADITIONAL-CLOSED GENERATION: ADOPTIONS BEFORE 1970

Before 1970, relatively little information existed about adoption, and what was available was poorly disseminated. As a result, adoptive parents had little to help them in creating their roles as adoptive mothers and fathers. Guided by normative family values, with its strong emphasis on the importance of biological ties between parents and children, and influenced by societal attitudes about unwed mothers and illegitimate birth, adoptive parents often struggled on their own to understand the similarities and differences between adoptive and nonadoptive parenthood and family life. In short, there was no cultural script readily available to guide parents in raising their adopted children. Kirk (1964) referred to this predicament as the "role handicap" of adoptive parenthood.

In addition, prior to the 1970s, little empirical data existed on the social and individual consequences of adoption on members of the adoption triangle (Sorosky et al., 1978). Moreover, what was available was based largely on clinical case studies offering limited insight into the complex nature of adoptive family dynamics or the reality of relinquishment for birth parents. As a result, adoptive parents often received advice and guidance from professionals that was influenced by social prejudice and stigma associated with out-of-wedlock pregnancy and nonnormative family life as well as the inherent value placed on genetic-based family relationships. In this context, adoptive parents often felt they had little choice but to minimize the differences of adoptive family life and to adjust to their "role handicap" by adopting an RD attitude (Kirk, 1964). They believed this pattern of coping would give the child the best chance for successful integration into the adoptive family and the surrounding community. As a result, the background of the child—that is, the biological parents and extended family and the circumstances of the relinquishment—were considered of little relevance to the adoptive family. In fact, when the American adoption activist Jean Patton first published her book *The Adopted Break Silence* in 1954 and when Kirk (1964) published his groundbreaking research on adoptive family dynamics, they were far ahead of their time. It would take another 15 to 20 years before other adoption professionals began to emphasize the importance of biological family ties for adopted individuals and for voluntary registers such as Reunion to be established to facilitate search and reunion between adoptees and their birth parents.

The first generation of modern adoptive parents was born in the 1920s and 1930s. They adopted their first child between the late 1940s and 1970s. This generation consisted of parents for whom adoption was an alternative means of having a child. Given that their first choice was to have a biological child of their own, adoption was viewed as a functional response to the emotionally painful reality of infertility or in some cases to the devastating experience of child death (Rowe, 1959). During this period, adoption was considered primarily a service for childless couples, a means by which they could satisfy their emotional needs or to cement their marriage (Tizard, 1977). It was less often viewed as a service for homeless and needy children, although the beginnings of a more altruistic perspective in the adoption field could be seen following World War II and the Korean War, when thousands of orphaned children were placed in the homes of North American and European families.

Because of the societal stigma associated with out-of-wedlock pregnancy and single parenthood, birth parents seldom were encouraged to keep their child during this period. Agencies routinely emphasized adoption placement as the only sensible solution to the problems confronting the unwed, pregnant woman and her "illegitimate" child. To protect the

birth parent from scrutiny of others and to minimize social stigma, agencies routinely engaged in confidential adoption placements in which
there was no contact between the birth parents and adoptive parents and
no sharing of identifying information with the parties. The cardinal principles of adoption practice were confidentiality, secrecy, and anonymity
(Brodzinsky, Smith, & Brodzinsky, 1998; Cole & Donley, 1990). Birth parents were even told that they would soon forget the entire affair once
their child was placed for adoption (Marcus, 1981). As a result, newborn
infants were removed from their birth mother's care as soon as possible.
In many cases, the birth mother never even had an opportunity to see,
hold, and/or feed her child and was discouraged from naming her baby.
The goal was to prevent any sort of emotional connection between the
birth mother and her infant so as to facilitate her ability to relinquish the
child without undue regret or emotional pain. The primary message to
the relinquishing birth parent was to place her child for adoption, put the
experience behind her, and get on with her life.

If adoption was a means of coping with unwed pregnancy and single
parenthood for the birth parent, it was also a means of simulating biological family life as closely as possible for the first generation of adoptive parents (Bussiere, 1998). To support this fantasy, adoption agencies
generally allowed only infertile couples to adopt a child. It was
assumed that a subsequent child born to the family would cause the
rejection of the adopted child given that parents "now had what they
wanted all along." This assumption was supported both by clinical
work (Schneider, 1995) and empirical research (Geerars & Hoksbergen,
1991) that suggested that the coexistence of biological and adopted children sometimes was a source of conflict and adjustment problems in the
family. Other research, however, failed to confirm this view (Brodzinsky & Brodzinsky, 1991).

The first generation of adoptive parents was a relatively homogeneous
group. Typically, they were married, infertile, Caucasian couples, 30 to 45
years of age, physically healthy and free of disabilities, and financially
stable. During this period, adoption agency criteria for determining suit-
ability for adoptive parenthood were quite strict and narrowly defined.
As a result, single adults, fertile couples, families of color, older or disabled individuals, lower- and working-class families, and gay and lesbian individuals were routinely rejected by caseworkers as viable
candidates for adoptive parenthood (Brodzinsky et al., 1998; Cole & Donley, 1990).

The first generation of adoptive parents also held quite conventional
values about marriage, family life, sexual behavior, law, and authority and
these values were reflected in their attitudes as adoptive parents. It was
rare for these individuals to challenge the existing regulations, values, and
norms of the adoption agency. The advice of social workers at the time

was to shield the child from his history and to protect the family from the curiosity of others. Consequently, as soon as the child had been placed in the family, the door often was closed to outsiders. Social workers even discouraged contacts with other adoptive parents (Mansvelt, 1967; Reitz & Watson, 1992). It was unusual during this period for adoptive parents to request and receive detailed information about their child's origins and the circumstances of the relinquishment. Even less frequent were efforts by the adoptive parents to seek contact with the birth family. Agencies emphasized the confidential nature of adoption, and adoptive parents and birth parents readily complied with this practice.

Because virtually all adoptions were along racial lines during this time, some families attempted to keep the nonbiological nature of the parent–child relationship a secret. Once a child was placed in their home, these parents made every effort to raise the youngster as if she were born into the family. The child was not informed of her adoptive status, nor were others outside of the family. In these families, simulation of the biological family was complete. In keeping with the emerging view of adoption professionals, however, the majority of adoptive parents did tell their children of their adoptive status. There was still much confusion, though, about the best time to share this information with the child (Schechter, 1970; Wieder, 1977), although agencies suggested that this aspect of the child's life should not be emphasized too much. This recommendation was consistent with the practice of not providing much background information on the child to the adoptive parents (Mansvelt, 1967; Sokoloff, 1993).

In summary, the first generation of adoptive parents was guided primarily by internal motives. Faced with infertility, miscarriage, and/or infant death and longing for the desired child they had been deprived of, these individuals sought the help of adoption agencies to complete their family. It was a time of secrecy and anonymity in adoption practice. Adoptive parents were encouraged to "think of the child as their own"—in short, to adopt an RD attitude (Kirk, 1964; Mansvelt, 1967). In this atmosphere, little thought was given by adoption professionals to the long-term impact of adoption on the child or, for that matter, to the adjustment of birth parents who had been promised they would soon forget about this part of their life. As result, no consideration was given to the need for postplacement services for adoption triad members. With time, this oversight would become readily apparent, especially as adoption practice changed and a new generation of adoptive parents emerged.

THE OPEN AND IDEALISTIC GENERATION: ADOPTIONS BETWEEN 1971 AND 1981

Beginning in the mid-1970s, intracountry adoption began to decline in both western and northern European countries as well as in the United

States and Canada. The greater availability of birth control and abortion, coupled with the growing societal acceptance of single parenthood, resulted in a gradual reduction in the number of infants available for adoption. For example, in the United States between the early 1950s and early 1970s, approximately 19 percent of unmarried, Caucasian women placed their newborn babies for adoption, whereas by the late 1980s, this figure had dropped to about 3 percent (Bachrach, Stolley, & London, 1992). A similar pattern of decline in the relinquishment of infants for adoption during this period has been noted in most European countries (Selman, 2000). These demographic changes in infant relinquishment had a dramatic effect on couples seeking to adopt children. With fewer adoptable babies available, couples began looking beyond their own country and even beyond their own race and ethnicity in their search to adopt a child. This shift in adoption practice created a new generation of adoptive parents.

The emergence of the second generation of adoptive parents was supported, in part, by profound changes in cultural values and mores in the late 1960s and early 1970s. Starting with the student revolt in Paris in 1968 and spreading over other parts of Europe, students and laborers rebelled against authority and the Establishment. Existing attitudes, beliefs, and values related to sexuality, women's rights, parental authority, governmental control, and religion were openly criticized. Concurrent attacks on traditional values and the Establishment also occurred in North America. This cultural revolution, described as a "neoromantic phenomenon" (Becker & Hermkens, 1993), had a profound influence on the practice of adoption and ultimately on the second generation of adoptive parents, who, compared to the first generation, were much more open, questioning, and idealistic.

The most important societal changes influencing this group of adoptive parents were those related to the place of women in society, ideas about sexuality and abortion, the decreased influence of religion and authorities, and the rise and gradual acceptance of the one-parent family. The decreased influence of religion in European countries resulted in greater acceptance of birth control and abortion. As a result, the birthrate in the Netherlands declined 39 percent between 1970 and 1975. Furthermore, despite the opposition of the Catholic Church, the use of the pill and other forms of contraception became quite common in Europe after 1968. Sex education for children and adolescents also was beginning to be incorporated into the schools in the 1960s and today is an integral part of the school curriculum. This "cognitive pill" was perhaps even more effective in reducing unwanted pregnancies than the contraceptive pill. The ready availability of contraception, the growing societal support for sex education, and the more open attitude toward sexual behavior in the Netherlands contributed to the fact that the number of teenage pregnancies and abortions among the native Dutch population was the lowest in the world during this period. In short, a wide range of societal changes occurring in the 1970s created a climate in European and North American countries in which fewer domestically born infants were being relinquished for adoption as well as a climate in which traditional values in adoption were being challenged by both social service professionals and adoptive parents.

As intracountry adoption declined, prospective adoptive parents in western and northern Europe and North America slowly began to adopt children from other parts of the world, especially from Southeast Asia and South America. In the United States, following the Korean War, Harry Holt was a pioneer in facilitating placements of thousands of orphaned and unwanted American Korean children with American families. However, it wasn't until the early 1970s that European social service agencies began to make similar intercountry adoption placements in any significant numbers. Since the mid-1970s, intercountry adoption has been the primary road to the adoption of young children for northern European couples as well as in other parts of Europe. In the early 1980s, for example, approximately 10,000 intercountry adoptions occurred in northern and western European countries. Although there was a decline in intercountry adoption in the mid-1980s, by the 1990s there was a clear upward trend in these types of placements due largely to the significant number of children adopted from China and more recently from Russia and other eastern European countries. Norway, Sweden, and Denmark had the highest rates of intercountry adoption (11.0, 9.4, and 8.5 per 1,000 live births, respectively) during this period. As a comparison, the rates for the Netherlands and the United States were 3.7 and 2.0, respectively (Selman, 2000).

Of course, intercountry adoption was not a new phenomenon, especially in North America. Beginning in the 1800s, because of the Irish potato famine, thousands of Irish children were sent to the United States and Canada to be raised and, often, legally adopted by nonrelative families. Between 1866 and 1915, for example, 25,779 children living in institutional environments in the United Kingdom were sent to Canadian families and about 200,000 children to families in the United States (Kittson, 1968). This practice of placing orphaned and destitute children from the United Kingdom in American and Canadian families continued into the twentieth century and ended only prior to World War II.

The difference in the practice of intercountry adoption that began to emerge in the 1960s and 1970s was that it typically involved interracial and interethnic placements. The vast majority of these placements involved children of Asian or Hispanic/South American descent being placed with Caucasian couples. In contrast, intercountry adoptions from the nineteenth and early twentieth centuries almost always involved intraracial placements.

How did this important change in adoption practice become possible? What factors led social service professionals and prospective adoptive parents to challenge traditional adoption values and practices? One essential component underlying this change was, of course, the impact of the civil rights movement on society in general, leading to improved racial relations and a growing tolerance for racial, ethnic, and cultural diversity. As a result, a growing number of prospective adoptive parents, especially those with a more liberal social and political orientation, were willing to consider adopting a child of a different race and ethnicity. In addition, the media played a major role in the shifting of adoption attitudes and practices. Television, radio, and print media routinely presented intercountry adoption as a means of "helping children in need." Adoption was promoted as the last possibility for these children to survive and develop normally. As societal pressure for intercountry adoption grew, politicians and governmental regulators gradually began lifting the barriers to these placements.

Another important change affecting this new generation of adoptive parents was the emphasis on the influence of nurture over nature in the development of the child. Confidence in the ability to overcome the negative effects of social class and cultural differences in school performance, for example, could be seen in the strong support for Head Start and similar programs in the late 1960s and 1970s. Social scientists were optimistic that with well-designed, early intervention programs, children could be helped to overcome the impact of social deprivation and other early adverse rearing conditions. This optimism soon began to find its way into the attitudes and beliefs of parents, including those seeking to adopt foreign-born children who had been exposed to war-related trauma, early malnutrition, and other negative life experiences. These adoptive couples generally were of middle- to upper-middle-class backgrounds (Feigelman & Silverman, 1983; Hoksbergen, 1982; Verhulst & Versluis-den Bieman, 1989). They were financially able to help children and were motivated to mitigate the problem of poverty in the Third World. Compared to the first generation of adoptive parents, the motives of these individuals for adoption were more often externally oriented, being strongly influenced by factors coming from outside the family.

The results of early adoption research, especially those studies focusing on intercountry and interracial placements, also served to bolster the confidence of the second generation of adoptive parents and to support their decision to adopt a child of a different race or ethnicity. Although there were many critics of interracial adoption (see Altstein & Simon, 1991), the results of the vast majority of these studies suggested that intercountry adoptees and interracial adoptees showed very positive patterns of adjustment (Cederblad, 1981; Fanshel, 1972; Feigelman & Silverman, 1983; Gardell, 1979; Hoksbergen, 1982; Rathbun, McLaughlin, Bennet, & Garland, 1965; Raynor, 1970; Weyer, 1979). For example, in their study of black, Colombian, and Korean children adopted by Caucasian parents, Feigelman and Silverman (1983) concluded, "Our evidence indicates that whatever problems may be generated by transracial adoption, the benefits to the child outweigh the costs. There is no evidence that any of the serious problems of adjustment or racial self-esteem suggested by the critics of transracial adoption are present in any meaningful proportion of nonwhite children who have been adopted by white parents" (p. 239). Such results served to reinforce the optimism of adoptive parents that they could overcome whatever obstacles they faced in raising their child.

The attitudes and beliefs of adoption caseworkers also influenced this new generation of adoptive parents. There was a growing awareness among professionals of the importance of telling children about their adoption rather than keeping it a secret and of sharing some background information. As a result, prospective adoptive parents were now given more information about their child's background and the circumstances of the relinquishment than the previous generation of adoptive parents. Although the practice of sharing some background information was an important step toward increased openness in adoption (Grotevant & McRoy, 1998), in the vast majority of cases relatively little information was collected at the time of relinquishment, and what was shared with adoptive parents often was censored. At this point in time, the sharing of identifying information and the facilitation of contact between the adoptive family and birth family was still considered taboo. In fact, the decision of some adoptive parents to seek a child from another country rather than adopt domestically undoubtedly reflected, in part, the desire to avoid having to cope with too much information about the child's background as well as the possibility of the birth parents making contact with the adoptive family. For these parents, the motivation for adoption resembles some the internally driven motives of the first generation.

With the advent of intercountry and interracial adoption, adoptive parents found it increasingly more difficult to minimize or deny the inherent differences associated with adoptive family life. For one thing, it was virtually impossible to hide the adoption when there were obvious, racially based physical differences between parents and child. Thus, couples who adopted across racial lines lost the privacy of their adoptive family status. The physical differences were an open advertisement of the nature of the parent–child relationship. Consequently, the RD attitude, so dominant in the first generation of adoptive parents, began to give way to a more open, AD attitude (Kirk, 1964). In fact, research by Hoksbergen, Juffer, and Waardenburg (1987) on Dutch parents who adopted children from Thailand between 1974 and 1979 showed a significantly greater AD orientation compared to the data reported by Kirk a decade earlier.

The open-idealistic generation of adoptive parents had few doubts about their motives for adoption or about their adoption plans. They maintained highly optimistic expectations that they could overcome whatever obstacles they faced associated with interracial placements, older child placements, and/or the effects of early adverse social conditions experienced by their child. Their attitudes and beliefs were reinforced by the cultural revolution sweeping across Europe and North America. It was a time of optimism and willingness to challenge tradition and authority.

The second generation of adoptive parents, however, were not adequately prepared for the responsibilities they were undertaking. The information available about the challenges of intercountry and interracial adoption was quite limited (Hoksbergen, 1991). Consequently, adoption agencies did a relatively poor job preparing prospective adoptive parents regarding the realities associated with these types of placements—for example, the difficulties associated with integrating an older child into the family, the long-term impact of child neglect and abuse, and the challenge of fostering a secure and healthy racial identity in a child placed across racial lines. Too often, this open and idealistic group of parents developed very unrealistic expectations about their capacity to meet the challenges of adoptive family life and/or about the capacity of their children to cope with these challenges. Too often, their day-to-day experiences resulted in disappointment and heightened stress. By the end of this period, the problems associated with adoption were beginning to be recognized by both adoption professionals and parents, but the second generation of adoptive parents simply was not prepared for this reality and experienced inadequate support from adoption agencies. However, as the parenting challenges associated with adoption and the psychological vulnerabilities of adopted children became clearer, agencies began to respond more effectively to the growing needs of adoptive (and birth) family members. These changes signaled the transition to a third cohort of adoption parents—the materialistic-realistic generation.

THE MATERIALISTIC-REALISTIC GENERATION: ADOPTIONS BETWEEN 1982 AND 1992

During the 1980s and into the early 1990s, there was a substantial increase in the number of research and clinical publications on the psychology of adoption (Barth & Berry, 1988; Brodzinsky, 1987; Brodzinsky & Schechter, 1990; Egmond, 1987; Hoksbergen, Spaan, & Waardenburg, 1988; Kuhl, 1985; Nickman, 1985; Verhulst & Versluis-den Bieman, 1989). Much of this literature focused on the psychological, behavioral, and academic problems experienced by adopted children, especially those youngsters involved in international placements, as well as children coming out of the foster care system. Defiant and oppositional behavior, aggression, impulsivity, hyperactivity, inattention, attachment problems, and learning difficulties were the most common symptoms reported for these children. Research also highlighted the psychological risks associated with older child placement as well as early orphanage life, prenatal exposure to alcohol and drugs, and child maltreatment (Barth & Berry, 1988; Hoksbergen,

1991; Verhulst, Althaus, & Versluis-den Bieman, 1992). The risk for these children is exemplified in a study reported by Hoksbergen and colleagues (1988). Using data from 670 institutions, these investigators noted that in the Netherlands, between 5 and 6 percent of intercountry adoptees ended up in residential care because of the serious nature of their psychological problems—five times the rate for Dutch-born children.

As the findings from research and clinical work emerged, it began to be disseminated to adoption agency personnel as well as to the general public through various forms of media. The plight of international adoptees as well as children lingering in foster care was the focus of numerous television shows, newspaper articles, and books during this period. So too was the long-term adjustment problems of birth parents. As a result, this new generation of adoptive parents was exposed to much more detailed and even controversial information about adoption and its impact on adoption triad members than previous generations.

As society in general became more pragmatic during the 1980s (Becker & Hermkens, 1993), the previous romantic and idealistic perspectives associated with adoption declined. For the first time, adoption was viewed in a more realistic way. In this context, adoption agencies began to inform parents about the risks of adopting a child, especially the risks related to inherited psychopathology, early biological and social adversity, and older child placements. For some individuals, at least in parts of northern Europe, this information appears to have lessened their interest in intercountry adoption. For example, in the Netherlands, there was approximately a 50 percent decrease in intercountry adoption from 1979 to 1990 (Hoksbergen, 2001), with a substantial decrease also seen in Sweden during roughly the same period. On the other hand, the decrease in intercountry adoption was less dramatic in Denmark and was not observed in Norway.

A more realistic view of adoption during this period also had another impact: fewer fertile couples expressed a desire to adopt children, at least in northern Europe. For example, in Sweden in the 1970s, among families adopting through two large organizations, approximately 20 percent also had biological children (Johansson, 1976). By the early 1990s, the figure had dropped to 12 percent. Similarly, in the Netherlands in 1980, 32 percent of adoptive parents had one or more biological children. By 1993, the comparable figure was 23 percent (C.B.S., 2003).

The 1980s witnessed a growing concern about the impact of long-term foster care on the emotional well-being of children. Rather than being a form of temporary care, for which it was designed, foster care slowly was becoming a way of life for thousands of children in many European countries as well as in the United States and Canada. In response, governmental agencies sought ways of supporting greater permanence in the lives of these children either through more timely reunification with their birth families or through adoption. One consequence of this policy shift was that adoption agencies became more active in recruiting families to adopt foster children, most of whom had special needs associated with physical health problems, prenatal difficulties, and/or various forms of neglect and abuse. Although initially the agencies met with some reluctance among their clients, over time they became increasingly successful in making special needs placements.

As agencies became more successful in making special needs placements as well as international adoption placements, they found that they also needed to spend more time educating and preparing their clients for adoptive parenthood. Consequently, the third generation of adoptive parents received more initial support from adoption agencies than previous generations of adoptive parents. However, the availability of post-adoption services was still rather limited. As a result, in the years following the adoption placement, adoptive families too often found themselves struggling with adjustment issues they did not understand and were ill prepared to manage.

With greater information available on the risks associated with adoption in general and with special needs and international adoption in particular, the expectations of adoptive parents regarding their children began to be altered. No longer could they ignore the impact of genetics and preplacement experiences on their child as well as the inherent differences of adoptive compared to nonadoptive family life (Kirk, 1964). Adopting children who were older and who experienced early institutional care or multiple foster placements as well as children of a different race and those who had been neglected or abused forced adoptive parents to reconsider their "ideal child." Parents had to adjust their expectations to the reality of the special needs manifested by their children. As a result, the shift toward an AD coping pattern among the third generation of adoptive parents grew even stronger than was observed for previous generations.

A growing desire for professionalism and accountability in adoption also emerged in the 1980s, especially with regard to intercountry adoption, where an increasing number of systemic abuses were being reported in the media (e.g., baby selling and bribing of officials). In response, the United Nations began to establish guidelines and standards for international adoption, culminating in 1993 with the Hague Convention on the Protection of Children and Co-operation in Respect of Intercountry Adoption. The Hague Convention, which to date has been ratified by 60 countries and signed but not ratified by another six countries, sets a framework for regulatory practice for intercountry adoption (http://hcch.e-vision.nl).

In summary, the rise in international adoption and special needs adoption during the 1980s, coupled with the growing availability of information on the psychological risks associated with adoption, supported a more realistic view of this form of family life not only in northern Europe but elsewhere as well. In turn, the need for greater professionalism was emphasized in the adoption community, including better guidelines for adoption practice. As adoption became more complex, families began to require more preparation and education. Although this period witnessed a clear trend toward increased support for adoptive families, the needs of adoption triad members still outpaced the development of preplacement and postplacement services. Only in the last decade, with the emergence of the fourth generation of adoptive parents, have adoption professionals begun to respond more effectively to the needs of the adoptees and their families.

THE OPTIMISTIC-DEMANDING GENERATION: ADOPTIONS SINCE 1993

Since the mid-1990s, there has been a significant rise in intercountry adoption in northern and western Europe as well as in the United States and Canada (Freundlich, 2002; Selman, 2000). In the Netherlands, for example, a total of 3,049 adoptions of foreign-born children were made in 2002, the majority of them involving infants and toddlers from China, Taiwan, and other Far Eastern countries (Minister of Justice, 2003) By contrast, over 20,000 intercountry adoptions occurred in the United States in 2002, up from approximately 9,000 a decade earlier (Federici, 2003). In northern Europe, intercountry adoption constitutes the vast majority of adoption placements, with very few domestic infant adoptions or special needs adoptions occurring over the past decade. In other European countries (e.g., Spain, France, Germany, England, Ireland, and Scotland), adoption of special needs children from the foster care system continues. Only in the United Kingdom are there a reasonable number domestic infant adoptions still taking place.

The increase in intercountry adoption and the emergence of a fourth generation of adoptive parents in northern Europe was fueled by several factors. First, improved economic conditions made it possible for many more couples to afford the relatively high costs of intercountry adoption. Second, there was a growing trend toward individualism during this period, leading more and more couples to believe that having a child was their "right." Third, rates of infertility also have risen over the past few decades (Lieblum, 1997; Te Velde, 1991). The struggle to conceive a child, coupled with the belief that parenthood was a "right," resulted in many prospective parents exploring not only assisted reproductive techniques (e.g., artificial insemination, egg donation, and surrogate parenting) as a means of becoming a parent but also adoption.

The fourth generation of adoptive parents is more internally motivated and less focused on the best interests of the child compared to the second and third generations. In fact, a shift toward an RD attitude can be seen in these individuals. More and more northern European adoptive parents are insisting on young, healthy children. They are making their demands in a more direct manner to adoption agencies and are less willing to accept older and medically "at-risk" children. As a result, it has become increasingly more difficult in many northern European countries to place older children for adoption. Whereas an "older child" typically was defined as six years of age or greater for the second and third generations of adoptive parents, for the current generation being three years of age or more is considered "old."

The fourth generation also appears to be less concerned about racial and cultural issues in the identity development of their children. There is more of an emphasis on integrating children into the culture of their adopted country rather than acknowledging the differences between the culture their children live in and the ones into which they were born.

The past decade or so also has witnessed a continued professionalism in the preparation and education of adoptive parents. For example, in the Netherlands all prospective adoptive parents are now obligated to attend preparation courses regarding intercountry adoption, at their own expense, sponsored by the government. Building on the knowledge base about adoption that emerged in the 1980s and supported by new information derived from more sophisticated adoption and child development research over the past decade, these courses are offering adoptive parents a wealth of information about family life and adjustment issues associated with adoption. Although much of this research continues to focus on risks related to older child placement as well as the impact of biological and social adversity on the developing child, other research (see chapter 4), this volume) has focused on the ability of adopted children to overcome the initial problems in their lives. The latter research seeks to identify protective factors internal to the child (e.g., intelligence, temperament, and coping strategies) and resource factors external to the child (e.g., support from family, friends and other caregivers; extent and quality of education; and availability of medical, psychological, and/or social services) that help ameliorate the adverse effects of biological vulnerabilities and early social stress. The information emerging from this body of research is providing the fourth generation of adoptive parents with reason for increased hope and optimism.

CONCLUSIONS, IMPLICATIONS, AND FUTURE DIRECTIONS

From the late 1940s until the present, four generations of adoptive parents can be distinguished. The first was highly focused on creating a biological family and sought adoption only in response to the emotionally painful reality of infertility. Once a child was in their home, they chose to downplay adoption as much as possible. The second generation was more idealistic and romantic in its view of adoption. Motivated by a desire to help "children in need," many of these individuals chose to adopt children of a different race and from foreign countries. This generation also was much more willing to acknowledge the inherent differences of adoptive compared to nonadoptive family life. The third generation, in response to the growing information regarding the impact of adoption on adoption triad members, was much more sophisticated and realistic in its assessment of adoptive family life. An AD orientation toward adoption characterized the majority of these individuals. Finally, the most recent generation of adoptive parents, emerging in the early part of the 1990s, appears more internally driven compared to the two previous generations. These individuals appear characterized both by a more demanding attitude—that is, a determination to fulfill their need for a young, healthy child—as well as by an optimistic view of adoption—that is, believing that with an early placement and good caregiving, the problems associated with adoption can be overcome. For many of these individuals, we see a shift toward an RD perspective.

Our analysis suggests that the emergence of these generations of adoptive parents is associated with major changes in attitudes and value orientations about adoption. In turn, the latter changes are firmly connected to the evolving changes in the demography, culture, and structure of Western society over the past half century. Today, more and more couples are facing medical and psychological problems associated with infertility (Lieblum, 1997; Te Velde, 1991). In turn, adoption has become an increasingly viable option for these couples in their struggle to become parents. Although in North America and the United Kingdom there continues to be significant numbers of domestic infant adoption placements occurring each year, in most parts of Europe these types of adoption are relatively rare. Couples seeking to adopt young and healthy children increasingly are applying for intercountry placements, many of which turn out to be interracial placements as well. In fact, in northern Europe international adoption constitutes the vast majority of adoption placements at the present time. Virtually no domestic infant placements and only small numbers of domestic, special needs adoptions are occurring in northern European countries.

Although we assume that many of the characteristics of the four generations of adoptive parents outlined here can be found in adoptive parents in countries beyond northern Europe, there also are clear differences in adoption practice across Western society that may limit the generalization of our findings. As noted previously, domestic infant adoption continues in North America and to some extent in the United Kingdom as well as in Australia and New Zealand. Most of these placements are intraracial in nature. Furthermore, as a result of legislation passed during President Bill Clinton's administration, domestic special needs adoptions are on the rise in the United States and continue to be reasonably prevalent in many European countries. In addition, the increasing prevalence of open adoption in North America, the United Kingdom, Australia, and New Zealand is only slowly finding its way to the majority of European countries. Given the considerable differences today in adoption practice among Western societies, we would certainly expect some differences to be observed in the attitudes, values, and behavior of adoptive parents and their children. To date, however, there has been virtually no cross-national or cross-cultural examination of adoption and its impact on adoption triad members. It is hoped that future researchers will begin to explore this neglected but important area of inquiry.

Despite the apparent differences in adoption practice across Western societies, there also appear to be many similarities in the attitudes, values, behavior, and needs among adoptive parents today. Adoption has lost its taboo in virtually all Western countries. It is no longer a topic of secrecy and shame. In the world today, with the prevalence of diversity in family arrangements, adoption is now seen as simply one of a number of alternative ways of forming a family and living one's life. Moreover, children are routinely informed of their adoption status, and there is a growing recognition of the normality of children's curiosity about their origins. In short, the role handicaps associated with adoption have been lessened for the current generation of adoptive parents (although not eliminated) compared with previous generations.

Adoptive parents today also have much more information about adoption than ever before. They are aware of the risks associated with adoption and generally have more realistic views about adoptive family life. They also are becoming increasingly aware of the ability of children to at least partially overcome early biological and/or social adversity. This awareness has fostered more hope and optimism among individuals adopting older and special needs youngsters as well as those adopting children from foreign countries who have experienced early institutional rearing and other forms of social, material, and/or nutritional deprivation.

Despite the increased information about adoption available to adoptive parents and the improved preparation of these individuals prior to the child's placement, there continues to be a tremendous need for better services for these individuals, especially in the postplacement period. The current generation of adoptive parents in northern Europe is experiencing considerable challenges in raising their children and often feel ill prepared to manage the family conflicts that emerge over time. Similar experiences are reported for families in other parts of Europe (Triseliotis, Shireman, & Hundleby, 1997) and in North America (Brodzinsky & Pinderhughes, 2002). Too often, adoption agencies place children for adoption without adequate support being available to help the families cope with the unique challenges they often experience in the years to come. When problems emerge, adoptive parents often feel reluctant to return to the agency for fear of being viewed as a "failure." When they turn to professionals outside the adoption system, they often find individuals who are poorly trained in adoption and lack adequate insight into the dynamics of adoptive family life. In short, for all the progress that has been made in the adoption field, too many adoptive parents, adopted children, and birth parents find that they lack adequate professional support and guidance as they struggle with adoption-related issues in the years following the placement. This is an area that needs much more attention from the adoption professional community.

Adoption in northern Europe as well as in other parts of Europe also has become complicated in recent times because of a growing prejudice against foreign immigrants. Since the 1980s, there has been a tremendous influx of foreigners emigrating to many European countries, such as the Netherlands, Belgium, France, Germany, and Spain (Committee Blok, 2004; Sociaal en Cultureel Planbureau, 2003). In the Netherlands in 2003, 10 percent of the total population consisted of non-Western inhabitants. By 2020, this percentage is expected to increase to approximately 14 percent (Committee Blok, 2004). The attitudes of European citizens to the rapid rise of foreign immigrants has changed dramatically over the past decade or so. Increasingly, conservative media have promoted negative views of these individuals, suggesting that, on average, they are less economically productive, less respectful toward women, more involved in criminal activities, more likely to abuse the social service system, and not particularly interested in becoming assimilated into European culture (as indicated by their tendency to choose marriage partners from their own ethnic group and their limited knowledge of the language of their host country). Given that intercountry adoption, which often involves interracial placements, is the norm in northern European countries and extremely common in other parts of Europe as well, there is concern about whether the growing prejudice against foreigners, especially those of a different race or ethnicity, will impact on societal acceptance of these types of adoption placements. There also are questions about how to protect intercountry adoptees from the prejudice that is emerging against foreign-born individuals. This societal problem requires much more thought and attention from the adoption community than currently exists.

Finally, another area requiring attention is improving adoption practice for older, domestically born, special needs youngsters. Many of these children are the products of neglect and abuse and have resided for periods of time in foster care and/or institutional settings. In northern Europe, there is a reluctance of most prospective adoptive parents to adopt these children. The current generation of adoptive parents typically are seeking healthy, young children and consequently apply for intercountry adoption rather than express a willingness to take on the responsibility of these older, special needs children. In North America and other parts of Europe, special needs adoptions are more common. Clearly, adoption professionals in northern Europe must do more to actively recruit and educate prospective adoptive parents so as increase the possibility of making these type of adoption placements.

In summary, our historical analysis suggests different cohorts of adoptive parents, with different attitudes, values, and behavior regarding adoption. Moreover, the past decade has witnessed the emergence of a new generation of adoptive parents in northern Europe. Although this generation shares many experiences and attitudes with adoptive parents in other parts of Europe and North America, the diversity in adoption practice across Western countries suggests the likelihood of some unique experiences for these individuals (and their children) as well. Our analysis is rooted in the belief that adoption can be understood only in the context of the culture and historical period in which it is being practiced. This belief suggests the need for increased cross-national examination of adoption practices and outcomes. It is only by examining adoption in context that we will be successful in understanding the impact of this social service practice on adoption triad members and be prepared to support these individuals in the postplacement period.

ACKNOWLEDGMENTS

This chapter is an adaptation and extension of the chapter "Changes in Attitudes in Three Generations of Adoptive Parents: 1950–2000" (Hoksbergen, 2000).

Without the help of the editors, this chapter would have been less clear and informative. We therefore thank them very much.

Chapter 3

Prenatal and Postnatal Risks to Neurobiological Development in Internationally Adopted Children

Megan R. Gunnar and Darlene A. Kertes

Last year, families in the United States adopted over 20,000 children from foreign countries (U.S. Department of State, n.d.). Thousands more are adopted into western European countries annually, including Belgium, Cyprus, Denmark, Finland, France, Germany, Iceland, Italy, Luxembourg, the Netherlands, Norway, Spain, Sweden, and the United Kingdom. Many of these children, especially those adopted from institutional settings, experienced conditions hazardous to healthy physical, cognitive, and emotional development. With approximately 75 to 85 percent of all internationally adopted children coming from institutional settings, primarily orphanages (Johnson, 2000a), international adoption has become a bold experiment in developmental plasticity. Given time, love, and money, can families reverse the impact of adverse early life experiences?

Questions about the ways and extent to which early experiences shape later outcomes are central to developmental psychology. Throughout the history of the field, children fostered or adopted from institutions have served as test cases to address these questions in humans. Developmental research with these children has provided valuable insights into the effects of early adversity on physical growth, IQ, and social relationships (see review by Rutter, 1981; see also chapter 4). However, little is known about the impact of adverse early experiences on brain development more directly. The field is poised to bring the tools of developmental cognitive and affective neuroscience to bear on this issue. Work on neurodevelopmental outcomes in internationally adopted children is just beginning. To date, little is known about the impact of institutional rearing on the development of specific neural systems and the capacity of affected systems to respond therapeutically to the postadoption environment. The time, however, may be ripe to review the theory and research that will guide the work on neurodevelopmental outcomes following early adversity and adoption and to consider its potential ramifications for intervention and social policy.

Accordingly, in this chapter we will first outline some of the general principles of brain development and plasticity as well as the hypotheses guiding behavioral neuroscience and developmental psychobiological research on adverse, depriving, or stressful early life conditions. Next we will enumerate the varied risks posed before and after birth for children adopted from institutional and other adverse preadoption conditions, considering both the animal and the human literature on how these risks impact brain development. We will then briefly describe the emerging literature aimed at beginning to understand the impact of early adversity on neurophysiological systems in internationally adopted children. Finally, we will consider the potential ramifications of this work for intervention and policy.

BRAIN DEVELOPMENT AND NEURAL PLASTICITY

The human brain begins to develop around the sixth week of gestation. Its development involves a tightly orchestrated cascade of events: (1) the birth of nerve and glial cells in generative zones of the developing brain, (2) the migration of these cells to where they will be located in the mature brain, (3) differentiation into the type of nerve or glial cells that they are to become, (4) the growth of axons and dendrites on nerve cells, (5) the growth and then pruning of the synaptic connections among communicating nerve cells and the organization of functional cell assemblies, and finally (6) the myelination of fiber tracts that improve the conduction of neural activity (Purves & Lichtman, 1985). These events occur in overlapping waves at different times in different regions of the brain. Generally, neural systems that need to be functional at birth develop very early, while systems underlying behaviors that emerge later in development take longer to reach maturity. In humans, most brain cells are born, migrate, and differentiate during prenatal development, although there is now good evidence that in one area of the brain, the hippocampus, new nerves cells continue to be produced throughout life (Eriksson et al., 1998).

Beginning in the last trimester of pregnancy, humans, like other mammals, experience a largely endogenously driven proliferation of synapses, occurring in waves in different regions of the brain. Synapses are the sites where nerve cells communicate with one another. Communication or activity at synaptic junctions is what determines whether a connection between two nerve cells will be retained or pruned. Although in some cases neural activity during critical or sensitive periods is endogenously driven, in many cases this activity is the product of the nervous system processing information and acting on the environment. Once a region of the cortex has experienced this exuberant proliferation of synapses, stabilization and pruning of synapses is based largely on interactions with the environment. In this way, disturbances that affect the prenatal environment may alter early neural development with the effects depending on the timing and severity of the insult.

In humans, the wiring and fine-tuning of the neural systems involved in visual, auditory, and sensory processing begins early and is largely complete by the preschool years. In contrast, the development of systems that are involved in higher-order cognition continues well into adolescence. Overlaid on this developmental progression is a continual change in wiring that is the basis of all learning throughout life. Thus, adverse postnatal experiences can also affect neural development.

Adverse events can affect the structure and function of the brain in three general ways, each of which is relevant to the development of children adopted from conditions of early neglect and privation. First, strokes following premature delivery, severe malnutrition, and maltreatment (e.g., shaken baby syndrome) can injure neural tissue, producing lesions in the brain. Second, a lack of stimulation or abnormal stimulation can affect the basic wiring plan of the brain and brain chemistry. Third, morphological and neurochemical adaptations to a nonoptimal preadoption environment may produce maladaptive responses to the postadoption environment that limit development and enhance risks for the emergence of behavioral and emotional disorders.

The impact of early brain insults depends both on the timing and on the extent of the damage. In some cases, the consequences of these insults for later functioning are less than one might suppose based on the magnitude of the injury; in other cases, the consequences are greater than would be expected. Both patterns reveal important principles of developmental plasticity that may help us think about the potential impact of early adverse life experiences. Kennard (1942) performed some of the earliest and best-known studies on the impact of early brain injury on later behavior. According to Kennard's principle, the consequences of early brain injury are less severe than would be observed if the same injury were sustained by the mature brain. The developing brain is capable of reorganizing to compensate for injury by creating novel neural networks. In contrast, Hebb (1947) argued that early brain injuries have more severe consequences than late injuries because early injuries can result in a failure of the brain to organize neural systems supporting mature behavior, particularly socioaffective behavior. According to Hebb, later neural organization grows out of earlier, less mature neural systems. If less mature systems are damaged, later maturing systems would be disorganized. Furthermore, the full effect of the earlier damage might not be observed until many years later when the maturing neural systems that communicate with the damaged area begin to come "online."

As reviewed recently by Kolb and Gibb (2001), both views are partially correct. Neuroscience studies with a variety of animal species have shown that if a lesion is produced in a region of the brain that is still undergoing the birth of new neurons, outcomes tend to be very good. If the damage is produced when these neurons are migrating to their cortical locations, outcomes may be dismal. Damage produced during periods of maximal synapse proliferation tend to lead to good functional outcomes, while damage produced during periods of synaptic pruning tends to have progressively worse functional outcomes the longer the brain is allowed to develop abnormally. Mapping the results of these animal studies onto periods of human brain development, the third trimester of pregnancy may be the period when the human brain may be most vulnerable to injury with long-term functional consequences. In addition, damage or abnormal wiring during the first years after birth may produce progressively greater functional abnormalities. As with prenatal insult, the effects of the damage depend on the system as well as the severity, timing, and duration of insult. Furthermore, damage or alterations in wiring produced in structures that feed into later-developing structures may affect the development of those structures. With regard to children deprived in their first years of life, this last point may be of particular relevance to the late-developing prefrontal cortex.

The prefrontal cortex is a brain region whose development starts in infancy but does not reach full functional maturity until sometime in adolescence. It supports cognitive processes that have been collectively termed executive functions, which include the ability to hold ideas in working memory, plan and sequence means of solving problems, inhibit desired actions to achieve long-term goals, and effortfully regulate attention. This region of the brain is richly interconnected with regions that reach maturity earlier in life. Thus, it is possible that although much of the development of this region of the brain may take place after a child is adopted, alterations in other brain regions that developed prior to adoption may influence the ways in which this region becomes organized.

While animal studies show that early adverse conditions may harm the healthy development of the brain, they also reveal the capacity of postinsult manipulations or therapies to stimulate functional recovery or compensation. Two types of therapy have been examined extensively in rats by Kolb and his colleagues: stroking and complex environments (for a review, see Kolb & Gibb, 2001). Both of these environmental manipulations were chosen as therapies because they are known to stimulate neural growth in normally developing animals (i.e., those that have *not* sustained neural insults; Fernandez-Teruel, Escorihuela, Castellano, Gon-zalez, & Tobena, 1997; Kolb, 1995). In one study, Kolb and Gibb (cited in Kolb & Gibb, 2001) caused damage to the cortex or top layer of the brain of infant rats during the first week after birth, a period roughly equivalent to the third trimester for humans. If they stroked the infant rats for 15 min-utes three times a day for the next two weeks (roughly equivalent in human development to the first few years of life), the tactilely stimulated infants sustained few behavioral effects of the lesions. Similar effects have been shown for severely malnourished infant rats (Wiener & Levine, 1978). Most strikingly, analyses of the infant animals' brains revealed that in stroked infants, the remaining neurons had formed rich cortical con-nections. This stands in contrast to the infant animals without the stroking intervention, whose remaining neurons died.

The second therapy, called the complex environment, involves placing a young animal along with peers into an environment designed to offer opportunities for social, motor, and visual exploration (Greenough, 1987). Objects in the environment are changed frequently so that there is always something novel to explore. This type of environment is capable of stimu-lating neural development at all points during life, even into old age in animals. However, young animals take to these environments with great vigor and enthusiasm. Kolb and colleagues found that when they took juvenile rats that had sustained brain insults and placed them into these environments early in life, they showed increased thickness or size of the cortex of the brain along with dramatic reversals of behavioral deficits induced by the brain insults (Kolb & Elliot, 1987). If they waited until the early-lesioned animals were adults before placing them in these stimulat-ing environments, the effects were less dramatic. These findings raise the possibility that when neural insults are sustained early in life, moving children into enriching environments where they receive physical and intellectual stimulation may have profound therapeutic effects, with the effects being greater for those who make the transition earlier in their development.

Risks to Healthy Brain Development

In this section we will briefly outline the risks to healthy brain develop-ment encountered by internationally adopted children or children adopted domestically from conditions of neglect and maltreatment. Not all internationally adopted children will have encountered these risks. To some extent, it may be possible to estimate the likelihood of risk by know-ing the child's country of origin and circumstance prior to adoption. In most cases, however, it is difficult if not impossible to know with certainty whether a given child has been exposed to a particular risk factor. Our review of these risks will focus on risks during three periods of development: prenatal, perinatal, and postnatal. This review is meant not to be exhaustive but rather to highlight some of the most likely risks to healthy neurodevelopmental outcomes.

Prenatal Risks

Healthy prenatal development is fostered when the mother is well nourished, does not engage in consumption of alcohol or other drugs of abuse, and does not encounter threats to her emotional and physical well-being. Maternal malnutrition is associated with fetal growth restriction and subsequently low birth weight. (Georgieff & Rao, 2001). Alcohol consumption and stress have also been linked with low birth weight and/or prematurity (Becker, Randall, Salo, Saulnier, & Weathersby, 1994; Killingsworth-Rini, Dunkel-Schetter, Wadhwa, & Sandman, 1999). Low birth weight and preterm delivery, which may have different antecedents but often co-occur, are major risk factors for poor developmental outcomes (Hack, Klein, & Taylor, 1995; McCarton, Wallace, Divon, & Vaughan, 1996). Birth records available from children adopted from Russia and eastern Europe indicate that 20 percent of infants are reported to be premature and 40 percent as small for gestational age (Jenista, 2000b). Rates of prenatal malnutrition and low birth weight are likely to be higher in Asian countries than in other regions of the world (UNICEF, 2001). Interest in the impact of low birth weight, prenatal malnutrition, and prenatal alcohol exposure initially focused almost exclusively on cognitive (and, in the case of low birth weight, neurosensory) outcomes. The majority of studies noted reduced IQ, but in recent years problems in various aspects of executive functions (i.e., working memory, attention regulation, planning, and sequencing) have also been documented. Researchers are only beginning to address deficits in social and emotional processes, including difficulties in peer relationships and in emotional self-control (e.g., Strupp & Levitsky, 1995). Since many of these problems overlap with those reported for children adopted internationally (Kreppner, O'Connor, Rutter, & the E.R.A. Research Team, 2001; O'Connor, Rutter, Beckett, et al., 2000), we should be aware that it is not only postnatal circumstances but also the prenatal environment that may contribute to behavioral and cognitive challenges encountered by internationally adopted children and their families.

Because of its potentially devastating effect on development, prenatal alcohol exposure perhaps deserves special notice. Teratogenic effects of alcohol on the brain are possible throughout pregnancy, with specific effects dependent on the dose, timing, and conditions of exposure. Neurobehavioral problems associated with prenatal alcohol exposure include hyperactivity, inattention, memory problems, visual and auditory perceptual disorders, perseverations, eating and sleeping disorders, and motor and learning problems (for a review, see Streissguth & Conner, 2001). Structural anomalies in the brain following prenatal alcohol exposure are well documented in human children and include microcephaly, abnormal cerebellar development, and atypical development of the major fiber tracts connecting the left and right hemispheres of the brain. In animal models of fetal alcohol exposure, altered production and migration of nerve cells and fewer synaptic connections among nerve cells have been observed. These effects are likely to be present in humans but are difficult to assess in the living brain. In the absence of information about maternal drinking habits during pregnancy, fetal exposure to damaging levels of alcohol is difficult to assess. If exposure occurs during fetal periods when the face is developing, children display minor facial anomalies that can be measured. Problems in growth following adoption in combination with such facial anomalies add to confidence in diagnosis. However, significant brain effect of prenatal exposure may be present in the absence of facial anomalies, and growth problems in children may be due to factors other than maternal drinking during pregnancy. Unfortunately, for these reasons, families may never get an unambiguous diagnosis and thus may always be uncertain as to whether cognitive and social problems observed in their adopted child are due to prenatal alcohol exposure.

Prenatal malnutrition is another risk factor affecting development of the brain that can lead to permanent deficits in learning and behavior. Protein-energy malnutrition is of particular concern because in addition to their involvement in protein synthesis, the amino acids that are deficient in this type of malnutrition are precursors to neurotransmitters, structural proteins essential for growth, enzymes, peptide hormones, and peptide neurotransmitters (Morgane, Mokler, & Galler, 2002). Protein-energy malnutrition may result in deceleration of intrauterine fetal growth, which is in turn associated with poor developmental outcomes, including low IQ (Georgieff & Rao, 2001). In studies with animals, prenatal protein malnutrition has been linked with a general loss of curiosity and initiative and a lack of interest for exploring and investigating the environment (Morgane, Austin-LaFrance, Bronzino, Tonkiss, & Galler, 1992). A wide range of effects on brain growth and development have been documented, including decreased neurotransmitter production, profoundly altered fatty acid profiles, reduced synthesis of growth factors critical for normal brain development, and decreased number of synapses and neural activity (Georgieff & Rao, 2001; Nishijima, 1986). Certain areas of the brain, including the cerebral cortex, cerebellar cortex, and hippocampus, appear particularly vulnerable to the effects of prenatal malnutrition. Animals exposed to severe prenatal protein deficiency learn more slowly and have difficulty with remembering specific pieces of information (Morgane et al., 2002).

Prenatal deficiencies in micronutrients such as iron, zinc, and iodine can also impact brain and behavioral development. The impact of several micronutrient deficiencies have been well documented in animal studies, though their generalizability to human conditions in which multiple deficiencies may occur is limited. Deficiencies in zinc are linked with a variety of neurochemical and neurophysiologic changes, particularly in areas typically rich in zinc, including the cerebellum, limbic system, and cerebral cortex (Frederickson & Danscher, 1990). Reduced spontaneous motor activity and poor short-term memory are suggested by animal studies. Iodine is particularly critical for central nervous system development in early fetal life, with severe deficiencies linked with mental retardation, spastic diplegia, and deaf-mutism and less severe deficiencies linked to impaired verbal and motor abilities. Endemic areas of severe iodine deficiency include India, Iran, Zaire, and parts of China. Insufficient iron is among the most well-studied micronutrient deficiencies. Iron is essential in carrying oxygen to the brain, and when iron is too low in the diet and anemia results, the developing brain may be deprived of the oxygen it needs for normal functioning. In the fetus, low iron has its biggest effects on brain regions such as the hippocampus that have large requirements for oxygen. Effects are more marked when other insults, such as periods of hypoxia due to problems in blood flow through the placenta, reduce fetal blood oxygenation. Iron is also essential for normal myelination; thus, iron deficiency may be associated with less efficient neural functioning. Clinical studies show that early iron deficiency is associated with impaired motor and cognitive abilities. While the highest risk for iron deficiency includes the fetal and neonatal periods, infancy, and following menarche, cognitive effects from early iron deficiency appear to be the most permanent and resistant to later supplementation.

More elusive to document but likely more pervasive in children who are abandoned is the effect of maternal stress during pregnancy. There is increasing evidence from animal and human studies that emotional stress to the mother affects the development of her fetus (Lemaire, Koehl, Le Moal, & Abrous, 2000). Maternal stress in pregnancy appears to impact the brain circuits and neurochemistry associated with problems in regulating attention and emotions (see reviews by Schneider & Moore, 2000; Wadhwa, Sandman, & Garite, 2001). In particular, animal studies suggest that chronic stress to the mother during pregnancy leads to changes in the hippocampus, reduced cell proliferation in the dentate gyrus, and enlargement of the basolateral amygdala in offspring (Lemaire et al., 2000; Salm, Pavelko, Krouse, Webster, Kraszpulski, & Birkle, 1999; Vaid et al., 1997). Prenatal stress in rodents has been shown to alter level or function of monoamines in the brain, including norepinephrine and dopamine (for a review, see Kofman, 2002). Notably, however, the work on animals suggests that a positive postnatal environment can do a great deal in reversing the impact of prenatal stress (Maccari et al., 1994). Thus, it is important to consider the nature and quality of care provided following birth.

Perinatal Risks

The perinatal period encompasses the late fetal and early postnatal life. It is characterized by rapid brain growth and development, with continued neuronal proliferation and the beginning of myelination (Volpe, 2001). Risks during the perinatal period are increased for infants born prematurely. In industrialized countries, it is now possible for infants to survive who are born as early as 24 weeks' gestation. However, health care conditions in many nonindustrialized countries make it less likely that children available for international adoption were born extremely premature. We will, therefore, focus on the risks associated with being born only a few weeks prematurely (e.g., between 34 and 37 weeks' gestation). During the last several weeks prior to a normal full-term birth, the mother's body transfers substances to the fetus that will protect it during the first months following birth. Three are particularly important: fatty acids, IgG, and ferritin or iron (Connor, 1994; Hobbs & Davis, 1967; Larque, Dammelmair, & Koletzko, 2002). Long-chain polyunsaturated fatty acids typically transferred across the placenta aid in myelination of the nervous system, brain lipid composition, and learning ability. Fatty acids are not supplemented in conventional infant formulas (Carver, 2003); even low-risk premature infants have been observed to have poorer cognitive performance by two years of age (e.g., de Haan, Bauer, Georgieff, & Nelson, 2000). As discussed earlier, if prenatal malnutrition is also present, it also confers risk of altered fatty acid profiles.

IgG is an immunoglobulin that enhances newborns' natural immune response. Infants are not able to make their own IgG until around three or four months after birth. So, the premature infant can be considered somewhat immune compromised with increased risk of becoming sick and remaining sick longer. Illness often reduces appetite, increasing problems in physical and mental growth. Febrile illnesses can cause brain damage if the fever is prolonged and uncontrolled. Chronic low-grade infections can reduce the baby's interest in its surroundings, further limiting its opportunities to gain the stimulation it needs for normal neural development.

Iron is essential for healthy brain development, as noted previously. Typically, full-term newborns rely on ferretin acquired in the last several prenatal weeks to supplement milk consumed postnatally in meeting its needs for iron (Georgieff & Rao, 2001). If an infant missed the opportunity to acquire sufficient ferretin because of premature birth and supplementation is not provided, iron deficiency anemia may be observed by several months postdelivery. Iron deficiency may also be a concern for full-term infants who are not provided with iron-rich foods by six to eight months of age when their prenatal iron stores are depleted. As noted in the discussion of prenatal risk factors, the effects of low iron early in life on the developing brain appear to be permanent and have repercussions for cognitive developmental outcomes.

Postnatal Risks

Postnatal factors that are essential for healthy neurodevelopmental outcomes include adequate health and nutrition, sensory stimulation, social interactions, and opportunities to form relationships. Postnatal risks are numerous for abandoned infants (for a review, see Johnson, 2000a), and institutions such as orphanages vary in the extent to which these needs are met. Risks to basic health and nutrition include malnutrition due to inadequate food intake and/or intestinal parasites and infectious illness due to poor sanitation and overcrowded child care conditions. Even when basic health needs are met adequately and the ratio of adults to infants is relatively good, it is difficult in institutional settings to provide adequate and quality experiences necessary to support optimal brain development (Rutter, 1981). This is partly due to the fact that human infants are motorically immature for many months after birth; they require the aid of a caregiver to interact with the world. The inability of infants to actively seek out sensory stimulation is exacerbated in many institutions by the lack of things to look at and explore and very limited access to the few objects that are available. Delays in motor development that are common among institutionalized infants further impede infants' ability to explore and to provide themselves with visual and tactile stimulation needed for brain development. All these forms of deprivation can be reduced if a child is frequently held and engaged in social interaction. Social engagement with adults also would prevent the language deprivation that presumably results in the significant language delays noted among institutionalized children prior to adoption.

Even in institutions where social stimulation can be considered adequate, it is rare that children experience the type of continuity in caregivers that may be needed for normal social development. In a family setting, even if there may be several young children to care for, children interact with a small number of (usually) unchanging caregivers. Under these conditions, adults and infant can develop consistent patterns of interaction within which a child can begin to organize rudimentary self-regulatory competencies (Gianino & Tronick, 1987). These conditions are also essential for infants to form attachment relationships with specific adults, a species-typical human propensity that typically emerges by the latter part of the first year (Bowlby, 1969). Even in institutions that provide sufficient stimulation to support normal cognitive and language development, the lack of consistent adult–infant relationships has been shown to increase the likelihood of difficulties in forming intimate and secure emotional relationships following adoption into stable homes (Hodges & Tizard, 1989b).

Sadly, while in most cases adverse preadoption care is due to inadequate resources and thus benign neglect, some internationally adopted children also experience physical and sexual abuse prior to adoption.

This abuse may have been at the hands of parents and relatives and may have served as a factor in the termination of parental care. It may also have occurred while the child was in foster or institutional care. Most often, unless parental rights were terminated or a physical examination provides evidence consistent with physical or sexual abuse, abuse will be suspect but unproven. Stress associated with abuse can impact brain development in multiple ways, including the down-regulation of growth factors and the development of posttraumatic stress disorder (PTSD). There are a host of growth factors that translate potential nutritional value into tissue synthesis and function, affecting myelination as well as neuronal number and complexity (McMorris & Dubois-Dalcq, 1998; Saneto, Low, Melner, & de Vellis, 1998). Even with adequate nutrition is provided, the effects of stress on growth factors inhibit the utilization of nutrients for normal neural development (M. K. Georgieff, personal communication, June 10, 2003).

PTSD is a syndrome characterized in adults by vivid reexperience of the trauma, emotional upheaval or numbing when exposed to stimuli associated with the trauma, avoidance of these cues, and hyperphysiological arousal (American Psychiatric Association, 1994). PTSD is difficult to diagnose in preverbal children who cannot name the trauma and may not have laid down memories of the event in a preverbal format that is comprehensible to themselves or others (Scheeringa, Zeanah, Drell, & Larrieu, 1995). Studies with older children, however, whose abuse began when they were infants or young children suggest that such maltreatment early in life can have adverse consequences for brain development. In particular, reduced brain volumes, atypical patterns of development in the left hemisphere, and reduced volume of the major fiber tracts that connect the left and right hemispheres of the brain have all been noted (Carrion et al., 2001; De Bellis et al., 1999).

The trauma of abuse is believed to produce its effects through intense and long-term activation of stress-responsive neural circuits. In infants and young children, separation and loss are also believed to be traumatic (Bowlby, 1973) and may activate similar circuits in the brain. In animal studies, infant monkeys who experience separation followed by deprivation exhibit similar brain changes to those noted in physical and sexually abused children, even if the monkeys are not subjected to bodily harm (Sanchez, Hearn, Do, Rilling, & Herndon, 1998). Whether or not they are traumatic, transitions in care are frequent in the preadoption lives of many internationally adopted children. In our survey of internationally adopted children in Minnesota, 72 percent had experienced two or more transitions in care prior to adoption (Gunnar, Grotevant, & Johnson, 2002). In another large study of internationally adopted children in the Netherlands, Verhulst and colleagues (Verhulst, Althaus, & Versluis-den Bieman, 1992) found that children who had experienced many transitions in care prior to adoption were at greater risk of developing behavioral and emotional problems than children who had experienced fewer transitions. Thus, frequent changes in care arrangements can be considered a significant postnatal risk factor for internationally adopted children.

It is also worth noting that the older a child is at adoption, the more postnatal risks the child is likely to have encountered. In our survey of children adopted internationally, the correlation between preadoption risks and age at adoption was $r = .53$, $n = 2,287$, $p < .001$ (Gunnar & Kertes, 2003). Verhulst and colleagues have reported a similar association in their study of children adopted internationally (Verhulst et al., 1992). Unfortunately, early adoption reduces but does not eliminate the possibility that a child has experienced significant postnatal risks to healthy development. In addition, it certainly does not alter the likelihood of having experienced significant prenatal and perinatal risks. The younger the child is at adoption, however, the sooner the child can be exposed to care that is likely to promote healthy brain development.

As noted earlier, in most cases it is difficult to know with certainty whether a particular child has been exposed to the various risks described here prior to adoption. However, even if a child has been exposed to particular adverse circumstances, risks are only probabilistically related to particular outcomes and do not determine they will occur with certainty. Children exposed to the same risk factors will exhibit a variety of outcomes. Enumeration of the various risk factors that may impede healthy brain development in internationally adopted children is sobering. What is equally striking is that in the face of all these potential risks, many internationally adopted children appear to develop into reasonably intelligent and adjusted young people. This fact, which has been well documented in all the studies of internationally adopted children, including those of postinstitutionalized children (see other chapters in this volume), should not be forgotten. Resilience is probably not so much a characteristic of the child as it is an amalgam of factors, including chance events that influence human development (Masten & Reed, 2002). The frequency with which postinstitutionalized children show good developmental outcomes despite a myriad of early adverse experiences challenges us to understand the resilience of the human brain and the factors in the postadoption experience that help children reorganize compromised neural systems to support healthy adaptation and more optimal development.

NEUROBIOLOGICAL STUDIES OF INTERNATIONALLY ADOPTED CHILDREN

Behavioral studies of children who have been fostered or adopted from institutional settings have appeared since the early 1930s (for a review, see Rutter, 1981). To our knowledge, however, there are only two published neurobiological studies of postinstitutionalized children, although there are several studies in progress. Chugani and colleagues conducted positron emission tomography (PET) scans on 10 children adopted following 22 to 90 months of institutional care in Romania (Chugani et al., 2001). Neuropsychological evaluations on these children indicated cognitive functioning in the low average range (full-scale IQs averaged 81), with low scores on attention and concentration, language, and ability to control impulses. Parents reported significant behavioral problems in nearly all the children. At adoption, nearly all the children were severely growth retarded, and head circumferences averaged more than 1.5 standard deviations below the mean. Furthermore, nearly half were reported to have injuries at adoption indicative of physical abuse. In short, these children appeared to have been very poorly cared for over a long period of time prior to adoption. The PET scan results revealed low glucose metabolism (i.e., impairments) in multiple regions of the brain. These included the prefrontal cortex, infralimbic cortex, amygdala and head of the hippocampus, and brain stem. Importantly, these brain regions are richly interconnected, and their activity underlies the types of behavioral problems and cognitive deficits displayed by children in the study. Moreover, all the regions exhibiting impairments in this study are known to be regions affected by chronic stress exposure during development (Sanchez, Ladd, & Plotsky, 2001).

Our laboratory has examined salivary cortisol levels in Romanian postinstitutionalized children 6.5 years after adoption (Gunnar, Morison, Chisholm, & Schuder, 2001). Cortisol is produced by the hypothalamic-pituitary-adrenocortical system and is one of the two major stress-related hormones in the body. Cortisol typically peaks in the early morning hours and declines across the day, reaching its nadir around bedtime. Chronic elevations in cortisol may be a risk factor for the development of affective disorders later in life (Heim & Nemeroff, 2001). Consistent with the hypothesis that institutionally reared children may experience prolonged periods of stress, we found elevations in cortisol over the day. The magnitude of these elevations was roughly comparable to those reported recently by Carrion and his colleagues (Carrion et al., 2002) for children of the same age who had been maltreated (abused, subjected to separation/loss experiences, neglected) earlier in childhood. The idea that institutional care might be highly stressful for young children and that elevated stress hormone activity might compromise stress-sensitive neural systems is reasonable given the stress and early experience literature in animal studies (for a review, see Sanchez et al., 2001). However, studies of young children living in orphanages in Romania and Russia have failed to provide evidence that cortisol is chronically elevated (Carlson & Earls, 1997; Gunnar, 2000). Instead, a lack of a normal daytime rhythm in cortisol has been observed with early morning levels being abnormally low. An atypical diurnal rhythm in cortisol has also been reported in nonhuman primate models of maltreatment and/or repeated, unpredictable mother–infant separation (Sanchez, Winslow, Plotsky, & McCormack, 2002) as well as in abused children (Cicchetti & Rogosch, 2001; King, Mandansky, King, Fletcher, & Brewer, 2001). It is not known how such atypical yet generally low cortisol levels impact the developing brain or whether they might be associated with chronic increases in other parameters of the stress system that, in turn, might have deleterious impact on neural development. What is now apparent, though, is that findings from the Romanian children adopted in 1990–1991 may not generalize to children adopted from less extremely depriving institutional settings. In as-yet-unpublished data, the authors of this chapter examined salivary cortisol levels over the day in children adopted from institutions in Russia/eastern Europe, Asia, and Latin America. Internationally adopted children who had received primarily foster or family care prior to adoption served as the comparison group. Elevations in cortisol levels were small and were observed primarily around the time children awakened in the morning, at the peak of the daily rhythm (Kertes & Madsen, 2003). Children who had experienced severe preadoption deprivation, as indicated by reports of poor preadoptive care and stunted growth at adoption had higher early morning cortisol levels relative to children not experiencing extreme deprivation. Because this sample of postinstitutionalized children was larger (nearly 90 children) and more representative than the earlier study of Romanian postinstitutionalized children (16 children), it seems likely that most children adopted from institutional settings exhibit very small, if any, changes in daily cortisol production. This says nothing, however, about their cortisol responses to stressful events. To date, hormonal stress reactivity of postinstitutionalized children has not been studied. Furthermore, the literature on the effects of early deprivation on stress-sensitive systems points to stress reactivity as being more likely to be compromised by early deprivation than basal or daily cortisol production (Sanchez et al., 2001).

The likelihood that the effects of institutional care on behavior are at least in part due to chronic stress is increased by another set of unpublished data obtained by B. J. Casey and colleagues (Tottenham et al., 2003). Chronic increases in cortisol and/or corticotropin-releasing hormone are expected to reduce the size of the hippocampus and increase the size of the amygdala. According to this model, the more intense and/or prolonged the stress experienced, the larger the ratio of amygdala to hippocampal volume. Casey and colleagues have conducted a small study on 14 postinstitutionalized children, most of whom were girls from China. Using magnetic resonance imaging to visualize hippocampal and amygdala volume (size), they found the expected inverse ratio associated with longer periods of institutional care in the children who had been with their adoptive families for several years at the time.

As noted earlier, there are too few neurobiological studies of postinstitutionalized children to draw any conclusions about the impact of early institutional deprivation on brain development. The data that are available suggest that some effects will be found, most likely in neural systems that underlie the behaviors noted to be affected by early institutional rearing. However, we will need to be cautious about extrapolating from studies with small sample sizes. As more representative samples of children are studied, we can become more confident in the generalizability of results. An additional concern in interpreting results from postinstitutionalized children is to whom these children should be compared. Comparison groups are always critical in developmental research, but they are a particular challenge in studying children who enter their families through international adoption. The ideal comparison group would consist of children who experience risk factors except the one that is the focus of the research. However, because risks often accumulate in some groups more than others, including institutionalized versus noninstitutionalized children, it is often difficult to find a comparison group that is similar on all risk parameters except the one of interest. Furthermore, because it is often impossible to reliably know what has happened to children in their countries of origin prior to adoption, attempts to devise adequate comparison groups will need to be considered in light of inevitable uncertainty of some children's preadoption history. Finally, as we have indicated throughout this chapter, the developing brain is a dynamic entity that adapts and changes with maturation and experience. Thus, results obtained on children of one age may or may not hold for children of another age. Notably, all the neurobiological studies so far conducted have examined primarily prepubertal children. Puberty brings a host of neurobiological changes that may further ameliorate or exacerbate the neural impact of early deprivation, relationship disruption, and abuse. All this should caution us from drawing conclusions about the neural impact of children's preadoption care histories without a good deal of developmental, neurobiological data. Interest in this area is strong, however, and we can expect to see such data becoming increasingly available in the near future.

INTERVENTION AND POLICY

While much remains to be learned about the impact of early adversity on brain development, knowledge of the myriad risk factors that many internationally adopted children may face and the potential repercussions of those risk factors enable us to consider the ramifications for social policy regarding the care of abandoned children. In this section we will outline some suggestions for social policy regarding care of children in countries of origin, practices surrounding international adoption, and support for families with internationally adopted children.

The multiple and often permanent changes produced by prenatal risk factors such as malnutrition, alcohol exposure, and maternal stress clearly implicate the urgency of good prenatal care. At present, the World Health Organization and UNICEF play key roles in increasing access to good prenatal care in developing countries. UNICEF (2001) reports that with efforts to improve access to prenatal care following the World Summit for Children, the proportion of women with at least one antenatal care visit rose from 53 percent in 1990 to 64 percent in 2000. The rise was greatest in Asia (excluding China) and smallest in sub-Saharan Africa. Current estimates indicate that about 65 percent of women in the developing world see a health professional at least once during pregnancy, with the highest rates in Latin America and the Caribbean (83%) and the lowest in South Asia (51%). While these improvements are laudable, more work is needed to improve *regular* access to prenatal care and to ensure that these services reach sectors of the population who, for various reasons, give up their children to institutions or international adoption.

Efforts should also be directed at improving the nature and quality of care for children living in institutional settings such as orphanages. First, adequate environmental input is essential for normal development of neural systems related to sensory, motor, and language skills. Improved visual, auditory, and tactile stimulation would help promote normal development of these systems that are otherwise often severely delayed in institutionalized children. Importantly, material objects such as toys are useful but not critical in this regard. Rather, the sensory and social stimulation that caregivers have the potential to provide are as good or better than nonsocial stimuli in promoting healthy brain development in these domains. However, it is not enough to have caregivers present; rather, the consistency of caregivers and the meaningfulness of their interactions with children (i.e., interaction that goes beyond physical care) are the determinant factors in children's developmental outcomes. Consistency of caregivers is also of critical importance in enabling children to develop reasonably normal social skills and attachment relationships. All these changes would be facilitated by the establishment of expanded in-country foster care or adoption services. In the absence of such services, however, there have been some efforts to implement intervention play therapy programs and training for caregivers in select orphanages to provide better sensorimotor and social stimulation to children (Groark, McCall, Muhamedrahimov, Nikoforova, & Palmov, 2000; Taneja et al., 2002). The effectiveness of such programs in improving developmental outcomes is likely to hinge, at least in part, on the stability of the caregivers in the institutions.

In terms of policies regarding intervention such as foster care and adoption, the principles of neural plasticity described earlier would suggest that the earlier the intervention (i.e., placement in a stable and permanent home), the better the eventual recovery from the detrimental effects of early adverse circumstances (prenatal and postnatal). Therefore, concerted efforts should be made to place children in permanent care as early as possible. This is not to suggest that children who remain in orphanages are irrecoverable. Children stay in institutions for a variety of reasons, including political changes in adoption policies in their countries of origin. In fact, the longer the duration and the more severe the delays, the more dramatic the "catch-up" children show in the first years post-adoption. Thus, while early placement may be desirable, the bottom line is that permanent or stable family care environments, provided they afford better-quality care than institutional settings, are beneficial in ameliorating or reversing the potentially detrimental effects of early adverse experiences on brain development. It is worth noting, however, that while improved quality of care associated with a stable family environment often provides a supportive environment for dramatic growth, there is a notable lack of research exploring *particular* parental characteristics that are associated with positive developmental outcomes in internationally adopted children.

With respect to international adoption, there are several recommendations that would facilitate intervention efforts and the ability of families to meet the particular needs of individual children. First, information needs to be provided to parents both prior to and following adoption regarding the potential adverse experiences that their children may have encountered. In addition, efforts should be made by international agencies or institutions in countries of origin to provide better documentation of children's health and developmental status, including exposure to parasites and other illnesses, prenatal exposure to teratogens, or adverse environmental factors that may affect brain development. In adoptive countries, efforts should be expanded to disseminate information to primary care physicians such as those provided by Johnson (2000b; see also Hostetter & Johnson, 1990) and Jenista (2000a; see also Mitchell & Jenista, 1997) regarding the kinds of illnesses and experiences children may have encountered in their countries of origin and the types of delays sometimes observed in postinstitutionalized children. This will enable parents and physicians to be more proactive and intervene early to address child-specific, preadoption adverse experiences.

Accurate information and training also needs to be disseminated beyond physicians to key adoption personnel, such as caseworkers and mental health professionals. Stereotypes exist both in the professional adoption community and among adoptive parents regarding the impact of early adversity on children's development, and parents often have unrealistic beliefs (both positive and negative) regarding the possibilities of ameliorating the effects of early adversity. Since realistic parental expectations are key in placement stability and family adjustment and since parental expectations are greatly affected by the input they receive from key adoption professionals, it is imperative that these professionals have up-to-date, accurate information as well as the skills to translate it into meaningful and useful information for parents.

Correspondingly, research efforts and monies should be aimed both at understanding the potential consequences of early adversity on brain and behavioral development in internationally adopted children and toward the development of effective intervention strategies for children adopted from conditions of deprivation and maltreatment more broadly. The development of effective intervention strategies needs be coupled with education of adoptive parents to encourage them to seek evaluation and treatment early rather than ignoring problems that manifest early in the postadoption years in the hopes that children will grow out of them.

At the same time, parents need to be informed that preadoption history is often uncertain; thus, they may never know with confidence what experiences may have contributed to cognitive and behavioral problems that they may observe in their adopted children. Support services are essential to provide the social support that families of internationally adopted children need, as they may face continued challenges through childhood and adolescence unlike those of birth children. It is worth noting, however, that given the complexity of development, uncertainty as to what "caused" delays or behavioral problems is not restricted to adoptive families but is often experienced by parents of birth children as well.

As a final note, the brain is a remarkably resilient organ, capable of reorganization with effective intervention. This chapter emphasized the potential detrimental effects that pre- and postnatal adverse experiences often encountered by internationally adopted children may have on the developing brain. While some effects may be permanent, at no point should a child who has languished in an institution for much of his or her young life be considered lost or completely incapable of recovery. In fact, there are numerous children who have been adopted internationally, including those reared in institutions, and who are doing very well in school and are reasonably well-adjusted young people. Most children, regardless of their upbringing, are likely to encounter some cognitive or behavioral difficulties at some point during development, including those with relatively typical early care experiences and, presumably, brain function. We should not lower our expectations for what could be with regard to postinstitutionalized children's brain development, cognitive skills, and behavioral adjustment. With improvements in care and effective intervention strategies for children whose quality of care has been less than ideal, we should expect and work toward facilitating optimal developmental outcomes.

ACKNOWLEDGMENTS

Preparation of this chapter was supported by a National Institute of Mental Health Research Scientist Award (MH00946) to Megan R. Gunnar and a National Science Foundation Fellowship to Darlene A. Kertes. The authors wish to thank Christopher Coe for his help in sorting through the literature on prenatal stress and premature birth.

Chapter 4

Adverse Preadoption Experiences and Psychological Outcomes

Michael Rutter

Over the past three decades, there has been a marked fall in the number of within-country adoptions in infancy and a parallel rise in the number of children adopted from abroad, often from very depriving backgrounds, and in the number of adoptions of older children with special needs (Cohen, 2002; Selman, 2000). The empirical findings indicate that, despite their unfortunate starts in life, many of these higher-risk adoptees have a relatively good psychological outcome. However, the changed pattern of adoption has meant that questions need to be asked about the ways in which adverse preadoption experiences may affect children's development and psychosocial functioning after adoption and about the types of interventions that could ameliorate the situation postadoption. The empirical research literature on this topic is decidedly limited, but a few studies have begun to identify some of the key issues, and the purpose of this chapter is to review what these studies show. It will be appreciated that similar questions need to be asked about genetic risk factors, but they fall outside the scope of this chapter; genetic research findings will be noted here only in relation to environmentally mediated risks.

RISK AND RESILIENCE

Traditionally, adoption has tended to be viewed as a means of providing a high-quality rearing environment for children not wanted by their biological parents or whose care by those parents has broken down for one reason or another. When most adoptions took place in infancy, the risks experienced by adopted children were thought to be mainly genetic. In recent decades, however, adoptions in infancy have become the exception rather than the rule. Accordingly, the conceptualization of risk has had to be broadened in a major way to include those resulting from adverse experiences in early life. The issues that have to be addressed involve two key questions (Rutter, 2000b, in press a; in press b). The first concerns the nature and extent of such environmentally mediated preadoption risks (including the query of the degree to which such early risks operate in a way that is independent of later risk experiences). The second concerns the degree to which the children may show resilience or recovery of psychological functions as a result of positive, or compensatory, postadoption experiences. These questions constitute both the context and the focus of this review of the limited empirical evidence available that could begin to provide answers.

THE "NATURAL EXPERIMENT" OF ADOPTION

Adoption has been used by behavior geneticists as a research strategy that pulls apart the effects of genes and of environments (see Rutter et al., 1990; Rutter, Silberg, O'Connor, & Simonoff, 1999). The need for such a strategy arises because, ordinarily, the biological parents who pass on their genes also provide the rearing environment for their children. As a consequence, any correlation between a family feature and the children's psychological functioning could be due to either genetic or environmental indicators or to a combination of the two. With adoption, the parents who pass on their genes are not the same parents who provide the children's rearing; accordingly, it is possible to determine whether the main effects stem from the biological heritage or from the pattern of rearing. The research design is not free of problems (see Rutter, Pickles, Murray, & Eaves, 2001), but it has been informative in confirming the genetic effects identified through the use of twin designs.

What has been less recognized until recently is that adoption also provides an invaluable natural experiment to study hypotheses about environmental risk mediation (Rutter, Pickles, et al., 2001). That is because it pulls apart the effects of pre- and postadoption experiences. A major limitation in most longitudinal samples of nonadopted studies is that it is not only difficult to separate genetic and environmental effects but also extremely problematic to differentiate the effects of earlier and later environments because the two are so closely associated. Adoption of children from high-risk backgrounds differs in that there is a sharp discontinuity between serious adversity preadoption and a generally somewhat better-than-average rearing environment postadoption. The causal hypothesis (with respect to environmentally mediated risk) is put to test by (1) the extent to which psychological functioning improves following the move from the adverse environment preadoption to the good conditions of the adoptive home, (2) the extent to which individual differences in psychological outcome are a function of variations in the severity or duration of the preadoption depriving experiences, and (3) the extent to which individual differences in outcome are a function of variations in the quality of the adoptive home environment. Clearly, the strength of these tests is much increased by having a comparison sample of early-adopted children who have not experienced severe deprivation. Maximum leverage is provided by the combination of across-group comparisons and within-individual change over time.

This use of the natural experiment of adoption has been described in terms of its scientific value in testing hypotheses about environmentally related protective processes. However, it is obvious that the same design provides invaluable findings on the policy and practice issues that have to be considered with respect to the adoption of children who have experienced severe adversity in early childhood. The issues to be addressed include the frequency of major (or minor) problems deriving from serious deprivation in early childhood, whether such problems show a recognizable pattern, the extent to which they persist if rearing conditions are good, and the nature of interventions that might best foster normal development in such circumstances. Before considering either the theoretical or practical implications, the findings from some of the key studies using the natural experiment design need to be presented.

EFFECTS OF PRENATAL DRUG EXPOSURE ON COGNITIVE PERFORMANCE

Several studies of babies born to substance-abusing mothers and adopted or fostered soon after birth have been undertaken. These include both intensive studies of small groups and questionnaire studies of large samples.

Toronto Study

Nulman et al. (1994) compared 23 prenatal cocaine-exposed adopted children and 23 matched controls (also adopted and also referred for post-adoption counseling after gestational exposure—in the case of controls—to nonteratogens such as penicillin). The cocaine-exposed infants had a gestation that was 3 weeks shorter (37 weeks vs. 40 weeks) and weighed a lot less at birth (2,597 vs. 3,415 grams). The groups did not differ in weight or height at the 3-year follow-up, but the head circumference of the drug-exposed children was significantly lower (31st percentile vs. 63rd percentile). The groups did not differ on IQ, but the cocaine-exposed children had significantly lower scores on the Reynell language scales, this difference not being accounted for by gestational age or weight at birth. The groups of children studied were small, but the samples were well chosen, and the findings clearly point to adverse effects of prenatal cocaine exposure on intrauterine growth, with sequelae evident on measures of both head circumference and language.

Göteborg Study

Aronson et al. (1985) studied 21 children born to alcoholic women together with a matched control group. Psychological testing was undertaken between 1 1/2 and 9 years. The mean IQ score of the alcohol-exposed children was 95 as compared with 112 in the control group. The mean score for those in foster homes (96) did not differ from that for those in biological families (93). The mean IQ was lower for those with physical stigmata of the fetal alcohol syndrome (89) than in those without (100). The small sample size and large spread of ages call for caution in drawing conclusions, but the findings are consistent with some small effect on IQ.

California Long-Range Adoption Study

Barth and Needell (1996) used as their starting point contact with the adoptive parents of 2,589 children placed in 1988–89. Questionnaires were completed on 1,396 children at 2 years after placement and 1,008 at 4 years after placement (i.e., a participation rate of only 39%). The 1,008 were subdivided into the 220 exposed prenatally to drugs, 201 not so exposed, and 587 unknown (the categorization being on the basis of questionnaire responses of the adoptive parents). The median age at placement of the drug-exposed group was 6 months as compared with 1 month for the non-exposed. This led, among other factors, to the drug-exposed group being substantially older (76 vs. 59 months) at the 4-year follow-up. On the Behavior Problem Inventory, the drug-exposed children showed a higher rate of hyperactivity, but otherwise the groups did not differ. The findings suggest few long-term sequelae of prenatal drug exposure, but the low participation rate and the weak measurement call for caution in the conclusions.

Norwegian Study of Fostered and Adopted Children

A recent Norwegian study (Moe, 2002; Moe & Slinning, 2001) has provided somewhat fuller findings on the effects of prenatal exposure to drugs. A drug-exposed group comprised 64 children born to mothers with heavy use of illegal drugs (mainly heroin but also a mixed range of other substances, including alcohol and tobacco) and who had been placed in foster care ($n = 37$) or adopted ($n = 27$), in most cases (85%) in infancy. A volunteer comparison group of 52 was made up of children born without any known biomedical risk to mothers and without alcohol or illicit drug use during the pregnancy. About half the nonbiological mothers who reared the drug-exposed children had a college-level education, and half did not. Because the comparison group was stratified on socioeconomic status (SES) to be comparable to the foster/adoptive groups, their educational level was similar. Both groups were assessed at 4 1/2 years of age on the McCarthy Scales.

The drug-exposed children had a lower mean general cognitive index (GCI) than the comparison group (103 vs. 114), the difference being most marked on perceptual skills, on which there was a difference of about one standard deviation. As would be expected, the drug-exposed group was the only one in which the children showed the neonatal abstinence syndrome (observed in 80%), and a much higher proportion (27% vs. 0%) were born before 38 weeks of gestation (with an associated marked difference in both weight and a smaller head circumference).

In order to examine possible mediating influences, possible predictor variables were correlated with the outcome measures. Gestational age and parental SES had substantial, statistically significant correlations with outcome (.33 and .25, respectively, in relation to the GCI); curiously, the effects of head circumference were not examined. A simultaneous regression analysis showed that only parental SES had an independent effect on the GCI (the effects of drug exposure was marginal, with a p value of .08). However, both drug exposure and parental SES, together with gestational age, had independent effects on perceptual performance. There were significant interactions with gender in the case of both outcomes, boys showing the greater adverse effects of prenatal drug exposure on cognitive functioning.

Moe (2002) interpreted her findings as indicating that prenatal drug exposure (involving a mixture of illicit drugs plus alcohol and tobacco) increased the likelihood of premature gestation, low birth weight, and low head circumference. The subsequent effects on perceptual functioning were partially but not entirely accounted for by the effects on duration of gestation and birth weight, with boys apparently more vulnerable to the sequelae of prenatal drug exposure. Moe and Slinning (2001) argued that a good caregiving environment had provided a buffering effect on the grounds that, between 1 and 3 years of age, there was a rise in scores on the Bayley Scale. However, this was also found in the comparison group, and there was not a significant interaction; accordingly, there is no empirical support for the buffering claim.

The design used almost rules out postnatal drug-related influences as a cause of the relative cognitive impairment (not entirely because a few of the children spent some time with drug-abusing mothers). Because the comparison group came from a similar SES background, it is also unlikely that genetic factors accounted for the prenatal drug exposure effect on IQ. An alternative design, which seems not to have been used up to now, would be to compare the outcomes of children born to substance-abusing mothers and substance-abusing fathers, the rationale being that both transmit genes but that only the mothers can give rise to prenatal drug effects.

Because (as is usually the case) the mothers used a variety of different drugs, it is not possible to conclude whether the effects derived from the heroin, alcohol, tobacco, or other substances. The pattern of findings suggests that part of the effect on later cognition was mediated through drug effects on fetal growth, but that does not appear to be the whole story, and the analyses undertaken did not quantify the extent of such mediation (see Baron and Kenny, 1986). From a practical point of view, it may be concluded that prenatal drug exposure probably carries some risk for later cognitive functioning (at least in early childhood) but that the effects tend to be moderate rather than marked, that they appear to be greater in boys than girls (for unknown reasons), and that it is not clear whether the effects apply generally or rather only on some vulnerable subgroup. Although the evidence base is inadequate, it may be tentatively evaluated that the risks are probably least in girls born after at least 38 weeks of gestation, with a normal birth weight for gestational age, and whose head circumference is normal.

EARLY PARENTAL NEGLECT OR ABUSE

French Adoption Study

The effects of parental neglect or abuse on the later cognitive performance of adopted children have been most systematically investigated by Duyme and his colleagues (Duyme, Areseneault, & Dumaret, 2004; Duyme, Dumaret, & Tomkiewicz, 1999). They identified children in France who met six criteria: (1) removal from home because of parental abuse or neglect, (2) placement in multiple foster families or institutions prior to adoption, (3) an IQ assessment in the year preceding adoption with a score above 60 but below 86, (4) aged between 4 and 6 years at the time of adoptive placement, (5) aged between 11 and 18 years at the psychometric follow-up, and (6) raised by two adoptive parents.

The mean IQ score before adoption was 78, with no significant variation according to the SES of the adopting families, rising to a mean of 91 at follow-up. The implication is that the good rearing environment of the adoptive families had led to an increase in cognitive level. The design does not allow a strong conclusion on this point because there was no comparison group providing evidence on developmental (or time) trends in IQ. Nevertheless, it seems highly unlikely that there would have been a comparable rise in IQ if the children had remained with their abusing/neglecting parents.

The particular, unique strength of the design lies in the opportunity to test whether the degree of cognitive gain was a function of the SES of the adoptive parents. The findings showed that it was, with gains of 8, 16, and 19 points, respectively, for children placed with low, middle, and high-SES adoptive parents. This significant effect substantially bolsters the inference that the gain in IQ over time was attributable to the change in the quality of the rearing conditions.

Despite this, strong normative stability of IQ was found. There was a correlation of .39 between the preadoption IQ and the follow-up IQ; this increased to .67 after correction for restriction in range. The strength of correlation was uninfluenced by the SES level of the adoptive parents. In short, the move to an adoptive family had resulted in a considerable rise in the overall *level* of IQ, but it had had no effect on preestablished individual differences, however caused (genetic factors are likely to have been the most important, but obstetric factors and postnatal experiences may well have played some part).

It might be supposed that adoption should have a beneficial effect on the cognitive level of abused/neglected children regardless of initial IQ. In order to determine whether that was the case, Duyme et al. (2004) used the complete preadoption IQ range (above 60) to select those with an initial IQ between 60 and 85, termed the low-IQ group ($n = 98$), and those with an initial IQ above 106, the high-IQ group ($n = 30$). In each case, outcome was compared according to whether the SES of the adopting family was low or high. The findings were striking in showing a *fall* in mean IQ for the high-IQ group but a *rise* in the low-IQ group. Nevertheless, in both groups there was a significant effect from the adoptive family SES. Thus, the high-IQ group showed a fall from a mean of about 113 to one of about 107 if the children were in a high-SES adoptive family and to about 98 if they were in a low-SES adoptive family. Both 98 and 107 were well above the respective follow-up means of about 93 and 84 in the low-IQ group. The data do not provide an answer on the reasons for the fall, but it is important to note that the high-IQ group already had a preadoption IQ above the general population mean (so that regression to the mean is almost certainly part of the explanation) and that this means that they were highly atypical for abused/neglected children.

It may be concluded that preadoption cognitive level (reflecting genetic and early environmental influences) continues to exert important effects postadoption. Adoption does not (and almost certainly cannot) eliminate preexisting individual differences. On the other hand, when the adverse effects of preadoption parental neglect/abuse lead to low IQ, adoption can have an important effect in countering cognitive impairment, and the extent of such buffering is a function of the qualities of the adoptive home.

Dutch International Adoption Study

The Dutch International Adoption Study (Verhulst, 2000a, 2000b) used a quite different approach. A sample of over 3,000 children adopted from abroad (mostly Korean, Colombian, and Indian) by nonrelatives in the Netherlands in the early 1970s constituted the starting point. Usable information on adverse environmental influences in the country of origin were available on just under two-thirds of the sample (n = 2,148) who were aged 10 to 15 years at the time of follow-up. The adolescent assessment comprised the Child Behavior Checklist (CBCL) completed by the parents (n = 1,538) and the Youth Self Report (YSR) version of the same scale (n = 1,262). The scores were compared with those of 933 nonadopted children of the same age.

The proportion of adopted boys showing delinquent and hyperactive problem behavior (assessed by the parental questionnaire) was approximately twice that in the nonadopted boys; the differences for girls were quite minor. The increase in problem behavior was quite strongly related to early adverse experiences, with the rate of marked problems (scores supposedly in the clinical range) somewhat higher in the case of those placed in the adoptive home after the age of two and markedly higher in those experiencing many changes in the caregiving environment (50% problem behavior) and in those with five or more placements or in those experiencing neglect (24% in those suffering severe neglect) or abuse (31% in those severely abused). The findings on the YSR showed that 22 percent of the boys and 18 percent of the girls had scores in the deviant range as compared with 10 percent of adolescents of both sexes in the general population (Verhulst, 2000a). The increased scores in the internationally adopted boys were especially evident for delinquent behaviors (although the individual items on the scale suggested rather atypical delinquency). The increased scores for girls were most evident in relation to aggression.

The initial findings were supplemented by further questionnaires some 3 years later, when the subjects were aged 14 to 18 years. The total problem mean score in the adopted group increased from 21.4 to 24.8, whereas those in the nonadopted group fell from 20.8 to 16.3, with the consequence of a widening of the difference between the two groups. The rise appeared to be greater in girls than boys.

The findings are important in showing substantial effects of the preadoption environment on behavioral functioning in adolescence. Nevertheless, some caution is needed in the interpretation of the findings because (1) the information on the early environment derived from the adoptive parents, with the consequence that the same informant provided data on both the predictors and the outcome variables; (2) the measures were confined to questionnaires; and (3) there was substantial sample attrition (thus, the parental CBCL was available on only 1,538 subjects—just 44% of the original sample of 3,519—and the YSR on just 39%).

Other International Adoption Studies

A Swedish study similarly used the CBCL to study the emotional/behavioral adjustment of international adoptees (three-quarters from Asia and one-quarter from Latin America) at 13 to 16 years of age, the findings being compared with those for a similar-aged youth random sample (Cederblad, Hook, Irhammar, & Mercke, 1999; Irhammar & Cederblad, 2000). Overall, the mean scores of the two groups did not differ significantly. However, there was a significant effect of the preadoption situation, the scores being about twice as high in the small group ($n = 20$), who had spent 7 months or more in orphanages or foster homes in their country of origin. This effect was most evident with respect to social problems, withdrawn behavior, and attention problems.

Minnesota International Adoption Survey

Gunnar and Kertes (2003) undertook a postal questionnaire survey, including the CBCL, of over 3,000 families of 4- to 19-year-old children adopted in Minnesota from abroad between 1990 and 1998; their response rate was 60 percent. The majority of the children were adopted from Asia, and only 16 percent came from Russia and eastern Europe. Most of the children in the latter group had been institutionalized for more than 4 months, whereas most of the former had not. All the analyses focused on the factors associated with problems, as assessed on the CBCL, within this large sample of international adoptions. Institutional care was associated with a higher rate of "externalizing" problems (incorporating inattention, delinquency, and aggression). It was found that both the duration of institutional care and the extent of health problems at the time of adoption predicted a higher risk of externalizing problems. However, multivariate analyses showed that the apparent effect of health problems was accounted for by the duration of institutional care. The increase in disruptive behavior was less evident in children under the age of 11 years (being associated mainly with inattention in this younger group) but was marked in adolescence. The elevated risk was clearest in those adolescents who had spent more than 2 years in institutions. The education of the adoptive parents did not predict outcome, but a high family income had a slightly protective effect, and the simultaneous adoption of another child somewhat increased the risk.

The findings of these studies, considered together, suggest that international adoption is associated with an increased risk for disruptive behavior (including inattention, some kinds of delinquency, and some kinds of aggression) and that, to an important extent, this increased risk is a function of adverse experiences (especially institutional rearing) preadoption.

REARING IN DEPRIVING INSTITUTIONS

The international adoption studies in the Netherlands and Scandinavia have been limited by their reliance on questionnaire scores. Much richer data on psychological outcomes are available in prospective studies of children initially reared in institutions of some kind.

Hodges and Tizard Study

One of the earliest systematic studies of possible enduring effects of early institutional care was that undertaken by Hodges and Tizard (1989a, 1989b). The basis for their investigation was provided by a small group of children who had experienced an institutional upbringing in residential nurseries and who had been assessed there. The children were followed up at age 16 years, with the main comparison between the 21 who had been adopted, the 8 restored to their biological parents, and the matched comparison samples for both these groups.

The children adopted between 2 and 4 1/2 years showed a substantial rise of IQ by the time of the age 4 assessment (the rise is implied rather than demonstrated because there was a change in IQ test and because there was a similar, albeit smaller, rise in those children restored to their biological parents or who remained in institutional care), and at both 8 and 16 years their mean IQ was 114 (Hodges & Tizard, 1989a). The children adopted after the age of 4 had a mean IQ of 102 at age 16, and those restored either before or after the age of 4 had a mean IQ of 96 to 98. It was concluded that early institutional care, in the relatively good circumstances of the residential nurseries studied, had no marked effect on later IQ but that early adoption might bring cognitive benefits.

Overall, both the adopted and the restored groups tended to show somewhat more emotional/behavioral disturbance than their matched controls, but the two ex-institutional groups did not differ markedly in the level of difficulties at 16. On the other hand, the restored adolescents were more likely than the adopted children to have been in trouble with the police and/or referred to psychiatric/psychological services.

The findings on the adolescents' social relationships at 16 showed a disparity between relationships with peers and those within the family. The restored children were more likely than adopted children to have marked difficulties getting on with their siblings and more likely not to show physical affection to their parents. Although both groups showed more family relationship difficulties than controls, this difference was more marked in the case of restored children. It seemed that both intrafamilial problems and antisocial behavior were related to the worse current psychosocial situation in the biological families to which the children had been restored.

By contrast, both the adopted and the restored children differed from their controls with respect to the quality of their peer relationships. The particular features were adult orientation, difficulties with peers, lack of a special friend, little turning to peers for emotional support, and little selectivity in choosing friends. Half the ex-institutional children showed at least 4 of these 5 features as compared with only 1 (4%) of the 24 matched comparisons. Hodges and Tizard (1989b) noted the variety of explanations that could be proposed to account for these findings. However, whatever the mechanism, what was striking was that the experience of institutional care (with a very high level of turnover of caregivers) in the first few years of life was associated with persistent effects on peer relationships at 16 that did not appear to be accounted for by their current circumstances in adolescence (because of the lack of differences between the adopted and the restored children).

Roy Study

Roy, Rutter, and Pickles (2000, 2004), in their comparison of children reared in foster families and those reared in institutions, focused on the hypothesis that institutional rearing constituted the key risk factor (rather than on the quite different question of whether the risk effects persisted after a radical change of environment). Nineteen primary school children admitted to residential group care before the age of 1 year were compared with 19 similar-aged children reared in foster families from the same age, together with classroom controls for both groups. Both the family-fostered and the institution-reared children came from very high-risk family backgrounds, but they did not differ in that respect. The children in these groups were assessed in the same way at about 80 months of age.

The institutional and family foster groups did not differ in their mean IQ (108 and 106, respectively), but the institutional children had elevated rates of emotional and behavioral difficulties, particularly characterized by inattention and overactivity at school (Roy et al., 2000). In addition, the institution-reared children showed a marked lack of selective relationships with both caregivers and peers, this lack of selectivity being associated with inattention/overactivity (Roy, Rutter, & Pickles, 2004). This pattern of a lack of selective relationships was not found in the family-fostered group, and it was concluded that it derived from some feature of an institutional upbringing.

Canadian Study of Adoptees from Romania

Elinor Ames and her colleagues (Ames, 1997; Chisholm, 1998; Chisholm, Carter, Ames, & Morison, 1995; Fisher, Ames, Chisholm, & Savoie, 1997;

Morison, Ames, & Chisholm, 1995) in British Columbia, Canada, under-took a systematic study of 46 children adopted from Romania who had spent at least 8 months in institutional care (the median length of time was 17.5 months), plus 29 noninstitutionalized children adopted from Romania before the age of 4 months, together with 46 nonadopted Canadian-born (CB) children. In obtaining this sample, Ames et al. were able to make contact with 131 children adopted from Romania. As the official Canadian records indicated that 142 children came to British Columbia during the comparable period of time from Romania, it is highly likely that their sample was reasonably representative. The adoptive families of the early-adopted (EA) group had a higher educational level than the Romanian orphanage (RO) group. In order to ensure meaningful comparisons, there were 29 matched pairs of RO and EA children and 29 matched pairs of CB and EA children. The groups were first studied when the children had been in their adoptive homes for about 11 months and reassessed again when most of the children were aged about 4 1/2 years. The attrition rate was low (6.5% to 8.5%), but to compensate, new subjects were added.

The mean Stanford-Binet IQ for the 4 1/2-year-olds was 109 in the CB group, 98 in the EA group, and 90 in the RO group. However, the spread of scores in both the EA and RO groups was wide (65 to 127 in the RO group). The between-group differences were greater for children older than 4 1/2 (and, therefore, who had been adopted at an older age). The mean IQ was 69 in the RO group as compared with 106 in the CB group. There was no particular pattern of cognitive skills and deficits.

The Home Observation for Measurement of the Environment (HOME) was used to assess qualities of the adoptive family rearing environment. The findings showed that the RO families provided the least stimulation and support, but it seemed that this may have derived from having to deal with the children's other manifold problems. Be that as it may, the HOME score showed a significant correlation with the child's IQ in the RO and EA groups but not in the CB group.

The main factors associated with lower cognitive performance were the length of time spent in institutions and whether the family had adopted two Romanian children at the same time. The effects of institutional care on IQ were particularly marked in those who had spent at least 2 years in depriving institutions.

At the time of adoption, according to parental reports, 59 percent of the RO children had a weight below the fifth percentile. At the time of the 4 1/2-year follow-up, 18 percent of the RO children were still below the 10th percentile for weight. On average, the RO children were 5.1 centimeters shorter than the CB children and 2.5 centimeters shorter than the EA children.

The majority of RO children had at least one major health problem, of which intestinal parasites, hepatitis B, and anemia were the most common. Most of these (apart from hepatitis B) had been overcome by the time of the second follow-up.

On the CBCL, at the time of the second follow-up, just over one-third of the 20 children had scores above the clinical cutoff, these being mainly externalizing problems. The rate of problems in the RO group was significantly higher than in the CB group but did not differ from the EA group. However, it was found that the longer the duration of institutional care, the greater the level of behavioral disturbance.

In the period shortly after adoption, eating problems were very frequent in the RO children, but these were much less evident at follow-up. Stereotyped behavior, however, was much increased in the RO children (as compared with the EA and CB groups) both initially and at follow-up. Problems in relationships with other children were significantly higher in RO children than the CB children, those in EA group being intermediate. Like other outcomes, social relationship difficulties were associated with having spent a long time in institutional care.

A modified separation–reunion procedure was used in the family home to assess attachment insecurity, using the coding scheme devised by Crittenden (1992). Secure attachment was equally frequent in the CB and EA groups (58% and 67%, respectively) but less common (37%) in the RO group. However, the most striking difference lay in the "atypical insecure" category; this applied to 33 percent of the RO children but only 7 and 4 percent, respectively, in the CB and EA groups. It was particularly striking that, at the time of the second follow-up, parents described indiscriminate friendliness as evident in 60 percent of RO children, this being much higher than in either the CB or EA groups. Indiscriminately friendly behavior in RO children was particularly shown by a tendency to wander without distress and a willingness to go home with a stranger. Within the RO group, such behavior was associated with having been a favorite in the institution (as reported by the adoptive parents) and with greater behavioral and social problems at follow-up. It was, however, unrelated to the duration of institutional care.

Ames (1997) sought to combine the various psychological outcome measures to provide an overall assessment of serious problems. One-third of the RO group had no serious problems, but one-third had at least three (as compared with none in the CB group and only one child in the EA group). The number of serious problems was related to the length of time spent in institutional care but not to the institutional conditions as reported by the adoptive parents. In addition, the families who had adopted two children from Romania at the same time were more likely to have a child with a large number of serious problems (probably because of the resulting burden on the family), as were families of lower SES or lower total family income. Interestingly, too, multiple serious problems were more likely when the father alone had been to Romania to select a child, perhaps because the mother felt that she might have made a different choice.

British Study

The British study differed from the Canadian study in that it employed a random sampling design, stratified only on the child's age at the time of coming to the United Kingdom and in its use of a comparison group of 52 within-U.K. adoptees who had not experienced institutional care and who were placed in their adoptive family prior to the age of 6 months (Rutter, 2000a; Rutter & the E.R.A. Research Team, 1998; Rutter, O'Connor, et al., 2004). The Romanian adoptees sample of 165 children (who came to the United Kingdom at ages varying from infancy to 42 months) included a few children adopted from home settings, but particular attention was paid to the 144 reared from infancy in very depriving circumstances. The adoptive families of both U.K. and Romanian children were slightly better educated than the general U.K. population but did not differ in this respect from one another. Within the Romanian group, there was no association between adoptive family characteristics and the children's age at entry into the United Kingdom. In addition, those who entered the United Kingdom young and those who entered when older did not differ in the age when they were placed in an institution (85% were placed in the first month of life) or in their level of subnutrition at the time of U.K. entry.

The conditions in the Romanian institutions at that time were extremely bad in all respects. The children were generally confined to their cribs for much of the time, few if any toys and playthings were available, there was little interaction between caregivers and children (there being a very poor staff-to-child ratio), feeding was usually gruel provided by propped-up bottles with large teats, and washing usually consisted of being hosed down with cold water (see Castle et al., 1999; Johnson, 2000b; Kaler & Freeman, 1994). Not surprisingly, this was reflected in the children's state at the time of coming to the United Kingdom. Over half had a weight below the third percentile, and three-fifths were functioning developmentally in the severely retarded range.

The first question was the extent to which recovery was possible when the children moved from these dreadful institutional conditions to a good-quality adoptive family. The findings showed that, even for those who were markedly malnourished at the time of leaving Romanian institutions, there was virtually complete catch-up in weight by the age of 6 years in those who came to the United Kingdom before the age of 2 years. There was a similarly dramatic catch-up in those who remained in institutions until after the age of 2, but it was not quite complete by age 6 (Rutter, O'Connor, et al., 2004). Even for those initially functioning developmentally in the severely retarded range, cognitive catch-up was remarkable so that by 6 years their mean level of cognitive functioning had almost (but not quite) come up to the U.K. population mean by age 6.

The extent to which the children's psychological functioning was normal by age 6 years was assessed by examining seven main domains of functioning—spanning features such as cognitive level, emotional disturbance, behavioral disruption, and social relationships (Rutter, Pickles, et al., 2001). Nearly half (45%) of the children adopted from Romania showed no impairment on any of the seven domains as compared with 78 percent of those adopted in infancy within the United Kingdom (the fact that 22% of this very low-risk group showed impairment on at least one domain reflects the stringency of the criteria employed). However, the extent to which functioning was normal was strongly influenced by the children's age at the time of entry to the United Kingdom; of those entering below 6 months, 70 percent showed no impairment—a figure almost the same as in the U.K. group. By contrast, of those entering between 24 and 42 months, only a quarter (24%) showed no impairment in any domain. Nevertheless, it was striking that a substantial minority of the children who spent the longest period of time in severely depriving institutions were functioning without measurable problems at age six. Moreover, considering the opposite extreme, it was notable that, even in this highest-risk subgroup, only just over a fifth (22%) showed impairment in three or more of the seven domains.

On the whole, research findings have shown little specificity in the patterns of psychopathology associated with psychosocial stress or adversity (McMahon, Grant, Compas, Thurm, & Ey, 2003; Rutter, 2000a). It was necessary to consider whether this apparent lack of specificity also applied to profound institutional deprivation. Perhaps surprisingly, it was found that it did not—at least in terms of the findings at 6 years of age (Rutter, Kreppner, et al., 2001). There were just four psychological patterns that both showed a marked difference in rate between the Romanian and within-U.K. adoptees and that showed a dose–response relationship with the duration of institutional deprivation. These were, first, attachment disturbances characterized by a relatively undiscriminating social approach, a seeming lack of awareness of social boundaries, and a difficulty in picking up social cues on what is socially appropriate or acceptable to other people (O'Connor, Brendenkamp, Rutter, & the E.R.A. Research Team, 1999; O'Connor, Rutter, & the E.R.A. Research Team, 2000; O'Connor, Marvin, et al., 2003). Second, there was inattention/overactivity of a kind that seemed, possibly, to be more a problem in dealing with group situations than with pervasive hyperactivity as such (Kreppner, O'Connor, Rutter, & the E.R.A. Research Team, 2001). It was noteworthy that inattention/overactivity in the Romanian children was more often associated with attachment problems than with cognitive impairment. Third, there was a pattern that was made up of autistic-like features, especially including marked circumscribed interests, but that tended to improve as the children grew older (Rutter, Silberg, et al., 1999). Fourth, there was cognitive impairment, usually associated with either quasi-autistic patterns or attachment disturbances.

Analysis of the findings of the further follow-up at 11 years of age is still under way, but one important difference from the situation at 6 is clearly apparent. At 6, there was no increase in either emotional or conduct disturbance (unless associated with one of the four specific patterns), and neither showed any association with duration of institutional care. At 11, by contrast, there was a marked between-group difference in emotional and conduct problems (Rutter, in press a). Such problems were most frequent in the Romanian adoptees who had one of the four deprivation-specific problems at 6, but the rate was also substantially higher than in the within-U.K. adoptees group for those without deprivation-specific problems at 6. Moreover, such problems were significantly higher in those who entered the United Kingdom between 6 and 24 months of age than in those who came in infancy. There were too few children who entered the country after 2 years and who did *not* show one of the deprivation-specific patterns for a valid assessment of the rate of emotional/behavioral disturbance, but the rate appeared to be lower than in the subgroup who came to their adoptive family between 6 and 24 months of age.

One of the most striking findings of this study was the extent to which the effects of duration of institutional care continued to be the main mediator of psychological outcome several years after the children had been with their adoptive families. Because the children had usually moved directly from an institution to their adoptive family, it was not initially clear whether the finding reflected the continuing risk effect of duration of institutional care or rather the protective effect of a longer time in the adoptive home. The availability of follow-up data at both 4 and 6 years of age enabled these two variables to be disconfounded. Considering only children who had had 2 1/2 to 4 years in their adoptive home, it was found that those who experienced 24 to 42 months institutional deprivation had a mean IQ at 6 that was some 20 points below those with a shorter period of institutional care (Rutter, O'Connor, et al., 2004; Rutter et al., 2000). Similarly, after equating for time in the adoptive home, disinhibited attachment was much more frequent in those experiencing over 2 years' institutional deprivation. It might be thought that the effects would have largely washed out by the time of the follow-up at 11, but that proved not to be the case. The effects of duration of institutional care on cognitive level at 11 were broadly comparable to the effects as assessed at 4 (Rutter & the E.R.A. Research Team, 1998) and at 6 (O'Connor, Rutter, Beckett, et al., 2000).

Accordingly, it was necessary to consider what mechanisms might be involved in this remarkable persistence of effects stemming from preadoption institutional deprivation. The possibilities have been examined in relation to the 6-year follow-up findings for two contrasting outcomes: cognitive impairment and disinhibited attachment (Rutter, O'Connor, et al., 2004). The key findings with respect to cognitive impairment were the following: (1) no cognitive deficit was apparent in those who left Romanian institutions before the age of 6 months; (2) even after 2 to 3 1/2 years' institutional deprivation, there was a marked cognitive catch-up by the age of 6 following adoption; (3) cognitive functioning at 6 was strongly associated with the duration of institutional deprivation; (4) subnutrition had a significant effect on cognition, but this was less than the effect of duration of institutional care; (5) cognitive functioning at 6 was significantly associated with the head circumference both at the time of U.K. entry and at follow-up; (6) the catch-up in head growth was significantly less than that for weight; (7) cognitive functioning at 6 was unrelated to the educational level of the adoptive parents; and (8) there was great heterogeneity in cognitive outcome even for those children suffering the most prolonged institutional deprivation.

The associations with both subnutrition and a low head circumference point to the likelihood of abnormal brain development (because it is brain growth that largely determines head size). That could reflect active neural damage from stress, or it could derive from the passive effects of a lack of the experiences that are needed for normal brain growth.

The findings on disinhibited attachment were similar in some respects but different in others. Thus, at age 6 (1) there was a strong association with duration of institutional deprivation, but (2) there was no effect of subnutrition and (3) no association with head circumference either at U.K. entry or at follow-up. As with cognition, (4) there was marked heterogeneity in social outcome and (5) no association with measured aspects of the adoptive family environment.

Attachment insecurity is often conceptualized as being a function of a negative internal working model that has developed as a result of the cognitive and affective processing of relationship experiences. However, that did not seem to be the case with respect to disinhibited attachment. In the first place, blind rating of the videotapes of a modified separation–reunion procedure did *not* indicate an increased rate of the two "ordinary" varieties of insecurity (the so-called A and C patterns). Rather, there was an increase in a different nonnormative pattern, primarily evident in the response to the stranger and by coy, silly, overexuberant, or overexcited behavior (O'Connor, Marvin, et al., 2003). It was inferred that the disinhibited attachment pattern represented a relative failure to develop selective attachment relationships rather than insecurity in established attachments. Second, if mental processing was crucial, it might be anticipated that the disinhibited attachment pattern would be less likely to arise in those who were most cognitively limited at the time of U.K. entry. However, the rate of disinhibited attachment did not differ between those with a mental age below 12 months at U.K. entry and those with a higher mental age.

In view of the lack of association with either subnutrition or head circumference, neural damage does not seem likely to constitute the key mediating mechanism for the persistence of disinhibited attachment. On the other hand, the apparent lack of responsivity to variations in adoptive family environment and the persistence of effects does suggest that some form of developmental programming may be involved—an issue considered later in the chapter.

Animal Studies and Longitudinal Investigations of Nonadopted Humans

In interpreting the adoption findings in relation to preadoption experiences factors, we need to turn to experimental studies with animals in order to consider possible biological mediating mechanisms involving neural effects. There is a very substantial research literature on possible prenatal effects on brain development, summarized by Rice and Barone (2000) and by Grossman et al. (2003). On the whole, environmental hazards tend to have their greatest impact if the period of exposure coincides with a phase of rapid active development. Brain growth involves a mixture of proliferation of nerve cells, their migration within the brain, the development of synapses (the substrate of cell-to-cell communication), the increase in support cells for neurons, the myelination of nerve fibers, and apoptosis (the programmed cell death that provides a pruning of neurons in order to fine-tune brain development). In parallel, there is the development of a range of neurotransmitters—the chemicals that provide for transmission of messages through the central nervous system. The timing of these various developmental processes varies across different brain systems and extends over a period beginning in the first months of gestation, peaking in the months leading up to birth and continuing over the infancy stage, but going on right up to and through adolescence (Curtis & Nelson, 2003; Huttenlocher, 2002).

It is clear that neurotoxic agents (such as alcohol, smoking, lead, irradiation, and methylmercury) can have marked effects on brain development and functioning. In severe cases, this may be indexed by congenital abnormalities, such as those associated with the fetal alcohol syndrome, but also it is evident that there may be important functional sequelae in the absence of such physical stigmata. What has been very difficult to determine is whether there is a threshold below which the neurotoxins have no effects and, if there is, at which level of exposure it is to be found. Longitudinal studies of human infants exposed prenatally to toxins such as alcohol (Olson et al., 1997; Streissguth & Kanter, 1997; Streissguth et al., 1994) or cocaine (Chasnoff et al., 1998) or who suffered prenatal irradiation (Igumnov & Drozdovitch, 2000; Nyagu, Loganovsky, & Loganovskaja, 1998) confirm the adverse psychological sequelae but also emphasize the huge heterogeneity in outcome. The evidence points to both prenatal and postnatal risk effects. The few adoption studies that have been undertaken, summarized in this chapter, point to the reality of prenatal effects that may sometimes persist despite a good rearing environment in an adoptive family. However, for the most part, the effects are modest, with most children functioning well despite their prenatal risk experiences. It should be added that most mothers who take drugs use a wide mixture of substances, with the consequence that it has been impossible so far to quantify the relative importance of tobacco, alcohol, cocaine, opiates, marijuana, and other substances. Certainly, it should not necessarily be assumed that the effects of "hard," illegal drugs (such as cocaine or heroin) are worse than those of heavy alcohol exposure or heavy smoking.

In recent years, there has been increasing evidence that severe stress during pregnancy can, in some circumstances, have long-term effects on later behavioral, neuromotor, and physiological development (Francis, Diorio, Liu, & Meaney, 1999; Henry, Kabbaj, Simon, LeMoal, & Maccari, 1994; Schneider & Moore, 2000; Schneider, Roughton, Koehler, & Lubach, 1999). O'Connor, Heron, et al. (2003) have shown, using data from the Avon Longitudinal Study of Parents of Children, that children whose mothers experienced high levels of anxiety in late pregnancy had somewhat higher rates of behavioral/emotional problems at 81 months of age, even after controlling for a range of possible confounding variables. They argued that this indicated some kind of biological programming effect on the fetus. The findings suggest this possibility, although prenatal programming could not account for the fact that there were also some effects of maternal postnatal anxiety or depression. The evidence to date is much too meager for any firm conclusions on the lasting effects of prenatal stress, but, equally, it is apparent that severe stress needs to be included in the list of possible prenatal factors that may sometimes have lasting effects.

Animal studies have provided much more evidence on the structural and functional consequences of postnatal experiences of various kinds (see Greenough, Black, & Wallace, 1987; Grossman, Churchill, Bates, Kleim, & Greenough, 2002; Grossman et al., 2003). Four rather different processes are operative. First, there is "experience-expectant" programming (Black & Greenough, 1986), by which particular experiences that are typical for a species and universally available in all ordinary environments guide brain development during a particular sensitive period when key structures are being laid down. The role of visual input in shaping the development of the visual cortex (Hubel, Wiesel, & LeVay, 1977; LeVay, Wiesel, & Hubel, 1980) provides the best-known and best-documented example. Some commentators have seen this as a model for how all early experiences influence psychological functioning through their effects on brain development. This view, however, is mistaken because experience-expectant programming does not apply to environmental variations within the normal range (Rutter, 2002; Rutter, O'Connor, et al., 2004). In other words, variations in the extent to which children are read stories, or go on outings, or engage in play or conversation are unlikely to affect structural brain development in a permanent fashion.

Second, there is "experience-adaptive" programming, which does apply to normal as well as abnormal environments (Rutter, 2002; Rutter, O'Connor, et al., 2004). The notion in this case is that experiences during a relatively sensitive period of development influence biological develop-ment in such a way that there is optimal adaptation to the specifics of the environment operating at that time (Bateson & Martin, 1999; Caldji et al., 1998; Sackett, 1965). The concept has been discussed most extensively in relation to the role of early subnutrition in bringing about a much increased risk of heart disease in later life (Barker, 1997; O'Brien, Wheeler, & Barker, 1999), although there are also similar effects in relation to immu-nity and infection (Bock & Whelan, 1991). The psychological parallel is provided by the role of language input in relation to psychological dis-criminations as they develop in different languages (Kuhl, 1994; Kuhl et al., 1997).

Third, there are "experience-dependent" effects (Black & Greenough, 1986), by which experiences associated with learning trigger the forma-tion of new synapses as opposed to selecting from cell connections already in place. In a real sense, this simply reflects the fact that all learning must have a neural basis of some kind. In animals, the brain changes as well as the functional effects have been shown through studying the effects on rats of specially controlled complex environments (Greenough & Chang, 1988). In humans, brain imaging studies have shown parallel effects asso-ciated with various forms of intense learning in adult life (see Elbert, Pan-tev, Weinbruch, Rockstroh, & Taub, 1995; Maguire et al., 2000). Unlike the first two processes, this type of neural plasticity extends well into adult life and is not limited to sensitive periods of brain development. Like experience-adaptive programming, it concerns experiences within as well as outside the normal range.

Fourth, there is evidence that, in some circumstances, severe stress can lead to neural damage, especially in the hippocampus (Bremner, 1999; McEwen, 1999; McEwan & Lasley, 2002). It seems that the damage is brought about largely by high levels of cortisol, one of the hormones closely associated with stress, although glutamate (a chemical messenger) is probably also implicated. Human studies evidence is much more sparse, but findings suggest that processes similar to those observed in rats are found with severely stressful experiences. It should also be noted that chronic stress does not necessarily lead to high cortisol levels; sometimes it is associated with low levels or with unusual patterns of diurnal variation. Accordingly, there must be caution in any invoking of neural damage due to cortisol as a mediating mechanism for the long-term sequelae of stress. In addition, it remains uncertain how far the damage is irreversible.

Animal studies are also pertinent with respect to the effects of severe malnutrition on later psychological functioning (Dobbing & Smart, 1974). Both human and animal studies have shown important adverse psychological sequelae (Grantham-McGregor, 1987), but it has not proved easy to separate the effects of subnutrition as such from the effects of the numerous psychosocial adversities with which it tends to be associated in human populations. It has been suggested that the ill effects of malnutrition tend to be greatest when it occurs in the early months of life when brain growth is particularly great, but the evidence on this postulated sensitive period effect is contradictory and inconclusive (Drewett, Wolke, Asefa, Kaba, & Tessema, 2001). On the whole, it seems that the duration and severity of malnutrition is probably more important than the details of its precise timing in the first few years. However, it should be noted, in addition, that the breast-feeding findings suggest that nutritional effects tend to be most marked in preterm infants (Anderson, Johnstone, & Remley, 1999). Whether this derives from their developmental immaturity or from some other aspect of their vulnerability is not known.

NATURE–NURTURE INTERPLAY

In the past, arguments tended to focus on the quantification of the extent to which psychological features were due to the effects of genes or the effects of the environment. It is now clear that this is a misleading oversimplification of the interplay that takes place over the course of development (see Ridley, 2003; Rutter, 2002; Rutter & Silberg, 2001). The point is that genes influence people's sensitivity to environmental stress and adversity, and environments can modify an individual's response to genetic risk. Thus, Grossman et al. (2003) discuss the examples of the fetal alcohol syndrome (FAS) and the fragile X anomaly. FAS is due to environmentally mediated prenatal damage, but the effects appear to be moderated by a particular gene involved in alcohol metabolism (Viljoen et al., 2001). In addition, there is some indication that, although the psychological sequelae derive from actual brain damage, the effects may be reduced by rearing in a nurturing household (Streissguth & Kanter, 1997). Similarly, the fragile X anomaly is a wholly genetic condition, but there are suggestions that the rearing environment may somewhat modify the psychological consequences (Dyer-Friedman et al., 2002; Hessl et al., 2001). There is also some suggestion that the adverse outcomes seen in some children exposed to drugs in utero derives as much from postnatal experiences as from prenatal drug exposure (Accornero, Morrow, Bansdtra, Johnson, & Anthony, 2002) and that an early home intervention program may reduce the risk of psychological problems. (Butz et al., 2001). Unfortunately, the evidence available to date is not sufficient for even tentative conclusions on the extent to which a good rearing environment or well-planned therapeutic interventions can counter the persisting ill effects of seriously adverse preadoption experiences. However, the implication is that postadoption experiences probably can serve to ameliorate the effects of preadoption adversities even if we lack knowledge on just what is needed to enable that to happen.

OVERVIEW OF EFFECTS OF PREADOPTION EXPERIENCES

The number of studies using research designs that could test hypotheses about the postadoption effects of adverse preadoption experiences is quite limited. Nevertheless, certain provisional conclusions are possible. First, the range of adverse preadoption experiences with possible long-term consequences includes prenatal exposure to toxins and hazards of various kinds, postnatal abuse and neglect, postnatal malnutrition, and an institutional rearing. The true range of adverse environments carrying risk is likely to be very much broader than that, but it is these that have been studied, and already the list points to a substantial variety in the types of experiences that have to be considered.

Second, the psychological outcomes that can be attributed to preadoption risks include quite diverse patterns. Some seem relatively specific to particular risk experiences. Thus, profound institutional deprivation has been found to be associated with quasi-autistic patterns, atypical syndromes of inattention/overactivity, a particular kind of attachment disorder, and cognitive impairment. However, institutional deprivation is also associated with delayed-onset conduct and delayed-onset emotional disorders. The effects of other preadoption stresses and adversity seem much less specific in pattern.

Third, the mechanisms or processes that underlie the long-term sequelae are likely to be heterogeneous. The evidence from the studies of adoptees from institutions suggests that substantial cognitive impairment is largely a consequence of depriving conditions in the institutions rather than institutional upbringing as such. Thus, the children reared in British residential nurseries studied by Hodges and Tizard (1989a) and by Roy et al. (2000) did not show significant cognitive impairment. The studies of adoptees from Romanian institutions, by contrast, showed quite marked cognitive impairment that was strongly associated with the duration of institutional deprivation. The finding that the children's cognitive level at age 6 years was associated with head circumference and, to a lesser extent, with their nutritional level at the time of U.K. entry pointed to the likelihood that cognitive impairment was due either to neural damage or to experience-expectant biological programming (Rutter, O'Connor, et al., 2004). The rather different findings for disinhibited attachment pointed to a different mechanism because, although it was strongly associated with duration of institutional deprivation, it was *not* associated with either subnutrition or head circumference. Neural damage seems a less plausible mediating mechanism, but some form of biological programming (perhaps experience-adaptive in type) does seem to be needed to be invoked in view of the strong persistence of the effects of duration of deprivation and the relatively strong temporal stability of the attachment pattern. If the programming is experience-adaptive in type, there is the implication that it may have been adaptive in the institutional environment and that, if so, too sudden and too radical a shift to a warm intimate family setting may provide stressful challenges. Counterintuitive though that may seem, it demands serious consideration.

Fourth, all the studies have shown remarkable psychological recovery following removal from stressful depriving environments and placement in a good-quality adoptive family. This was evident not only in the studies of institution-reared infants but also in Duyme et al.'s (1999) studies of French abused and neglected children. Even when the deprivation has been both severe and prolonged, the possibility of major resilience and recovery remains strong. It is clear that a good rearing environment, even when it is not provided until after the postinfancy period, can make a big difference to children's psychological functioning.

Fifth, however, despite remarkable major improvements in children's functioning postadoption, significant deficits attributable to preadoption adverse experiences remain in a substantial minority. It might be supposed that these would lessen greatly with the increasing duration of time in an adoptive family, but the British study of Romanian adoptees indicates that this did not happen, at least not by age 11 years. Those parents adopting children with prolonged seriously adverse preadoption experiences must expect that in some (but not all) cases, postadoption difficulties may go on a long time.

Sixth, with all manner of preadoption stresses and adversities there is a remarkable heterogeneity of responses. The British and Canadian studies of Romanian adoptees showed that, even with the most severe and prolonged institutional deprivation, some children appeared to develop normally with respect to cognition, behavior, emotions, and social relationships. Moreover, the spread of functioning (both cognitive and social) was as great in those suffering prolonged deprivation as in those adopted in infancy. The reasons for this individual variation remain largely unknown. The qualities of the adoptive home appear related to the degree of functional recovery following early parental abuse and neglect (as shown in the study by Duyme et al., 1999) but not following profound and prolonged institutional deprivation (as shown in the British study of Romanian adoptees (Rutter, O'Connor, et al., 2004).

Seventh, it is likely that, particularly in later childhood and adolescence, children's thoughts about their background and experiences and their mental sets, or models, of all that has happened to them will influence their self-concepts and their psychological and social functioning. However, remarkably little is known on the extent to which this is the case with young people whose preadoption experiences were exceptionally awful.

Eighth, just because of the evidence that preadoption experiences can have long-lasting effects, there is a danger that all difficulties will be attributed to adversities in the early years. The reality is that it is certain that some difficulties will be attributable to the challenges implicit in being adopted, and many may well stem from the ordinary problems associated with development and from the range of stresses that may be encountered over the course of the postadoption years. Often it will not be easy to assess the relative importance of these different factors, but any adequate clinical assessment will need to consider this complex admixture of possible causal influences.

Ninth, it should not be presupposed that, just because adopted children may have had unusual stresses and adversities preadoption, this necessarily means that ordinary means of therapeutic intervention will not be helpful. Systematic studies of the treatment of adopted children are few and far between, and there are no controlled studies of interventions designed to remedy the particular sequelae of seriously adverse preadoption experiences (Cohen, 2002). There may be methods that are particularly useful in fostering good social relationships, but some of the more extreme approaches have given rise to more extravagant claims that lack sound evaluations. The development of better methods of treating attachment disorders is much needed (Minde, 2003), but so far there are no clear indications that any one approach is superior to others.

Tenth, the findings on the long-term effects of seriously adverse preadoption experiences should not be viewed as indicating unalterable effects. Children can and do change and they remain responsive to qualities of rearing and to psychological intervention. Parents and professionals need to have a realistic sense of the challenges that may need to be faced in adopting a child who has suffered dreadful preadoption experiences, and most of all, both need to be aware that help and support may be needed over many years and not just during the immediate postadoption period. On the other hand, all the studies have emphasized the resilience shown by many children and the resourcefulness, patience, persistence, and ingenuity of many adopting parents in dealing with severe challenges.

IMPLICATIONS FOR RESEARCH AND PRACTICE

The main practice implication derives from the combination of findings that (1) preadoption adverse experiences can sometimes have long-lasting (including delayed) effects, (2) there is huge heterogeneity in outcome, (3) there is substantial resilience and restoration of normal function even after severely adverse early experiences, and (4) psychological outcomes will be influenced by postadoption as well as preadoption experiences, by responses to the fact of being adopted, and by normal developmental changes. Clearly, it would be desirable to have a reliable and valid means of assessing the relative importance of different risk and protective factors in relation to different psychological outcomes. Unfortunately, such knowledge is largely lacking at the moment. Equally, we lack adequate evaluations of specific interventions that have been devised to alleviate particular types of problems (such as attachment disorders) that are especially associated with the deprivation backgrounds of high-risk adopted children. That definitely does not mean that nothing can be done to prevent or treat such problems, but it does mean that there should be caution with regard to the acceptance of unsubstantiated claims.

The research implications stem fairly directly from these considerations. The main need is *not* for further descriptive studies; rather, what are required are research designs that can test specific hypotheses on mediating mechanisms and that, in particular, can pit one hypothesis against competing hypotheses, together with systematic evaluations of prevention and intervention strategies. We need to differentiate the effects of preadoption and postadoption experiences, determine the particular aspects of experiences that carry risk or provide protection, test the possibility that effects vary according to the age when they occur, consider possible sex differences in susceptibility and the reasons for them, and determine the extent to which there are specificities in risk and resilience effects. In tackling all these questions, it will be crucial to test for the possibility that susceptibility to experiential risk effects is moderated by genetic vulnerabilities (see Caspi et al., 2002, 2003; Rutter, 2003a; Rutter & Silberg, 2002). One of the very consistent findings in studies of stress and adversity is that there are large individual differences in response. Evidence is accumulating that genetic influences are important in such differences (Rutter, 2003a). Behavior geneticists have been inclined to emphasize the role of genetic factors in response to environmental risk, but the equally important message is that many genetic effects are indirect and, therefore, open to modification from the right kind of interventions.

As far as evaluations of prevention and treatment are concerned, one of the key issues is whether the fact that some mental disorders have their origins in adverse experiences in early childhood means that they require forms of intervention that are different from those ordinarily employed. For example, how should the relationship problems, quasi-autistic patterns, or inattention of children reared in poor-quality institutions be treated? Should the focus be on the *current* problems or, rather, their origins in earlier life? Satisfactory answers are not yet available, and it is important that they be found. As ever, that means that there is a need for a good functional integration between research and practice and a two-way flow of ideas and findings between the two (Rutter, 1998, 1999).

Chapter 5

Change and Continuity in Mental Representations of Attachment after Adoption

Jill Hodges, Miriam Steele, Saul Hillman,
Kay Henderson, and Jeanne Kaniuk

Many adopted children enter their new families after experiences of mal-treatment or neglect and a subsequent period in public care in which they may move through a succession of foster placements. These experiences can have a major impact on their relationships and development within their new families. Government policies aim to increase further the pro-portion of such children who are placed for adoption. This chapter reports part of a detailed study of a group of these children, examining the way in which their expectations and perceptions of attachments and relation-ships were affected by their earlier experiences and how these altered over their first two years in adoptive families.

NATIONAL VARIATION IN ADOPTION FROM CARE

In this chapter, "adoption from care" refers to children adopted after being in residential or in foster care. Adoption from care is more common in the United States and United Kingdom than in many other countries (PIU, 2000). In Portugal and France, between 1 and 2 percent of the in-care population is adopted, but in Norway, Luxembourg, Denmark, Austria, Finland, and Sweden, as well as in Australia and New Zealand, the pro-portion is less than 1 percent.

In contrast, the figure for England is around 4 to 5 percent (2,200 children in 1998–89 from a total in-care population of 55,300 children, 2,700 in

1999–2000). The proportion is higher among the younger children in this population; thus, in 1999–2000, the figure was 5 percent of all children in care but 12 percent if one examined only the population of children under 10. While the overall number of U.K. adoptions has fallen drastically over the past 30 years, from around 20,000 per year in 1970 to just over 4,000 in 1999, this reduction reflects the sharp fall in the number of illegitimate infants given up for adoption. The percentage of children adopted from care has remained relatively constant over this period. For the United States, the proportion of children in care who are adopted is still higher; every year, around 6.6 percent of the in-care population are adopted. In the United States, a much larger proportion of young people are in care (75 per 10,000 of under 18s compared to 47 per 10,000 in England). In both the United States and the United Kingdom, the great majority of children in care live with foster carers, and a high proportion return to their birth families.

In both countries, children in care may wait a long time for adoption. In the United Kingdom, 65 percent of children adopted waited over a year between coming into care and being placed in their prospective adoptive family; the average was two years and 10 months in 1999. In the United States, in any one year the proportion of in-care children awaiting adoption is about 20 percent, of whom only 30 percent are actually adopted within the year (PIU, 2000).

A CHALLENGING POPULATION

Children leaving care to enter adoptive families are more challenging than the general population of children in care. The U.K. figures for 1996 indicate that 44 percent of the children adopted from care had entered care because of abuse, neglect, or risk; this was true of only 17 percent of the total of children leaving care that year. While 66 percent of the total of children leaving care had experienced only one placement, only 38 percent of the children who left to be adopted had experienced such stability while in care, and 14 percent of them had had six or more moves. Compared to children who left care for other reasons, children who were adopted were also much more likely to have entered care under emergency protection orders, indicating the severity of concerns about abuse or neglect (PIU, 2000).

Children adopted are thus those with the more difficult histories, both before and during care, so-called children with special needs. In addition, the population of children in care is becoming more challenging as a whole. Between 1995 and 1999, the proportion of children entering care because of abuse or neglect rose from 19 to 29 percent, an increase of 53 percent. There was a parallel increase in the proportion of children coming into care under emergency protection orders or under care orders, where it has to be proved in court that the child has suffered significant harm attributable to the care the child has received (PIU, 2000).

Most children adopted from care will thus have experienced one or more major form of adversity, including physical, sexual and/or emotional abuse and neglect, multiple placements, and multiple losses, before joining their adoptive family.

MENTAL HEALTH DIFFICULTIES

Not surprisingly, in view of these adversities, children in public care are a population at high risk of mental health problems. In the United Kingdom, the Department of Health recently surveyed the mental health of young people in public care in England (including residential care, foster families, children living with birth parents under a legal order, and young people living independently under a legal order (Meltzer, Corbin, Gatward, Goodman, & Ford, 2003). This survey reported that 45 percent of those aged 5 to 17 years were assessed as having a mental disorder, using ICD-10 diagnostic criteria with strict impairment criteria—the disorder causing distress to the child or having a considerable impact on the child's day-to-day life. This prevalence was five times higher than for children not in care, living in private households. Over a third of the children had been in touch with a child mental health specialist.

If we take only the 5- to 10-year-olds, since the great majority of adoptions from care in the United Kingdom are of children under the age of 10 (PIU, 2000), there is no indication that these younger children are any less disturbed: 42 percent showed mental health problems compared to 8 percent of those living in private households. Conduct disorders were most common, reported in 36 percent of children compared to 5 percent of private household children. Of children in public care, 11 percent showed emotional disorders (compared to 3%), and 11 percent showed hyperactivity (compared to 2%). So in this age-group too, children in public care were about five times more likely to have a mental health disorder than children in private households. The risk is greatest for boys; in the 5- to 10-year-olds, 50 percent of boys and 33 percent of girls had a mental health disorder.

This survey did not examine posttraumatic symptoms or difficulties in forming attachments and relationships. Both of these are often comorbid with the difficulties identified and both, especially attachment difficulties, are often reported clinically and to postadoption services. Thus, these figures may well understate the degree of these children's difficulties.

PLANNED INCREASES IN ADOPTION FROM CARE

Both the United States and the United Kingdom are now taking steps both to increase the numbers of children adopted from care and to speed up the adoption placement process. In the United Kingdom, the government recently announced the aim of increasing adoptions of children from care by 40–50 percent and set in place numerous measures to recruit more adopters, streamline and speed the process of matching, and support adoptive placements (PIU, 2000). In the United States, the Adoption and Safe Families Act of 1997 aims to speed the process of achieving permanency, and the United States also aims greatly to increase the number of adoptions from care.

There is thus a plan to greatly increase adoption of this very disturbed population of children. This is an excellent aim in terms of providing for children's needs: it is clear that children do remarkably well in adoptive families relative to their earlier experiences (Brodzinsky, Smith, & Brodzinsky, 1998; Hodges, 2003; chapter 6 in this volume). However, this progress is very often at a high cost to families (Livingston Smith & Howard, 1999), and in many cases there is inadequate provision to support families and provide the therapeutic and educational services that such children may require. As more children are placed who show a high prevalence of emotional and behavioral difficulties and "attachment disorders" as sequelae of their earlier maltreatment experiences, there will be an increased need for services, including detailed assessments, that can help parents and professionals address children's particular needs.

This chapter presents some of the findings from a recent research study aimed at assessing the effect of earlier experiences of maltreatment on children's mental representations and expectations of relationships as they moved from care into their adoptive families and how these changed over the next two years. Broadly, we take children's mental representations of relationships as equivalent to what Bowlby, in formulating attachment theory, referred to as "internal working models." From infancy onward, the child mentally organizes reality experience, constructing generalized representations of expectable interactions with others (Bowlby, 1973; Stern, 1985). These developing representations guide the child's expectation of new interactions and perception and understanding of current experience. Bowlby describes the young child mentally "constructing working models of how the physical world may be expected to behave, how his mother and other significant persons may be expected to behave, how he himself may be expected to behave, and how each interacts with all the others" (p. 419). Thereafter, these models bias perception and influence how experience is evaluated. These models combine different forms of registration of experiences with the attachment figure, including nonverbal and nonconscious "habit" memories, as well as generalized memories that can be verbally recalled as expectable "scripts" for experience, and specific verbal memories. As these models develop and stabilize, they tend to become automatic, operating increasingly outside conscious awareness (Bretherton, 1985). Crittenden (1994) notes that if children routinely experience abuse, these abusive experiences may no longer be represented as occasion-specific episodes but instead become a part of the child's "unscrutinised, taken-for-granted understanding of the nature of relationships" (p. 116). Such models can thus have a powerful effect on how a previously maltreated child can perceive and react to the new relationships that an adoptive family offers. Crittenden (1988) and others have emphasized how attachment models that are adaptive in one situation may become maladaptive if conditions change.

Children's internal representational models are, however, not open to easy scrutiny or assessment, and thus, as we shall outline in the next section, research on children moving into new families has tended to rely on adult reports about children in assessing change. However, there is now increasing interest in narrative assessments as a technique for examining children's mental representations of social and emotional relationships and attachments. These offer the possibility of a more direct exploration of the child's understanding and responses. Although children's narrative completions are structured by the child's earlier experiences, they are not simply a mirror reflection of them. Representations displayed in children's narratives may reflect imagined possibilities as well as other defensive and emotional aspects. However, if what appears in the narrative is "imagined," this implies that it forms part of the child's possible repertoire of internal representations. This can be an important indicator for future development; an abused child who nonetheless has some mental representation of what can be expected from a good-enough parent may be better able to recognize and use good-enough parenting once the opportunity arises in a new family than a child who has no such representation.

In the study we describe here, we used the narrative technique to assess directly the children's expectations and understanding of family relationships, examining the impact of their earlier maltreatment as they entered their new families. As Livingston Smith and Howard (1999) comment, what the child has learned to expect about trust, intimacy, and caretaker dependability may be quite different from what the adoptive parent wishes to provide. Being able to chart the child's expectations can provide valuable information for the new adoptive parents. In separate clinically based work, we have found that narrative assessments early in placement can be used to guide parents and professionals in understanding children's particular areas of vulnerability, planning appropriate management of difficulties, and thus assisting the parents' handling of behavior and the children's developmental recovery. In the research study we report here, we did not intervene in this way but tracked changes in the children's attachment representations over the next two years as they settled into their adoptive families.

Barth and Berry (1988), in studying placement stability, pointed to the importance of the adoptive parents being able to maintain realistic expectations about the child and about family interactions. A picture of the "natural history" of how children's attachment representations expectably change and develop after placement can also be helpful in providing a realistic view to reassure and guide adopters, a point we shall return to later in this chapter.

ASSESSING CHILDREN'S DEVELOPMENT AFTER ADOPTION PLACEMENT

Studies of community samples, both longitudinal and cross sectional, have not pointed to any consistent pattern of differences in behavior and adjustment between infant-adopted children and others but tend to find the infant-adopted group at greater risk for some externalizing problems, including aggression and hyperactive behavior, and some school adjustment difficulties. Differences are generally small, compared to differences accounted for by demographic variables (Brodzinsky et al., 1998; Hodges 2003; chapter 6 in this volume). Later-adopted children, who have also suffered maltreatment and discontinuities of care, unsurprisingly show considerably greater levels of difficulty. Levels of mental health difficulties in children in care have been outlined previously, with conduct disorders, emotional disorders, and hyperactivity all substantially higher than children living in their own homes. Posttraumatic difficulties are often comorbid with various of these disorders. Thus, on entering their adoptive homes, these children are likely to be already showing difficulties.

A study by Quinton, Rushton, Dance, and Mayes (1998) that followed 61 children found that after a year in placement, there was little change in the children's emotional or behavioral adjustment. Despite some positive changes, children tended to remain oppositional and still to show high levels of fearfulness and anxiety as well as restless, inattentive behavior. At school, high levels of problem behavior did not decrease and indeed tended to increase over the year. An earlier study in this research program (Rushton, Treseder, & Quinton, 1995) that followed 18 late-adopted boys over eight years found most boys showing steadily improving affectionate relationships with the adoptive parents by the end of the first year and did find improvements in behavior problems, though restlessness and an inability to play creatively remained. By eight years into placement, nearly a fifth of placements had broken down, but half the remainder had a good outcome. Restless, distractible behavior seems an especially persistent feature for late-placed children, and some difficulties in peer relationships and in school also appear to persist. This is a rather similar picture to the children followed up by Hodges and Tizard (1989a, 1989b) whose first years were spent in institutional care before they were placed for adoption or restored to their biological parents.

As Quinton et al. (1998) note, the research literature on adoption outcomes in older children suffers from limitations in outcome measures. Prospective studies of the progress of later-adopted children in placement have used various measures such as parental and school observations of behavior, family functioning, the child's behavior, self-esteem, and cognitive development (e.g., Hodges and Tizard, 1989a, 1989b; Quinton et al., 1998; Rushton et al., 1995; Rutter, 1998). To date, these studies have not attempted direct assessment of children's mental representations of attachment relationships.

However, the developing attachment relationship between adopters and child is critical in the viability of adoption (Quinton et al., 1998; Tizard, 1977). It is based on the interaction between what the present carers bring in terms of their own expectations and attachment histories (Steele, Hodges, Kaniuk, Hillman, & Henderson, 2003) and what the child brings. What the child brings is the set of expectations and perceptions derived from past experiences and relationships—the lessons life has taught the child up to the point of adoption. These lessons have often been harsh ones about the unavailability, rejectingness, or abusiveness of attachment figures, the powerlessness and vulnerability of the child, and the defensive behaviors, cognitions, and emotional attitudes needed for survival.

As children become part of their adoptive family, we hope that they will discover the new and positive possibilities of relationships with their new parents. But as the child's existing set of attachment representations governs not only expectation and prediction but also the perception of current experience, the new parents' behavior will inevitably be perceived at times as repeating past experiences with abusing or rejecting attachment figures, thus confirming and strengthening the child's existing model.

In studying changes in the organization of attachments, research and clinical practice has relied on reported and observed behavior in the absence of any other way of examining the child's mental representations. However, narrative stem assessments provide a means of making a more direct assessment of the child's mental representations—in attachment theory terms, their "internal working models" of attachment and family relationships (Bretherton, Ridgeway, & Cassidy, 1990).

An increasing number of studies are now available that have used narrative techniques to make more direct assessments of children's mental representations of attachment relationships. These have examined both children living in their own, nonmaltreating families (e.g., Bretherton et al., 1990; Oppenheim, Emde, & Warren, 1997) and children in families where the parent has maltreated the child (e.g., Buchsbaum, Toth, Clyman, Cicchetti, & Emde, 1992; McCrone, Egeland, Kalkoske, & Carlson, 1994; MacFie et al., 1999; Toth, Cichetti, MacFie, Maughan, & Van-Meenen, 1997; for a review of findings in risk and clinical populations, see

Warren, 2003). Narrative assessments allow detailed examination of the mental representations of family life that children are left with when *removed* from situations of abuse and neglect, and we have used them to examine children recently removed from maltreating families into foster care (Hodges & Steele, 2000).

None of the previous work, however, has examined what happens when maltreated children, whose attachment representations are founded on their previous adversities, are placed in new adoptive families. The obvious next step was to use the assessment for systematic tracking of changes in attachment representations as such children began to settle into new families, and it is this research that we outline in this chapter.

Clearly, in examining the attachment representations of maltreated children as they enter their new adoptive families, it is not particularly useful merely to establish the child's global attachment category—maltreated children are very unlikely to show "secure" attachment organization and very likely to be "disorganized" (Carlson, Cicchetti, Barnett, & Braunwald, 1989). What is of interest is the more fine-grained picture, the component elements subsumed under the general construct of a "secure" or other attachment organization. For example, a secure organization suggests that there is a representation of parents as providing help and comfort, being responsive to the child's need and aware when the child may be distressed; that parents are not seen as likely to respond to the child with aggression or rejection; and that children have a reasonable sense of self-efficacy and self-esteem. A securely attached child will be able to respond to the narrative stems with a relatively coherent story without their response either being inhibited by anxiety or becoming extremely aggressive (Main, Kaplan, & Cassidy, 1985). Conversely, an insecure organization of attachment would involve expectations that parents would not be consistently responsive in providing help or comfort and could possibly be aggressive or actively rejecting.

Equally, in examining changes in attachment during placement, there is not an expectation of simply finding that a child shifts from an "insecure" category of attachment organization to a "secure" one. This would be too gross a categorization to be useful; developmental recovery in maltreated children can take a very long time, and it is likely that some of the effects of their earlier experiences will remain with them permanently or at least well into adulthood (Howe, 1998). We aimed rather to find a way of examining more subtle changes in the components of a child's attachment organization. Would some of the negative representations show themselves more readily altered than others, and were there discernible patterns in how children's attachment representations changed as they settled into adoptive families? We examined changes in the individual ratings, the component elements described previously, so that we could see, for example, whether children became more likely to represent adults as offering help or less likely to show them as rejecting. We also grouped these components in theoretically meaningful ways to form composite scores so that we could see, for example, whether the composite of various indicators of security, outlined previously, increased over the course of placement.

AN OUTLINE OF THE NARRATIVE ASSESSMENT TECHNIQUE

We first outline the assessment technique. The story stem assessment we use consists of a structured series of 13 narrative stems. It draws on the MacArthur story stem battery, which has been widely used in the United States and elsewhere with young children from both clinical and research populations (Bretherton & Oppenheim, 2003).

What is a narrative assessment? In brief, it consists of giving the child, individually, a series of "narrative stems"—the beginnings of stories, played out with doll and sometimes animal figures and simultaneously spoken, dramatizing them so as to engage the child emotionally in the attachment-related scenario presented—and then inviting the child to "show me and tell me what happens next."

Children's narrative responses are based both on their experiences and on how they as individuals deal with and can portray with those experiences. They are not direct reports on autobiographic incidents but a combination of representation of underlying expectations of interactions and indicators of emotion and emotional regulation. Children's responses provide a "window" into their underlying basic scripts for human relationships and how they affect the child, particularly relationships between young children and their caregivers. This allows assessment of the child's expectations and perceptions of family roles, attachments, and relationships.

As a whole, the assessment battery is designed to elicit themes concerned with the child's expectations of relationships between parents and children, including those most central to the construct of security of attachment, namely, whether the child displays an expectation that parents will be aware when children need protection or comfort and will respond appropriately to this need. Besides indicators of attachment and of representations of maltreatment, it covers such areas of parent–child interactions as giving affection and setting boundaries. It also elicits indicators of other important aspects of the child's functioning, such as the modulation of aggression, and certain defensive maneuvers, such as avoidance and denial.

Two particular features of story stem assessments, displacement and the possibility of nonverbal as well as verbal narratives, are worth emphasizing. Both are aspects of the technique that make it very different from direct self-report measures.

Displacement

The narrative technique avoids asking children direct questions about their own experiences or their own parents, as this might cause the child conflict or anxiety. Rather, it allows the child to represent these in displaced form. Investigations of doll play techniques conducted in the 1940s showed that using doll families that duplicated the child's own generally produced more identificatory themes but that in some children play became inhibited if the experimenter explicitly suggested these identifications (Woolgar, 1999). Thus, it is helpful (and probably particularly so with maltreated children) to use a standard doll family rather than trying to replicate the child's own family configuration. Maltreated children sometimes seem to experience even dilemmas portrayed with the doll figures as too "near the bone" and anxiety provoking, and two of the story stems use animal figures, providing a further step of displacement from the child's personal experience. Children often show enjoyment and great involvement in the task, and even initially reluctant children usually get drawn in and tolerate it without great anxiety.

Nonverbal as Well as Verbal Narrative

Beside displacement, the technique facilitates the child's narrative in another important way. It allows both verbal and nonverbal means of representation, allowing children to display memories and expectations that are not part of verbally based memory or, alternatively, that the child is fearful or anxious about putting into words. Child clinicians know well that play can provide access to feelings, thoughts, and memories that cannot be recalled verbally.

Memory that operates automatically, outside conscious awareness, requires assessment by other means than conscious verbal recall or description, and memories that cause anxiety will be repressed or the child will resist reporting them. Thus, in the nonverbal narrative, the child can reveal underlying expectations of interactions and relationships that have been established preverbally, that are part of so-called procedural or habit memory rather than verbally based memory or that may be at odds with the way in which expectations and events are portrayed verbally to the child or in which the child attempts to portray them to him- or herself or to others.

Crittenden (1994) notes that if abuse is part of children's routine everyday experience of family life, it comes to form part of the child's "unscrutinised, taken-for-granted understanding of the nature of relationships." In such cases, the clearest evidence of a history of abuse may be how these taken-for-granted expectations guide the child's behavior in the present. The child's behavior may reveal their fearful or aversive expectations of parents without their necessarily being able, let alone willing, to recall specific events.

The Story Stem Assessment

Story stem assessments have been used for clinical assessment and for research in numerous centers (Emde, Wolf, & Oppenheim, 2003). The battery we use consists of five stems (the LP, or "Little Pig," stems, so nicknamed after one of the stories) originally devised, with a preliminary rating scheme, on the basis of clinical experience in the assessment of abused children. Eight additional stems were selected from the MacArthur Story Stem Battery (MSSB) (Bretherton & Oppenheim, 2003), which was devised for much wider research uses and has been employed primarily with nonclinical populations The stems are always administered in the same order, using a standard doll "family" and also animal figures in two stories. The interview is designed for use with children between the ages of four and eight, although we have used it in research for children slightly older than this, and generally takes about one hour to complete (for details including a protocol for the LP stems and summaries of the eight MSSB stems, see Hodges, Steele, Hillman, & Henderson, 2003; Hodges, Steele, Hillman, Henderson, & Kaniuk, 2003). Interviews were video and audiotaped and the tapes transcribed, producing a verbal "script" consisting of what the child and interviewer said and "stage directions" describing what the child did—that is, the nonverbal narrative. Transcripts were then rated in accordance with a manual (Hodges, Steele, Hillman, & Henderson, 2002) with each of the child's 13 stories rated for the presence of around 30 themes, covering representations of parents, representations of children, aggressive manifestations, indicators of engagement or avoidance, aspects of positive adaptation, and indicators of disorganization.

The rating manual (Hodges et al., 2002) provides detailed criteria and benchmark examples; raters trained on this system for research purposes achieved good levels of reliability on a three-point rating, percentage agreement overall being 87 percent. From these detailed ratings we also constructed composite scores that showed high internal consistency, representing more global constructs. Thus, the "Security" composite combines aspects of representations associated with security of attachment, where a young child has developed the expectation that a parent will reliably respond to provide a sense of safety when needed. It consists of the following scores: *Child Seeks Help, Siblings/Peers Helping, Realistic Mastery, Adult Provides Comfort, Adult Provides Help, Adult Shows Affection, Limit Setting, Coherent Aggression, Acknowledgment of Distress of Child and Adult,* and *Realistic/Pleasurable Domestic Life.*

The "Insecurity" composite consists of the ratings for *Child Endangered, Child Injured/Dead, Excessive Compliance, Adult Unaware When Child Distressed, Adult Actively Rejects, Adult Injured/Dead, Extreme Aggression, Neutralization* (of a negative theme arising in the story), and *Throwing Away*. The "Disorganization" composite draws on research on children in middle childhood whose attachments were rated "disorganized" in the Strange Situation assessment in infancy, which noted the presence of chaotic, catastrophic fantasy in their narratives and controlling behavior toward their parents (Main & Cassidy, 1988) and consists of the ratings for *Child Parents/Controls Adults, Catastrophic Fantasy, Bizarre/Atypical Material, Magic/Omnipotence,* and *Bad/Good Shift* (unexplained shifts between a figure being represented as good and as bad or frightening). The "Defensive Avoidance" composite score consists of the ratings for *No Engagement, Disengagement, Initial Aversion, No Closure, Premature Foreclosure, Changes Constraints, Avoidance of Conflict,* and *Denial of Distress*.

A RESEARCH STUDY TRACKING CHANGE IN ATTACHMENT REPRESENTATIONS

The study described here is a prospective longitudinal study that included interviews and questionnaire measures with the adoptive parents prior to placement. As soon as practicable after placement, videotaped narrative assessments and other assessments were carried out with the child—the "year 1" assessment. At the same time, the parents were interviewed, and other data were collected via questionnaire from the parents. This assessment was repeated (with minor modifications) in the "year 2" and "year 3" assessments, one and two years later.

The Sample and Comparison Group

The total sample of previously maltreated children consisted of 63 children in 42 different families. Fourteen children were placed alone, and 49 were part of a sibling group. Just over half were boys. They had been placed for adoption at a mean age of six years (ranging from four years to eight years, eight months). The great majority were white British. They had been in placement approximately four months when the year 1 assessment took place.

Most children had experienced multiple changes of caregiver before their adoption placement. The average number of placements prior to adoption was 5.3, ranging from 2 to 18. Most children had also suffered multiple abuse before coming into care. Fifty-six had suffered neglect, 42 had been exposed to domestic violence, 19 had been physically abused, and 14 were believed to have suffered sexual abuse. Social workers reported virtually all the children, 60 out of the 63, as having experienced emotional abuse, and 9 were seen as having been singled out for rejection in their families of origin, which appears to be particularly associated with instability in adoption placement (Quinton et al., 1998). These children were therefore at the most disadvantaged end of the spectrum in terms of previous abuse and discontinuity of care, compared to the figures outlined earlier in this chapter for U.K. children adopted from care as a whole. This reflects the fact that they were placed through specialist family-finding agencies for "hard to place" children.

We also compared these late-adopted maltreated children with a group of children adopted in infancy. This comparison group allowed us to take account of adoptive status per se and focus on the differences between the groups, that is, preadoptive maltreatment and discontinuity and age at adoption. Children in the infancy group had not experienced the abuse and discontinuities of care that characterized the earlier lives of the prospective group and had lived with their adoptive families for all but a small part of their lives, while the late-adopted children had only recently joined their families. The total sample in the infancy-adopted group consisted of 48 children, half of them boys, placed in their adoptive families below the age of 12 months. Ten were singletons, and the rest were part of a sibling group. The mean age at adoption was 3.73 months, ranging from a child placed at birth to one placed at 11 months. The mean age at first assessment was 5 years, 9 months, and they were followed up for two years in the same way as the previously maltreated group.

The results reported here are based on samples of 56 previously maltreated children and 41 children placed in infancy. In this analysis we excluded from both groups children with major learning difficulties or diagnoses of pervasive developmental disorder (e.g., Asperger's syndrome), those who showed extreme outlying scores on behavioral measures, and, from the infancy-adopted group, a couple of children who were almost a year old at placement, as all the others were placed before 10 months.

DIFFERENCES AT FIRST ASSESSMENT

At the first assessment, soon after the previously maltreated children had entered their adoptive families, we found clear and statistically significant differences between the previously maltreated group and the infancy-placed group, which meaningfully reflected the different life experiences of the two groups. All the results reported here were statistically significant at the level of $p < 0.05$ at least.

Avoidance and Disorganization

The previously maltreated group showed more avoidance maneuvers, either unwillingness to begin the task or to continue with it or trying overtly or more subtly to avoid engaging with certain parameters of the story stem presented to them. Such avoidance apparently functions as a means of emotional regulation. Not only did the attachment-related dilemmas or conflicts presented in the stems elicit more avoidance from these children, but their own story continuations sometimes led them to further anxiety and avoidance because of their frightening or negative content. They also showed significantly greater "disorganized" character-istics, such as the sudden eruption of dysregulated aggression and catas-trophes into their narratives. Here is an example of some of these characteristics from a boy aged six who had suffered physical and emo-tional abuse and neglect and two changes of caregivers before adoptive placement. The narrative is his response to the third of the story stems, "stamping elephant." The interviewer says that "the family are having a picnic outside the house, and the animals are there too. A big elephant comes (the interviewer dramatizes the elephant stamping loudly) and sometimes this elephant gets a bit fierce and goes stamp, stamp; and the children and the animals feel scared when the elephant goes stamp, stamp." The child first responded by saying that all the animals and peo-ple were asleep (apparently a way of trying to prevent anything further happening in the story). Then the two boys went for a walk. The child did not mention the elephant here, but the next event in his story was that the crocodile ran up and knocked the boys down and ate them up. He contin-ued his story by saying that the children were not dead, but one had blood on him. In other words, while avoiding the potential threat presented in the story stem, his narrative at once introduced another danger, much worse than the potential threat from the elephant and producing death and injury. Then he again said that everyone went back to sleep, as though trying to neutralize the fearsome themes that he had just represented. Asked about the elephant in the story, which he had avoided mentioning at all so far, he again produced more violent aggressive themes; the ele-phant woke up and stamped on the animals; the alligator hurt the ele-phant, and then the elephant killed it. Reminded via a standard prompt that the children and animals were scared of the elephant, the child flatly denied this: "no, they are not scared, cos they had a ride on him"—another effort to avoid the threat presented in the narrative, through a distortion of what was given, rather than being able, for example, to show any protec-tion or help for the children within the story.

Solomon and George (1999) describe the same phenomena in the responses of children with disorganized attachments; on the one hand "frightening and explosively angry" themes, disorganizing the represen-tational process itself, and on the other a marked constriction and inhibi-tion of content and play, "as if the child is struggling to 'flee' mentally from the situation as quickly as possible" (pp. 17–18). In the former, the child appears flooded by affect and images, related to the fear and rage resulting when the attachment system is strongly activated but its needs are then left unmet. In the latter, extreme constriction is the only way of preventing themselves being overwhelmed in this way. Inevitably, children often veer from one alternative to the other.

In comparison to the defensive avoidance and disorganization shown by the later-placed group, the infancy-placed children did not avoid dealing with the dilemma or conflict in the stems; they could maintain organized functioning in the face of the attachment-related stress presented, and their narratives were not derailed by the eruption of catastrophes and violently angry themes. One would expect that not only had the maltreated children's traumatic experiences provoked much greater rage and fury in them (Eth & Pynoos, 1985) but that their relationships had not helped them develop emotional self-regulation in the way that the normal experiences of the nonmaltreated group had done.

Representations of Adults

It is not surprising, given the high incidence of disorganized attachments in maltreated children, that we should have found these features. But of more immediate use to parents and professionals may be an understanding of the detailed set of expectations and perceptions of adults that the child brings to the new placement and that forms the starting point for the development of their relationships with the new parents.

In terms of their representations of adults, these children more often showed adults as unaware when children needed their help and more often as explicitly rejecting children while less often showing adults being helpful to children or affectionate to them. They were also less likely to show ordinary levels of physical punishment by adults, such as a smack, but more likely to show catastrophes and "extreme" aggression. "Extreme" aggression is the term we used for manifestations of aggression and violence, including punishment, that appeared excessive and/or senseless, not related to the stem or in proportion with it. We distinguished this dysregulated aggression from "coherent," expectable aggression that remained contained and made sense within the story context.

Representations of Child Figures

We also found that the maltreated children's representations of child figures differed from the nonmaltreated children. They more frequently showed children as injured or dead. They were significantly more likely to show figures or objects being thrown out or thrown away; maltreated children and those who have experienced changes of carer often do feel that they are rubbish and have been discarded and sometimes wish to retaliate in kind. Kidnapping, usually of the child, was another theme more common in the maltreated group. Psychoanalytic studies of adopted children have identified this as a common theme (Hodges, 1990); in this late-adopted group it is likely in particular to reflect uncertainty about their permanence in their new family and perhaps their sense of powerlessness over the changes that others brought about in their lives.

As well as less often showing adults helping, the previously maltreated group were also less likely than infancy-adopted children to show children helping peers or siblings. However, this did not mean that the children felt themselves self-sufficient and competent to cope on their own. Rather, they were *less* likely than the infancy-adopted group to show children being able realistically to cope with a dilemma themselves. They were also less likely to acknowledge any distress of the child in the story. It seems probable that for these children whose internal representations predict that attachment needs will be unmet, that the child can expect rejection rather than help, this nonacknowledgment serves a defensive function; by not recognizing a need or wish for help, the child deactivates the attachment system, does not seek a response from adults, and avoids the possibility of further rejection or disappointment. However, if the child enters a new adoptive family, this defense becomes maladaptive because a child who avoids showing attachment needs makes it very hard for the new adoptive parents to recognize the times when they could respond to the child's need by offering comfort and security—responses that disconfirm the child's underlying expectations of rejection and that could help the child begin to develop new and happier expectations.

MORE ABUSE LEADING TO GREATER DIFFICULTIES

Given the degree of abuse and subsequent discontinuity of care that these children had suffered, it is not surprising that a few months after placement, the narrative assessments showed them to be a much more troubled group than the children adopted as infants. But even within this group, where most children had suffered multiple forms of abuse, we still found statistically significant differences between those who had experienced less abuse and those who had suffered more. In their story completions, the children with higher levels of previous abuse showed more themes of adult aggression, more adult unawareness when children needed them, more sexual material, more magic/omnipotent responses, and more bizarre/atypical material.

RELATIONSHIPS BETWEEN STORY STEM
ASSESSMENTS AND OTHER MEASURES

It has been shown that children's narratives are related to maternal reports of behavioral difficulties (Oppenheim et al., 1997). We compared the children's story stem assessments to parental reports of their behavior using the Strengths and Difficulties Questionnaire (SDQ) (Goodman,

1997), which examines children's behavior across various domains. We found clear meaningful relationships between the two, supporting the view that the assessments based on these children's stories were indeed tapping some forms of mental representation that also found expression in the child's behavior and relationships in real life. For example, children scoring higher for conduct problems on the SDQ showed more adult aggression, catastrophes, denial of distress, and avoidance in their story completions and less realistic mastery. Children scoring higher for peer problems also showed more denial of distress and catastrophes and less realistic mastery as well as fewer instances of children helping other children. Children scoring higher on the Prosocial subscale, on the other hand, showed more realistic mastery, more acknowledgment of distress, more children helping other children, more realistic/pleasurable domestic life, and less avoidance.

CHANGE OVER TIME IN ADOPTIVE PLACEMENTS

How did these attachment representations change as relationships developed in this new setting? We assessed the children again after one year and then two years in their adoptive families. One year later there were some positive changes, though it was clear that the children's internal working models of attachment relationships were far from transformed (Hodges, Steele, Hillman, Henderson, & Kaniuk, 2003). It appeared that aspects of new and more positive representations had begun to develop but did not automatically transform the already established representations. Two years into placement, it was clear that the consolidation of positive aspects was continuing but that there was considerable stability in various negative representations. The early-adopted group, who had shown significantly more positive representations than the previously maltreated group at the first assessment, showed a similar pattern of consolidation.

Figures 5.1 and 5.2 show changes over time in the maltreated and the early-placed group for the composite scores representing the constructs of attachment security and insecurity, defensive avoidance, and indicators of disorganization.

Increased Indicators of Security

As figure 5.1 illustrates, there was an increase, for both groups, in the overall score, which combined ratings indicating security. The overall score for insecurity, however, remained virtually unchanged. This may seem paradoxical if one is thinking in terms of using children's story stem responses to categorize their attachments into "secure" or "insecure" forms of organization (e.g., Bretherton et al., 1990; Green, Stanley, Smith, &

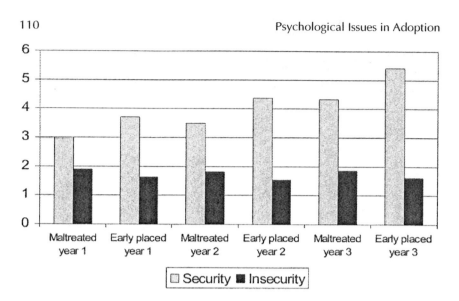

Figure 5.1 Changes over time: indicators of security and of insecurity.

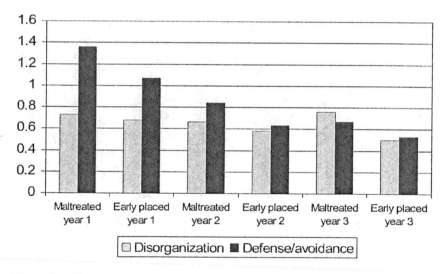

Figure 5.2 Changes over time: indicators of disorganization and defense/avoidance.

Goldwyn, 2000). How can children be both more secure and continuingly insecure? However, as outlined earlier, we used children's ratings not to classify them into categories but rather to examine changes in the various aspects of children's expectations and perceptions that go to make up the constructs of attachment security or insecurity. We expect any child's representations to include some negative ones, even if their attachment organization is a secure one. Our nonmaltreated group showed "insecure" aspects too. Reality and imagined possibilities contain negatives as well as positives even for children whose life experiences and family relationships are essentially benign. With children whose adverse earlier experiences had left them with many negative and insecure representations, we expected to find more negatives and fewer positives initially than the nonmaltreated group, as was the case. Their increasing security as they settled into their adoptive family was reflected in their increasing "secure" scores, but other possibilities and experiences remained part of their mental representations. (We should also note that the rating procedure, whereby each story was rated for the presence or absence of each theme, may impose a kind of ceiling effect, reducing extremes by ignoring any multiple occurrences of the same theme within a story, whether positive or negative.)

Many of the individual ratings also showed significant changes. Compared to the first assessment, the maltreated group more often showed adults providing not only practical help but also emotional comfort and affection; there were significant increases too both in limit setting and in physical punishment, suggesting that the latter could perhaps be thought about more "safely" than before, without the child having to resort to avoidance or alternatively being overwhelmed with imagery of extreme violence and death. Children were no longer so likely to show adults as unaware when children needed help or comfort than they had been at first assessment.

Parallel with these more positive expectations of parents was an increase in the maltreated children's capacity to acknowledge distress in children as well as in adults. A more secure sense that attachment needs would be met, that help and comfort would be available, and that adults would know when they were needed seemed to mean that children could now afford to acknowledge those needs. There was also an increase in representations of realistic/positive domestic life previously shown to be significantly higher in nonmaltreated and, specifically, in securely attached children compared to maltreated groups (Hodges & Steele, 2000).

There were significant increases too in representations of children seeking help, helping other children, and managing to cope realistically themselves with difficulties or dilemmas with a corresponding decrease in magic/omnipotent "quick fix" solutions to problems and excessive compliance at the expense of the child's own needs.

These positive changes are important indicators of the child's response to the adoptive family placement. Toth et al. (2000) showed in narrative assessments of younger children that maltreated children's representations of parents and self became consolidated and increasingly negative over a one-year assessment period between ages 3 1/2 and 4 1/2 compared to nonmaltreated children. It is therefore striking that this process can be reversed once maltreated children are placed in an adoptive family and that consolidation of positive representations can be demonstrated.

The previously maltreated adopted group also showed significant decreases in many of the avoidance maneuvers, which had been such a clear characteristic of the narratives of the maltreated group at first assessment. We distinguished various forms of avoidance, from outright refusal to continue a story at all to much more subtle changes of the constraints within a story so as to avoid the actual dilemma or anxiety; many of these individual forms decreased significantly as well as the overall score. This may be an important step in developmental recovery, as these children become able to use play, as in the story stem narratives, in the manner of normal children as a way of safely exploring feelings and cognitions about counterfactual possibilities. As we described previously, their narratives were beginning to demonstrate more expectation that attachment needs would be met; and, given this, they could apparently relinquish the avoidance, inhibition, or constriction of content, forms of emotional regulation that had guarded them against being overwhelmed by angry or fearful feelings (see figure 5.2). As a consequence, they may be becoming more able to use representational means to experiment with and perhaps to adjust their understanding of relationships between the self and attachment figures. In the Strange Situation it is securely attached infants who have the freedom to engage in physical exploration of their surroundings (Ainsworth, Blehar, Waters, & Wall, 1978). As these older children develop an increasing sense of the availability of the attachment figure, it may become more possible for them to turn their attention to this "representational" form of exploration of emotional and attachment relationships, which in turn should further help their gradual recovery.

As shown in figure 5.2, indicators of disorganization had been significantly higher at the outset in the maltreated children's stories compared to the stories of the infancy-adopted children. However, many characteristics indicative of disorganization remained unchanged over the two years. These included "extreme" aggression and catastrophes, bizarre and atypical material, and themes such as throwing away and children being injured or dead. The fact that these did not decrease indicates that the previously maltreated children were still struggling with disorganizing emotional responses, but the reduction in avoidance suggests that they had become rather more able to represent these in the narrative, acknowledge the dilemmas, and manage to maintain better functioning in the face of stress.

Despite these positive changes, when the maltreated group and the nonmaltreated children were compared two years after the first assessment, many of the original differences between them remained significant. In other words, children in the maltreated group were progressing but had not made up the gap that separated them from the nonmaltreated children.

Effects of Age at Placement

Younger children (four to six years at placement) showed more changes after one year than older ones, with a reduction in avoidance and an increase in positive representations. Change in the older children, six to eight at placement, was less marked and slower, but some of the same changes did occur by two years. It is particularly worth stressing that the positive changes were greater and took place more quickly in the children aged four to six at placement than in those aged six to eight. Sometimes, scarce social work resources may be concentrated on rapid placement of children in the first few years of life on the basis that with older children a little more delay will not create further damage; the findings indicate that even in these already "older" children, delay in placement damages future development.

We aim to follow these children up into adolescence to look at how far they maintain this path of developmental recovery. It will also be possible at that point to look at whether there are particular indicators at placement, including particular constellations of attachment representations, that can predict later difficulties, probably in combination with parenting factors. In the future this could allow the targeting of intervention and support where most needed.

IMPLICATIONS FOR RESEARCH AND INTERVENTION

Narrative assessments have proved a valuable technique for systematic assessment of children's internal representations of their relationships as well as often providing vivid insight into individual children's perceptions. The validity of the technique is also attested by numerous studies showing narrative responses to be related to children's CBCL scores, the Teacher Report Form, maternal attachment organization, of the mother, child's self-esteem, and other behavioral, attachment, and family measures (for a review, see Bretherton & Oppenheim, 2003).

Further research will be able to examine how a child's earlier patterns of representations relate to the subsequent development of their family and social relationships and other aspects of their functioning. Studies of the later social development of children with adverse early experiences (e.g., Hodges & Tizard, 1989b; Howe, 1998) have shown that individuals vary greatly in how well they can overcome these earlier difficulties. However, they have lacked techniques for detailed assessment of the children's internal representations in childhood, which might go some way toward explaining this variability. We plan to follow up the children in the study reported here in early adolescence, examining some of these issues. Although numerous factors may impact a young person's ability to make appropriate moves toward independence from parental care and control and to negotiate the different peer relationships of adolescence, the extent to which they have achieved a "secure base" from which to set out on these new developmental steps may be important. Expectably, children growing up in their families from birth are able to develop this secure base very early, unlike children placed for adoption later in childhood. One might, for example, hypothesize that those late-placed children whose narrative completions after two years in placement showed the development of more secure representations in their narratives may have more success in negotiating the tasks of early adolescence than those who were less able to develop security. The latter may still be struggling with the task of developing attachments at a point when it runs counter to some of the developmental tasks of their chronological age.

This study suggests that the technique may also be helpfully used to examine the effects following major change in the child's external situation. Besides placement changes, such as those studied here, such external changes can also include therapeutic intervention with a parent, aimed at improving their relationship with the child, and also therapeutic help for children themselves. Boston and Lush (1993) commented that one of the difficulties in evaluating the effectiveness of psychoanalytic psychotherapy has been "the relationship between the concepts and aims of psychotherapy, and the scope of currently available research techniques"; reduction in symptoms is not the only aim of psychodynamic forms of therapy. They comment, "Psychotherapists have placed considerable emphasis on change in the structure of the personality with fundamental implications for perceptions, internalised relationships and sense of self, and have argued that these are only loosely related to symptomatic change" (p. 117). The information provided by narrative assessments seems well suited for examining changes of this nature in younger children.

Turning to implications for practice, the study reported here demonstrates that change in children's attachment representations after adoption is complicated, uneven, and heterogeneous. Over the two years studied, children made significant progress in terms of their underlying expectations and perceptions of family relationships *and* still displayed significant, lasting damage, representing continuing vulnerabilities for the child and potential difficulties for the parents. As new and more positive representations had begun to develop, it appeared that they did not automatically transform the already established negative representations.

This is important because it suggests that children develop new and more positive sets of mental representations *in competition* with the existing negative representations rather than the new replacing the old. The old expectations and perceptions remain as vulnerabilities in that they can easily be triggered by events and interactions that seem to confirm their validity. It is all too easy for adoptive parents inadvertently to provide such triggers; they may have no idea of the way in which the child, on the basis of their abuse history, construes a particular interaction. The job of adoptive parents is one of active disconfirmation of the negative models that the children have brought with them and the building up of competing models that eventually, if all goes well, may become the predominant ones.

We have found that for many adopters this is a helpful way of thinking about the process they are struggling with. Although during the preadoption preparation new adopters may have accepted in the abstract that children's difficulties will persist, many adoptive parents retain an underlying belief that once the child settles into their family, the child's old life will soon be left behind. The belief or wish is that representations and expectations based on maltreatment and losses will fade and vanish, allowing "normal" family relationships to prevail. The story stem technique allows us to map areas of difficulty so that both parents and professionals have a clearer idea of the child's needs and vulnerabilities and the distorted underlying expectations that affect their perceptions and responses in the new family. Adopters can be helped to redefine their task and their expectations once they can see that the child still shows evidence of many negative representations and reassured moreover that this kind of stability is normal, at least over the two-year period we studied. They can also see clear evidence of the positive changes that their care has brought about in the child.

Whether consciously or not, children often seek to re-create interactions such as rejection or punishment because these are what feels familiar in terms of their underlying expectations. Adopters sometimes describe, in these interactions, the feeling of being pushed into roles in which they feel uncomfortable; the child's behavior may begin, for example, to evoke a response that makes them feel like a punishing, depriving parent. One could see this as the child's underlying negative representations driving them to behave in ways that will evoke a parental response confirming and consolidating the negative representation. Adopters can be helped by having, as it were, a preview of the script that the child's behavior is using and the roles that they are being allotted within it. This may allow them more easily to perceive when they are being placed in a particular role and to avoid and disconfirm the child's underlying expectation of a negative interaction. We are piloting the use of narrative assessments to help adoptive parents with children in placement. These are not necessarily families where there are major difficulties leading to a clinical referral but are designed to help the parents, together with their adoption social worker, consider their parenting in the light of what can be learned about the child's representations of attachment relationships.

It is not uncommon for adopters to feel some self-blame for their children's continuing difficulties, and in our experience it does also happen that professionals and the authorities responsible for the child may blame the family and begin to doubt the adequacy of the placement and whether the adoption should go ahead. We think it is helpful to have a method of direct assessment of the child's damaged view of family possibilities as they enter the placement so that both adopters and professionals can have a more realistic and detailed view of the damage to the child; ideally, this would occur before placement so as to inform the process of identifying the adoptive family best able to meet the child's needs.

The focus of this chapter is on what the child brings to the placement, but it goes without saying that what the adopters bring is equally important in terms not only of their expectations about the child but also of their own attachment histories and vulnerabilities. The development of new attachment relationships depends on the interaction of the two. We found some particular areas of vulnerability in adopters that led to their own attachment organization being classified on the Adult Attachment Interview as "Unresolved" with respect to losses or trauma they had experienced and that seemed to interact with their children's difficulties in ways that prevented the consolidation of positive representations in those children (Steele et al., 2003). Quinton et al. (1998) found that children who had been severely rejected developed attachments in the same way as other children to adopters with a sensitive parenting style but not to parents who showed less sensitive parenting.

As greater numbers of "special needs" children are adopted after histories of severe maltreatment and neglect, with a correspondingly high prevalence of emotional and behavioral difficulties and "attachment disorders," the need for postadoption services will increase further. In our view, one important component is the kind of detailed individual understanding of the child's "inner world" that story stem assessments provide. With such information, parents and professionals can more sensitively tailor their parenting and their support to fit children's particular individual needs.

ACKNOWLEDGMENTS

We are grateful for the generous support of the Sainsbury trusts (the Tedworth Charitable Trust and the Glass-House Trust) and the help and interest of the adoption agencies and the many families who together made this research possible.

Chapter 6

Beyond Adopted/Nonadopted Comparisons

Jesús Palacios and Yolanda Sánchez-Sandoval

During the past few decades, adoption research has proven to be a valuable source of information about very important matters, such as the development of adopted children and their problems, the role of early experiences, the possibilities for recovery after initial adversity, and the short-term and long-term consequences of being raised in environments marked by tension and lack of stimulation. As Howe (1998) points out, "Adoption studies take us to the heart of matters concerning human social development" (p. 125). However, psychological research about adoption has been encumbered by an overemphasis on comparing adopted with nonadopted children. Undoubtedly, such comparisons are appropriate and provide very valuable information. However, the results from these comparisons inadequately reflect the complexities of adoption, largely because of the type of design and the comparison measurements used in the research. Moreover, it is uncertain whether the type of information obtained from comparisons between adopted and nonadopted children is very useful for adoptive families, adopted children, and the professionals who interact and work with them.

This chapter has two sections. In the first one, our longitudinal research data from a wide range of adoptive families and their adopted children are presented. In contrast to similar research, our study is longitudinal, focusing on national adoption cases in Spain on boys and girls adopted mostly in their first year of life, although a significant percentage of children in the sample were considered special needs adoptions in our context. Regarding the design of the study, we collected data not only comparing adopted children to their current nonadopted peers but also comparing these youngsters to peers who remain institutionalized instead of being adopted. Comparisons among the groups of children were made for behavioral problems as well as self-esteem, life satisfaction, and coping strategies. Additionally, data were collected from adoptive parents who responded to a long semistructured interview and to different scales and measures. Teachers of the studied children also provided information on school adjustment and behavioral problems. We conclude this section by evaluating adoption as a resource for boys and girls within the child protection system.

In the second section, we analyze some topics that, while less prevalent in adoption research, are nonetheless very significant for the adoptees, their families, and professionals who work with them. These are issues that concern all adoptive families, such as communication about adoption, the sensitivity of the adopted child to being adopted, the problems that adoptive families have to confront with their children, acknowledgment of differences, the stress related to adoptive parenthood, and satisfaction with adoption. Frequently, families need help with these issues, but research offers little information and guidance. If adoption research should serve not only the interests of researchers but also those of adoptive families and adopted children, it would seem reasonable to hope for a better balance of research topics in the future.

ON THE COMPARISON OF ADOPTED WITH NONADOPTED CHILDREN

Adoption research has been—and in large part still is—dominated by comparisons between adopted and nonadopted children. Adoption provides a sort of natural experiment whereby it is possible to analyze important issues like the role of early experiences and the possibility of recovery after initial adversity (see chapter 4 in this volume). Therefore, it is hardly surprising that researchers have concerned themselves with comparing children raised in regular circumstances (born and raised into their own family) with children raised in a more adverse environment (born into a family in which they were not well received or experienced abuse or neglect but later placed with other families).

The basic question that much research has considered is how adopted children compare with nonadopted children. The answer varies significantly depending on whether research is carried out with clinical samples (e.g., Brodzinsky & Steiger, 1991; Goldberg & Wolkind, 1992; Kotsopoulos, Walker, Copping, Coté, & Stavrakaki, 1993; Kotsopoulos et al., 1988), or nonclinical samples (e.g., Brodzinsky, Schechter, Braff, & Singer, 1984; Fergusson, Lynskey, & Horwood, 1995; Miller, Fan, Christensen, et al., 2000; Sharma, McGue, & Benson, 1998; Verhulst, 2000a). The former studies tend to present an image of greater problems and maladjustments in adopted children than in nonadopted children, with a higher incidence of learning and behavioral problems. The latter studies tend to give a less dramatic view of the difference, but they still show adopted children to be a more problematic group than nonadopted children. Behavioral problems of an externalized nature (impulsiveness, hyperactivity, or attention problems), as well as greater difficulty in adjusting to school, are the most common findings in adoption research. Nonetheless, although the differences are significant, the overall effect of these variables between adopted children and other groups tends to be of a small to moderate magnitude (Bimmel, Juffer, van Ijzendoorn, & Bakermans-Kranenburg, 2003; Miller, Fan, Christensen, et al., 2000; but see chapter 11 in this volume). Some factors that are associated with greater problems are the child's age when adopted and life experiences prior to adoption. There have also been studies that have found no difference between adopted and nonadopted children or between adoptive and nonadoptive parents (e.g., Borders, Black, & Pasley, 1998). Finally, other researchers have found that adopted children, while performing worse in some areas, actually have higher performance in some other areas than nonadopted children (Sharma et al., 1998).

SOME LIMITATIONS OF THE USUAL COMPARISONS BETWEEN ADOPTED AND NONADOPTED

One of the problems related to the comparison between adopted and nonadopted children is that often considerably unequal situations are compared. It is clear that if we compare the school performance and adjustment of children with a long and rich school experience to that of children with very limited contact with school contexts, it is almost tautological to say that the first ones will show better performance and adjustment than the latter. And if we compare the emotional and conduct adjustment of children whose early life experience is marked by nurturance and continuity with children whose early lives are filled with social adversity—such as neglect, abuse, institutional rearing, and separations from biological family, friends, and classmates—finding more problems among the latter than among the former group of children is once again almost inevitable.

In our opinion, the comparison that does the most justice to understanding the implications of adoption is not only the one with current peers or classmates but also the comparison to those youngsters who could have been their classmates if their life had taken a different turn. The case of children who are in institutions is a good candidate for a comparison group since they also have had adverse early experiences and a history of separations but, because of many circumstances (generally of a legal type), have not been adopted. This is precisely the reason why we have included this third comparison group in our design. Although this approach is not new (see, e.g., Hodges & Tizard, 1989a, 1989b), we think that it still has merit for achieving a more complete view of what adoption means in the life of the children involved.

Another problem that we believe exists in many of the comparisons between adopted and nonadopted children is the limited nature of the content areas that are subject to comparison. Most research of this type deals with behavioral problems, which is undoubtedly a very relevant area to explore. Other content areas of considerable psychological relevance are analyzed less frequently, such as self-esteem, life satisfaction, and coping strategies. Consequently, we have included these variables in our study. The exclusive focus on problems is, in our view, one of the shortcomings of adoption research.

Availability of longitudinal information has also allowed us to solve a third problem that is frequently found in adoption studies: the use of small samples and cross-sectional designs. By having information for a relatively large sample and for two different points in time (with a six-year interval), we can focus on stability and change of patterns of behavior and adjustment.

Our Sample and Methods

The data presented in this chapter come from our research about adoption in Andalusia, a region in southern Spain. Since 1987, all adoptions in Spain go through the public authority, and it was with its collaboration that we approached all Andalusian families who had adopted a child in the period 1987–1993. Of those, 18.7 percent could not be contacted (problems with postal address), and 15 percent decided not to participate in the study. Thus, from the population of 568 families, a sample of 393 families who had adopted a total of 484 children were studied (78% of families had adopted a single child, 20% had adopted two, and the rest had adopted three or more). In families that had adopted more than one child, we chose to study only one of them, selected at random. Of the 393 adopted children, 166 were also studied in the schools that they were attending, where two of their schoolmates, selected randomly, were also studied ($n = 314$). Finally, a sample of children raised in institutions was included. The latter are boys and girls who, like the adopted children, had to be separated from their families because of early relinquishment or some sort of maltreatment but who for some reason had not been adopted or placed into foster care but rather into residences ($n = 122$). These residences no longer are big orphanages but rather take the form of small groups of children (generally between 5 and 20) living in small facilities or in family-type living arrangements, like apartments. Very often, staff outnumbers children. Additionally, a good part of these children's lives take part out in the community, where they attend school as well as after-school activities (e.g., swimming, dancing, and arts and crafts). In the case of adoptive families, a long interview (never less than two hours) was conducted in order to explore their experiences during the entire process of adoption (the initial motivation, the waiting period, the arrival of the child, problems of adaptation, later development, and the current situation) as well as key issues in adoptive families (communication with regard to adoption, acknowledgment of similarities/differences with biological families, and satisfaction with adoption). In addition, parents answered a series of questionnaires related to the behavioral problems of their children and their educational styles (technical details to be presented later as data are reported). Educators in centers where the children were institutionalized responded to some of these questionnaires. In addition, the teachers of the children who were studied at school (adopted children, schoolmates, and institutionalized children) filled out questionnaires about motivation, performance, school behavior, and behavioral problems. Finally, self-esteem information was obtained for all children more than four years old.

With respect to the adopted children's characteristics, the proportion of girls (52.5%) to boys (47.5%) was nearly equal. At the time of the first data collection, 67 percent of adopted children were under 9 years of age, 26 percent were between 9 and 15 years, and the remainder (7%) were older than 15. A large proportion of children in the study were adopted shortly after birth (40.8%) or before turning one year of age (21%). Children adopted when they were 6 years or older account for 15 percent of the sampled children. The remaining children (23, or 2%) were adopted between 1 and 6 years of age. Thirty-eight percent of our subjects fell within the group known as "special adoptions" in Spain; of these, 42 percent were children with some type of special need or disability, 40 percent were children with 6 or more years of age when adopted, and 29 percent were children adopted together with a sibling. The total exceeds 100 percent because some of these children are included in more than one special adoption subgroup. All are national adoptions since international adoption was uncommon in Spain until 1997, 2 years after our first data collection. Results of this study have been presented elsewhere (Palacios & Sánchez-Sandoval, 1999; Palacios, Sánchez-Sandoval, & Sánchez-Espinosa, 1997).

Six years after the initial study, we recontacted the adoptive families studied in 1995. Given that a significant part of the children in our study were quite young when we first studied them, we were very interested to learn about their progress and their situation as they approached or entered adolescence. On this occasion, we were able to study 273 families (13% of the 393 initial families could not be located, and 17% preferred not to participate again). Data analysis showed that this was not selective attrition and that the sociodemographic characteristics of the families studied in 2001 were not statistically different from those studied six years before. In each one of these families, we studied the same child as in 1995. In addition to the instruments used for previous data collection, new self-esteem and life satisfaction scales were added, as was an assessment of children's coping styles and a stress assessment of adoptive parents.

In this second phase of data collection, 273 adopted children were studied, along with a total of 169 of their current peers and 198 children living in institutions. However, only the adopted children were studied longitudinally. Therefore, their current peers and the children from institutions from time 2 are not the same as those studied in time 1. The results of this data collection wave will be reported in articles now in preparation.

SOME COMPARISON DATA

With regard to *conduct problems*, parents and teachers completed the respective version of Rutter scales (*Rutter Parents' and Teachers' Scales*—Rutter, Tizard, & Whitmore, 1970; *Revised Rutter Parent and Teacher Scale*—Hogg, Rutter, & Richman, 1997). These scales have been successfully used in various studies on adoption and foster care (see, e.g., Hodges & Tizard, 1989a; O'Connor, Rutter, & the E.R.A. Research Team, 2000; Quinton, Rushton, Dance, & Mayes, 1998); deal with contents very similar to the ones covered by CBCL (Achenbach, 1991), such as behavior problems, emotional problems, hyperactivity problems, and prosocial behavior problems; and are much shorter and thus less time consuming than CBCL.

The comparison between the three groups in our study did not show important differences during the preschool years in the majority of the areas, although the group of children from institutions already showed significantly higher scores regarding hostility/aggressiveness. For schoolchildren, the data show a more differentiated profile. The children from institutions show higher scores in conduct problems as well as in the subscales for hostility/aggressiveness, emotional problems (anxiety, fears), prosocial behavior problems, and hyperactivity–distraction. In this last subscale (but not in the rest or in the total score for problems), school-age adopted children also obtained scores significantly higher than their current classmates, a finding often reported in adoption research (see, e.g., the review by Wilson, 2004). We also found an even more remarkable difference: the accumulation of problems of a diverse type among the children growing up in institutions, whose difficulties seem widespread more than limited to a specific domain. In addition, quite interestingly, if in time 1 we analyze the adoptees' scores for hyperactivity–distraction depending on their institutional experience, significant differences are found between those who did not go through institutions, those who were at institutions for less than one year, and those who were at institutions for more than one year. The amount of institutional experience was positively correlated with hyperactivity-distraction scores.

On the other hand, it is interesting to analyze the differences between the adopted children and their current classmates in hyperactivity–distraction depending on the age at which the adopted children reached their new families. For example, in the data from time 2, the effect size for hyperactivity–distraction in the total sample of adopted–classmates is .56. If we compare with their current classmates only those who were adopted under three years of age, the differences are also significant but with a lower effect size of .42, and something similar happens with those who were adopted with less than one year of age (significant differences, effect size .40). But if the comparison is between those who were adopted from birth and their current classmates, the differences in hyperactivity are no longer significant (effect size .36). So for the diverse variables analyzed, if the comparison is made between the two maximum comparable groups (those adopted from birth and their current classmates), there are no significant statistical differences in any of the areas studied by us.

The use in time 2 (and with children aged 10 or over) of the *Coping Scale for Children and Youth* (Brodzinsky, Elias, et al., 1992) has allowed us to evaluate the *problem-coping strategies* for our three groups of comparison. The scale requests that subjects identify one major problem they have had in the last weeks and then choose the type of strategies they have used to cope with it. The alternatives that are offered fall into four specific strategies: assistance seeking (asking family members or friends to help or advice as well as sharing feelings with others), cognitive-behavioral problem solving (attempts to generate and enact possible resolutions to the problem or to reframe the problem in a less disturbing way), cognitive avoidance (wishful thinking and thought suppression), and behavioral avoidance (attempts to avoid reminders of the problem). The analysis of variance gender × group × age for each one of the variables shows that while the gender does not relate significantly to the use of the different coping strategies, group and age are associated with significant differences. Although there are no differences among the three groups in the use of cognitive avoidance strategies, adopted children and their classmates report using behavioral avoidance strategies less often compared to those in institutions (effect size of the adopted–institutions comparison –.48) but display significantly greater use of assistance seeking strategies (effect size of the adopted–institutions comparison of .36) and of problem-focused or cognitive-behavioral problem-solving strategies (effect size adopted–institutions comparison of .34). These differences seem to increase with age: while in the group of children aged 10 to 11 the differences are found only in behavioral avoidance, in the 12-to-16 group the significant differences also affect the assistance-seeking and the problem-focused strategies.

With regard to *performance at school,* we have three indicators offering complementary and coherent information. We have the teacher-reported *Classroom Behavior Inventory* (CBI) (Schaefer, Edgerton, & Aaronson, 1978), with its subscales for intelligence, creativity–curiosity, task orientation, distraction, independence, dependence, extroversion, introversion, consideration, and hostility. We also have the evaluation made by teachers regarding motivation and pupils' performance (adoptees, classmates, and children from institutions). If we take the data from time 2 as a reference, in which the differences in CBI are more appreciable, we find significant differences between adopted children and their classmates, with the effect size −.47 in favor of the classmates. If we carry out the comparison with those children who were adopted before the age of three, the effect size decreases to −.29, and the differences are not significant. Similar, non-significant results are obtained if the comparison is carried out only for those adopted under the age of one. When those adopted are compared to children from institutions, however, the difference is significant in favor of the adopted children, with an effect size of .50 for the general sample of those adopted, .71 for those adopted under the age of three, and .72 for those adopted in their first year of life.

If we compare the scores for motivation and performance at school, the differences adopted–classmates are not significant. But when the comparison is carried out between the adopted children and the children from institutions, the differences are significant with a medium to high effect size in motivation (.49 for the total of those adopted, .86 for those adopted under the age of three, and .89 for those adopted with one year of age or less).

Finally, in the area of *self-esteem and life satisfaction,* we once again find very similar arguments to the previous ones. Self-esteem was assessed using Harter's (1980, 1985) scales. In our first collection of data, under eight years of age, the adopted children obtained scores that were higher on the Harter scale than those of their classmates and the children from institutions. For older children, the differences between the groups tended to disappear. In time 2 we once again used the Harter scale, adding the Rosenberg scale (Rosenberg, 1965) for children 10 years and older. Adopted children and their classmates scored higher on both scales compared to children from institutions. The effect size for the differences between adoptees (whatever the adoption age criteria taken into account) and those from institutions are of a medium size, ranging from .40 to .50.

A similar pattern was found for *life satisfaction,* assessed with a self-reported scale developed by Hueber (1991). Adopted children and their classmates obtained significantly higher scores than those from institutions (effect size 1.13 for the comparison adopted–institutionalized children and 1.04 for the comparison adoptees' classmates–institutionalized children). In addition, life satisfaction was lower in the three groups for children entering adolescence, but while the decrease was slight for adopted children and classmates, it was clearly marked for children from institutions. The effect size for the adopted–institution comparison indicates, in this case, a very marked difference regardless of the child's age at adoption.

In summary, the set of data presented in this chapter is based on the longitudinal study of a wide sample of adopted children, their classmates, and a comparable sample of children at institutions. The data suggest that in the contents examined and for the developmental periods and the time lapse considered, adoption serves the needs of children in a highly favorable manner. The adopted children are well integrated into their families and schools, show good psychological adjustment, and are quite comparable in psychological outcomes to nonadopted community classmates, at least for those youngsters adopted at birth or within their first year of life. However, as the age of adoption placement increases, the presence of adjustment problems also raises, although these two groups continue to be more similar than different in their pattern of development and adjustment. When group differences do occur, they are of a small to medium magnitude and usually are in areas of hyperactivity–distraction and school adjustment.

If there are still any doubts regarding adoption as an acceptable solution for those children who experience early separation from biological parents and/or early adversity, it is enough to analyze the comparisons of these youngsters with those children who, for various reasons, cannot be adopted and remain at institutions. In our research, institutionalized children are the ones who are systematically worse off in virtually all areas of adjustment, frequently with a medium- to high-magnitude difference. We have seen this with regard to the areas of behavior problems and academic performance as well as with regard to coping strategies, self-esteem, and life satisfaction of these children. Although adoption is commonly stereotyped as being associated with significant problems, our data suggest a more positive view of adoption as a stable solution for children whose initial life circumstances are marked by adversity or would otherwise be marked by adversity if they remain in their biological families.

ADOPTERS AND ADOPTED: CHALLENGES AND REALITY

We will now turn our attention to a set of issues that are notably less often explored in adoption research. Through a long, semistructured interview with the adopters from our sample group, we have been able to examine the details of the adoption process, its joys and concerns, and its challenges and realities. Our longitudinal data provides information not only for the initial period of study but also for how adoption was experienced over time.

Communication about Adoption

Research on communication about adoption with adopted children is rather scarce despite the fact that the "talking and telling" process is considered as one of the key parts for successful adoption (see chapter 7 in this volume). Looking at it on the negative side, secrecy and denial have a negative impact on the adjustment, well-being, and identity of the adopted children (Rosenberg & Groze, 1997; Triseliotis, 1973). And from the perspective of communication, the degree of comfort with which the adopted children face the knowledge about their adoptive status seems to depend on the age at which the communication process started—earlier ages being associated with more positive outcomes (Raynor, 1980)—as well as on the ease with which the adopted children feel they can talk about the matter with their adoptive parents (Feast & Howe, 2003; Howe & Feast, 2000). The need for communication affects not only those who were adopted as babies and, therefore, do not have memories or direct knowledge regarding their previous history but also those who were adopted at ages that allow them to have knowledge and memories of their past; in fact, as noted by Howe and Feast (2000), it is more likely for the latter youngsters to find the communication process with their parents more difficult than those who were adopted when they were younger. The communication process is considered essential for the well-being of the adopted children and is seen as a key part in the formation of their identity (Triseliotis, 2000). The most common recommendation is that the communication process should start as early as possible with a simple and credible history that is told before the age of four and that will later still be talked about and to which information elements will be added as the cognitive and emotional capacities of the adopted child allow for efficient communication (regarding children's understanding of adoption, see Brodzinsky, Singer, & Braff, 1984).

Although communication about adoption is universally recommended by adoption professionals and is viewed as morally compulsory for adoptive parents (Triseliotis, 2000), this process undoubtedly is one of the most challenging tasks found by adopters and also is one that gives raise to considerable anxiety and uncertainty (Brodzinsky & Pinderhughes, 2002). For the child adopted as a baby, parents often question the need to alter the child's well-being with information that may bring about a sense of instability and confusion. For the child adopted at a later stage in life, parents often believe that if the child is aware of the past, there is no need to bur-

Table 6.1
Percentage of children whose parents had talked to them about their adoption, depending on age (longitudinal data, six-year span)

Age of the child at time 1	Children who had been spoken with at time 1 (%)	6 years later (%)
1	0	83.7
2	0	95.7
3	12.5	94.4
4	25	96.4
5	48.7	89.5
6	52.9	88.6
7	64	80
8	77.8	92.9
9	75	94.1
10	64.3	90
11	66.7	87.5
12	100	100

den him with discussions about events that not only are distant but also are associated with painful memories.

The data from our investigation point out the difficulties that parents face regarding communication with the child when the subject is adoption. As shown in table 6.1, half of the six-year-old children in our first wave of data collection had not yet received the information regarding their adoptive status from their parents, and a third of the 11-year-old children were still in the same situation. These results are, undoubtedly, far from the experts' recommendations. Six years later, the majority of the children had been given the information (although 16.3% of the seven-year-old children still had not).

Regarding the frequency with which parents talked to their children about adoption, at time 2, 10 percent of the parents stated that they had held only a single conversation with their children regarding adoption, while 56 percent reported that they had spoken about the matter on very few occasions. In contrast, 21 percent of the parents stated that they talked about adoption every few months, and 12 percent stated that they did so at least once a month.

These results are interesting for a number of reasons. First, they show the difficulty that parents have in approaching communication about adoption at early ages. In addition, the data suggest that parents view "telling" not as a process to be engaged in throughout the child's formative years but as a series of discrete events that allow for the imparting of key information. It should be noted, however, that parents in this group did not go through adoption training programs that would inform them of the need and the strategies for early communication. Quite interestingly, the majority of the parents told us that nobody had explained that it was important to talk to the children about their adoptive status. Curiously, when we interviewed the professionals who had been involved in those adoptions, they said that "of course" they had given parents this information. Both are probably telling the truth: the professionals informed the parents, but they did so in a context and manner that did not allow the parents to "hear" the information.

The data also show a certain tendency toward generational changes in such a way that the percentage of children in our sample group who were seven in 1995 and to whom parents had spoken about adoption (64%) is clearly lower than the percentage of children who were seven years old in 2001 and to whom parents had spoken about adoption (83.7%). This difference probably reflects changes in general social assumptions regarding adoption as well as better preparation of adoptive parents by social casework and mental health professionals.

When adoption was discussed in the adoptive homes in our sample group, it was the children who normally brought up the conversation (44% of the cases) as opposed to either parents or children (29%) or only the parents (24%); in the remaining 3 percent, other people started the conversations. The conversations typically came about more in response to news or events linked to other people than in response to specific adoption issues in the family. In addition, although knowing that they were adopted or having spoken with their parents at some stage about adoption, 56 percent of the children in the sample group did not bring up any questions about the matter again after the initial conversation with their parents. Those who had raised the matter or questioned their parents did so with a frequency related to age. Figure 6.1 indicates that questions about adoption increased between 6 and 18 years, with a clear decrease after this age. Furthermore, data from time 2 suggest that children whose parents show more closed communication attitudes demonstrated greater difficulties when it came to talking about adoption. Undoubtedly, this pattern reflects a reciprocal influence between parents and children regarding communication problems about adoption: as parents are less inclined to talk about adoption, the children feel less free to ask questions related to this matter; in turn, when parents perceive that their children do not ask any adoption-related questions, they are likely to believe that the matter does not bother them, in turn reinforcing their tendency to limit adoption communication. In contrast, the data also show that those adopted children who show an interest in their biological family have parents who are more open and communicative in their ideas and practices regarding adoption (see chapter 7 in this volume).

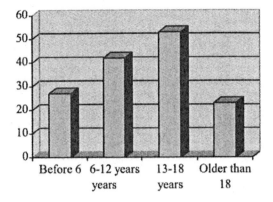

Figure 6.1 Frequency of questions about adoption by adopted children at various ages as reported by their parents.

In wave 2 of our data collection, we spoke to 44 boys and girls about communication with their parents regarding adoption; 64 percent of these youngsters stated that they recalled the first conversation that they had about adoption. Their recollection of the age at which this first conversation took place correlates well with the memories of their parents, with a maximum discrepancy of one year. A third of these children said that they imagined or suspected their adoptive status before they were told about it. After a first conversation about adoption, 23 percent of the boys and girls interviewed (as opposed to 14% of their parents) told us that they had never again spoken about the subject, while 49 percent of the adopted children (as opposed to 44% of their parents) were of the opinion that the subject had been dealt with very few times throughout the years, and 28 percent of the adopted children (and 40% of their parents) thought that communication about the matter occurred very frequently. The divergence between the perception of these matters by the adopted children and their adoptive parents has also been found by other investigators (McRoy, Grotevant, & Zurcher, 1988; Wrobel, Kohler, Grotevant, McRoy, & Friedrick, 1998). In any case, it is evident that, according to the adopted children as well as their parents, the percentage of adopters in our sample that take the initiative of dealing with matters related to adoption with their children is clearly low.

Attitudes of Adopted Children about Adoption

The way in which adopted children experience the meaning and implication of being adopted has been studied by Brodzinsky (see, e.g., Brodzinsky, Smith, & Brodzinsky, 1998) using a developmental approach that takes into consideration both the emergent cognitive capacities of the children as well as their experiences over time. According to Brodzinsky's developmental model, there would be two periods of greater sensitivity for the child about adoption. The first occurs around six to seven years of age, when most children discover that belonging to a family implies biological links with parents and when the adopted children face, for the first time, the feeling of loss of their biological parents (a feeling of loss caused both by cognitive maturation and by the interiorization of a cultural definition of family linking family and biology, as stressed by Leon, 2002); the second period of enhanced sensitivity occurs when access to the cognitive capacities of adolescence and the importance of solving essential concerns linked to identity cause new doubts about oneself (see also Kohler, Grotevant, & McRoy, 2002; Wilson, 2004).

Among families whose children knew about their adoptive status, 44 found that their children have gone through a period of greater sensitivity related to the fact that they are adopted. The most frequent manifestations are verbal expression of doubts, of lack of satisfaction and of sad emotions (34%), and of the negative expression of these emotions through crying, bad moods, or complaints (34%). Other parents noticed this heightened sensitivity through social isolation, shyness, or the lack of communication during this period (22%). Finally, 10 percent manifested absenteeism (or attempted absenteeism) from home in a more or less prolonged manner.

As shown in figure 6.2, the periods of greater sensitivity detected by parents is at the age of 6 to 9 years and, to a lesser extent, at the age of 12

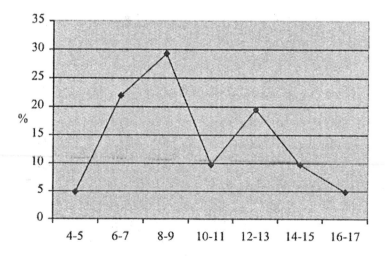

Figure 6.2 Ages of greatest sensitivity among children with respect to adoption, according to their parents.

to 13 years. Forty-five percent of the parents attributed this greater sensitivity to their child's growing awareness of the meaning and implications of being adopted, while the rest attributed it to other factors, including feelings of being rejected (24%); an important family event, such as the birth or death of a relation (13%); or meeting with a member of the biological family (8%). An additional 1 percent of parents had no explanation for the heightened sensitivity to adoption displayed by their children.

The results are quite consistent both with the data and developmental speculation reported by Brodzinsky, Singer, et al. (1984) and with Leon's (2002) proposals. These results suggest that the concern of the adopted children regarding adoption is not linked exclusively to the construction of identity during adolescence but also to feelings of loss that begin to emerge in earlier developmental periods, usually around six to nine years. Although our data suggest a lesser sensitivity to adoption issues in the adolescent years than during earlier developmental periods, this finding does not necessarily mean that adolescents are less concerned with adoption than they once were; rather, they could be simply less transparent in the expression of feelings.

Parents' Perception of Children's Problems

As well as the communication problems around adoption, parents have to face other matters related to their children. When we asked them to identify the main problems that they had come up against, both at time 1 as well as at time 2, the most frequent response referred to behavioral difficulties, which probably is not only due to the adoption but also common to the experiences in many families, be they adoptive or not. Because of our longitudinal design, we were able to collect data not only on parents' perception of their children problems at two different time periods but also on the changes in the behavioral adjustment over time. Parents' reports of their children's problems using the Rutter scale were used as the source of information, and figure 6.3 shows some of the data.

Problems related to hyperactivity are those that stand out among the concerns of the adoptive parents, and this seems perfectly consistent with the greater incidence of this problem in these children, as was mentioned previously. Our results also found a moderately strong correlation (normally in the order of .50) between the manifestations of problems by the children between both assessment phases, which is probably not very surprising. More interesting, however, is the tendency for children to present a lower level of problem behavior in time 2 (when a greater percentage of children are in their adolescence) than in time 1. The differences are statistically significant in the case of behavioral problems and hyperactivity. The reduction of problems occurs in boys as well as in girls, without significant differences between them, except in relation with prosocial behav-

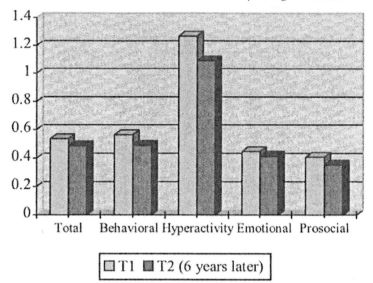

Figure 6.3 Evolution of children's problems encountered by parents in the collection of initial data and six years later.

ior, for which problems decrease significantly more in girls as compared to boys.

The presence of more or less problems is related to several characteristics of the adopted children and their parents. For example, families who adopted children with special needs scored higher for total of problems, as measured by the Rutter scale for parents, than families who adopted children without such needs; their scores were also higher for emotional problems but not in the other areas explored. Families who adopted children with chronic illnesses also perceived more behavior problems than those who adopted children without this characteristic; in this case, differences are statistically significant for total number of problems, hyperactivity, and behavioral and emotional problems but not for problems related to prosocial behavior. Finally, families who adopted children with previous experience of abuse and neglect reported more total problems as well as more behavioral and emotional difficulties.

The problems identified in the children are not related to such characteristics of their parents as age or type of family structure (single or two parent), but they are significantly linked to other variables. The less educated the parents, the higher the total problem score as well as the hyperactivity and emotional problem scores. In addition, the rearing styles of the parents correlate significantly with the manifestation of problems in the children: higher scores in affection and communication correlate with lower total score of problems ($r = -.31$) as well as lower scores in behavioral ($r = -.29$), emotional ($r = -.22$), and hyperactivity ($r = -.13$) domains. In addition, parents who show an authoritative style and a preference for inductive educational styles are less likely to have children who manifest behavioral problems.

The presence of more behavioral problems in the children of less educated parents is undoubtedly more understandable when other information is added. According to our data, the babies assigned to families in our sample appear to be distributed somewhat equally among parents of differing educational levels (40% to less educated parents, 26% to parents with a medium level of education, 34% to well-educated parents). However, the distribution of children older than six years shows a marked imbalance with regard to their assignment: 60 percent of these children were adopted by less educated families, 23 percent by medium-educated families, and 17 percent by well-educated families. Therefore, the greater presence of problems among the children of less educated families must be interpreted in the light of the fact that their children have greater difficulties present from the moment that they join the family.

Acknowledgment of Differences

Ever since the pioneering work of Kirk (1964), interest has been shown in the perception that adoptive parents have of the similarities and differences between their families and nonadoptive families. According to Kirk, when coping with adoption-related issues, some parents deny or minimize the differences, whereas others acknowledge them and seem more ready to face the specific challenges of adoption. Kirk's initial hypothesis suggests that acknowledgment of differences is a positive way for the adoptive family to operate and for the adjustment of the adoptees, while rejection of differences is negative regarding the same variables. This hypothesis has been empirically supported only in a limited way, as Brodzinsky et al. (1998) pointed out. In addition, it seems logical to suppose that parental attitudes are likely to change during different periods of the family life cycle; at times, parents may need to minimize differences between their families and others; in contrast, at other periods, parents may willingly (or reluctantly) acknowledge the differences in their families that are related to adoption. For example, when a baby joins the family, there may be a definite tendency to act as if differences between adoptive and nonadoptive families do not exist: a major effort is made to integrate the new member into the family and build family bonds, without considerations of their adoptive status. Later on, adoptive parents must begin to recognize and acknowledge the differences in their families as they assume responsibilities specific to adoptive family life, such as talking with the child about adoption, his or her previous life circumstances, how he or she feels about the past, and so on. Once the differences have been recognized, however, it is important that they are not insisted on (Brodzinsky, 1990), as that would give the adopted child the message that his or her adoptive status is *the* problem in the family.

In our study, adoptive parents' acknowledgment of differences was explored through several questions in the semistructured interview in which parents were asked their opinion on a series of specific issues: Do adopted children have needs that nonadopted children do not have, do they have reasons for specific worries, and do adoptive parents need to face problems that are specific to adoptive families? The more positive answers parents come up with, the higher the acknowledgment of differences score they obtain.

Information from our study confirms that parental attitudes about adoption are not something unalterable among those who adopt. On the contrary, it seems that these attitudes are adjusted and readjusted with the passage of time and through various circumstances. Thus, for example, in time 1 of our investigation, we found that parents with children between 7 and 11 years perceived less differences in the nature of adoptive family life than parents of children over 16 years. A similar pattern was observed at the time 2 assessment, six years later. Additionally, in time 1, the older the children were when they arrived in the home, the greater their parents acknowledge the differences inherent to adoption ($r = .40$). This pattern, however, was not repeated at the time 2 assessment.

Parents' attitudes on this dimension seem to be also related to characteristics of their children such as their behavior problems. As shown in figure 6.4, both at time 1 and time 2 assessments, parents of children in the first quartile of problem behavior scored lower on the acknowledgment-of-differences dimension than parents of children in the intermediate or the upper quartiles. Parents of the latter children (those with the total highest score for problem behavior in our sample) were the ones with the highest score in acknowledgment of differences, a score that is probably telling us something about their insistence on differences, a way of explaining child's problematic behavior due to her adoptive status (which, simultaneously, takes responsibility for the problems away from the parents).

Another interesting piece of information shows that as an adoptive family increases its time together, acknowledgment of differences tend to diminish. Although there is a positive correlation between the scores for acknowledgment of differences at both data collection times ($r = .29$), 60 percent of the values had changed, becoming lower at time 2 as compared to time 1. This indicates that adoptive families, on average, perceived fewer differences six years after the first data collection. It would therefore seem that strengthening family relationships results in a decrease of the recognition of differences.

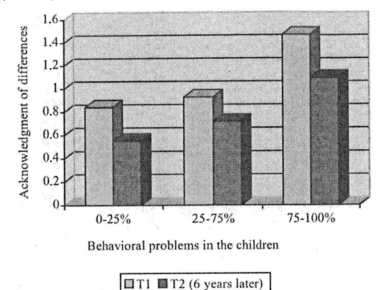

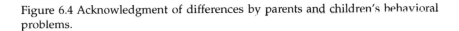

Figure 6.4 Acknowledgment of differences by parents and children's behavioral problems.

The way adoptive parents perceive the differences existing between them and nonadoptive parents seems then to be result of a combination of factors. There seem to be ages of the adoptive children when their adopters perceive greater differences, and the fact that, in our data, acknowledgment of differences seems to be lower for parents of children between 7 and 11 years probably tells something about more tensions associated with adoption-related issues in the preschool years and later in the adolescence. In addition, the presence of more problematic behavior may make some parents more aware of the difficulties very often associated with experiences in the child's early life, a life before the arrival of the child to the family that does not exist when a child is born to the family and remains in it throughout his or her formative years. Additionally, our data show that strengthening family relationship results in a decrease of acknowledgment of differences. It would then seem that acknowledgment of differences is not a single or a simple dimension but rather the result of many different child and family-related variables interacting over time.

Stress in Adoptive Parenthood

Adoption entails a number of specific tensions and sources of stress reviewed by Brodzinsky and Pinderhughes (2002). However, it is frequent to refer to stress linked to adoption as if it were specific only for the transition to adoptive parenthood period, including decision making, going through the home study to qualify for adoption, waiting for the child's arrival, forming bonds once arrived, and so on. In their study of transition to adoptive parenthood, Levy-Shiff, Goldschmidt, and Har-Even (1991) have shown that, despite this additional stresses, most adoptive parents do well in this phase. But little is known about stress and adoptive family life beyond the transition period. As an exception, Mainemer, Gilman, and Ames (1998) evaluated stress in parents who had adopted Romanian children with different length of stay in institutions, also comparing them with a group of biological parents. They found no differences between biological parents and those adoptive parents with children subjected to short institutionalization, but there were differences between those who had adopted children after longer institutionalization. The authors therefore concluded that adoption in itself is not a source of special stress, although there are circumstances (like long institutionalization of the children they adopt) that may make life of the adoptive parents to be more stressful.

In the second data collection, we obtained information about the stress associated with adoptive parenthood using Abidin scales (*Parenting Stress Index*—Abidin, 1995; *Stress Index for Parents of Adolescents*—Sheras, Abidin, & Konold, 1998). When both father and mother in the same family answered the scale (as happened in 64 families), it was possible to estimate to what extent the experienced stress was shared, or not, by both. The correlation of .79 between father and mother shows clearly that the stress level is definitely shared. Bearing this in mind, and as we have information from more mothers than fathers—the former had answered the stress scales in greater numbers than the latter—in the following we will focus on the data produced by mothers in order to analyze which aspects of our data are related to experiencing stress.

The age at which the adopted child joins the family, the adoption of an individual child or a child with sibling(s), previous institutional experiences, and abuse before adoption were found to bear no relationship to stress levels in the mother in time 2 of our assessment. However, stress increases significantly when dealing with males, with special needs, and with older children. Stress is also higher when the adoption was of a child with whom the parents have had a previous relationship (e.g., part of the extended family) as well as among the mothers of lower educational level. The experience of stress in our sample of adoptive mothers also related to their child-rearing styles: mothers characterized by a more affectionate and communicative style reported less stress ($r = -.45$), whereas mothers who more openly acknowledged differences associated with adoptive families experienced more stress ($r = .28$).

It is then clear that those who adopt face stressful circumstances not only in the transition to parenthood but also during the years thereafter.

Adoptive parents might experience increased stress in handling the telling process, helping their children understand and adjust to adoption-related loss, helping their children resolve adoption-related identity issues, and coping with attachment-related issues (especially in late placements) (Brodzinsky & Pinderhughes, 2002). Our findings indicate that the level of stress is associated both with some structural characteristics of the adoption (certain characteristics of the adopted child and the adoptive parents) and with some process variables (child-rearing style and acknowledgment of differences). Although more research seems necessary to further clarify the role and level of stress in adoptive families, what we have learned from our study points to some practical implications to be discussed at the end of this chapter.

Satisfaction with Adoption

The degree of satisfaction that adoptive parents have with their adoption is a sufficiently important indicator to have lead Tizard (1977) to suggest that it is, in itself, an indicator of the success or failure of an adoption. In general, studies tend to agree on the high levels of satisfaction among the adoptive families (Barth & Brooks, 2000; Borders, Penny, & Portnoy, 2000; Groothues, Beckett, & O'Connor, 1998; Palacios, 1998). Data show that satisfaction is affected by the age of the children on their arrival with the family, with a decrease in satisfaction as that age increases (Rosenthal & Groze, 1992). Satisfaction is also seen to be negatively affected by the greater presence of problems in the children (Fernández & Fuentes, 2001; Groothues et al., 1998). However, satisfaction within families who adopt children with serious medical problems is very high (Glidden, 1992, 2000). Other factors associated with satisfaction give rise to more contradictory evidence from one study to another like, for example, the adopted child's gender (Nelson, 1985; Rosenthal & Groze, 1992), the fact of having adopted a single child or a group of siblings (Palacios et al., 1997; Rosenthal & Groze, 1992), the children's previous institutional experience (Mainemer et al., 1998; Rosenthal & Groze, 1992), and diverse sociodemographic characteristics of the adoptive families (Groothues et al., 1998; Mainemer et al., 1998).

In our study, parents answered a number of questions related to their satisfaction with their family life (how satisfied they feel with their current family life and how this compares to their life prior to adoption) as well as with adoption-related matters (how satisfied they feel with adoption in general and with the specific child they adopted). According to our data, the level of the adoptive parents' satisfaction with their adoption is very high both in time 1 and six years later. Thus, on a scale from 5 to 15, the average satisfaction rating in time 1 was 13.46 (with a standard deviation of 1.40) and in time 2 was 13.12 (with a standard deviation of 1.70). A quarter of the families rated their satisfaction as the same at both times, while 30 percent were more satisfied by time 2 than they were six years earlier, and 45 percent were more satisfied at the earlier date. The correlation between the satisfaction ratings at both times is therefore low ($r = .18$) although statistically significant. The difference between the ratings at both times allows us to analyze other variables that are related to the increase or decrease in satisfaction with the adoption.

The level of satisfaction does not appear to vary with regard to the following variables: the child's gender, current age, special needs or chronic illness, and previous institutional experiences. Nor does it vary with regard to whether the family has one parent or two or with the educational level of the parents. Satisfaction with the adoption appears higher with those who adopted a younger child, those who adopted a single child rather than a child with sibling(s), and those who adopted children who had not been badly treated before their adoption. Satisfaction levels are also related to the presence of problems in the child so that the more problematic the parents evaluate their child, the lower their satisfaction with the adoption. In addition, greater satisfaction is positively correlated with more affectionate and communicative parenting styles. Finally, the mothers who displayed increased acknowledgment of differences between time 1 and time 2 were less satisfied with the adoption and its repercussions in their lives.

Therefore, it seems clear that although adoptive families generally have a high degree of satisfaction with the adoption, such satisfaction is not indiscriminate but rather is related to the child's individual circumstances and to the dynamics of the family. To this conclusion one could add the analysis regarding satisfaction with the adoption from the perspective of the adoptees. From the previous analysis on adopted children's life satisfaction (which indicates an essentially high feeling of life satisfaction), it would appear that they also experience a high level of satisfaction with their adoption.

IMPLICATIONS FOR RESEARCH AND PRACTICE

Adoption research should not be some sort of competition between researchers finding more and less differences between adopted children and their nonadopted peers. In our view, the results of these comparisons depend largely on the perspective of the research. It seems clear that the more the investigation is based on a hypothesis of adoption as a mild psychopathological condition and the more clinically biased the sample and the measurement methods are, the more likely it is that the results will show deficiencies and clinical problems in adopted children. Conversely, investigations without a clinical bias that employ a wider variety of measurements (most of them related to the healthy and normal functioning of people) and that view adoption not only as a risk factor but also as a means of providing stability and nurturance for those who otherwise would be raised under adverse circumstances tend to highlight the benefits and obvious advantages of adoption over alternatives such as institutionalization. Clearly, our work derives from the latter perspective. Our data indicate few differences between children who have been adopted and their nonadopted peers, especially for those youngsters adopted as newborn babies, with whom no differences were found. For children who were older at adoption, some relevant differences do appear, although these children tend to be more similar than different to their nonadopted peers, both groups being in sharp contrast with the more problematic situation of children reared under institutional arrangements. It seems clear that in general the differences between adopted children and their nonadopted classmates, if they exist, are of low or moderate magnitude and that they affect a limited number of areas. Probably, whether one finds differences or not between one group and the other has a lot to do with the samples used, the contents and methods of measurement, and the various groups used for comparison. Thus, for example, when children raised in institutions are compared, such as in our case, the gains and benefits of adoption seem perfectly clear.

Apart from this, the fact that the children who have grown up under more difficult circumstances and have had broken and disturbed histories and, frequently, have suffered abuse and abandonment presents a slightly higher incidence of problems when compared to those who have grown up in more favorable circumstances, and this can be taken as good news: in spite of adversity or of the accumulation of setbacks, the great majority of those affected develop and function as normal people. Logically, the more adverse and prolonged the previous situation, the more they will move away from values generally considered normal (as shown, e.g., by the data of Rutter et al., 2000; see also chapter 4 in this volume).

The fact that the current study found fewer differences between adopted and nonadopted children compared to other studies (e.g., Verhulst, 2000a) could also be viewed from another perspective. As Triseliotis (2000, p. 95) indicated, "adoption is bound by time and context." If we bear in mind, for example, that the way adoption-related losses are experienced is rooted in the social construction and actual practice of adoption (Leon, 2002), it should not be surprising that different outcomes may be observed at different times and in different cultures. To our knowledge, a comparative study examining the social representation of adoption in different cultures has yet to be carried out. Such a study would include the differences in adoption practices and the consequences of these differences on family functioning and the adjustment of both the adopters and the adoptee. Undoubtedly, this type of study would provide enlightening information. If we study our own data as detailed in this chapter, some of our discoveries are surprising when viewed in the light of what might have been expected from the results of other investigations. For example, secrets and lies surrounding adoption have been shown to have a negative effect on the adopted child. Rosenberg and Groze (1997) and Triseliotis (1973) found that there were more problems in adopted children who had not been appropriately informed about their adoption. Under these circumstances, suggests Leon (2002), feelings of loss are increased, giving way to increased difficulties regarding identity and self-esteem. However, the girls and boys in our sample were affected not by one but by two secrets: all their adoptions were closed or confidential, and in many cases they were told very late and in a very limited manner about their adoption. As shown in the first column of table 6.1, up to six years old, around 50 percent of the adopted children studied by us ignored the fact that they were adopted, and of the parents who had talked to their child on the subject, 10 percent had mentioned it only once and 56 percent only in passing. These conditions are consistent with what Brodzinsky (chapter 7 in this volume) has described as a closed communication system, a type of family environment that is considered the basis for individual and family problems. However, the data for adjustment, self-esteem, and relationships between parents and children in our sample were very positive. Perhaps our methods were unable to show up difficulties, or perhaps those difficulties will be manifested later. Neither of these alternatives seems very likely, however, as the methods used were standard for a study on adoption, and the adopted children in our sample were studied over a long period, well into their adolescence. So, other possibilities must be borne in mind. Are our data influenced, for example, by the fact that children in our sample were adopted domestically, were not treated differently by their parents and friends, and therefore were less likely to feel different? Is there something about Spanish cultural attitudes about adoption that makes it easier for children to become integrated into their adoptive families and for parents to cope with adoption-related tasks? At this point, we do not have answers for these questions.

We are convinced, as is Howe (1998), that adoption outcome studies are particularly well placed to illuminate matters of risk, resilience, and recovery in human development. We believe, however, that one of the defects of the frequently and implicitly used psychopathological or deficiency model is an excessive emphasis on losses and risk factors, with scarce consideration of the gains and protection factors associated with adoption. In this, we share the views of researchers such as Leon (2002) and Quinton et al. (1998). From a research point of view, perhaps more illuminating than those comparing adopted and nonadopted children would be the results from studies comparing children and families (biological or adoptive families) that are functioning well with similar children and families that are not working appropriately. In addition, there is a remarkable lack of investigation into the dynamics and functioning of adoptive families and the analysis of the extent to which these aspects relate to the adjustment of those involved, adopters and adoptees (Rushton, 2004). In this we agree with the proposals of investigators such as Borders et al. (1998).

If research is to be closer to practice, we probably need fewer of those studies comparing adopted and nonadopted children and more emphasis on investigating how adoptive families are meeting the needs of children and how adoption services are meeting the needs of families. For example, to what extent do families have appropriate answers to their child's questions, particularly during sensitive periods, regarding their adoption? To what extent do less educated parents, who more frequently receive the most difficult children, with only their own resources and without additional support, manage to cope with the challenges that they will inevitably encounter? Do the families that adopt children with special needs receive additional support and resources with which to face up to the increase in their children's problems, as has been shown in this study?

If the value of studies on adoption were to be measured by the extent to which we have sound information on the comparison between adoptees and nonadoptees, we believe that, with some limitations, such studies have thoroughly advanced our knowledge. However, if the value of adoption research is measured by the extent to which the needs of adopters and adoptees (and professionals who work with them) are currently met, then our evaluation is clearly more negative. Another wave of investigations will have to be carried out in order to have more balanced results. Now may already be the time for that new wave. When it takes place, we will probably see not only how much adoptive families have benefited from studies on adoption but also that we have gained a more comprehensive and balanced vision of what adoption means and how adoptive families work.

Results presented in this chapter also allow for the consideration of some implications for adoption professional practice. From the first section, two implications seem clear to us. The first one refers to the need to find alternatives to the institutionalization of children and, when children have to be institutionalized, to find other caregiving options as quickly as possible. Even when placed in small and well-staffed institutions like the ones we have visited, children who do not live in a family environment seem to be doing much more poorly than those in family contexts. This does not necessarily imply that the institution is the source of all their problems, but it clearly implies that institutionalization is not the solution for the problems they may have as a consequence of the negative impact of their previous experiences and that these may be aggravated because of the more depersonalizing and less nurturing atmosphere of the institutional rearing.

The second implication of our first section deals with the "love is not enough" message. If there was a time when idealistic views were held about adoption as a solution for all problems of the adoptees (see chapter 2 in this volume), that time is now over. No doubt, there are many crucial problems and emotional wounds that love can heal, and this is also true for adoption. But in order to deal with their children's behavior problems, chronic illnesses, special needs, hyperactivity, impulsivity, school difficulties, feelings of loss, and so on, adoptive parents very often need advice and support, and the adoptees may also need the type of specific professional support that better helps them to overcome the problems associated with early adversity and experiences of separation and loss. This is especially so for those parents with more difficulties dealing with their children's problems and for those children whose early life came with more mishaps. And when these two circumstances (parents with less personal resources and children with more difficulties) coincide in the same family, the need of support is compounded, which should be obvious but unfortunately sometimes is not recognized. In our research, we found that families with very different circumstances and problems were receiving the same postadoption support: very little. If this can be acceptable in the case of families facing minor problems or with a high level of personal and family resources, it does not seem adequate when the circumstances are more problematic. Our postadoption services should be more sophisticated and more readily available for those who need them, both parents and children.

The implications of the second section of the chapter parallel those of the first one. We can take issues of communication about adoption as a good example. Parents in our sample talked to their adopted children about adoption little and late. They claimed not to have received professional advice on communication issues, although the professionals who worked with them claimed the contrary. But the whole issue of communication about adoption is rather complex and cannot be adequately tackled in the context of a conversation in which many other topics (e.g., paperwork that is needed or judicial procedures and how to deal with them) are addressed. Not only did parents in our sample receive very limited postadoption support, but they also received very little preparation for adoption. Adoptive parents do not come into life with a gene for adoptive parenthood, and there are many times in the life of an adoptive family when love and common sense are just not enough. Adoptive parents need information and guidance to help them cope with the many challenges of adoptive family life. Unfortunately, as our data show, they do not get it. This is not because the information is not available but, in many cases, because the relevant information has not been made accessible to those professionals who provide the practical help for these families, both in the preplacement and in the postplacement period. Researchers need to do a better job of translating their findings into a "user-friendly" format and disseminating the information to social casework professionals, mental health professionals, and adoptive parents. For example, one consequence of our study was the development of an adoption training program in which communication about adoption occupies a relevant position (Palacios et al., 1999). Groups of parents who wish to adopt meet together in at least four sessions of three to four hours and with the guidance of two adoption experts. They work together, explore their feelings, get familiar with the needs and challenges of adoption, and listen to what other parents with experience in different types of adoption have to tell them, and in this way they feel and are better prepared to be adoptive parents that adequately meet their future children's needs.

In the course of this preparation, adopters-to-be also get better prepared to understand the unique characteristics of adoptive families. The issue of acknowledgment of differences and its variations along the adoptive family life cycle is another central topic. Between the extremes of totally ignoring the differences or insisting on them, there seems to be a healthy pattern that needs to be tuned to the specific characteristics of the child and the specific moment in the adoptive family life cycle. There is a risk in only acknowledging differences when problems related to adoption do appear. But this lack of appropriate acknowledgment of differences may precisely be the cause of some problems. And, again, adoptive parents are not automatically equipped with the information and the attitudes needed to deal with this complex issue. They need help from the professional community to handle it.

Something very similar could be said regarding other adoption-related issues. Helping adoptive parents develop and maintain realistic expectations about themselves and their children in relation to adoption is another critical goal for adoption professionals. Research and clinical experience indicate that unrealistic expectations about adoption among adoptive parents is a key predictor of adjustment problems in the family as well as a predictor of adoption disruption (Brodzinsky & Pinderhughes, 2002). The results of our research support this conclusion. By disseminating the results of adoption research to social casework and mental health professionals, we can increase the likelihood of bolstering their counseling interventions in ways that will help adoptive parents become more realistic about adoption. This outcome can only have positive benefits for adopted children.

But the preparation for adoption should not be done in an atmosphere of fear and dread. Our longitudinal study of adoptions in southern Spain has proved that most adopted children do quite well both when young and when older. In addition, adoptive families seem to be very satisfied with their family life, and this holds true for a considerable length of time and for a wide range of children's ages. These very positive facts should then permeate the process of preparation for adoption, in which those who are planning to adopt need to become aware of the many challenges and the many joys of adoption.

ACKNOWLEDGMENTS

Research reported in this chapter was made possible by funding from the Department of Social Affairs of the government of Andalusia, Spain. Its active collaboration and parents' and children's involvement and patience are acknowledged with great gratitude.

Chapter 7

Reconceptualizing Openness in Adoption: Implications for Theory, Research, and Practice

David M. Brodzinsky

There can be little doubt that adoption, as a social service practice, is moving decidedly toward increased openness not only in the United States and Canada but in many European countries as well and that agencies are offering a wider array of placement options for birth parents and adoptive parents (Grotevant & McRoy, 1998; Henney, Onken, McRoy, & Grotevant, 1998; Hughes, 1995; Sykes, 2001). There also can be little doubt of the growing openness within the adoption kinship system. But what is meant by openness in adoption, and what implications does this trend have for the adjustment of adopted children and their families? In this chapter, two different perspectives on openness in adoption will be explored, and research linking these two constructs to children's psychological adjustment will be reviewed. This chapter also will conclude with a focus on the theoretical, research, and practice implications of this analysis.

HISTORICAL PERSPECTIVES ON OPENNESS IN ADOPTION

The rise of the adoption agency system in the United States, in the early part of the twentieth century, brought about many changes in adoption practice (Sokoloff, 1993; Sorosky, Baran, & Pannor, 1978; Wegar, 1997). Although it was not uncommon prior to this period for birth parents and adoptive parents to know one another and to maintain some degree of contact even after the adoption placement, a new philosophy based on secrecy and anonymity soon began to alter the way in which adoption was practiced. The newly emerging adoption agencies began to prevent adoptive and birth family members from meeting and sharing identifying information. Agency caseworkers also began counseling the parties against attempting to make contact with one another in the post-placement period. In addition, all records of the adoption proceedings, including the original birth certificate, were now sealed by court order, and an amended birth certificate for the child was issued to the adoptive parents. These confidential adoption practices, which were supported eventually by statutory law and regulations throughout the United States and in most European countries, were instituted by social workers in the belief that they would protect the child from the stigma of illegitimacy, preserve the birth mother's anonymity and protect her from the stigma of out-of-wedlock pregnancy and single parenthood, and maintain the privacy and integrity of the adoptive family. In keeping with this focus on secrecy, many adoptive parents during this period did not even inform their children of their adoption status. Rather, many of these youngsters were raised as the parents' biological children (see chapter 2 in this volume). Moreover, for those families that did tell the children about their adoption, it was not uncommon for parents to share as little background information as possible and to treat adoption revelation as a one-time event rather than as a process to be explored throughout childhood and adolescence.

In the 1970s, however, questions concerning the impact of secrecy and the sealing of adoption records on the adjustment of adopted individuals and birth parents began to be raised both by members of the adoption triad and by a small group of adoption professionals (Sorosky et al., 1978; Wegar, 1997). These questions were fueled and supported by profound changes in social mores occurring in most Western societies at the time and in the United States were especially influenced by the civil rights movement, the women's movement, and the passage of the Freedom of Information Act (Cole & Donley, 1990; Hoksbergen, chapter 2 in this volume). In addition, during this period a growing number of adult adoptees and birth parents were returning to agencies and requesting additional background information and in some cases seeking to reunite with one another (Wegar, 1997). For the first time in nearly half a century, the fundamental principles underlying confidential adoption were being challenged. At the heart of the challenge was a demand for greater openness in adoption. Over the past three decades, these initial pioneers in open adoption have gathered substantial support for their position and have had a major impact on the way adoption is practiced today not only in this country but around the world as well (Grotevant & McRoy, 1998; Henney et al., 1998; Hughes, 1995; Sykes, 2001).

CONTEMPORARY DEBATE AND RESEARCH
EVIDENCE ON OPEN ADOPTION

Although the practice of open adoption is becoming much more commonplace than in the past, it certainly is not universally accepted as being in the best interests of adoptive parents, birth parents, or the adopted child. Critics of open adoption, for example, have argued that ongoing contact between the two families will result in greater insecurity in adoptive parents and undermine their sense of control and entitlement to their child (Kraft, Palumbo, Mitchell, Woods, & Schmidt, 1985a). Concerns that open adoption will compromise the grief process for birth parents and increase the risk for adjustment difficulties following the relinquishment of their child also have been raised (Cocozzelli, 1989; Kraft, Palumbo, Mitchell, Woods, & Schmidt, 1985b). So too have concerns about the impact of open adoption on children's attachment security as well as their self-esteem, identity, and general psychological adjustment (Byrd, 1988; Kraft, Palumbo, Woods, Schmidt, & Tucker, 1985).

In contrast, proponents of open adoption believe that eliminating the secrecy in adoption is not only morally appropriate but will have positive effects for all members of the adoption triad (Baran & Pannor, 1993; Chapman, Dorner, Silber, & Winterberg, 1986, 1987a, 1987b; Gritter, 1997; Hughes, 1995; Silber & Dorner, 1990; Sykes, 2001). In particular, these professionals have suggested that greater openness will reduce the anxiety and insecurity of adoptive parents and foster a more realistic and empathic view of the birth parents. In addition, individuals favoring open adoption believe that this type of placement arrangement will reduce the birth mother's fears and anxieties as well as her grief and postplacement adjustment problems, especially if she is given some control over who adopts her baby. Finally, it also has been argued that greater openness in adoption will reduce the child's sense of rejection and loss by fostering a more empathic understanding of the circumstances surrounding the relinquishment, which in turn should support more positive self-esteem and fewer adjustment difficulties.

Although research on the impact of open adoption is still rather limited, the data collected, to date, largely support the benefits over the drawbacks of this placement practice (for reviews of the literature, see Brodzinsky, Smith, & Brodzinsky, 1998; Grotevant & McRoy, 1998; see also chapter 8 in this volume). In brief, research suggests that most adoptive parents who choose an open adoption are quite satisfied with the arrangement and generally have positive relationships with their child's birth parents. They also have more empathic views of the birth parents and worry less about the attachment to their child (Grotevant & McRoy, 1998; Silverstein & Demick, 1994). Moreover, adoptive parents in open placements communicate more with their child about adoption, display more empathy toward their child, are more accepting of the child's curiosity about his or her background, and are less fearful that their child will be reclaimed by the birth parents (Grotevant & McRoy, 1998). On the other hand, adoptive parents in open adoptions worry, at times, about the impact of ongoing contact with the birth parents on their children (Siegel, 1993). Research also has found that open adoption generally benefits birth mothers by increasing their sense of control, reducing unresolved grief issues, and diminishing adjustment difficulties in the postplacement period (A. B. Brodzinsky, 1992; Grotevant & McRoy, 1998). No research has been conducted, however, on the impact of open adoption on birth fathers or extended birth family members. Finally, although there still are rather limited data on the impact of open adoption on children, what is known suggests that having contact with birth family members does not appear to have the negative consequences for children predicted by the critics of this placement practice. In fact, there is evidence that children in open adoptions, compared with those youngsters with little or no contact with birth family, have a better understanding of the meaning and implications of being adopted (Wrobel, Ayers-Lopez, Grotevant, McRoy, & Friedrick, 1996), display greater curiosity about their adoption and ask their parents more adoption-related questions (Wrobel, Kohler, Grotevant, & McRoy, 1998), and are more likely to be involved in an active search for birth family members (Wrobel, Grotevant, & McRoy, 2004). Furthermore, adopted adolescents have been found to be more satisfied with the extent of information and degree of contact they have with birth parents when their contact is ongoing (Mendenhall, Berge, Wrobel, Grotevant, & McRoy, 2004). Finally, at least one study has shown that children in open adoptions are rated by parents as manifesting fewer behavior problems than children in confidential adoptions (Berry, 1991). Although the latter finding is encouraging and certainly in keeping with the predictions of those professionals who favor this type of adoption placement, it is important to note that some studies have found little difference in adjustment between children involved in open adoptions compared to those youngsters in other types of adoptive family arrangements (Berry, Cavazos Dylla, Barth, & Needell, 1998; Grotevant & McRoy, 1998). Furthermore, Kohler, Grotevant, and McRoy (2002) reported no difference in adopted adolescents' perceptions of family functioning for those youth experiencing different levels of openness in adoption.

In summary, although there remains considerable controversy regarding the impact of open adoption on the various members of the adoption triad, the general trend of the data suggests that this practice is associated with either more favorable or neutral results than problems. However, what the research has not addressed, to any great extent, are those factors associated with open adoption that are linked to the beneficial effects of this practice (for some initial attempts to explore family and systemic factors associated with adjustment of adoption triad members to open adoption placements, see Grotevant, Ross, Marchel, & McRoy, 1999; Grotevant, Wrobel, van Dulmen, & McRoy, 2001).

In addition, there are few studies exploring the basis for the variability in outcome for adoption triad members who choose different types of placement arrangements. Why is it that many families who choose an adoption arrangement in which there is only limited information shared between the birth family and adoptive family and no direct contact between the parties appear to do quite well, whereas other families who choose an open adoption display adjustment difficulties in the postplacement period? In the following sections, a reconceptualization of openness in adoption will be offered in an attempt to broaden research and practice perspectives of this construct and to offer some speculations on the variability in outcome for families choosing different adoption arrangements. The final section of this chapter will explore future directions for research, social casework, and clinical practice in relation to openness in adoption.

OPEN ADOPTION VERSUS OPENNESS IN ADOPTION

For most professionals—researchers and practitioners alike—as well as most adoptive parents and birth parents, open adoption refers to a specific type of adoption placement involving the sharing of identifying information between the adoptive and birth families as well as some degree of direct contact between the parties, which may or may not involve the child. Grotevant and McRoy (1998) refer to this type of adoption as a *fully disclosed placement*. In this context, open adoption is defined primarily in terms of a specific type of *family structure*—that is, a specific family arrangement within the adoption kinship system. In contrast, openness in adoption is a far broader and, in my opinion, more relevant construct in relation to issues of adoptive family life and adoption adjustment. Openness in adoption refers, first and foremost, to a state of mind and heart (Gritter, 1997). It reflects the general attitudes, beliefs, expectations, emotions, and behavioral inclinations that people have in relation to adoption. It includes, among other things, a willingness on the part of individuals to consider the meaning of adoption in their lives, to share that meaning with others, to explore adoption related issues in the context of family life, to acknowledge and support the child's dual connection to two families, and perhaps to facilitate contact between these two family systems in one form or another. Furthermore, openness in adoption is linked not only to content-based communication—that is, the exchange of adoption information—but, just as importantly, to the experience of affective attunement and the sharing and supporting of adoption-related emotions both within the adoptive family and between the adoptive and birth families. Thus, openness in adoption has more to do with *intrapersonal, interpersonal,* and *systemic process* than with a specific type of family or systemic structure. Its emphasis is on the adoption communication process, both informational and emotional, within the individual, between adoptive family members, and, for those individuals involved in a structurally open arrangement, between members of the two family systems (for a similar distinction in relation to the exploration and development of adoption identity, see Grotevant, Dunbar, Kohler, & Essau, 2000).

In support of the distinction between the construct of openness in adoption and what traditionally has been called open adoption, two hypothetical case examples are offered. First, consider the situation in which a family adopts a young child and there is very little, if any, information about the child's background. Perhaps the child was abandoned, perhaps the birth parent refused to provide any information other than a few basic facts about herself and the child's father, or perhaps the adoption involved an international placement and the social service agency or the orphanage in the child's country of origin did not collect much information about the child's birth family and what was collected is of dubious value in terms of its validity. In any case, the child is being raised in an adoptive family that has little information about the child's origins and no contact with the birth family. Most professionals would consider this placement arrangement to be a closed or confidential adoption, and from a structural perspective, it is. Now consider a second family that adopted a little girl at birth, has met the child's birth parents and exchanged identifying information with them, and has had periodic contact with various birth family members in the years following the child's placement. In this case, even the child has been involved in these contacts and has been informed of the identity of the birth parents and her relationship to them. Most professionals would characterize this type of placement as an open or fully disclosed adoption, and from a structural perspective, they would be correct.

The complexity of openness in adoption becomes evident, however, when the following family dynamics are considered. In the first family, despite the lack of information about the child's origins, the adoptive parents create a family atmosphere characterized by open, honest, and emotionally attuned communication. They are empathic and respectful of their child's needs, talk openly but not excessively about adoption issues, acknowledge the frustration of not knowing more about the birth family, accept the reality and validity of their child's confusion and sadness regarding adoption-related loss, talk respectfully about the birth family, support a positive connection between the child and her origins, and do whatever is possible to explore the various options for finding out more about the child's background and the circumstances of her relinquishment. In contrast, in the second family, although there has been a sharing of identifying information and periodic contact over the years between the adoptive and birth families that included the child, the adoptive parents felt pressured into accepting the original adoption arrangement. They were afraid that unless they agreed to an open placement, they would have been rejected by their daughter's birth mother. In the years since the placement occurred, however, they have become less sure of the wisdom of their decision and the value of the open adoption for their family's well-being. As a result, although they continue to allow periodic communication and contact between the two families, they do not talk much to their child about her birth parents. When their daughter raises questions about her birth mother and why she was placed for adoption, the adoptive parents tend to evade her questions or at best provide somewhat superficial and emotionally unattuned responses. For example, expressions of sadness, embarrassment, and feelings of rejection on the part of the child, especially in relation to not being raised within her biological family and feeling different from other children because of this fact, are responded to by the adoptive parents with reassuring reminders such as "there is no reason to feel that way...mommy and daddy love you so much." Such a comment is undoubtedly true, but from the perspective of what the child has shared, it reflects a lack of emotional sensitivity and responsiveness on the part of the parents.

How are we to understand these two families? The first is structurally a closed adoption, but the communicative process is extremely open. The second is structurally an open adoption, but the communicative process is quite closed. From the perspective of the child's emotional well-being, which of these factors is more important—family structure or family process?. Research generally suggests that family process variables such as parental warmth, emotional sensitivity, nurturance, involvement, stimulation, support, and communicative openness play a much more important role in children's psychological development and emotional well-being than the specific type of family structure within which the child lives, such as single versus two-parent family, intact versus nonintact family, mother-headed versus father-headed household, single-earner versus dual-earner household, heterosexual-headed versus homosexual-headed household, or adoptive versus nonadoptive family (Bradley, 2002; Brodzinsky & Pinderhughes, 2002; Gottfried, Gottfried, & Bathurst, 2002; Hetherington & Stanley-Hagan, 2002; Parke, 2002; Patterson, 2002; Weinraub, Horvath, & Gringlas, 2002). In short, what is being suggested is that regardless of whether a child grows up in a traditionally closed or open adoption arrangement, what is primary for healthy psychological adjustment is the creation of an open, honest, nondefensive, and emotionally attuned family dialogue not only about adoption-related issues but in fact about any issue that impacts on the child's and family's life. In my view, this is the essence of openness in adoption as well as one of the critical factors underlying the variability in adoption adjustment for adopted children and their parents. Let me turn now to some of the underlying assumptions associated with the concept of openness in adoption.

ASSUMPTIONS UNDERLYING OPENNESS IN ADOPTION

First, openness in adoption is best understood as a communicative continuum (Grotevant & McRoy, 1998; Wrobel, Kohler, Grotevant, & McRoy,
1999, 2003). At one end of the continuum are those individuals characterized by a greater willingness to explore adoption-related issues in their
lives, to share their thoughts and feelings with others, and to be empathically attuned to those around them; at the other end of the continuum are
those individuals who are reticent to acknowledge and discuss adoption
related issues and who are cut off from their own feelings and the feelings
of others regarding these issues. It is assumed that members of the adoption triad are likely to be distributed widely across this communicative
continuum.

A second assumption underlying the principle of openness in adoption
is that the exploration of adoption-related issues, regardless of the structural arrangement that exists between the families, occurs on three separate but interrelated levels (see also Grotevant et al., 2000). The first level
is *intrapersonal*, reflecting the individual's own self-exploration of his or
her thoughts and feelings about adoption (see Dalen's discussion of inner
search in chapter 10 in this volume). For the child, this process obviously
begins only after they have been informed of their adoption status; for
adoptive parents, the process begins when they first consider the possibility of adoption, often in response to the crisis of infertility (Daly, 1988,
1989); and for birth parents, the process begins when they are confronted
with an unexpected and unwanted pregnancy and first consider the possibility of adoption as a solution for their dilemma. For all parties of the
adoption triad, however, the personal exploration of adoption is assumed
to be a lifelong process (Brodzinsky, Schechter, & Henig, 1992). The second
level of adoption communication is *intrafamilial*, reflecting the exploration
of adoption issues among adoptive family members as well as among
birth family members. Within the adoptive family, this process occurs
both between the parents and, perhaps more important, between the parents and children. Much has been written about the importance of parents
maintaining an open, active, and emotionally attuned dialogue with their
children about adoption-related issues (Brodzinsky & Pinderhughes,
2002; Brodzinsky et al., 1998; Kirk, 1964; Nickman, 1985; Wrobel et al.,
1998, 1999, 2003; chapters 6 and 8 in this volume). Of particular concern is
the way in which adoptive parents portray the birth parents and the circumstances of the relinquishment in discussions with their children.
Finally, the third level at which adoption communication occurs is *interfa-
milial*, reflecting the exploration of adoption issues between adoptive and
birth family members. It is assumed that successful open adoption
arrangements require open, honest, respectful, and emotionally sensitive

dialogue among members of the adoption kinship network not only in the preplacement and early postplacement periods but also throughout the entire family life cycle (Grotevant et al., 1999; chapter 8 in this volume).

Third, openness in adoption is assumed to involve not only the exchange of adoption information but also the expression and support of adoption-related emotions. The ability of children to express their feelings about being adopted, as well as the empathic attunement of parents to those feelings, is viewed as a critical process in healthy adoption communication. In fact, facilitating the child's feelings about adoption in family (or clinical) dialogue is especially important in situations in which the background information on the child is viewed as somewhat problematic (e.g., when there is a history of neglect, abuse, abandonment, parental psychopathology, and so on) and in those situations in which there is very little, if any, information available about the child's origins. In the latter case, parents and clinicians are urged to explore the child's confusion, frustration, sadness, resentment, and/or anger in relation to the lack of available background information.

Fourth, as a communicative continuum, openness in adoption is assumed to reflect the attitudes, beliefs, expectations, emotional needs, personality characteristics, behavioral inclinations, and experiences of each member of the adoption triad. Individuals who are more introspective, more aware of their feelings and emotionally attuned to others, more open to new ideas and willing to explore options, more emotionally secure and self-confident, and perhaps even more inclined to take risks are assumed to be more likely to manifest a higher degree of openness in relation to adoption in terms of both the type of adoption arrangement they choose and the extent of communicative openness they manifest—and especially in the context of parent–child communications. In other words, it is assumed that individuals with a more open, empathic, and secure personality style are more likely, on average, to choose an adoption arrangement that is structurally open and to be more willing to explore adoption issues within themselves and with others, including their children. In contrast, individuals with a more closed, cautious, and self-protective personality style can be expected, on average, to choose a placement arrangement involving less contact between the two family systems and to have more difficulty creating an open, nondefensive family environment in relation to adoption communication.

Although many of the attitudes, beliefs, and personality characteristics noted previously are assumed to have some degree of temporal stability, a fifth assumption underlying openness in adoption is that the extent of communicative openness created at any one time within the adoptive kinship system reflects the evolving needs of all parties within the system—the adoptive parents, the birth parents, and especially the adopted child. Because the needs of each of these individuals may well change over the course of the family life cycle, it is assumed that each of the parties may need more or less openness in communication and/or contact at different periods in time, a point that has been emphasized previously by Wrobel et al. (1999, 2003).

Sixth, because people's needs change over time, it is assumed that openness in adoption is likely to be fluid, that is, ever changing (for a discussion of the stability of openness and contact in foster parent adoptions, see Frasch, Brooks, & Barth, 2000).This means that the extent of communication about adoption within the adoptive family system or between the adoptive and birth family systems will vary from time to time as a function of various factors (for a more detailed discussion of this issue, see Wrobel et al., 1999, 2003).Within the adoptive family, the ebb and flow of adoption communication undoubtedly will be connected to the developmental changes in children's understanding of adoption and to the various adoption-related tasks that emerge at different periods of the adoptive family life cycle (Brodzinsky, 1987; Brodzinsky & Pinderhughes, 2002; Brodzinsky, Schechter, & Henig, 1992; Brodzinsky et al., 1998). For example, it is generally not until children begin to appreciate the inherent loss in adoption—typically around six to eight years of age—that they begin to question their parents about the reasons for the relinquishment. In addition, exploration of adoption identity and the need to search for one's origins typically does not emerge until the adolescent period (Grotevant, 1997; Wrobel et al., 2004). Adoption communication—especially in relation to feeling states—also is very likely to be influenced by developmental changes in children's capacity for self-reflection, empathy, and affective expression and regulation. Finally, adoption communication is assumed to vary as a function of new information and/or contact that is experienced within the adoption kinship system, such as when adoptive parents receive updated information about the child's background from the adoption agency or when a previously closed adoption gradually becomes more structurally open. New information requires processing, both intrapersonally and interpersonally, which is likely to result in fluctuations in the extent of communication within each member of the adoption triad as well as between the members of the two family systems (for additional comments on this process, see Wrobel et al., 1999, 2003).

A seventh and related assumption is that there will be times when the parties are in synchrony with one another regarding their evolving needs and tolerance for various levels of adoption openness and times when their needs will be in conflict with one another (Grotevant & McRoy, 1998; Wrobel et al., 1999, 2003). Regarding the latter situation, for example, it is not uncommon to find some families in which children are very curious about their origins and want to discuss their birth parents and the circumstances of the relinquishment but have adoptive parents who, at least for the time being, are still feeling uncertain and reluctant to talk about these issues and so remain rather silent or, at best, provide very cursory answers to the child's questions (Wrobel et al., 1998, 1999, 2003). Similarly, adoptive parents and birth parents may desire differing levels of information or contact, only to have the other party resist or express ambivalence. It is assumed that greater congruence among adoption triad members regarding their need and tolerance for openness in adoption will result in greater satisfaction and adjustment in relation to adoption issues.

Eighth, it is assumed that the quality of adoption communication and the level of openness achieved within the adoptive and birth families, respectively, as well as between the two family systems reflects the mutual influence of adoption triad members on each other. In other words, communicative openness reflects a process of reciprocal influence (Grotevant & McRoy, 1998; Wrobel et al., 1999, 2003). Individuals who manifest greater openness in their attitude and communication style not only model greater openness for others but also are assumed to facilitate greater openness in dyadic conversations. Conversely, individuals who are emotionally insensitive to others and display less openness in their attitude and communication style are assumed to inhibit open adoption communication in the people with whom they interact.

Ninth, although the adoption communication process is assumed to be reciprocal, from a developmental perspective it is expected that children's attitudes, curiosity, and openness in adoption initially will reflect the attitudes and openness of the adoptive parents rather than vice versa (for additional discussion of this point, see Wrobel et al., 1999, 2003). In other words, the way in which parents initially share adoption information with their child, the extent to which they support the child's questioning, and the success they achieve in remaining emotionally attuned to their child's adoption needs is likely to determine the extent to which children explore adoption-related issues not only within themselves but also with others. As children get older, it is assumed that the family communication process regarding adoption will become increasingly more reciprocal in influence.

Finally, a tenth assumption related to the concept of openness in adoption is that although greater openness is likely to be related to better adjustment for most adoption triad members, what is even more predictive of healthy psychological adjustment, at both the individual level and the family systems level, is the degree of satisfaction that these individuals experience in having their desires and needs met regarding openness (Mendenhall et al., 2004). Simply put, this means that some individuals will desire and need greater openness at specific times in their life, whereas at other times they may desire and need less openness. To the extent that they are able to achieve their goal—whether that means gaining more information about their origins, having more contact with birth family members, or pulling back somewhat from the adoption exploration process—they are likely to feel more in control of their life and more satis-fied and experience a greater degree of psychological stability. Conversely, when the individual's need for a specific level of openness is not sup-ported by actual experience—such as when children or teenagers are pre-vented from gaining information about themselves and their heritage or when they are exposed to information and/or contact prematurely—psy-chological adjustment may well be compromised. In short, this final assumption suggests that no one level of openness is inherently better all the time for all individuals (see also Brodzinsky et al., 1998; Grotevant & McRoy, 1998; Wrobel et al., 1999, 2003). What must be kept in mind is the reality that the need for varying degrees of openness in adoption is con-stantly evolving in all three parties of the adoption triad and not always in ways that are congruent with one another. Thus, although advocates for open adoption may wish for some clear, straightforward guideline such as "greater openness is always better," this is assumption appears to be naive, overly simplistic, and clearly not supported by casework and clini-cal practice as well as by research (see chapter 8 in this volume).

THEORETICAL BASIS FOR ADOPTION COMMUNICATION OPENNESS

The theory underlying adoption communication openness derives from the work of Kirk (1964), who was the first to empirically explore adoptive family dynamics and the first to emphasize the importance of open com-munication within the adoptive family system. According to Kirk, under-standing adoptive family life begins with the recognition that adoptive parents and their adopted children share a common experience: loss. For the adoptive parents, it is the loss of fertility and the desired biological off-spring; for the child, it is the loss of his or her origins. Kirk emphasized that adoption-related loss creates "role handicaps" for adoptive parents and challenges their ability to handle a variety of family life cycle tasks, such as telling children about their adoption, discussing their dual connection to two families, remaining empathically attuned to their children's feelings, and so on. To manage the stress associated with these "role handicaps," Kirk argued that parents adopt one of two coping strategies or communi-cation styles. Some parents, in an effort to simulate nonadoptive family life as closely as possible, choose to minimize, deny, or reject the differences associated with adoptive family life. Other parents, though, appear better able to acknowledge adoption-related loss as well as the additional chal-lenges inherent in raising adopted children. Kirk suggested that the latter strategy, which he termed "acknowledgment-of-difference," was a more adaptive way of handling the challenges of adoptive family life since it pre-sumably allowed parents and children to explore adoption issues more openly and supportively. In contrast, the "rejection-of-difference" strategy was thought to create a child-rearing atmosphere that inhibited communicative openness in relation to adoption.

The construct of adoption communication openness also has been influenced by adoptive family life cycle theory (Brodzinsky, 1987; Brodzinsky, Schechter, & Henig, 1992; Hajal & Rosenberg, 1991), which emphasizes the unique, interactive adoption-related tasks encountered by parents and children at each stage of the family life cycle. For example, as parents begin to share adoption information, typically in the preschool and early school years, children slowly begin to understand the implications of the information presented (Brodzinsky, Schechter, & Henig, 1992; Brodzinsky, Singer, et al., 1984; Brodzinsky et al., 1998). In turn, children's curiosity grows, and questions about their origins are raised, requiring parents to talk about the children's connection to their biological family. For healthy adjustment to occur, this interactive, communicative process must remain open, focus on the child's evolving needs, and support a positive connection to the birth family as well as a positive adoption identity (Brodzinsky, Schechter, & Henig, 1992; Grotevant, 1997).

Adoption communication theory also is strongly influenced by Bronfenbrenner's (1992) developmental ecological systems theory, which emphasizes the contextualistic and interactionist nature of human development. Applied to adoption theory, this approach focuses attention on the relationship and mutual influence that occurs at both the microsystemic level (i.e., within the adoptive family) and the mesosystemic level (i.e., between the adoptive and biological families).

Finally, the current conceptualization of adoption communication openness has been greatly influenced by the work of Grotevant, McRoy, Wrobel, and their colleagues (see chapter 8 in this volume) and specifically by their recent development of the Family Adoption Communication (FAC) model (Wrobel et al., 1999, 2003). Conceptually rooted in Bronfenbrenner's (1992) ecological systems theory and Kirk's (1964) social role theory as well as adoptive family life cycle theory (Brodzinsky, 1987; Brodzinsky, Schechter, & Henig, 1992) and developmental theory (Brodzinsky, Singer, et al., 1984), FAC attempts to "capture the dynamic nature of family systems by accounting for the inter-connected relationships of adopted children, adoptive parents and birth parents" (p. 19). In fact, many of the assumptions of the current model outlined in this chapter parallel those assumptions underlying FAC. However, there are at least two important differences between these models. First, compared with FAC, which, at least to date, tends to emphasize content-based adoption communication, the current model gives greater weight to the role of affective attunement and emotional communication between parent and child and, in the case of structurally open adoptions, between adoptive and birth family members as a basis for healthy adoption adjustment. This relative difference probably reflects the different origins of the models. FAC is primarily a theory-driven, research-based model, whereas the current model of adoption communicative openness, although certainly influenced to a great extent by adoption theory and research, has additional roots in the author's clinical and consultative work, where parental empathy and the capacity for reflecting and supporting children's emotional states is viewed as a crucial intervention goal. Second, FAC places greater emphasis on the connection between structural openness and communicative openness, whereas the current model tends to deemphasize this connection. Thus, although greater structural openness is likely to provide more opportunities for adoption triad members to exchange adoption information, the expression and support of adoption-related emotions is believed to be more closely tied to the attitudes, personality characteristics, and developmental level of the adoption triad members. For example, as noted previously, it is assumed that individuals with a more "open, emotionally attuned, and secure personality style" are more likely to choose a structurally open adoption arrangement and be more willing to explore adoption issues with others compared to individuals with a more "closed, cautious, and self-protective personality style." Furthermore, children's level of cognitive and emotional development is viewed as an important factor underlying their sensitivity to and engagement in emotion-based adoption communication. Once again, this difference between the two models— which appears to be more a matter of emphasis than substance—probably reflects their different origins.

RESEARCH FINDINGS ON ADOPTION COMMUNICATION OPENNESS

Despite the importance placed on adoption communication in adoption theory and practice both in North America and in Europe (see Brodzinsky & Pinderhughes, 2002; Brodzinsky et al., 1998; Grotevant & McRoy, 1998; Howe, 1998; Howe & Feast, 2000; Kirk, 1964; Reitz & Watson, 1992; Triseliotis, Shireman, & Hundleby, 1997; Wrobel et al., 1999, 2003; chapters 6, 8, and 9 in this volume), to date there have been only a small number of studies published on the relationship between communication patterns and the adjustment of adopted individuals. This is especially surprising given that Kirk's (1964) original work in this area, which has been very well received by adoption professionals and which laid the theory and empirical groundwork for the importance of adoption communication, was published 40 years ago.

Consistent with adoption communication theory, Stein and Hoopes (1985) reported that families with a more open communication style had teenagers with fewer identity problems. In contrast, Kaye (1990; Kaye & Warren, 1988) found that families manifesting high levels of acknowledging differences in relation to adoption had adolescents with lower self-esteem and poorer adjustment. The latter finding, though, is consistent with Brodzinsky's (1987) revision of Kirk's theory of adoptive family dynamics. Brodzinsky suggested that the relationship between "acknowledgment of difference" and patterns of adjustment is curvilinear rather than linear. In other words, the inability to acknowledge the differences inherent in adoptive family life as well as an overemphasis on such differences—termed "insistence of difference"—were thought to create more problems in the family leading to increased adjustment difficulties compared to communication patterns in which there was a moderate level of acknowledgment of differences.

Although not focusing on adoption communication per se, Kohler et al. (2002) reported that adopted adolescents who perceived greater communication in the family also reported more trust of their parents, fewer feelings of alienation from them, and better overall functioning of the family. Interestingly, quality of communication in the family was not reported to be different for adolescents living in homes with varying levels of contact with birth family members. In addition, perceived quality of family communication was found to be unrelated to adolescents' preoccupation with their adoption.

Other research has found that adult adoptees who reported growing up in homes in which adoption was a relatively open and comfortable topic for family discussions were more satisfied with their adoption experience. For example, Howe and Feast (2000) noted that 77 percent of adult adoptees who were comfortable as children asking their parents for adoption information rated their adoption experience as positive, whereas only 44 percent of adult adoptees who experienced discomfort in discussing adoption with their parents stated that their adoption experience was positive. These results are consistent with earlier research by Raynor (1980), who found that adult adoptees were more satisfied with their adoption if their parents were viewed as having been comfortable discussing adoption issues with them when they were children.

Still other studies have linked adult adoptees' interest in searching with patterns of adoption communication experienced while growing up in the adoptive family. Sobol and Cardiff (1983) reported that adoptees who were dissatisfied with the way adoption communication was handled in the adoptive family were more likely to search for their birth origins than individuals who felt their informational needs were better met by the adoptive parents. In addition, Sobol, Delaney, and Earn (1994) reported that open adoption communication was related to adult adoptees feeling close to their adoptive parents.

Finally, a recent study by Brodzinsky (2004) examined the contribution of adoption communication openness versus family structural openness in relation to the adjustment of adopted children. Sixty-seven adopted children, ranging in age from 8 to 13 years, and their parents participated in the study. Seventy-three percent of the children were placed in-racially and 27 percent were placed transracially; 73 percent were adopted domestically and 27 percent were adopted internationally. All children were placed for adoption under 1 1/2 years of age. Adoption communication openness was measured by a 14-item, child-report instrument, adapted from the Parent-Adolescent Communication Scale (Barnes & Olsen, 1985). Family structural openness was assessed by a newly developed, 20-item, parent-report instrument measuring the extent to which the adoptive family had information about and contact with their child's birth family. Children's report of their self-esteem was assessed by the Global Self-Worth subscale from the Self-Perception Profile for Children (Harter, 1985). In addition, parents provided an assessment of children's behavioral problems using the Child Behavior Checklist (Achenbach & Edelbrock, 1983). Results indicated that adoptive families with greater openness in adoption communication had more information about and contact with their child's birth family. In addition, children's rating of their self-esteem was positively correlated with both family structural openness and communication openness, whereas parents' rating of children's behavior problems was negatively associated with communication openness but unrelated to family structural openness. Finally, regression analyses indicated that adoption communication openness was the only variable that independently predicted children's behavioral problems. In contrast, both adoption communication and child's age at adoption placement were significant predictors of children's self-esteem. Regarding the latter finding, the older the child at placement, the lower the self-esteem rating. Both regression analyses indicated that family structural openness did not contribute to the child outcome variables independently of adoption communication openness.

In summary, although still rather limited in scope, the research on adoption communication indicates that it is a significant factor in the adjustment of adopted individuals. Openness and ease of discussing adoption in the family and the child's experience of parental empathy and respect not only are related to adjustment in the childhood years but also are viewed by adult adoptees as important factors in their satisfaction with their adoption experience and in their search motivation.

IMPLICATIONS FOR ADOPTION THEORY AND RESEARCH

The concept of openness in adoption has significant implications for adoption theory and research. Viewed in its broader sense—as a continuum of attitudinal, emotional, personality, and behavioral inclinations in relation to adoption characterizing each member of the adoption triad rather than as a specific family structural arrangement—adoption openness is believed to impact on a wide range of intrapersonal, interpersonal, and systemic processes. Its emphasis on the individual's search for personal meaning in relation to adoption parallels a similar emphasis found in psychodynamic explanations of adoption adjustment (Brinich, 1990) as well as adoption-related stress and coping theory (Brodzinsky, 1990, 1993; Smith & Brodzinsky, 1994, 2002). In addition, its emphasis on interpersonal processing of adoption information, both within the adoptive family and between the adoptive and birth family systems, clearly is connected to adoptive family systems theory (Reitz & Watson, 1992) and to the FAC model of adoption adjustment (Wrobel et al., 1999, 2003). Finally, the importance placed on emotional communication and empathic attunement in relation to adoption openness parallels a similar emphasis found in Kirk's (1964) social role theory of adoptive family dynamics. In short, the construct of openness in adoption is seen as a unifying principle, bridging many of the important contributions from previous adoption theories.

As noted previously, most of the research has focused on open adoption as a family structural arrangement. The results of this research has supported the belief that adoptive parents and birth parents generally benefit from mutual knowledge and contact with one another (Grotevant & McRoy, 1998; chapter 8 in this volume). Furthermore, knowledge about and contact with birth family also appears to benefit many adopted children. However, as noted previously in this chapter, as well as in chapter 8 in this volume, no one level of structural openness inherently appears to be better all the time for all people. This conclusion raises several questions: Who most likely benefits from an open adoption arrangement and under what conditions? Are there individual characteristics associated with better adjustment in one type of adoptive family arrangement compared to another? Earlier in this chapter, it was suggested that individuals with a more "open and secure personality style" would more likely choose an open adoption and be more satisfied with this type of family arrangement than individuals with a more "closed and insecure personality style." Clearly, this speculation needs to be examined empirically, as do other questions addressing individual difference factors related to the choice of and adjustment to different adoptive family arrangements. Another question of interest is whether there are family system characteristics that result in greater satisfaction with one type of adoption arrangement than another. Is it possible that open adoptions may be easier to manage at different points in the family life cycle than at other points? And what factors are likely to increase or decrease contact between the adoptive and birth families over the course of time? To date, these and related questions have received very little systematic attention in the research literature with the exception of the ongoing work being conducted by the Minnesota/Texas Adoption Research Project headed by Grotevant and McRoy. For nearly two decades, these investigators have been involved in open adoption research, including exploring different systemic issues related to patterns of information exchange both within the adoptive family and between the adoptive and birth family systems (for reviews of this research, see Grotevant & McRoy, 1998; chapter 8 in this volume). This research has begun to shed light on the circumstances under which different adoptive family structural arrangements are chosen as well as those individual, family, and systemic factors that influence the ebb and flow of structural openness over time. It is important, however, that others begin to pursue a similar line of inquiry and to confirm that the findings emerging from the Minnesota/Texas Adoption Research Project generalize beyond the single, albeit moderately large, sample of research participants whom these investigators are following.

From my perspective, however, the most important feature of adoption openness lies not in the extent of contact developed between the adoptive and birth families but rather in the extent and quality of adoption exploration that is achieved both within each member of the adoption triad and among these individuals. Adoption openness, conceived of as intrapersonal and interpersonal communicative processes, has received relatively little empirical attention, which is surprising given the prominence of this construct in existing adoption theory. As noted earlier, the few studies that have been conducted in this area indicate that open adoption communication during the childhood and adolescent years is extremely important for positive adjustment in adopted individuals, not only affecting the adjustment of adopted children but also influencing feelings of closeness to adoptive parents as well as feelings of satisfaction with adoption, even into adulthood. Furthermore, the research by Brodzinsky (2004) suggests that adoption communication openness may be a more important factor in children's adoption adjustment than the specific type of family structure in which the child lives. As noted previously, this research found that family structural openness had no independent predictive power in relation to children's adjustment after communicative openness was taken into account.

Just as with family structural openness, there are a host of questions that need to be addressed regarding adoption communication openness. Are there periods of development in which children and parents are more likely to be actively involved in adoption communication? Based on research conducted by Brodzinsky and his colleagues (Brodzinsky, Schechter, et al.,1986; Brodzinsky, Singer, et al., 1984) as well as Bronfenbrenner's (1992) ecological theory of development, the FAC model discussed earlier (Wrobel et al., 1999, 2003) provides some guidelines for making predictions regarding the developmental pathways related to patterns of communication within the adoptive family. These speculations need to be explored empirically, however. So, too, do questions related to a wide range of potential individual difference factors (as well as family and systemic factors) that are likely to influence the intrapersonal and interpersonal exploration of adoption issues. Why are some children and teenagers extremely curious about their origins and seek out information about unanswered questions, whereas others seem content not knowing much about their birth heritage (see Kohler et al., 2002)? How do parental attitudes about the birth family influence their child's questioning and search for new information about their origins? Are there predictable systemic factors that increase or decrease the adoption communication process? And how does adoption communication influence the development and maintenance of different types of adoptive family structural arrangements? These are but a few of the critical questions connecting adoption communication openness to issues in adoption adjustment and adoptive family life. Although Grotevant, McRoy, and their colleagues have begun to explore some of these questions and have reported some interesting findings regarding the role of communicative openness for individual and family adjustment (chapter 8 in this volume), it is hoped that others also will begin focusing their attention on this important research area.

IMPLICATIONS FOR ADOPTION PRACTICE

Let me turn now to some of the social casework and clinical practice implications related to the construct of openness in adoption as discussed in this chapter. First, in evaluating and preparing prospective adoptive parents during the preplacement period, it is important to focus more on their ability and willingness to acknowledge and explore adoption issues both personally and with others. How open are adoption applicants to examining their motives for adopting as well as their feelings about the similarities and differences between adoptive and nonadoptive family life and their feelings about the child's birth family and history? Exploring the applicants' ability to engage in the intrapersonal search for meaning in relation to adoption provides the caseworker with insight not only into the ease with which these individuals are capable of introspection but also into the likelihood that they will be open and accepting of different points of view in relation to adoption, especially the view of their child. For those individuals who appear more reticent or defensive regarding their thoughts and feelings in relation to adoption, caseworkers may need to consider additional counseling and preparation prior to placing children with them.

Another area that needs assessing during the preplacement and early postplacement period is the parents' ability and willingness to discuss difficult and emotionally charged issues related to adoption without undue judgment or embarrassment. Today, many children are being placed for adoption following very difficult and, at times, traumatic life experiences in the birth family, orphanage, or foster home. Prenatal exposure to drugs and alcohol, exposure to parental psychopathology, domestic violence, physical abuse, sexual abuse, and neglect as well as a host of other early adverse rearing experiences are all too common in the history of adopted children (see chapters 1, 3, and 4 in this volume). Parents who are overly judgmental in their assessment of their child's history or who find some topics too difficult to discuss with their child are less likely to create a family atmosphere reflecting truly open, empathic and supportive adoption communication. Of critical importance is the way in which parents portray the birth family and the circumstances of the child's relinquishment (Brodzinsky & Pinder-hughes, 2002). Unless adoptive parents can find ways to help their children feel positive about their origins, these youngsters are likely to have more problems with self-esteem and identity. A family environment characterized by openness in communication and parental empathic attunement to their child's needs is much more likely to support positive self-esteem and healthy psychological adjustment than a family environment in which parents and children are uncomfortable discussing sensitive adoption-related topics or where the child's background is portrayed in unnecessarily critical or demeaning ways. Parents must always remember that to feel worthy as a human being, their child needs to feel valued—even by the birth parents who did not want to or could not care for them (Brodzinsky et al., 1998). Translating a child's adverse history into information that is supportive of positive self-esteem and psychological growth can be a challenging task for adoptive parents. It is clear that they need much more help from caseworkers and clinicians in achieving this goal.

Adoption professionals also need to ensure that structurally open adoptions are communicatively open as well. We cannot assume that this will be the case either within the adoptive family or between the adoptive and birth families. At times, adoptive parents simply assume that because children have been given a great deal of information about their background or have access to members of their birth family, the goal of creating an open adoption has been achieved. Yet openness in adoption is about meeting not only children's informational needs but also their emotional needs. Openness in adoption requires that parents remain emotionally attuned to their children's feelings, provide them with opportunities to share those feelings, and have those feelings validated and normalized. Unless parents are aware of and are comfortable with their own feelings in relation to adoption and their children's history, they are likely to have more difficulty remaining emotionally attuned and supportive of their children's adoption-related emotional needs.

Adoptive families and birth families also need help in establishing effective means of communicating with one another as well as supporting realistic and effective conflict resolution strategies when differences of opinion between the parties occur regarding the nature and extent of contact and communication. Too often agencies promote an open adoption placement and then let the parties fend for themselves over the years in terms of making the placement arrangement work. This process can be quite challenging and often leads to frustration, resentment, and conflict between the parties, with children too often getting caught in the middle. To date, there has been very little discussion in the adoption literature regarding models of intervention for helping adoptive and birth families manage the dynamic nature of their open adoption arrangement.

Caseworkers and clinicians also need to ensure that families who enter into traditional confidential adoptions or who adopt children internationally and are unable to get much useful information about the child's history do not fall into the trap of believing that the lack of information about their child precludes openness in adoption. Parents need to be counseled about how to discuss adoption with their child when there is a dearth of reliable information about the birth family and the circumstances of the relinquishment. In short, it must be remembered that *a structurally closed adoption need not be—and should not be—a communicatively closed adoption.* Fostering and supporting open adoption communication must be a central focus of professional preplacement preparation and postplacement support, especially in those adoptions in which family members believe there is little information to discuss.

In addition to improved preplacement and postplacement services for all members of the adoption triad, there needs to be improved training for adoption caseworkers as well as clinicians who provide psychotherapy for adopted children, adoptive parents, and birth parents. Adoption has become incredibly complex over the past three decades (Brodzinsky & Pinderhughes, 2002; Brodzinsky et al., 1998; Henney et al., 1998), challenging the assumptions, beliefs, and stereotypes of the professionals who work with this diverse group of children and adults. Providing effective preplacement and postplacement services for adoption triad members, including supporting the need for openness in adoption—both communicatively and structurally—requires better training for adoption professionals. This is especially true in relation to social casework and clinical involvement with children coming out of the foster care system. In many cases, these placements are structurally de facto open adoptions in that the children know their birth parents and other birth relatives and often have had periodic contact with them during their time in foster care. However, because of the children's history of neglect and abuse, often at the hands of the birth parents, there is reluctance among many adoption professionals and adoptive parents to consider the possibility that some type of ongoing contact with birth family members following adoption could be in the children's best interests. Yet Berry (1991) found that adopted children coming out of the California foster care system who had contact with birth family members were rated as manifesting fewer behavioral problems than youngsters without such contact. Although it would be naive to assume that such contact will always benefit children, it is important not to foreclose on the option of an open placement during the adoption planning process. Unfortunately, there are no data available that directly address the issue of when and under what conditions to create open adoption placements for children coming out of the foster care system (regarding patterns of contact and communication between adoptive families and birth families in foster parent adoptions, see Frasch et al., 2000; Neil & Howe, 2004). Developing models of decision making regarding ongoing contact between children and their birth relatives in these cases, helping to support adoptive parents in recognizing the potential benefits and drawbacks of such contact, and developing intervention models for supporting a cooperative and respectful relationship between the adoptive family and birth family remains a significant challenge for professionals in the adoption field.

Finally, we need to support adoption policy and practices that allow for greater openness and honesty in adoption, including full documentation of a child's history and the sharing of that history with adoptive parents at the time of placement, access to adoption records and one's original birth certificate for adult adoptees, and full support for adult adoptees and birth parents who are seeking to reunite with one another. As the adoption process becomes freed from the veil of secrecy that characterized it in the past, the ability to meet the informational and emotional needs of adoption triad members will be enhanced, and this should translate into improved psychological adjustment for all.

ACKNOWLEDGMENT

Portions of this chapter were presented as a keynote address at the 10th Biennial Conference on Open Adoption, Lake Tahoe, Nevada, November, 2002.

Chapter 8

Openness in Adoption: Outcomes for Adolescents within Their Adoptive Kinship Networks

Harold D. Grotevant, Yvette V. Perry,
and Ruth G. McRoy

Since ancient times, adoption has made it possible for children who cannot be raised by their biological parents to grow up in nurturing environments. Around the world and across historical time, most adoptions have been handled informally within children's extended families. When parents were unable to provide appropriate care, they would be assisted by grandparents, siblings, or other members of the community. More recently, Western countries have established legal processes by which the parenting rights and responsibilities of a child's birth parents are legally terminated and transferred to other adults who would raise the child. In 1851, Massachusetts enacted a model adoption law that provided for the legal severance of the relationship between child and birth parents (Carp, 1998). Other states established similar laws, and by 1929 all states in the United States had adoption statutes in place. "The enactment of the Massachusetts Adoption Act marked a watershed in the history of Anglo-American family and society. Instead of defining the parent-child relationships exclusively in terms of blood kinship, it encouraged adoptive parents to build a family by assuming the responsibility and emotional outlook of natural parents" (Carp, 1998, p. 12).

There is much we do not know about factors contributing to successful adoptions, especially when success is defined in terms of the development of healthy, resilient children who become productive adult members of society. A large body of research has examined adjustment outcomes for children from adoptive families (for reviews, see Haugaard, 1998; Ingersoll, 1997; Peters, Atkins, & McKay, 1999). Virtually all this research was conducted with families experiencing confidential adoptions, in which there is no contact and no identifying information shared between birth and adoptive families. However, in recent years adoption practice has changed, making it possible for the legal transfer of parental rights to occur while retaining contact and communication between members of the child's birth and adoptive families.

There are currently four major types of adoptions in the United States, and issues about contact among members of the child's adoptive family and birth family (which we call the adoptive kinship network) vary among them. Openness refers to this continuum of contact and communication among members of the adoptive kinship network. The continuum ranges from confidential (no contact and no identifying information shared) to mediated (communication occurs but is conveyed without identifying information through a third party, such as an adoption agency) to fully disclosed (communication and contact occur directly between parties). These openness categories describe contact at any particular point in time. However, the level of openness (confidential, mediated, fully disclosed) or intensity of the contact (frequency, degree of disclosure) may vary over a family's life course.

One type of adoption is of healthy U.S. infants and young children, voluntarily placed by their birth mothers. Within this type of adoption, there is a trend toward fewer confidential adoptions and more fully disclosed adoptions (Henney, McRoy, Ayers-Lopez, & Grotevant, 2003; Henney, Onken, McRoy, & Grotevant, 1998). A second type includes kinship adoptions, in which children are adopted by other members of their birth families. Related to this are children adopted by a stepparent following remarriage of one of their biological parents. A third type consists of special needs adoptions, which include an array of children, most of whom are placed involuntarily because their birth parents' rights have been terminated through court proceedings. Contact in special needs adoptions is currently a topic of great interest because of the growing number of children in this category (e.g., McRoy, 1999; Neil, 2003; Smith & Howard, 1999). Practitioners and researchers are exploring innovative arrangements that allow children to maintain contact with kin. The final category includes children adopted from other countries. The number of internationally adopted children in the United States has risen dramatically over the past decade, and in most of these placements, adoptive families have either little or no identifying information about their children's birth parents (Gunnar, Bruce, & Grotevant, 2000). Contact between adoptive and birth family members is rare. Each of these types of adoptions presents unique challenges in terms of openness issues. Only the first category mentioned previously (voluntary placements) will be explored in this chapter, but the issues and conclusions explored here may have relevance to the other adoption situations.

Issues about contact in adoption have become increasingly more complex. The movement toward greater openness has been stimulated by adoption professionals and members of the adoptive kinship network who believe that such contact would be beneficial for the mental health and identity development of adopted children and for the well-being of birth parents. The Minnesota-Texas Adoption Research Project (MTARP), led by Grotevant and McRoy, was developed to examine these issues empirically with a sample of children placed as infants. This chapter summarizes and discusses the findings and policy implications of this longitudinal study of variations in openness in adoption, exploring the features and dynamics of this changing adoption practice.

The overarching purposes of the MTARP are (a) to understand the dynamics of adoptive kinship networks in which the connection between members of the adoptive family and birth family vary in level of openness, (b) to investigate the development of adjustment in adolescents who have grown up with varying openness arrangements, (c) to examine outcomes for birth mothers who placed children for adoption 12 to 20 years earlier, and (d) to examine the changing role played by adoption agencies.

The chapter begins with a description of the study's conceptual framework. It then describes the participants and methods and briefly presents the project's major conclusions on several key issues: openness arrangements, adolescent curiosity and searching, adolescent psychological adjustment, and adoptive identity development. The primary focus of this chapter is on the adopted children and adolescents. Readers interested in further information on outcomes for birth mothers should consult Christian, McRoy, Grotevant, and Bryant (1997) and Fravel, McRoy, and Grotevant (2000); further information about changing agency practices may be found in Henney et al. (1998, 2003). The second part of the chapter discusses some of the broad challenges of applying adoption research to policy and practice and outlines some specific policy and practice implications of MTARP findings.

THE STUDY

Grotevant, McRoy, and colleagues have been following 190 adoptive families and 169 birth mothers since the mid-1980s, when adoption agencies began offering options that included contact between members of the child's families of adoption and birth. These changes in policy and practice were considered radical and experimental at the time. Although they remain controversial in some circles, adoption practice involving domestically placed children has clearly moved toward more openness (Henney et al., 2003). The project is unique because it has studied changing family relationships within the context of changing social policies and practices.

The project is guided by an ecological framework that is both developmental and systemic in its focus (e.g., Bronfenbrenner & Morris, 1998; Grotevant, 1998). The framework acknowledges the developing personalities, motivations, and skills that individuals bring to their interactions within their adoptive kinship networks. It illuminates the individuals' transactions with others across time and the interdependencies in their relationships. It also highlights their connections with individuals in their proximal environments, such as friends; their embeddedness in activity settings, such as school, work, and organizations; and the influences of broader contexts, which include culture, history, and the social forces influencing adoption practice and policy. Individual outcomes relating to adjustment are viewed along a continuum, ranging from successful adaptation at one end to psychopathology at the other.

Each of the families in the project adopted a child in the late 1970s or early 1980s. Families and birth mothers were first interviewed between 1987 and 1992 and again between 1996 and 2000. Grotevant and colleagues at the Minnesota site have followed the adopted children and their adoptive parents (e.g., Dunbar & Grotevant, 2004; Grotevant, Ross, Marchel, & McRoy, 1999). McRoy and colleagues at the University of Texas at Austin have followed the children's birth mothers (e.g., Christian et al., 1997; Fravel et al., 2000). In addition, staff from private adoption agencies around the United States were interviewed at three points in time: 1987–89 ($N = 31$ agencies), 1992–93 ($N = 34$), and 1999 ($N = 29$). They provided information about their experiences with openness and other adoption practices, enabling us to look at historical changes in adoption practice as they were occurring (Henney et al., 1998, 2003).

Wave 1: 1987–92

Adoptive families and birth mothers were recruited for the study through 35 adoption agencies located across the United States. Families were sought in which there was at least one adopted child (the "target child") between the ages of 4 and 12 at the time of the interview who was adopted through an agency before his or her first birthday; in which the adoption was not transracial, international, or "special needs"; and in which both adoptive parents were married to each other. Transracial, international, and special needs adoptions were intentionally not included in the study so that the clearest possible conclusions about openness could be drawn without having to consider the additional complexities inherent in these other adoption arrangements. Simultaneously, birth mothers were sought who made adoption plans for children placed with these families. Participants in the study were located in 23 different states from all regions of the United States.

Each participating agency was asked to select all children who met the criteria outlined previously and then to sample randomly among them within levels of openness until they located a set number of families and birth mothers willing to be interviewed. A few families and birth mothers were recruited through advertisements in newspapers and periodicals. Wave 1 data were collected between 1987 and 1992. Although this sample is not a fully random one, participants were specifically not recruited on the basis of their success with adoption or their having an interesting story to tell, which is often a problem in volunteer samples.

At wave 1, the study's participants included 720 individuals: both parents in 190 adoptive families, at least one adopted child in 171 of the families, and 169 birth mothers. The vast majority of adoptive parents were Caucasian, Protestant, and middle to upper-middle class. Of the 190 adoptive couples interviewed, 185 were Caucasian, 3 were Latino, 1 was African American, and 1 was Latino and Caucasian. Virtually all adoptive parents in the study had adopted because of infertility. The average level of education was 16.2 years for adoptive fathers and 15.1 for adoptive mothers. Adoptive fathers ranged in age from 32 to 53 years (mean = 40.7) and adoptive mothers from 31 to 50 (mean = 39.1). Of the 171 participating adopted children, 90 were male, and 81 were female; their ages ranged from 4 to 12 (mean = 7.8 years). The sample was limited to infant placements in order to remove one possible source of variation in adoption outcomes. The mean age of placement was 4 weeks (range: immediately after birth to 44 weeks). Ninety percent of the children were placed by 9 weeks; all but three children were placed in the first half year of life. Because of this restricted range, age of placement was not an important contributing factor to outcomes in this study and will not be discussed further. Adoptive families were interviewed in their homes in one session that lasted three to four hours. The session included separate interviews with each parent and with the target adopted child, administration of several questionnaires, and a joint couples interview with the adoptive parents.

The birth mothers ranged in age from 14 to 36 years (mean = 19.3) when their children were born and from 21 to 43 (mean = 27.1) at the time of the first interview. The average number of years of education they had attained was 13.5. Most were Caucasian (92.9%), with four Latina, two Native American, one African American, one Asian American, and four who did not indicate ethnicity. At the time of the first interview, half the birth mothers were married. Birth mothers were interviewed in their home, at the agency, or by telephone. They also completed several questionnaires. For further details about the wave 1 sample and findings, see Grotevant and McRoy (1997, 1998).

Wave 2: 1996–2000

Participants were interviewed again approximately 8 years after their first interview. They included the parents and target adopted adolescent from 177 adoptive families: 173 adoptive mothers, 162 adoptive fathers, and 156 adopted adolescents (75 boys and 81 girls). The adopted adolescents ranged in age from 11 to 20 years (mean = 15.7). At wave 2, data are also available on 88 siblings (68 adopted, 20 nonadopted) and 127 birth mothers. Almost all adoptive parents who participated in wave 2 were still married, with the following exceptions: five adoptive mothers and three adoptive fathers were divorced, one adoptive mother and two adoptive fathers were separated, and one adoptive father and one adoptive mother were widowed. Adoptive families were once again seen in their homes during a single session that typically lasted four to five hours. The session included individual interviews with each parent and the target adopted child, administration of several questionnaires, and administration of a family interaction task. Some family members were interviewed by telephone when it was impossible to gather everyone together for the home visit (e.g., living out of the United States, adolescent away at college, and so on). The average age of the birth mothers at wave 2 was 35.4 years (ranging from 29 to 54). They reported an average of 14.2 years of education (range: 10 to 20 years). Almost 75 percent of the birth mothers were parenting at least one biological child. Birth mothers were interviewed by telephone.

KEY FINDINGS

Openness Arrangements

Our initial conceptualization of openness, based primarily on the existing literature and discussions with participating agency personnel, posited three levels of openness: confidential, mediated (or semiopen), and fully disclosed (McRoy, Grotevant, & White, 1988). We soon found that these categories did not adequately describe the experiences of our participants. Within the group of confidential adoptions, there were cases in which updated information was sent to the adoption agency for inclusion in the child's file. The information was not necessarily intended for transmission to the other party and could have been sent either once or a number of times. In most of these cases, either the birth mother or the adoptive parents sent information, such as an annual letter on the child's birthday. Within the categories of mediated and fully disclosed adoptions, in addition to cases in which the contact was ongoing, there were some for whom the contact had definitely stopped and others for whom the contact was temporarily paused. Our ultimate categorization of level of openness took these nuances into account. In addition, within each type of openness involving contact, there could be large variations in the intensity of contact (frequency, personal nature of the contact—e.g., a picture is more personal than a purchased gift), type of contact (e.g., letter, picture, gift, phone call, e-mail, visit), or participants' satisfaction. Although these variations were not registered in our openness categorization system, more detailed qualitative analyses have explored these factors (e.g., Berge, Mendenhall, Wrobel, Grotevant, & McRoy, in press; Dunbar et al., 2000).

Description of Arrangements in Families with Fully Disclosed Adoptions

The sample included 46 families whose adoptions involved direct or indirect contact at wave 2 and had continuously had contact—some since placement and others since the children were very young. (Most were in ongoing fully disclosed relationships.) The data from this group provide a profile of the nature and diversity of contact arrangements experienced by families with open adoptions. Family members had contact with a variety of birth family members. The adopted adolescents mentioned having contact with their birth mother (100%), birth grandmother (70.4%), birth sibling(s) (61.3%), birth grandfather (52.2%), the birth mother's spouse or partner (47.8%), and their birth father (29.5%). The pattern of contact for the child's adoptive parents was similar: the most contact was with the child's birth mother, an intermediate amount was with members of the birth mother's family, and the least was with the birth father. The type of contact included photos (93.5%), letters (91.3%), phone calls (87.0%), gifts (87.0%), face-to-face meetings (78.3%), and extended visits (54.3%). The frequency of contact varied across networks, but almost all reported contact among kinship network members more than twice a year.

We asked the adoptive mothers to describe the type of role the birth mother played in their child's life. The most common category mentioned was kin (such as aunt—40%). Other categories mentioned were nonkin (such as friend—16.7%), "birth parent role" (10.0%), parent (such as "other mother"—10.0%), "no role" (6.7%), role associated with actions or activities (6.7%), and other (10.0%). Most adoptive mothers indicated that the predominant way in which contacts were arranged was mutually between the adoptive parents and birth family (67.4%), whereas adoptive family members initiated primarily in 15.2 percent of networks, birth family members initiated primarily in 10.9 percent of networks, and the respondent couldn't tell in 6.5 percent of cases.

During the adoptees' childhood and early adolescence, the adoptive mother played the primary role in managing contact with birth family members. As time went on, the responsibility for contact tended to shift from adoptive mother and birth mother to adopted child and birth mother. In general, adoptive fathers were less involved than mothers in this process across time (Dunbar et al., 2000).

Satisfaction with Contact

High percentages of respondents having ongoing contact reported that they were either satisfied or very satisfied with the level of openness they were experiencing with the child's birth mother: 83.7 percent of the adopted adolescents, 93.5 percent of the adoptive mothers, and 84.8 percent of the adoptive fathers. The teens reported that they hoped their contact with the birth mother either stayed the same (55.8%) or increased (41.9%) in the future. Only one adolescent (2.3%) hoped it would decrease.

Considering the sample as a whole, adolescents who had contact with birth mothers reported higher degrees of satisfaction with their level of adoption openness and with the intensity of their contact with birth mother than did adolescents who had no contact. Satisfaction with adoption openness was lower during middle adolescence (ages 14 to 16) than during early or late adolescence (Berge et al., in press; Mendenhall et al., 2004). Birth mothers' satisfaction with openness also varied as a function of openness. Those in fully disclosed arrangements at wave 2 were more satisfied with their arrangements than were those in confidential or mediated arrangements (McRoy, Ayers-Lopez, Henney, Christian, & Gossman, 2001).

Detailed analyses of interviews were conducted for satisfaction with contact for adolescents who both had and did not have contact with their birth mother (Berge et al., in press; Mendenhall et al., 2004). Adolescents who had contact with their birth mothers and who were satisfied with the level of contact noted that contact (a) provided an opportunity for a relationship to emerge that would provide additional support for them, (b) felt that the contact helped them better understand who they are, and (c) made them interested in having contact with other members of their birth family. Adolescents who had contact with their birth mothers but were not satisfied with the level of contact they were having typically wanted more intensity in the relationship than they currently had, but they were not able to bring about this change. It was also clear that the adolescents in this group could want a deeper relationship with their birth mother while also being content with their adoptive families; they did not feel they were having to choose one family over another.

Adolescents who had had no contact with their birth mothers and were not satisfied about it typically had negative feelings toward their birth mother and assumed she had not made efforts to search for them. Their own efforts at searching had typically been unsuccessful. Finally, adolescents who were satisfied with having no contact typically felt that adoption was not an important aspect of their lives. They felt it was not necessary to have contact and feared that it might be a bad experience for them. They viewed adoption as a blessing and felt that they were better off where they were than had they been raised by their birth parents.

Changes in Openness over Time

Even before the first wave of data collection, a number of changes in openness had occurred since placement. Almost two-thirds of the fully disclosed adoptions did not begin that way: 51 percent began as mediated and 15 percent as confidential adoptions. In many of these cases, trust and mutual respect were gradually established between the adoptive parents and birth mother until they made the decision to share identifying information (Grotevant & McRoy, 1998).

The overall pattern of stability in major openness level is similar for both adoptive families and birth mothers. (Data are presented separately for adoptive families and birth mothers because our data set includes some adoptive families for whom we do not have birth mother data and vice versa.) The majority of cases remained within the same major openness level from wave 1 to wave 2 (71.2% of adoptive families and 78.7% of birth mothers). Smaller, and roughly equal, proportions increased in openness level (14.7% of adoptive families and 10.2% of birth mothers) or decreased in openness (14.1% of adoptive families and 11.0% of birth mothers). Relatively few fully disclosed cases stopped contact between waves 1 and 2 (13.2% of adoptive families and no birth mothers). Among adoptive families with ongoing mediated adoptions, almost equal numbers continued in this category (18), stopped contact (17), and increased to fully disclosed (15). Among birth mothers, 21 continued, 14 stopped contact, and 9 increased to fully disclosed. The majority of cases that were classified as confidential at wave 1 continued as confidential at wave 2 (89.5% of adoptive families and 91.2% of birth mothers).

When there were decreases in openness in adoptive kinship networks, the birth mothers and adoptive parents tended to have incongruent accounts regarding who initiated discontinuation of contact and divergent understandings about why contact stopped (Dunbar et al., 2000). Adoptive parents were more satisfied when birth mothers respected their family's boundaries and let the adoptive family initiate most of the contact.

Members of adoptive kinship networks involved in ongoing contact found that their relationships were dynamic and had to be renegotiated over time. Early in the adoption, meetings were especially important for the birth mothers, who were very concerned about whether they had made the right decision, whether their child was safe, and whether the adoptive parents were good people. After a while, birth mothers' interest in contact sometimes waned, especially as they were assured that their child was thriving. With the passage of time, many birth mothers became involved in new romantic relationships, sometimes taking attention away from the adoptive relationships. According to the adoptive parents, the ability of birth mothers to provide information when requested was not always in tune with the timing of the request (Wrobel, Grotevant, Berge, Mendenhall, & McRoy, 2003). Adoptive parents tended to become more interested in contact as they became more secure in their role as parents. As the children grew older and understood the meaning of adoption (see Brodzinsky, Singer, & Braff, 1984), their questions tended to put pressure on the adoptive parents to seek more information or contact (Wrobel, Kohler, Grotevant, & McRoy, 1998, 1999).

Thus, the maintenance of open adoptions is a complex dance in which the roles and needs of the participants change over time, affecting the kinship network as a whole (Grotevant, McRoy, & van Dulmen, 1998). There is no uniform pattern for open adoptions—kinship networks have contact by different means, among different people, at varying rates, and with varying degrees of interest. Successful relationships in such complex family situations hinge on participants' flexibility, communication skills, and commitment to the relationships.

Adolescent Curiosity and Searching

An important aspect of this work is that we have brought forward the voices of the children and adolescents who have participated. For example, adolescents' interviews have contributed to understanding of the process of searching for birth parents (for details, see Wrobel, Grotevant, & McRoy, 2004). This analysis included all adolescents in the study who did not have ongoing direct contact with their birth mother ($N = 93$). These adolescents were divided into four groups on the basis of their interview responses: (a) those who said they would definitely not search or left open a very small possibility that they might search (34.4%), (b) those who said they might search in the future (24.7%), (c) those who would definitely search in the future (28.0%), and (d) those who had already embarked on a search (12.9%). Older adolescents (ages 17 to 20) who experienced some openness in their adoption (such as mediated contact) and were the least satisfied with their level of openness were most likely to search. Importantly, search behavior was not related to family functioning (as measured by the Family Assessment Device—Epstein, Baldwin, & Bishop, 1983) or adolescent problem behavior (on the Achenbach Youth Self-Report [YSR] or Child Behavior Checklist [CBCL]), contradicting reports in the literature that adoptees searched for their birth parents because of unsatisfactory relationships with their adoptive parents or their own psychopathology (Wrobel et al., 2004). Consequently, we view decision making about searching as part of the normative developmental process for adolescent and young adult adoptees. This does not mean that every adoptee will search, but it does mean that they will need to consider the decision to search as part of the process of their development. The following quote, from an adolescent in a mediated adoption, illustrates how curiosity about birth parents and a strong desire to meet them does not negate the adolescent's positive views about her adoptive family:

I want to see what it's like. I want to see them. I want to meet them. I want to see what it's like to have a little brother. I think after I have contacted them once, I thought I'd talk to them more frequently. You know, I mean, I'd never ditch the family I have now for them.

The planned wave 3 will provide the opportunity to examine whether and how these young adults implement their intentions to search as well as how their birth parents and adoptive parents respond to this process.

Adolescent Psychological Adjustment

At wave 1, variations in adjustment among adopted children were linked to relationships within their adoptive families as well as to the quality of the connections across the adoptive kinship network in which they were members. There was no relation between level of openness and the children's socioemotional adjustment as measured by the Child Adaptive Behavior Inventory (Grotevant & McRoy, 1998). Subsequent analyses focused on family process predictors of adjustment, including acknowledgment of difference, compatibility, parents' sense of entitlement, and parenting competence. In these analyses, the strongest predictor of problematic adjustment outcomes (internalizing and externalizing) during middle childhood (wave 1) was the parent's perception of the child's incompatibility with the family (Ross, 1995). At wave 2, relationships were examined between adjustment outcomes and five patterns of change in compatibility (continuously high, continuously moderate, continuously low, increasing, and decreasing). Higher degrees of perceived compatibility maintained longitudinally from middle childhood to adolescence were associated with higher degrees of psychosocial engagement (defined as adolescents' active use of inner resources to interact positively with others in family, peer, and community contexts), greater attachment to parents, and lower incidence of problem behavior. The results were similar for male and female adolescents and regardless of whether compatibility change patterns were derived from mothers' or fathers' perceptions (Grotevant, Wrobel, van Dulmen, & McRoy, 2001).

Detailed qualitative analyses of the interviews from a subset of adoptive kinship networks who were experiencing contact between the adoptive family and birth mother and who had complete wave 1 data on adoptive parents and birth mother revealed an important construct on which the networks in the study varied. Collaboration in relationships was found to be an emergent property of the adoptive kinship network, characterized by the ability of the child's adoptive and birth parents to work together effectively on behalf of the child's well-being. It involves collaborative control over the way in which contact is handled and is based on mutual respect, empathy, and valuing of the relationship (Grotevant et al., 1999). Collaboration was rated on a 10-point scale, and ratings were correlated with children's scores (at wave 1) on socioemotional development (from the Child Adaptive Behavior Inventory). Spearman rank order correlations suggested that higher ratings on collaboration were associated with lower scores for the children on indicators of problematic adjustment.

At wave 2, the YSR (Achenbach & Edelbrock, 1987), CBCL (Achenbach & Edelbrock, 1983), and Brief Symptom Inventory (BSI—Derogatis, 1993) were used to assess adjustment of the adolescent adoptees in the study. Adjustment scores for the MTARP adolescents did not differ significantly from gender-specific norms on the YSR or CBCL (mother or father report). The MTARP males scored significantly better (i.e., fewer symptoms) than the norm group on the BSI. Overall, we ran 42 comparisons of adjustment scores against normative scores. Only three of 42 yielded statistically significant differences, and two of them were in the direction of the MTARP adolescents being better adjusted than the norm groups. Most of the non-significant differences were in the direction of the MTARP youth being better adjusted than the national norms. Our data provide no evidence that this sample of adolescent adoptees is less well adjusted than other youth on which the measures were normed. Analyses examining adjustment outcomes by openness level are in progress.

Adoptive Identity Development

In addition to dealing with the normative developmental issues of adolescence, adopted youth are confronted with the challenge of making meaning of their beginnings, which may be unknown, unclear, or otherwise ambiguous. Meaning making (e.g., Kegan, 1982; Klinger, 1998) involves constructing a story about oneself that attempts to answer many questions: Where did I come from? Who were my parents? Why was I placed for adoption? Do my birth parents think about me now? Do I have siblings? What does adoption mean in my life? This story, or narrative, helps the adolescent to make sense of the past, understand the self in the present, and project himself or herself into the future (Grotevant, 1993). Constructing this narrative is about the development of adoptive identity, the evolving answer to the question, Who am I as an adopted person? (Grotevant, 1997; Grotevant, Dunbar, Kohler, & Esau, 2000). This is part of the larger process of identity development, which is widely recognized as an important task of adolescence that lays a foundation for adult psychosocial development (Erikson, 1968).

The narrative approach to identity highlights the integration and coherence of the self through the evaluation of the structure, content, and function of the narrative (e.g., McAdams, 1987, 1993, 2001; Mishler, 1999). From this perspective, the adolescent is viewed as creating and recreating a life story that makes meaning of and gives purpose to his or her experience of adoption.

During wave 2, participating adolescents were administered interviews that examined adoptive identity. The interviews were coded for several dimensions. Exploration assessed how deeply an adolescent had considered his or her adoptive identity. High ratings indicated considerable depth in exploration with serious, reflective thinking that showed self-awareness and integration. Salience of adoptive identity indicated the level of importance and prominence of the identity; the degree to which the adoptive identity influenced behaviors, thoughts, decisions, and feelings; and adolescents' ranking of the adoptive identity in relation to five other identity domains. High ratings indicated that the adoptive identity may consume great psychic and emotional energy and may be the identity that is most prominent or a "leading theme" in the adolescent's sense of self. Internal consistency measured the completeness of the content of the narrative; the most consistent narratives showed complexity and detailed elaboration. Flexibility measured the adolescent's ability to view issues as others might see them and to explore new ideas and alternatives. Positive and negative affect were each coded in terms of how the adopted adolescent felt about being adopted and/or having an identity as an adopted person. Higher ratings indicated intense emotions, such as loving or hating.

Adolescents' narratives were categorized into types based on the narrative attributes mentioned previously (Dunbar, 2003; Dunbar & Grotevant, 2004). A cluster analysis based on the preceding variables revealed four groups of identity narratives. In the first group, unexplored adoptive identity, the adolescent had undertaken little or no exploration, adoption had low salience, and little affect around adoption was expressed. For example, one adolescent stated, "Because I feel like it's over and that I'm happy where I am and I just don't want to mess with that other part." Another noted that "I don't really think about adoption that much so it's just, I probably don't even realize that I am." In the second group, limited identity, adolescents were actively exploring ideas. As one young woman stated, "Sometimes it's important to me and sometimes it isn't." Adolescents in the third group, unsettled identity, had narratives that were coherent and integrated, marked by high exploration of adoptive identity, high salience, and strong negative affect. One adolescent stated, "My mom [adoptive] and I aren't very close and I know that's [adoption] the reason. I mean if, I'm sure if I lived with my real mom we'd be a lot closer, we'd talk about it and that's just hard because all my friends can talk to their moms." Finally, adolescents demonstrating integrated identity had coherent, integrated narratives in which adoptive identity was highly salient and viewed positively. For example, one teen said, "When I was little I worried I was placed because she didn't want me. Now I know I was placed because she cared enough."

Patterns of adoptive identity differed widely across adolescents, although, in general, more positively resolved patterns were found among older rather than younger adolescents and girls rather than boys (Dunbar & Grotevant, 2004). Frequencies of adolescents in the four identity types did not significantly differ as a function of openness level (Dunbar, 2003).

The process of adoptive identity development may involve a period of time when adoption issues are particularly salient, involving intense reflection and emotional engagement, perhaps preoccupation on the part of the adolescent (Dunbar, 2003). When this occurs, it may be accompanied by the adolescent's temporary emotional withdrawal from the adoptive family. On average, girls' levels of preoccupation (measured by the Adoption Dynamics Questionnaire) were higher than boys' (Kohler, Grotevant, & McRoy, 2002). Differences in degree of preoccupation with adoption were not related to the level of openness in the adolescent's adoption. However, differences in preoccupation were related to identity group. Mean scores for preoccupation with adoption were significantly higher for adolescents in the unsettled and integrated types than for adolescents in the unexamined type (Dunbar, 2003). Ongoing work with wave 2 data continues to examine the family predictors of identity types and the relation of identity to adjustment during adolescence. Longitudinal work will allow us to investigate the stability of adoptive identity across the transition from adolescence to young adulthood.

IMPLICATIONS FOR ADOPTION PRACTICE AND POLICY

A primary goal of the MTARP has been to characterize changing family relationships within the context of the changing institution of adoption in order to better inform adoption practice and policy. We have drawn two consistent general conclusions from this project with implications for practice and policy. First, one type of adoption arrangement is not "best" for all adoptive kinship networks, and, further, within a kinship network, what works well for one party at one point in time may not be the best for other parties (Grotevant & McRoy, 1998). Second, because adoption within the lives of the specific people touched by it is a dynamic process, the patterns of different needs and desires of different kinship members may shift over time (Grotevant & McRoy, 1997; Grotevant et al., 1998). These conclusions introduce complexities that make the historical debates about openness (for or against) appear oversimplified. Nevertheless, in the absence of data, adoption practices have continued to evolve, often without firm grounding in empirical research findings. Now that a critical mass of knowledge is emerging from this and other projects, future changes in practice and policy regarding postadoption contact and other adoption issues should be informed by research findings.

In the next two sections, we discuss examples of specific themes emerging so far from the MTARP relating to the general conclusions stated thus far that have implications for adoption practice and policy. In the concluding section, we highlight the need to strengthen links between research, policy, and practice.

Adoption Openness and "One Size Fits All"

Based on early debates about the desirability and undesirability of fully disclosed or confidential adoptions, adoption practice and policy would seem to benefit from a definitive answer about which type of placement arrangement is "best." However, our data suggest that such a conclusion of a "one size fits all" approach is not warranted. For example, MTARP findings suggest that the development of adoptive identity is quite varied, depending on individuals, families, and aspects of the kinship network. It may be marked by intense positive and/or negative affect, preoccupation, temporary emotional withdrawal from the family, and active exploration of relationships outside the adoptive family (Dunbar & Grotevant, 2004; Kohler et al., 2002). But as the discussion in the previous section suggests, this variation does not appear to be significantly dependent on level of openness.

Since there are such wide individual differences, professionals who work with parents of more than one adopted child should help them see that their children may not experience identity development in the same way in terms of issues such as timing, intensity of affect, or salience. Similarly, school personnel and clinicians should be acquainted with the diversity of ways in which adoptive identity may be explored. Support groups for adolescents exploring identity issues should be normalized and available. Together with MTARP findings related to the normative nature of search decision making, these findings argue for flexibility that allows information-access policies to be tailored to the differing disclosure and privacy needs of individuals who have been adopted.

In an additional example, the previous discussion about adolescent adjustment reveals that most measures of adjustment were not significantly related to variations in level of openness. Instead, family process variables, such as the adoptive parents' perceptions of child compatibility, appear to have greater implications for adjustment outcomes than openness level per se. We are continuing to explore processes such as empathic understanding, communication, and collaboration in relationships that are related to outcomes for adoptive kinship network members.

Different Needs: Patterns over Time

Adoptive families are unique in their specific positioning within changing social, legal, and historical contexts. The lives of the specific people touched by adoption should also be viewed dynamically—as an ongoing process rather than a discrete time-bound event. The process nature of adoption was evident in the MTARP sample. For example, the maintenance of open adoptions is a complex dance in which the roles and needs of the participants change over time, affecting the kinship network as a whole (Grotevant et al., 1998). There is no uniform pattern for open adoptions—kinship networks have contact by different means, among different people, at varying rates, and with varying degrees of interest. Successful relationships in such complex family situations hinge on participants' flexibility, communication skills, and commitment to the relationships.

One example of an ongoing process with key practice and policy implications is the construct of collaboration in relationships. The MTARP findings suggest that collaboration between a child's adoptive parents and birth parents plays a key role in successful management of contact and predicts positive socioemotional development for the child (Grotevant et al., 1999). We have noted the dynamic nature of relationships among the adults in the child's life, arguing that maintenance of contact after adoption requires a commitment to making ongoing relationships work despite their inherent ups and downs.

These findings imply that, although agency staff might want to match birth mothers and adoptive parents by their openness preferences at the time of placement, no one can predict what the parties' preferences will be in the future. Educational and therapeutic interventions and agency practices based on these findings should be developed for adoptive parents, birth parents, and adopted persons. One of the most important things that practitioners can do is educate adoptive kinship members to expect and prepare for change over the course of the adoption. Even though the major openness levels were largely stable over the eight-year period between waves 1 and 2, changes in the type of contact, frequency of contact, and individuals involved in the contact seemed to be the rule rather than the exception. By providing education, such as in the development of communication skills, agencies may help kinship members handle changes in openness and in relationships and negotiate difficulties that may emerge from these changes. Agency staff should find appropriate ways to assist the contact process and should offer postadoption services in the event that issues surrounding openness arise. These services should be designed to respond to a diversity of needs.

Further, the needs of children themselves—unknowable at placement in the case of infant placements—may also differ. At adolescence, for example, some youth desire contact but do not follow through on this desire for fear they might alienate or offend their adoptive parents. In this case, agency staff could facilitate the process by helping the adoptive parents and adopted child talk about their feelings concerning contact with birth family members. Other adolescents desire no contact with birth family members and are happy with their lives as they are. Agency staff should be aware that desire for contact can be influenced by many factors, including developmental level, understanding of adoption, prior experiences of the child with birth parents, and current circumstances. Therefore, staff should not assume that a present desire not to have contact is problematic (Wrobel et al., 2004). This is a legitimate feeling and indicates that openness is not necessarily indicated for every adoption arrangement at all time points in the life span.

Legal and policy initiatives should also be based on longitudinal research rather than myths and suppositions about openness. Legal procedures related to initiating and maintaining openness should provide mechanisms for voluntary agreements, for the ability of agreements to be renegotiated, and for the availability of professionals who can assist kinship networks experiencing difficult transitions. Future policy could also benefit from further research to understand how these processes play out over time.

Toward Stronger Links Connecting Research, Policy, and Practice

In an ideal world, research, policy, and practice are tightly interwoven. However, in the absence of research (or in the absence of access to it), practice and policy decisions are made on other grounds. In closing, we offer several recommendations to strengthen the links that connect research, policy, and practice.

First, whenever possible, researchers should engage multiple stakeholders in the formulation of research questions and the interpretation and dissemination of results. Relevant stakeholders for adoption research include members of adoptive kinship networks, clinicians, adoption workers, policymakers, community leaders, advocates, and educators. Involvement of such people in the research process will help ensure that the work is based on a broad understanding of the relevant issues and asks questions that will be useful for the adoption community.

Second, adoption researchers should explore nontraditional approaches that might result in more rapid collection or analysis of data or more rapid dissemination of findings to applicable policymakers. For example, Family Impact Seminars have been used in a number of states to bring research results directly to legislators and their staff members. The work is presented in order for the legislators to understand the potential impact on families of laws and policies that are under consideration (Bogenschneider, 2002).

Third, adoption professionals should find opportunities to respond with research-based information to adoption issues that receive sensationalized treatment in the media. Counteracting inaccurate media images is critical since 41 percent of Americans report that their main sources of information about adoption are the news, movies, and entertainment programs (Evan B. Donaldson Adoption Institute, 2002c).

Fourth, new or expanded services are needed to support adoptive kinship networks experiencing open adoptions. For example, preadoption services for prospective adoptive parents should acquaint them with birth parents and their needs. Both birth parents and adoptive parents should have access to supportive counseling about contact around the time of placement, when emotions may be intense. Following placement, ongoing services should be available to help birth family and adoptive family members renegotiate their openness arrangements over time, especially if competing needs or desires are present. In addition, ongoing training is needed for adoption and mental health professionals who work with families experiencing these new forms of adoption.

Finally, adoption researchers should develop long-term connections to policymakers and practitioners in order to respond to proposed legislation that may affect adoptive and birth families. Legislation that influences adoption practice is often proposed and passed with little or no consideration of the empirical research findings on the topic. For example, in 2003, the Texas legislature passed legislation stipulating that if the court finds it in the best interest of the child, the court may provide in a termination order, "terms that allow the biological parent to receive specified information regarding the child, provide written communications to the child, and have limited access to the child." When this openness initiative was proposed, limited (if any) attempts were made to receive input and guidance from adoption scholars who study long-term implications and practice issues associated with postadoption contact.

Much of the existing research on adoptive kinship is problem focused, assuming that adoption presents challenges to overcome and risks to avoid (Grotevant & Kohler, 1999). It emphasizes the negative, such as a higher rate of psychopathology among adoptees, risk of disrupted placements, trauma of searching for birth parents, and difficult interpersonal relationships (e.g., Haugaard, 1998; Peters et al., 1999; Smith & Howard,

1999). It is common for interventions, programs, and policies related to adoption to similarly grow out of a problem-focused perspective. The lens in the adoption field now needs to be widened to address the development of strengths (rather than simply the amelioration of problems) in all members of the adoptive kinship network as well as strategies for maintaining healthy kinship network relationships across time. Our research findings point to positive outcomes and processes, such as psychosocial engagement of adolescents and compatibility in parent–adolescent relationships, needing further investigation. Once more is known about them, implications for practice and policy will become even clearer.

Looking to the Future

The institution of adoption has served as "a clarifying lens, a way to discern the arbitrariness of...our received truths about family, identity, and kinship" (Melosh, 2002, p. 4). Recent changes in adoption policy and practice, such as increasing openness at placement, changing laws concerning adoptees' access to identifying information and birth certificates, and underground social movements supporting search and reunion, have contributed to adoption's unique dynamic force as both caretaker of and challenger to notions of family.

Further changes in family life on the horizon point to the need to consider the practice and policy implications of this and other such adoption research. In the area of assisted reproductive technology, for example, it is currently possible for children to be conceived from donated sperm or eggs, to be gestated in the uterus of a surrogate, to be born years after being "frozen" as a cryopreserved embryo, and all combinations of these scenarios. Several scholars have pointed to this high-tech family formation as an area with parallels to adoption that might be informed by the lessons of adoption research, policy, and practice (e.g., Perry, 2002; Shapiro, Shapiro, & Paret, 2001). In turn, the application of concepts and issues from adoption to new domains is encouraging reconceptualization of the nature of adoptive kinship itself (Perry, 2003). The work reported in this chapter and throughout this volume points to the need for adoption researchers to continue to think and work across disciplinary and international boundaries.

ACKNOWLEDGMENTS

We acknowledge, with gratitude, funding support from a number of agencies: the William T. Grant Foundation; the National Institute of Child Health and Human Development; the Office of Population Affairs; the U.S. Department of Health and Human Services; the Hogg Foundation for Mental Health; the John D. and Catherine T. MacArthur Foundation; the

Minnesota Agricultural Experiment Station; the Center for Interpersonal Relationships Research, University of Minnesota; and the University Research Institute of the University of Texas at Austin. Yvette Perry's contributions were made possible by the support of the Mary Ellen McFarland Assistantship in the Department of Family Social Science, University of Minnesota. We extend special thanks to the adoptive parents, adopted children, birth parents, and adoption agency staff members who generously gave their time to share their experiences with us. We also thank Susan Ayers-Lopez, our key project manager since the project's beginning, as well as the many students and colleagues who have worked with us to date.

Chapter 9

The Construction of Adoptive Parenthood and Filiation in Italian Families with Adolescents: A Family Perspective

Rosa Rosnati

The past decade has seen a renewed interest in the subject of adoption, especially in Italy. This can be seen in the media coverage that adoption has received as well as in the efforts to regulate this process as much as possible in order to guarantee respect for the rights of minors. The ratification of the Hague Convention of 1993 by the Italian government (Law 476 of 1998) and Law 149/2001 have brought about substantial changes in regulatory guidelines as well as profound transformations in adoption procedures, particularly with respect to international adoptions. In particular, the procedural time has been drastically reduced, a central authority with oversight functions has been instituted, and couples now are required to be accompanied and supported throughout the adoption process by agencies authorized by the Italian government.

This renewed interest in adoption also derives from the overall increase in the number of children adopted by Italian families, mostly from other countries. As a matter of fact, in 2003, 2,305 children came to Italy through international adoption (Commissione Adozioni, www.commissioneadozioni.it). The children's countries of origin have also changed significantly in the past decade in keeping with recent historical, political, and social transformations. Until the 1990s, the countries of origin of children adopted in

Italy were mainly Brazil, India, Peru, and Chile. In the period 2000–2003, in contrast, the majority of children have come from countries of eastern Europe (23.07% from Ukraine, 10.06% from Russia, 9.41% from Bulgaria, 8.35% from Byelorussia, 5.18% from Poland, 4.31% from Romania, and so on), and only a marginal percentage have come from Latin America (9.33% from Colombia and 7.07% from Brazil), Asia (5.43% from India), and Africa (3.34% from Ethiopia). As a consequence, most children adopted today do not show an evident and marked ethnic diversity and are more similar in physical appearance to Italian children than in a near past. Furthermore, in contrast to what parents would wish, the children who come to Italy to be adopted are by no means all infants: for the period 2000–2003, only 7.7 percent were under 1 year, while 47.7 percent were between 1 and 4 years old, 33 percent were between 5 and 9 years old, and 11.6 percent were even older than 10 (Commissione Adozioni, www.commissioneadozioni.it).

In 2003, 5,790 Italian couples were granted approval to adopt by the Courts for Minors (Commissione Adozioni, www.commissioneadozioni.it). In almost all cases, the couples did not have biological children (90.4%) and were decidedly older than biological parents when their first child is born: in Italy, the average age at adoption is 41.3 for husbands and 39 for wives, while first-time biological mothers range from 27 to 28 years old. This pattern of greater age for adoptive parents compared to birth parents is similar in other European countries as well as in the United States and Canada.

This brief account suggests that adoption is a multidimensional phenomenon where cultural, social, historical, and psychological factors intersect. But we must not forget that adoption originates above all as a *social* response to the problem of childhood abandonment and neglect. It constitutes a challenge to society since it sanctions a parental bond beyond biological ties. International adoption, in particular, stands out as being worthy of study in that it intersects and at the same time diverges from the phenomenon of multiethnicity; in fact, it allows us to analyze how people of different ethnic origins are able not only to integrate themselves into a given social context but also to coexist within the family unit. Thus, adoption can be seen to be a phenomenon of particular social importance.

This chapter focuses on the intergenerational and social dimensions of adoption from a family perspective, considering adoption as an event that requires a regulation of family bonds and the construction of an adoptive pact between parents and the child. The adoptive pact is viewed within the context of the intergenerational family network and is directly related to the process of inner legitimization of the parental role that adoptive parents have to accomplish. Finally, to highlight the points being made, results from research on Italian adoptive families with adolescents will be presented, focusing on the perception of adoptive parenthood and filiation in relation to the quality of family bonds and adolescents' well-being.

TRANSITION IN ADOPTION: A "RISKY" TRANSITION

From a psychological point of view, adoption represents a unique means to acquire a new family member since it establishes a parental relationship in the absence of blood ties (Scabini & Cigoli, 2000). Consequently, in adoptive families what gives continuity to the family history, connecting one generation to the next and the past to the future, is the construction of a psychological bond instead of a biological one (Sorosky, Baran, & Pannor, 1978).

Life span developmental theory (as well as stress and coping theory) has noted for some time that the arrivals and departures of members of the family group are of particular relevance in that they not only change the family structure but also radically modify its functioning (Brodzinsky & Pingerhughes, 2002; Scabini & Iafrate, 2003). Adoption represents, in fact, a "critical" moment for the entire family (and not only for the couple), a crucial turn of events that allows the family to modify its own functioning and activate the resources needed to face the challenge of incorporating a new individual into the family system.

The day when parents and child first meet (as well as the day when the adoption is legally finalized) deeply impresses themselves on the history of all family members. These are days that many adoptive families celebrate in the following years, along with the child's birthday. In contrast to these discrete events, the construction of the adoptive bond is a process that develops over time and sinks its roots into the life story of each person involved, continuing well beyond the arrival of the child. It is more appropriate to speak of a *transition to adoptive parenthood* in order to emphasize not only the dimension of process involved but also the element of risk intrinsic to all family transitions. In adoption, this risk is especially accentuated by the factor of unpredictability that it implies. We can thus affirm that the adoptive transition is in itself a *risky transition* in the etymological sense of the term, as a "crossroads, bifurcation." Successfully overcoming this critical process is not a given as if it were the only destination on a linear path. Although adoption represents an opportunity for growth for the entire family, it also presents each family member with various life obstacles that have the potential for interfering with building a shared family history.

Many factors may amplify this degree of risk, for example, the child's age at adoption, the number and quality of placements before adoption, traumatic experiences in the child's early life, the child's temperament and behavioral problems, the adoptive parents' disappointed expectations, the failure of the couple to work through the trauma of infertility, and so on (Brand & Brinich, 1999; Brodzinsky, Smith, & Brodzinsky, 1998; Cederblad, Hook, Irhammar, & Mercke, 1999; Howe, 1997; Marcovitch et al., 1998; Priel, Melamed-Hass, Besser, & Kantor, 2000). On the other hand, the research literature generally points to the positive quality of adoptive family relationships as the primary protective factor in the adjustment of the adopted child and the family as a whole (Brodzinsky & Schechter, 1990; Brodzinsky et al., 1997; Rosnati & Marta, 1998). An earlier study (Rosnati, 1998) has highlighted the sense of family belonging and the quality of communication with the adoptive mother as critical variables capable of reducing the psychosocial risk for adopted adolescents

The outcome of the adoptive transition thus depends on the interplay of variables located on intraindividual, interpersonal, relational, and social levels. It is also contingent on how all the participants involved (parents, children, families of origin, and adoption professionals) face and overcome the different pitfalls and developmental tasks that emerge in the course of the various phases of the family life cycle (Brodzinsky & Pinderhughes, 2002). Unlike other types of critical events that mark family's life cycles (e.g., a family member's illness), this event is chosen. This allows the family to think ahead about coping strategies and gather adequate resources to meet the challenge, but it does not eliminate the degree of risk already mentioned.

The etymology of "to adopt" underlines this dimension of choice: indeed, in Latin, "optare" means to choose, reinforced by the prefix "ad." The couple may perceive choice as an element that characterized only the initial phase of the adoption process. But faced with the real child, always different from the one they longed for and imagined, the adoptive couple must again choose to be father and mother of *this particular* child with his or her unique face and personal history. The child is also called on, over time and above all during adolescence, to make a choice to be the son or daughter of *these* parents and to belong to this particular family as he or she looks for a link, a connecting thread, between the different chapters of his or her own life history. The construction of the adoptive bond is therefore based on a reciprocal choice even if enacted at different times and in different ways by parents and children.

The reciprocity of the choice can be seen also in the exchange of gifts—to use the terminology of Godbout (1992)—that lies at the origin of the adoptive bond. The parents offer the child care, protection, and the security of a family, but the child also brings gifts by offering to the parents the possibility of experiencing parenthood and ensuring the continuity of the family. The cases of adoption in which the bond is "mortgaged" from the start are not rare: in these situations, parents do not welcome the reciprocity of the exchange and may even reject it. These parents see themselves as having "saved" the child from an adverse destiny—from neglect, violence, and often from poverty and hunger as well. As a consequence, the child remains imprisoned forever in the position of debtor (Greco & Rosnati, 1998). As much as the child strives to meet expectations, how can he or she ever repay a gift so great? In this case, only the aspects of the child's obligation and debt are allowed to surface in the exchange, and elements of a continually renewed reciprocal gift are obscured or even erased. We might refer to these as cases of "destructive indebtedness" in which the child ends up feeling crushed by the obligations to his or her parents. In contrast to other situations, this distortion of the exchange is less easily recognizable in that it is often cloaked in altruism, as the charitable action of one who wishes to provide a home to a needy and lonely child. In this way, the adult transforms the gift into a "poisonous" gift, that is, a gift that by its very nature cannot in any way be reciprocated (Scabini & Cigoli, 2000).

The reciprocity of the choice and the exchange must not obscure the *asymmetry of the responsibility*, however, that always flows from the first generation toward successive generations: parents and children, then, each make their own contribution although with differing degrees of responsibility (see also chapter 7 in this volume).

THE CONSTRUCTION OF THE ADOPTIVE PACT

The goal of the adoption transition is the construction of the *adoptive pact* (Bramanti & Rosnati, 1998). The pact is a curious and unique amalgam of needs, expectations, and the personal histories of all those who enter into the contract, that is, the child, the parents, and the parents' own families of origin (Scabini & Cigoli, 2000). The term "pact" underlines once again the aspect of reciprocity already emphasized: the pact is a relational modality drawn up among generations and is always subject to changes over time as the contracting parties' needs and expectations change (see chapters 7 and 8 in this volume).

The construction of the adoptive pact has as its critical point the way in which the different generations involved face the issues of difference as well as reciprocal belonging. Kirk (1964) states that the differences of adoptive compared to nonadoptive family life can be either denied and expelled or recognized and integrated into the family context. Brodzinsky (1990) has expanded on Kirk's ideas and maintains that adoptive families use different *coping strategies* in order to face this issue: these strategies exist in a "continuum" between the two extremes of the rejection of difference on one end and the insistence on it on the other. In the first case, differences are banished by the family and strenuously denied. At the other extreme, families show a tendency to blame the child's adoptive origin for all the difficulties and problems that sooner or later arise with respect to the parent–child relationship, with peers, or at school. In the middle of the continuum exists a functional area where differences are acknowledged. This strategy is founded on the acceptance of differences that are recognized and incorporated into the family history.

The pact that is drawn up between the two generations—parents and children—depends on the way in which the issue of difference is treated. We can therefore delineate differing types of pacts, as one of our recent studies on adoptive families with adolescent children has demonstrated (Greco & Rosnati, 1998). This study was based, first, on an in-depth interview carried out separately with adoptive parents and their adolescent child and, second, on a drawing (the Family Life Space) jointly created by all three family members representing the different people in the family, significant others and events in the family's life, the quality of the family relationships, and the closeness versus distance among family members (for an application of this instrument with adoptive families, see Gozzoli & Tamanza, 1998, and especially Greco, Ranieri, & Rosnati, 2003). The following aspects were taken into special consideration: the perception of similarity/difference with respect to biological families, the quality of the memory of the trio's first encounter, the intergenerational exchange with both parents' families of origin, and, regarding the execution of the drawing, evidence of references to the history of the adoption and the quality of family members' relationships.

In the pact that *negates differences,* we noted the expulsion, by both parents and child, of the adoption story, which was experienced by all concerned as being exceedingly painful. Thus, all references to the adoption were ignored, and all traces of the experience were pushed from one's memory over time. Moreover, any differences between adoptive and biological parenthood were vigorously denied.

In the *assimilation pact,* the adoption event was kept in mind but for the most part was neutralized as to any latent negative feelings regarding the child's unknown origin. Differences were admitted but immediately put "between parentheses" in an effort, on the part of the parents, to resemble a biological family as much as possible. It is not by chance that in these families adoption was often associated with a "physiological event" and equated with birth. As a consequence, adoptive parenthood was viewed as the same as biological parenthood. The effect was one of assimilating the adopted child to a biological child while trying to hush up all that may in some fashion recall his or her different origins. Thus, although differences were not denied, as in the preceding pact, they were juxtaposed to the family history and only superficially integrated into it.

The *pact of recognition and appreciation of differences* was found in those families in which the adoption not only was integrated into the family history but also brought to the family a richness enjoyed by all. These are families who believe that they have had an experience that has given "something more" to all involved with respect to normal family life. These couples viewed themselves as fully legitimate parents and not only acknowledged the difference between adoptive and biological parenthood but also attributed to the former a positive value, seeing it as a *plus* rather than a *minus*. This pact does not result from idealization but was founded on the awareness of having faced the often painful experiences of infertility and adoption and overcome these challenges. In these families, one senses a certain freedom not only in the retelling of the adoption story but also in expressing both positive and negative emotions connected to it. The children, by now adolescents and supported by their parents, have succeeded in putting together the disparate parts of their life stories and in giving them meaning as they take the difficult path of reappropriating their own origins and accepting the abandonment that has marked their personal histories.

In the *impossible pact*, parents and children occupied psychic positions so distant from each other that it was impossible to establish a pact between them. The disparity between expectations and reality was great on both sides. The process of taking on the parental role appeared to be blocked so that parents and children existed as if suspended in a void, so far apart as to be unable to establish shared ways of relating. The children were effectively experienced as strangers, and the negative aspects of their behavior were blamed on their origin. For their part, the children confirmed their estrangement from family relationships, often acting out in the process of individuating and separating from their parents.

The adoptive pact thus can be seen to be a relational modality that depends on the way in which the different components of the family unit succeed in "holding together" aspects of belonging and difference: the child is able to "put down roots" in the adoptive family and its history only on condition that his or her different origin is acknowledged and respected. The difficulty in integrating aspects of similarity and belonging with those of difference is precisely the challenge faced by adoptive families. The temptation to simplify reality by eliminating one or the other pole—similarity or difference—is always possible, especially in times of increased tension in the parent–child relationship. Thus, one's "own" child, assimilated to the status of a biological child, suddenly becomes the "child of others," more or less subtly rejected through the attribution of defects or deficiencies to his or her origins and heredity (Greco et al., 2003). This state of affairs can lead, in extreme cases, to the child's being expelled from the home: in these situations, belonging was never constructed, and difference was lived in terms of complete estrangement. This is the failure of the adoptive process inasmuch as it was not possible to establish the adoptive pact.

In defining the pact, the roles played by the relationships with families of origin and the parents' own representations of their childhoods (Greco & Rosnati, 1998) are not to be underestimated. These considerations converge with the attachment literature, pointing out the transmission of *internal working models* from one generation to the next (Ainsworth, Blehar, Waters, & Wall, 1978; Bowlby, 1969; Cassidy & Shaver, 1999). However, further aspects must be taken into consideration: a triadic relationship is established from the very beginning (mother–father and child), and the couple itself constitutes the crossing point of two intergenerational stories. As a consequence, parenting style is affected not only by the parent's own experience as a child but also by the conjugal relation and the partner's own past experience: the couple is able to elaborate, to a certain degree, what it inherits from previous generations and what it transmits to the following ones (Scabini & Iafrate, 2003). The intergenerational transmission therefore follows a very complex process and also plays a very important role in construction of the adoptive bond.

In fact, some couples see in adoption a way of passing on to the next generation the abundance of gifts received from both their families of origin. These couples live in a context characterized by positive relationships and mutually satisfying exchanges with both their families of origin. In these families, one witnesses a "choral" welcoming of the adopted child: grandparents, aunts, uncles, and cousins all gather around to celebrate the new arrival.

In other families, however, the couple's relationship with their families of origin are still characterized by conflicts. In such cases, adoption can be one of many ways in which the couple seeks to distance themselves from their families of origin and mark the rupture in relationships with their respective parents. For the most part, these couples perceive their family histories as characterized by deficiencies and a lack of nurturing and support that are difficult to forgive and about which deep grudges are still harbored. Consequently, they express the desire to differentiate themselves from their own parents and to behave in a completely different way with their own children. They believe that there is nothing positive in whatever their parents have given to them that is worth transmitting to their own children. Thus, a deep rupture is created between the generations.

Our research highlighted that in these cases of unresolved relational difficulties between the generations, there is an associated difficulty in establishing satisfactory relationships between parents and an adopted child on the one hand and grandparents and adopted grandchild on the other (Greco & Rosnati, 1998). Indeed, difficulties in being able to adequately address the issue of the child's difference are generally connected to difficulties experienced by the parents in the process of differentiation from their respective families of origin, whether this manifests itself as excessive closeness or, at the other extreme, as the complete breakdown of ties. Research suggests that grandparents play an important role in supporting their children and helping them keep confidence in the face of a choice as risky and challenging as adoption (Scabini & Cigoli, 2000). Thus, the support that grandparents give to the adoptive parents, whether emotional and affective in nature or organizational and material, constitutes an irreplaceable resource. They must also welcome the adopted child as one who will carry on the family's history and must accept that the family legacy, including the material inheritance, be entrusted to a genetically foreign individual. The bond that is established between grandparents and adopted grandchild is therefore critical to the process of his or her integration into the family unit.

The preliminary results of a recent study we have conducted in Italy reveal that, even if it happens in a minority of cases, paternal grandparents are more likely than the maternal relatives to express resistance or to refuse the idea of adopting. Later on, the former are less inclined to welcome the child and turn out to be less involved in his or her care (Rosnati & Bazzani, 2005). Evidently, the paternal branch of the family appears to have greater difficulty in accepting that its lineage, symbolically represented by its surname, will be carried on by an individual who is genetically foreign to the family unit. This resistance could be influenced by the Italian culture, which tends to attribute more importance to the paternal family line, and may not generalize to other cultures. It is evident, therefore, that the construction of the adoptive bond depends not exclusively on the relational network within the nuclear family but on the larger context of the extended family as well.

ADOPTIVE PARENTHOOD AND FILIATION: THE PROCESS OF RECIPROCAL LEGITIMIZATION

If these are the principal characteristics of the adoption transition, let us focus now on the building of adoptive parenthood and filiation since they are crucial elements for facing this challenge. Adoptive parenthood has a particular connotation in that it can be collocated in the realm of social generativity. By the term "generativity," Erikson (1982) meant "the concern to create and direct a new generation" that expresses itself in the "capacity of taking care of persons, products and ideas to which one has made a commitment." This concept is broader than that of procreation since it encompasses both the characteristics of *procreativity* and those of *productivity* and *creativity*. The latter usually refer not to the realm of biology but rather to the symbolic realm. Thus, the generative ethos, according to Erikson (1982), leads over time to a "more universal concern focused on the qualitative improvement of the life condition" of the next generation.

Snarey (1993) takes up the concept of generativity as defined by Erikson and identifies three types:

- *Biological generativity* indicates the giving of life.
- *Parental generativity* has to do with the care of one's own children and the capacity to develop their potential and autonomy.

- *Social generativity* refers to taking on the care of the next generation to which one's own children belong. If parenthood has to do with the care of children in the private sphere of the family, social generativity refers to a broader involvement with the next generation and a creative contribution to society in general.

The construction of the adoptive bond is therefore located "at the boundary," or, rather, at the intersection between parental and social generativity. Adoptive parenthood involves parental generativity in the sense of taking on the care of another's child as one's own; it involves social generativity in that it is a commitment that crosses the boundaries of one's own family group and becomes, in international adoption, the assumption of responsibility for an individual who belongs to another culture and often to another ethnic group. We can therefore speak about adoptive parenthood as a form of *social parenthood,* in which the parental bond is built in the absence of genetic continuity, family belonging is founded on the acknowledgment of a different origin, and parenthood itself is born from and legitimized as a response to a crucial social need.

Moreover, the construction of adoptive parenthood also requires both an inner and an interpersonal process of legitimization of the parental role. Even if the title of parent is conferred in a legal sense by the courts, there exists an inner process of assumption and legitimization of the parental role, that is, of *entitlement* (Cohen, Coyne, & Duvall, 1996). This term indicates that one has the right to exercise the role of parent and to designate the child as the one who will carry on his or her personal and family history. Entitlement is a process that has the effect of allowing the couple to feel they possess all the rights and privileges of parents, to accept the responsibility of the child's upbringing, and to experience the feeling of belonging to the family of that specific child. The construction of adoptive parenthood implies, therefore, the legitimization of oneself as the parent of that child with the acknowledgment of his or her own history and different origins. This legitimization is essentially an ethical dimension of the bond and it also has an interpersonal connotation: one legitimizes oneself but also one's spouse as the child's parent (Greco, Ranieri, & Rosnati, 2003).

Such a process of inner legitimization is also required in the case of biological parenthood, but in adoption it can be undermined by the absence of a shared genetic history or to the fact of not having experienced pregnancy and the first moments of the child's life. Entitlement also can be undermined when parents' expectations regarding the child diverge radically from the experience of actually raising the child. In addition, the legitimization process can be threatened by the adoptive parents' thoughts and feelings regarding their child's biological parents and by the related fantasy of having committed a "theft." In other words, adoptive parents may feel guilty, perhaps unconsciously, of having taken something (the child) that belongs to others. Thus, the challenge in adoption requires that one substitutes the logic of "either/or" (*either* one's own child *or* another's child) with the logic of "and/and" inasmuch as the adoptive child is at the same time one's own child (through adoption) and another's child (by birth). In short, adoptive parents must find a way of acknowledging and accepting the child's *dual connection* to two families (Brodzinsky et al., 1998; chapters 7 and 8 in this volume).

There is an aspect of reciprocity in the process of legitimization as well because the child is also involved in the task of legitimizing that specific man and that specific woman as his or her own parents and of acknowledging that he or she occupies a place in the continuity of the generations and belongs to a shared family history despite having different origins. This constitutes what it means to build adoptive filiation.

In order for this to happen, it is necessary that the child, over time, be able to answer the question, Why didn't they keep me? We know, in fact, that this is the crucial nexus around which the adoptive process evolves. Feelings of guilt, personal inadequacy, and rancor for what has happened are usually associated with abandonment and loss (Brodzinsky & Schechter, 1990; Brodzinsky et al., 1998; chapters 7 and 8 in this volume). These are the feelings with which the adopted child must come to terms. The sometimes compulsive search for one's biological parents, especially one's mother, has its roots in this question that remains unanswered.

Adoptive parenthood and filiation are, in truth, interdependent; Rosnati and Iafrate (1997) have revealed the existence of a significant correlation between these two aspects of family life. These researchers also have reported that adoptive parenthood and filiation are correlated with the quality of family relationships and, in particular, with parent–child communication and relational support. The more fluid the communication in the family and the more stable the relational bonds, the greater the sense of family belonging for both parents and the adopted child (see chapters 7 and 8 in this volume). In addition, adoptive parents who have a stronger sense of their own parenthood were shown to have children who felt a greater sense of belonging and were better able to "put down roots" in the adoptive family once there was a shared acknowledgment and acceptance of the child's different origin. For this reason, the construction of adoptive parenthood and filiation reveals itself to be a *joint* enterprise in which both parents and children are involved, even if in different ways.

THE ADOLESCENT TRANSITION IN ADOPTIVE FAMILIES: FROM THE FAMILIAL TO THE SOCIAL

Adolescent transition constitutes a crucial phase in the evolution of the adoptive bond because it discloses all the more clearly the family's relational scenario—laid down in prior phases—and also offers clues as to the success or failure of the adoptive process. The goal of this transition is to "ferry the younger generation toward the condition of adulthood" (Scabini & Iafrate, 2003). This phase therefore constitutes the critical nexus between the familial and the social and is, as already mentioned, particularly critical and salient in the case of adoption.

Adolescents are confronted with the challenging task of establishing a sense of personal identity. However, this process of individuation/differentiation from family usually is more complicated for teenage adoptees than their nonadopted peers, as there are two families that have psychological relevance for these individuals: the adoptive family, which is a part of the child's everyday life, and the biological family, about which he or she may have very little knowledge (Grotevant, 1997).

The task of the adopted adolescent is a "voyage backward" in time in order to reappropriate his or her own origins and find a deep sense of connection between present, past, and future. Personal identity cannot be built except by passing through this trial (Mackie, 1985). The adoptive family has a fundamental role to play in supporting the adolescent in facing up to this challenge.

Research in Italy and elsewhere that has focused on the quality of family relationships in this phase has revealed the existence of some elements common to adoptive and "biological" families as well as to relational patterns specific to each. It has been found that the two family forms share the centrality of the mother. The maternal figure stands as the principal point of reference: she is the one with whom children communicate more or to whom they go for advice and help when in need in both biological families (Carrà & Marta, 1995; Greene & Grimsley, 1990; Lanz & Rosnati, 1995; Noller & Callan, 1990; Youniss & Ketterlinus, 1987) and adoptive families (Lanz, Iafrate, Rosnati, & Scabini, 1999; Rosnati & Marta, 1997). Furthermore, in the case of adoptive families, research suggests that the mother–adolescent relationship constitutes the principal protective factor in relation to the development of psychological problems (Rosnati, 1998), while in nonadoptive families it is the bond between father and adolescent that provides the greatest degree of protection against adjustment difficulties (Carrà & Marta, 1995).

Furthermore, it is with respect to relationships with fathers that important differences emerge between the two family typologies, at least in Italy. It has been found that adopted adolescents of different ethnic groups experience communication with their father that is more fluid and less problematic and that they perceive a higher level of support compared to their peers who live in biological families (Rosnati & Marta, 1997): research carried out on Italian biological families has pointed out that the father usually has a more peripheral position in the relational network of his children, especially during adolescence (Carrà & Marta, 1995; Scabini & Iafrate, 2003). The adoptive father therefore demonstrates a greater involvement in the life and upbringing of his children that could also be ascribed to the task of mediating with the social domain—a task generally associated with the paternal figure—which is especially salient in adoption and even more so in interethnic adoption.

This finding also confirms the results obtained in other international studies on adoption. For example, research carried out in Canada by Sobol, Delaney, and Earn (1994) discovered that young adopted adults perceive their fathers as being emotionally closer and more supportive compared to nonadopted peers. In addition, research conducted in Israel by Levy-Shiff, Zoran, and Shulman (1997) revealed that in the case of international adoption, fathers turn out to be more involved in their children's upbringing than in cases of national adoptions. On the whole, these studies highlight the enhanced role played by fathers in interracial adoptive families.

Our results suggest that fathers equally share with their spouses not only the choice of social generativity through adoption but also the experiences involved in the preplacement period and the first meeting with the child. These experiences lead fathers to be actively involved with their adopted children from the very beginning.

Fava Viziello, Antonioli, Bartoli, Volpe, and Zancato (1996) and Greco et al. (2003) suggested that the construction of adoptive fatherhood in the early phase of the family life cycle is often more immediate and linear, whereas the process of the construction of adoptive motherhood resulted to be more complicated and nonlinear. In adoption, the mother must build a bond with the child even while "skipping" the biological factor, putting the woman in a situation of "advantage" in nonadoptive families.

In short, we could say that the child–mother relationship constitutes the sensitive point in the adoptive transition: if it is satisfying, it constitutes one of the fundamental protective factors for the child; if it is found to be wanting, it is without doubt the point of greatest weakness. The father, on the other hand, represents the main resource in adoptive families, especially in the case of interracial adoptions.

ADOPTIVE PARENTHOOD AND FILIATION IN ADOLESCENCE: A FAMILY RESEARCH STUDY

The research described in the remaining section of this chapter focuses on the construction of adoptive parenting, considered as a joint enterprise of parents and children. It is our intention to analyze and compare, from a family perspective, the perceptions of parents and adoptive children who are experiencing the challenging phase of adolescence. The literature on adoption is unanimous in discerning in family relationships the principal protective factor with respect to the risk connected to adoption (Borders, Black, & Pasley, 1998; Brodzinsky & Schechter, 1990; Brodzinsky et al.,

1998; see also chapters 6 to 8 in this volume). For this reason, we will explore possible links among family members' perception of the adoptive parenthood and filiation, the quality of family relationships, and various indicators of adopted adolescents' psychological well-being.

Our research focused on two dimensions of family functioning believed to be particularly crucial during the adolescent phase: parent–adolescent communication and support. According to Olson (1993), communication helps regulate emotional distance between family members during transition periods and especially during a young person's transition to adolescence (Olson et al., 1982). Through communication, parents and adolescents renegotiate their roles and relationships. Communication in the family should ideally provide an environment in which adolescents can learn appropriate social skills that will enable them to deal with interpersonal situations effectively and to find constructive solutions to their problems (Noller, 1995). Furthermore, some research has shown that children living in biological families perceive a lower level of openness and more problems in communication than do their parents (Barnes & Olson, 1985; D'Atena & Ardone, 1991; Lanz & Rosnati, 1995). This result could be interpreted as an indicator of the process of individuation/separation being carried out by adolescents. In other words, in their effort to differentiate themselves from their parents, these teenagers may become less open with their parents and view their family relationships as involving more difficulties. In contrast, Rosnati and Marta (1997) reported that adopted adolescents perceive a higher quality of communication with both mother and father than do their parents. This finding was interpreted as the tendency in adoptive children to idealize their parents as well as their difficulty in initiating the process of differentiation from the parental figures.

Parent–child support is also considered to be a crucial variable, especially during adolescence. Some studies have indicated that reciprocal support is inversely correlated with behavioral problems in young people, such as the use of illegal drugs (Wills & Clearly, 1996) and delinquency (Windle, 1992), as well as emotional problems and low self-esteem (Helsen, Vollebergh, & Meeus, 2000; Holahan & Moos, 1991; Holahan, Valentiner, & Moos, 1994). In our research, two variables of adolescent psychological well-being were used: self-esteem and an index of risk that reveals the presence of problems and difficulties connected the child's adoption status.

The choice of a family perspective in the study of family relationships carries with it various methodological implications. First of all, it is necessary to forge a unit of analysis based on the family that includes several members and generations (and not the single subject only). For this reason, our research is centered on the family triad composed of father, mother, and adopted child. In any case, only the comparison of the perceptions of multiple subjects makes it possible to fully delineate a picture as complex and multifaceted as that of the parent–child bond.

The designation of a family as unit of analysis is not in itself enough to guarantee coherence between the theoretically framed subject of interest (family relations) and the subsequent methodological choices: it is also necessary that the means by which data are processed be consistent with the family perspective (Lanz & Rosnati, 2002). In other words, one must identify procedures that are founded on the family unit of analysis and that utilize the nonindependence of family data as a source of information (Kenny, 1994; Kenny & Judd, 1986). In effect, subjects belonging to the same family have more similar perceptions than subjects belonging to different groups. As a consequence, the data furnished by members of the same family cannot be considered independent from either a theoretical or a statistical point of view: as a result, traditional statistical techniques such as analysis of variance and correlation cannot be used when the data derive from the same family unit (Lanz & Rosnati, 2002). Consequently, in our research we employed the multiple analysis of variance (MANOVA) for repeated measures as a means for analyzing the interdependent perceptions of family members in relation to adoptive parenthood and filiation. This analytical technique is considered well adapted to the type of family research we are conducting (Bray, Maxwell, & Cole, 1995; Lanz & Rosnati, 2002).

Based on the theoretical framework outlined previously and on the methodological considerations noted, our study had the following objectives:

1. To compare the perceptions of parents and children with respect to their perception of adoptive parenthood and filiation and to analyze if and to what extent they are affected by several structural variables, such as age, gender of the adolescent child, and his or her age at the time of adoption

2. To explore, on the one hand, possible connections between adoptive parenthood and filiation and, on the other, the quality of family relationships, here explored through communication and parent–child support

3. To shed light on the relationship existing between adoptive parenthood and filiation and the adolescent's well-being, using as indicators self-esteem and the existence of personal difficulties linked to adoption

The sample was composed of 230 adoptive families (father, mother, and child) with adolescent and young adult children between the ages of 12 and 24. Subjects were recruited through collaboration with associations working in the field of international adoption.

The distribution of the sample according to the child's age was as follows: 21.5 percent were younger than 14 years, 22.2 percent were between 15 and 16 years, 33 percent were between 17 and 19 years, and the rest, 23.3 percent, were older than 20 years. Adoptees were born in a foreign country and adopted by an Italian family when they were from 0 to 11 years old: the mean age at adoption was 4.3 years old. Slightly more than 40 percent of adopted adolescents were born in Latin American countries (Brazil, Chile, Bolivia, and so on), 58.2% in Asia (India, Sri Lanka, and so on), and 1.7 % in eastern European countries (the former Yugoslavia).[1] A slight majority of children were females (53%). Nearly half the adoptive families (45.7%) had only the target adopted child, 27.6 percent had two adopted children, and 2.4 percent had three adopted children. The remaining 24.3 percent were "mixed families" with one or two adopted children and one or two biological offspring. Adoptive fathers, on the average, were 47.8 years old and adoptive mothers 44.3 years old. The majority of families (87%) belong to a medium to high socioeconomic status, and only 13 percent can be defined as being of low socioeconomic status.

Subjects filled out a self-report questionnaire that was administered in three different versions for the adolescent, mother, and father. It provided information about age, gender, family composition, education, and socioeconomic status of the family. It included the following:

- *The Parent-Adolescent Communication Scale* by Barnes and Olson (1985) focuses on the free-flowing exchange of information between parents and their adolescents, the lack of constraint, degree of understanding and satisfaction experienced in these interactions, and the negative aspects of communication, such as hesitancy to share, selectivity, and caution in what is shared (e.g., "My father/mother/child is always a good listener," "When I ask questions, I get honest answers from my father/mother/child," "There are topics I avoid discussing with my father/mother/child"). The adolescents were requested to separately appraise communication with their mothers and with their fathers.

- *The Parent-Adolescent Support Scale* by Scabini and Cigoli (1992) aims to reveal the level of reliability of the bond between parents and adolescent, that is, reciprocal support and the extent to which adolescents can count on their parents and vice versa (e.g., "I can count on my mother/father/child when I need something," "My mother/father/child understands me"). Adolescents completed two versions of the scale: one focuses on the support between themselves and their mothers and the other on the support between themselves and their fathers.

- *The Perception of Adoptive Parenthood and Filiation Scales* by Iafrate and Rosnati (1998) measures the degree to which parents accept the adoptee as their own child, acknowledge his or her different origin, legitimize themselves as parents, and perceive the child as one who will continue the family history (e.g., "I feel at ease when I introduce my child as an adopted child," "I feel myself to be in every respect the mother/ father of my child"). The child's version measures the

---

1. The distribution with respect to country of origin is obviously different from that presented in the introductory paragraph since, as we are considering families with adolescents, we are referring to adoptions that occurred in Italy 10 to 20 years ago. In the 1980s until the mid-1990s, most adopted children in Italy came from India, Korea, and Brazil.

extent to which the adopted child perceives him- or herself as belonging to the adoptive family and to its history with respect to his or her different origin (e.g., " I feel guilty towards my parents when I dream of going back to my country of birth," "I consider my adoptive mother and father as my parents in every respect").

- *The Rosenberg Self-Esteem Scale and the Index of Adoption Related Difficulties*, the former of which is a well-known instrument measuring children's self-esteem and the latter of which assesses adoption-related difficulties in relationships with mother, father, siblings, friends, classmates, and boyfriends/girlfriends and indicates whether subjects have been victims of racial acts. Both can be considered indicators of the adolescent's well-being.

ADOPTIVE PARENTHOOD AND FILIATION: EFFECTS OF AGE, GENDER, AND AGE AT ADOPTION

Results indicated that adolescent's perception of adoptive filiation and parenthood were unrelated to their age and gender. It would appear, therefore, that perception of adoptive filiation and parenthood remains fairly stable throughout adolescence and that the construction of the adoptive bond is a task associated primarily with earlier developmental periods, with little evidence of additional evolution in the adolescent period.

Neither the gender of the adopted adolescent nor that of his or her parents appears to affect the adoptive bond. Males and females, mothers and fathers, all demonstrate analogous levels of adoptive parenthood and filiation. Thus, adopted males who, according to some studies, are at greater risk for the development of behavioral problems (i.e., Marcovitch et al., 1998; Stams, Juffer, Rispens, & Hocksbergen, 2000) do not seem to manifest additional problems in establishing the adoptive bond, at least in Italy.

The only discriminating variable was the age at adoption. The analysis of variance demonstrated that the age at the time of adoption (0 to 2, 3 to 5, and 6 to 11 years) affects both the perception of adoptive filiation and the perception of the parenthood of both mother and father. In particular, it emerged that children adopted early on, by the age of two, manifest as adolescents a higher level of adoptive filiation than those of children adopted when already school age. For both parents as well, the fact of having adopted a child younger than five years old facilitates the task of building a sense of parenthood. These parents as a consequence show a stronger perception of adoptive parenthood compared to parents who adopted school-age children (Table 9.1). In short, the earlier the child is introduced into the family, the easier the task of building the adoptive bond for both parents and child. This finding is in agreement with many other studies that have discerned a connection between the age at adoption and the development of relational difficulties and symptomatic

Table 9.1
Perception of adoptive parenthood and filiation as a function of age at adoption: means, standard deviations, and results of the analysis of variance

Perception of Adoptive Filiation Scale	means	standard deviation	F	p
0-2 years	4.28	.48		
3-5 years	4.09	.78	4.98	p < .01
6-11 years	3.84	.58		
Perception of Adoptive Parenthood Scale (mother)				
0-2 years	4.48	.45		
3-5 years	4.47	.50	5.82	p < .001
6-11 years	4.02	.76		
Perception of Adoptive Parenthood Scale (father)				
0-2 years	4.47	.43		
3-5 years	4.28	.71	4.92	p < .01
6-11 years	4.02	.72		

Superscripts ($^{a, b, c}$) show the group(s) with which differences are significant.

behaviors (Brand & Brinich, 1999; Brodzinsky et al., 1998; Howe, 1997; Marcovitch et al., 1998).

Logan, Morral, and Chambers (1998), however, note that it is not age of adoption placement per se that affects later adaptation and the appearance of symptomatic behaviors but rather the nature of the child's preplacement history (e.g., number of moves prior to the final placement, the experience of abuse or neglect, and so on). Clinical experience also confirms the importance of the quality of the child's preplacement history in relation to later adjustment patterns. Unfortunately, in the present study, we were unable to explore this aspect because of a lack of information regarding the children's lives while still in their countries of origin.

ADOPTIVE PARENTHOOD AND FILIATION IN A FAMILY PERSPECTIVE

A family typology was constructed using data from fathers, mothers, and adolescents regarding the Perception of Adoptive Parenthood and Filiation Scales. Each of the three subsamples (mothers, fathers, and adolescents) was divided in two groups: one that scored below its mean score (low parenthood/filiation) and one that scored above its mean score (high parenthood/filiation). Crossing data from parents and adolescent belong-

Table 9.2
Family types in relation to Adoptive Parenthood and Filiation Scales

	Number of subjects	Percentage
Type 1. All family members with low levels	36	17.9
Type 2. Child and one parent with low levels and the other parent with high level	21	10.4
Type 3. Child with low level and both parents with high levels	19	9.5
Type 4. Child with high level and both parents with low levels	23	11.4
Type 5. Child and one parent with high levels and one parent with low level	38	18.9
Type 6. All family members with high levels	64	31.8

ing to the same family unit, six types of families were constructed, as shown in Table 9.2.[2]

Data analyses focused on comparing the perception that children have of the communication with mother and with father among the family types (MANOVA for repeated measures). Results suggested that adopted adolescents in all family types assessed a better communication and a higher level of relational support with mother than with father. This result is consistent with other Italian research on adoptive families (Lanz et al., 1999) and with a number of Italian and international studies on biological families with adolescents (Carrà & Marta, 1995; Lanz & Rosnati, 1995; Noller, 1995; Youniss & Smollar, 1985).

Family typology was associated with either parent–child communication or relational support: it emerged that adolescents belonging to type 1 (all family members with a low levels of adoptive parenthood/filiation) and type 2 (child and one parent with low levels and the other parent with a high level of adoptive parenthood) scored significantly lower on the parent–child communication and support, either with mother or with father, than all other family groups. These differences emerged only when the adolescent's point of view is considered. In contrast, parents' perception of communication and support do not vary according to the family type. This result indicates that the adoptive bond and the quality of family relations—measured through communication and support—are strongly

---

2. The initial eight-type family typology was modified, as two groups were aggregated into type 4 and another two groups into type 5 following either theoretical assumptions or numerical considerations. There are no adolescent gender differences in the six types of families.

interwoven in the adoptee's point of view. In other words, the family relational network has a great influence on the child's process of inner legitimization, as other research has already pointed out (Brodzinsky & Schechter, 1990; Brodzinsky et al., 1998; Rosnati & Iafrate, 1997).

Adoptive Parenthood and Filiation and the Adolescent's Well-Being

Further data analysis was carried out in order to assess differences among family types concerning adolescents' well-being (as measured through self-esteem and an index of adoption related difficulties). It emerged that adolescents belonging to family type 6 (all family members with a high levels of adoptive parenthood/filiation) and type 5 (child and one parent with high levels and the other parent with a low level) scored significantly higher in self-esteem and had fewer adoption-related difficulties than adolescents of type 1 (all family members with low levels of adoptive parenthood/filiation) and type 2 (child and one parent with low levels and the other parent with a high level of adoptive parenthood).

In sum, the construction of the family typology revealed that the construction of adoptive bonds is a *family enterprise* in which both parents and children give their own contribution while playing different roles. First of all, it emerged that adolescents who belong to family units in which all members perceive high levels of adoptive parenthood and filiation (type 6) assess their family relationships as being more positive in terms of communication with parents and support and manifest higher self-esteem and fewer personal problems connected to adoption. These results could be partially extended to families in which the adolescent and at least one parent, whether father or mother, have a high level of adoptive parenthood and filiation (type 5).

It was also found that the families most at risk—in which adolescents experience unsatisfactory family relationships, low self-esteem, and a higher number of personal problems connected to adoption—are those in which the adoptive bond has not been consolidated among family members and in which all members or at least the child and one parent—whether father or mother—show very low levels of adoptive parenthood and filiation (types 1 and 2).

These results also shed light on the adolescent's perception of adoptive bond that turned out to be deeply affected by the quality of the family relational network. They also outline a particular "sensitivity" in the adopted child whose psychological well-being depends mostly on the quality of the relational context into which he or she has been integrated. We could infer that parents—or at least one of them—are expected to legitimize their adoptive offspring and transmit a deep sense of family belonging; otherwise, the adolescent is not able to "put down roots" in the family context. Indeed, many authors, as already mentioned, have stressed that the quality of family relationships constitutes the most important protective factor for the adopted child (Brodzinsky & Schechter, 1990; Brodzinsky et al., 1998; Rosnati & Marta, 1997). The results of the present study provide an additional confirmation of this finding. Future research should deepen our understanding of this relationship between adoptive parenthood and filiation, family relationships, and individual well-being, seeking to reveal the existence as well as the direction of a possible causal connection between them.

IMPLICATIONS FOR RESEARCH AND PRACTICE

The principal goal of this contribution has been to analyze the construction of adoptive parenthood and filiation from a family perspective with reference to the quality of family bonds and the well-being of the adolescent child. The assumption of a family perspective and consequently the use of a family unit of analysis has made it possible to compare the perceptions of several family members. This approach to research has been fruitful in the present study and should be implemented in the future because it allows one to grasp the truly relational aspects of the data. Moreover, this approach allowed us to highlight the parts played by different family members in the process of developing family bonds.

Considering adoption as a family transition involving several generations suggests numerous ideas for future research. First, one could broaden the perspective by taking into consideration the respective parents' families of origin in order to analyze if and to what degree intergenerational relationships affect the successful negotiation of the challenge presented by adoption. Greco and Rosnati (1998) have already pointed out the influence of grandparents on the construction of the adoptive pact. But there is still a lack of empirical evidence concerning whether and to what extent the attitudes, beliefs, and/or support offered by grandparents affect the adjustment of adoptive parents and/or their adopted children.

Second, it is becoming increasingly necessary that studies adopt a longitudinal scheme that makes it possible to monitor changes over time. This approach would facilitate the identification of not only risk factors associated with adjustment difficulties and symptomatic behavior but also, and more important, factors of resiliency that allow most families, even in the face of crisis and adversity, to find a constructive way of making the adoptive transition and build healthy family relationships. Although our results suggest that adoptive parenthood and filiation are probably resolved during the childhood years (and subsequently show a certain stability throughout adolescence), only a longitudinal study can confirm these findings and single out crucial turning points in the process.

Another question of interest having both theoretical and practical implications is related to international adoption. This type of adoption is more widespread in Italy today and often involves interracial and interethnic placements. It is unknown, however, whether the development of the adoptive pact differs in families in which parent and child do not share the same somatic traits and racial/ethnic heritage. Future research will need to find a way of disentangling interracial factors from other adoption-related issues in the adjustment process.

The reflections we have thus far offered also point to many useful considerations for professionals working in the field of adoption. Recent transformations in the legal procedures in Italy—as pointed out in the introduction—attribute to public service psychologists and social workers the responsibility for preparing and supporting adoptive couples throughout the adoption process. Unfortunately, these professionals often lack specific training in adoption. In order to better serve the needs of adoptive families, social workers and psychologists require updated training in social casework and clinical and parenting issues related to adoptive family life.

It also must be emphasized that because the process of adoption is indeed a risky transition, adoptive families need to be followed by adoption professionals over a protracted period of time that does not end immediately after the child is placed in the home. Unfortunately, most Italian families today are left alone—or they want to be alone—in face the challenges of adoption once the child is placed with them. Postadoption services are still in short supply and irregularly offered in Italy. Specific parent-training programs for adoptive parents need to be developed and disseminated widely in order to empower the resources and coping abilities of the adoptive family relational network. Adoptive families need to be supported in the development of the adoptive bond, not only immediately after the child's placement, but during the school-age years and adolescence, which research has shown to be critical developmental phases for adoptees (Brodzinsky & Pinderhughes, 2002; Brodzinsky et al., 1998). They also need help in facilitating more open and honest communication about adoption (see chapters 6 to 8 in this volume). In particular, adoptive parents often need help acknowledging and respecting the differences in adoptive family life, the child's dual connection to two families, and the value of the child's origins. In addition, they often feel dismay about how to handle sensitive topics associated with the child's past (e.g., parental psychopathology, neglect, abuse, and abandonment). Confusion also is experienced by adoptive parents regarding discussing the child's origins when there is little or no information about the birth family or the circumstances of the relinquishment or abandonment. These are critical areas in which adoptive parents need guidance and support from adoption professionals.

We also believe that adoptive parents could benefit from ongoing contact with others who have adopted children. In particular, parent groups could have a very positive influence on adoptive parents by not only providing them with relevant adoption and parenting information but also offering them emotional support. In addition, we believe that parent support groups could help prevent psychosocial maladjustment, especially during adolescence. To date, the availability of postadoption parent support groups is quite limited in Italy. However, this calls for the acknowledgment and the assumption of a certain responsibility on the part of society with regard to adoption. Indeed, as adoption constitutes the social response to the problem of abandoned children, society is required not only to control but also to support and empower adoptive families throughout the transition.

Another practical implication emerges from the study of intergenerational bonds: the exchange with the parents' respective families of origin is without doubt an area that needs special attention during the process of reviewing couples (when the court must declare that a couple is fit to adopt or not). Furthermore, as we have noted, grandparents directly influence family functioning during the adoption transition and their relationship with their grandchild is of fundamental importance for the process of integration in the adoptive family. Consequently, it would be advisable for grandparents to be involved in the postadoption training sessions either separately or along with adoptive parents.

Finally, one hopes that there will come about, in the area of research as well as in that of clinical intervention and support of couples, a change in professional perspective: from a "pathogenic" vision of adoption, that is, as constituting the cause of problems (as it has been considered in large part of the psychological literature on this topic), to a "salutogenic" vision, to borrow the term used by Antonovsky (1979, 1989). The latter perspective focuses on those factors within the individual, the family, and the social network that protect the individual from stress and facilitate the development of emotional well-being. For too long, adoption has been viewed through a negative lens. It is time to recall that adoption emerged as a solution to the problems confronting the abandoned, neglected, and/or abused child. Although we do not wish to ignore the reality of the challenges associated with adoptive family life, it is important to bring greater balance to the focus on adoption and to recognize that this social service practice has served children quite well and that the vast majority of adopted children and their parents show very normal patterns of adjustment.

Chapter 10

International Adoptions in Scandinavia: Research Focus and Main Results

Monica Dalen

In Scandinavia, international adoptions began at the end of the 1960s, and today there are around 76,000 individuals who have been adopted into these countries: Sweden 43,000, Norway 16,000, and Denmark 16,000. The first adopted children to arrive in Scandinavia came from South Vietnam and South Korea. Today, they come from several other Asian countries, Latin America, and Ethiopia. Since the collapse of the Soviet Union, children are also being adopted from Russia, Bulgaria, and Romania. During the past five years, most children have been adopted from China.

Research into this field started at the end of 1970s. Sweden and Denmark were the first of the Scandinavian countries to present some results about internationally adopted children's adaptation to their new families (Gardell, 1979; Pruzan, 1977). Sweden carried out more comprehensive research work in the 1980s and part of the 1990s (Cederblad, 1982, 1989, 1991; Cederblad & Hook, 1986; Cederblad, Hook, Irhammar, & Mercke, 1999; de Geer, 1992; Halldèn, 1981; Hene, 1987, 1988; Hofvander, 1978; Irhammar, 1997) as well as the twenty-first century (Hjern, Lindblad, & Vinnerljung, 2002; Irhammar & Cederblad, 2000). However, during the past 15 years, Norway has been the most active country in doing research on international adoptions (Botvar, 1995, 1999; Brottveit, 1996, 1999; Dalen, 1995, 1999, 2001, 2002; Dalen & Rygvold, 1999; Dalen & Sætersdal, 1987, 1992, 1999; Howell, 1998, 1999, 2001; Rygvold, 1999; Sætersdal & Dalen, 1991, 1999, 2000).

In this chapter, we focus on some main results from the research on international adoptions carried out in Scandinavia during the past 20 years. Reading through most of the research done in this region, we have picked out some main topics that should give a picture of the activity in this field. First we describe what we can learn from children arriving in extremely poor physical and mental condition, as exemplified by children who were adopted into Norway at the end of the Vietnam War. Then we will look more closely into internationally adopted children's language development and school performances. The next topic is related to the adoptees' identity formation, with a focus on how they handle their differences in outlook and ethnic background. We then describe different patterns of interaction in adoptive families, followed by a section on adoption outcomes in Scandinavia. The chapter concludes with some reflection about implications for further research and practice.

LESSONS LEARNED FROM CHILDREN ARRIVING IN EXTREMELY POOR CONDITION

The first studies on international adoptions in Scandinavia focused on the adopted children's physical health and psychosocial adaptation (Dalen & Sætersdal, 1992; Gardell, 1979; Gunnarby, Hofvander, Sjölin, & Sundelin, 1982; Halldèn, 1981; Hofvander, 1978; Proos, 1992). Results from these studies showed that most of the adopted children had problems in the initial period in the new families. Although the majority of the children came in pretty good physical condition, they had some psychological problems in meeting the new situation. Many of the children had sleeping problems, and going to sleep in particular was a problem. For others, the greatest problem was related to food and eating: some children did not want to eat at all, while others overate and were completely focused on food. Most of the children showed evidence of anxiety and insecurity. They wanted to lie in their parents' bed for a long time and reacted with fear toward strangers. However, after a period of three to six months, the adjustment difficulties diminished for most of the children, although for a small percentage, the problems lasted for a longer time. These were the children who arrived in the most poor condition both physically and psychologically and who had often had a difficult time in their native country because of war, violence, abuse, malnutrition, and other lack of care.

Studies in Norway have had a special focus on one group of these vulnerable children, the Vietnamese-born children who arrived in this country during the Vietnam War (Dalen & Sætersdal, 1992; Sætersdal & Dalen, 1999; Schjelderup-Mathiesen & Nytrøhaug, 1977). They were in extremely poor physical and mental condition and in many ways represent an extreme group. Few groups of adoptees have had more traumatic early childhood experiences, and their fate is of special interest in a discussion about the reversibility of early childhood trauma. Their story provides an interesting illustration of how children raised under difficult conditions develop and adjust socially and psychologically.

Descriptions of disorientation and bewilderment were typical in the parents' accounts of the initial adjustment period. In interviews with the adoptive parents, they described the children as passive, apathetic, frightened, retarded, underweight, and physically sick. The following description was typical:

When she came to us she was at least two years old, but we believe she was older. She was in a pitiful condition and weighed only seven kilos. The hospital told us she was enervated, dehydrated, and on the verge of shock. She had boils, infection, and diarrhea. She had no expression on her face of either joy or sorrow. I carried her close to me day and night for at least three months. She always carried a rusk and a tangerine in each hand, and whenever she dropped either of them, she became hysterical. She sometimes had convulsions and fits of temper at night, so we understood that she suffered.

Many parents expressed worry and anxiety about the heavy responsibilities they had undertaken. Medical authorities told the parents that these children had very little chance of growing up without mental and physical defects. Along with anxiety and feelings of inadequacy, many parents talked about how much they were moved by the helplessness and pathetic condition of their children. The adopted children's total dependence and vulnerability affected them in the same way as parents of newborns. The adoptees' total helplessness intensified the attachment and promoted the bonding between parents and children in a way that is difficult to achieve with older adopted children who arrive in better physical and age-relevant mental states. The initial period gave parent and child a chance to revive parts of the child's lost infancy.

The families adopting children from Vietnam were atypical of adoptive parents in general. Most of the couples already had biological children. This might explain their ability to cope with the strains and challenges of the adjustment period. Their previous experience as parents enabled them to rely on their own judgment and feelings about what was right and wrong in situations, enabling them to resist contradictory advice from both professionals and friends. One mother to a child arriving at the age of two and a half years put it this way:

And everybody said that she would become impossible if we continued to carry her with us everywhere. We had an uncle who was a child psychiatrist, and he also emphasized that. But we had to trust our own feelings. She needed us all the time then, and that was most important. Once secure, she remained so from the time she was five years old.

Another factor that helped these families cope was the presence of older siblings who often acted as intermediaries, especially in families where the child was too afraid of adults to relate to their adoptive parents. For most of the Vietnamese-born adoptees, the adjustment problems lasted for over a year. Then their development came "as an explosion." Once they had overcome their initial medical problems, they developed "iron health." Psychologically and socially, the majority of these children also developed well.

In interviewing these children as adolescents and young adults, it was evident that most of the group did very well (Dalen & Sætersdal, 1992; Sætersdal & Dalen, 1999). Although some of the adoptees told about some major problems during adolescence related to school performance, social relationships, and identity formation, we were impressed of their mastering of life, especially in view of their condition on arrival in Norway many years ago. In other words, they present a positive picture that indicates that early childhood traumas and deprivation can be reversed or modified by a caring and devoted family setting.

There are truly some lessons to learn from the adoptive parents' way of handling these traumatized children's initial adjustment problems. International literature supports the notion that risk to development competence is mediated by the family environment (Garmezy, 1987; McGuinness, McGuinness, & Dyer, 2000; Rutter et al., 2000; Sameroff, Seifer, Zax, Barocas, & Greenspan, 1992). One of the most important protective factors seems to be the establishment of a positive relationship with a competent adult, in this case, adoptive parents. This can be exemplified by findings from research carried out with children adopted from Romania (Rutter et al., 2000). Most of these children were also in very poor physical and mental condition. They were described as severely malnourished with weights below the third percentile, and over half functioned developmentally in the retarded range. The children were followed up and assessed at the age of four. The improvement with respect to weight and height was dramatic. The vast majority of the children had weights and heights within the normal range, and scarcely any were below the third percentile. The follow-up study of the Romanian children also showed that cognitive gains continued over quite prolonged periods of time. Claims that early privation inevitably leads to "irreversible deficit" are clearly wrong. Rutter and his coworkers argue that there can be no doubt that, from the point of view of the individual children, they have benefited enormously from adoption into U.K. families (see chapter 4 in this volume).

Another study carried out on children adopted from the former Soviet Union to the United States also supports these findings (McGuinness et al., 2000). Many of these children had experienced abuse, abandonment, or neglect between birth and entry into institutions. The results from this study also supported the idea that the adoptive environments can serve as buffers between the risks encountered by the children and the subsequent development of competence within the adoptive family.

SPECIAL ATTENTION TO INTERNATIONALLY ADOPTED CHILDREN'S LANGUAGE DEVELOPMENT

Scandinavian researchers have paid particular attention to the internationally adopted children's development and mastery of language (Berntsen & Eigeland, 1987; Dalen & Rygvold, 1999; de Geer, 1992; Hene, 1987, 1988; Lyngstøl, 1994; Rygvold, 1999). This may be due to the fact that the Nordic region is a small linguistic area and that a common language is one of the signs of belonging and attachment. It is also natural to bear in mind that language is an integral part of a person's cognitive, social, and emotional development.

Learning a new mother tongue is a vulnerable process, and a third of the internationally adopted children do have some language problems (Dalen & Sætersdal, 1992; Dalen & Rygvold, 1999; Rygvold, 1999). The researchers in this field have focused on two main forms of language skills: *day-to-day language* and *school language skills*. Day-to-day language is the contextualized language in which meaning and understanding are anchored in the here-and-now situation to the same extent as in the words themselves. It is the language form that is used in normal everyday speech, where the children can utilize situational and nonverbal cues.

School language is decontextualized language in which meaning and understanding are not imparted through the situation itself to any great extent. Examples of this are oral communication in the form of lecture-like teaching, messages given to the entire class, and written texts.

Several research projects have shown that the adopted children's language problems are particularly linked to the use of the language at a higher language-cognitive level (school language). Compared to Norwegian-born pupils, the internationally adopted pupils as a group have significantly lower school language skills (Dalen, 1995, 2001; Dalen & Rygvold, 1999; Rygvold, 1999). A few studies have focused on subgroups within the adoptees (Dalen, 2001; Dalen & Rygvold, 1999; Rygvold, 1999). The results from these studies show that there is a great disparity within the adopted group. Adoptees from Asia have better school language skills, some of them even better than their Norwegian-born counterparts, while adoptees from Latin America have lower performances. The same studies showed no significant differences between the adopted and nonadopted sample in their day-to-day language skills.

Studies have indicated that it is very difficult for most adopted children to continue to use their mother tongue, even for children who were slightly older when they were adopted and who came from Spanish-speaking countries (Dalen, 1995; de Geer, 1992). The children are very reluctant to use their mother tongue. They are eager to learn their new language and need the parents' support in the language acquisition.

Some studies find that children at risk for language impairment are the late adoptees (Berntsen & Eigeland, 1987, Dalen & Sætersdal, 1992; Gardell, 1979). However, even if the extent of language impairment seems to increase with adoption age, adoptees arriving in their first months of life exhibit these problems as well. Dalen and Rygvold (1999) found no connection between adoption age and language skills either in adoptees as a group or in the group of adoptees from Latin America and Asia. These results apply to both day-to-day and school language skills.

Research carried out in the United States confirms the Scandinavian results to a certain degree (Federici, 2003; Gindis, 1999; Gioia, 2003). However, these studies employ a more neuropsychological approach and view language in a broader sense. The researchers are often psychologists or neurologists and are seldom associated with language and speech professions. In describing the internationally adopted children's cognitive language deficiency, they use the term *executive dysfunction* as an umbrella term encompassing those interrelated skills necessary for purposeful, goal-directed activities, which also include mastery of language.

SCHOOL PERFORMANCE AMONG INTERNATIONALLY ADOPTED CHILDREN

Little research has focused on the educational achievements of internationally adopted children. In recent years, some studies in Norway have shown that internationally adopted children have poorer school performance than nonadopted children (Dalen, 1995, 2001; Dalen & Rygvold, 1999; Kvifte-Andresen, 1992). The results also documented a great diversity within the adopted group. Adoptees from Asia are performing very well, some even better than their native-born classmates, while adoptees from Latin America have lower school performances. The disparity is greater within the adopted group than within the nonadopted group. The Scandinavian results are supported by similar findings from international research on school performance among internationally adopted children (Hoksbergen, Juffer, & Waardenburg, 1987; McGuinness et al., 2000; Rutter et al., 2000; Verhulst, Althaus, & Verluis-den Bieman, 1990).

As a group, internationally adopted children are different from nonadopted children in many ways that could explain the differences in school performances. All have experienced a change in the persons with the prime responsibility for caring for them in early childhood. Many of the children were conceived and born under very difficult conditions. As mentioned before, they have also experienced an interruption in natural language development.

The knowledge about what the children have experienced before adoption is, however, often limited. There is also very little specific information about the child's biological parents. We know, however, that many of the children have spent their first year(s) in an institution or an orphanage. This may have serious adverse effects on the children because of the absence of a close and continuous relationship with a caring adult.

The Scandinavian studies on adopted children's school performance have also documented that a high percentage of them develop some sort of hyperactive behavior, such as restlessness and an inability to concentrate for long periods of time (Dalen, 1995, 2001; Dalen & Rygvold, 1999; Kvifte-Andresen, 1992). Hyperactive behavior affects the child's learning and social functioning in a school situation. Hyperactive children are easily distracted and have relatively short attention spans. As a result, they may be subjected to an increased risk of developing learning difficulties.

Research from countries outside Scandinavia confirms that some kind of hyperactive behavior is often found among internationally adopted children (Brodzinsky, Schechter, Braff, & Singer, 1984; Grotevant & McRoy, 1988; Hoksbergen, ter Laak, van Dijkum, Rijk, & Stoutjesdijk, 2003; Kenny et al., 1967; McGuinness et al., 2000; Roy et al., 2000; Rutter et al., 2000; Silver, 1989; Verhulst et al., 1990; Verhulst, 2000a; also, see also chapters 1 and 6 in this volume). The diagnostic term attention-deficit/hyperactivity disorder (ADHD) is often used in these studies, and Hoksbergen et al. (2003) showed that around 15 percent of children adopted from Romania clearly demonstrated symptoms of ADHD. McGuinness et al. (2000) also found a high percentage (13.3%) of children with the diagnosis of ADHD among adoptees from the former Soviet Union as compared to the U.S. population (3% to 6%). She relates this to the fact that children born to women who have used alcohol during pregnancy are at increased risk for symptoms consistent with ADHD. Many of the children adopted from eastern Europe show symptoms of fetal alcohol spectrum (FAS) disorders (Frederici, 2003; McGuinness et al., 2000; Mitchell, 2001) As a result, they may also be susceptible to an increased risk of developing learning difficulties.

The Scandinavian studies on school performances have documented that adoptive parents are far more supportive of the child's school situation than the parents of native-born children (Dalen, 1995, 2001; Dalen & Rygvold, 1999; Tessem, 1998). They more often helped their children with their homework and were more involved in the day-to-day life at school. This can easily lead to a positive effect on a child's school performances. One should, however, also be aware that adoptive parents sometimes set unreasonably high standards for their children's academic performances, and this in turn may have a negative effect on the child's self-esteem and learning process.

It is difficult to explain the differences within the group of adoptees because of the lack of information about the children's histories; knowledge of the factors that may confine or improve development and learning must be taken into consideration. Genetic as well as environmental factors may interact in a way that may lead to impaired skills in different areas. One should also know more about how children are selected for adoption in different countries.

IDENTITY FORMATION AND SEARCH FOR ORIGINS: NO KEY ANSWER

Research has documented that adoptees have "additional work" to do when forming their identities (Brottveit, 1999; Sætersdal & Dalen, 1999). They have to integrate the awareness of their background into their perception of their personality. At some time or other, they have to deal with the painful insight that being adopted means not only being "chosen" but also being "rejected" and that adoption not only is a way of *creating* a family but also involves the *loss* of a family. Grotevant (1997; see also chapter 8 in this volume) points to the adopted children's additional challenges of integrating their history as an adopted person into their emerging sense of identity. Identity development for them thus involves constructing a narrative that somehow includes, explains, accounts for, or justifies their adoptive status. In coming to terms with themselves as adults, individuals need to know who they are as adopted persons.

Another key aspect of internationally adopted teenagers' identity development is their attitude to their own ethnicity. If the manner in which the adoptees *themselves* feel they identify (ethnic self-identification) is the same as the way that *others* categorize them (external self-identification), then there is no problem. It becomes more of a conflict if a child feels Scandinavian but, because of his or her "different " appearance, is treated as being non-Scandinavian. Identity and formation of identity are closely connected to relationships with others. The ethnic component is a complicating factor in the same way the adoption component is.

Attitude to Appearance, Culture, and Background

The adoptees' appearance is the *ethnic marker* that sets them apart from their own families from the beginning and that later puts them in category of being "alien," like immigrants or refugees. Other markers that otherwise distinguish ethnic minorities, such as their language, cultural behavior, dialect, body language, clothes, cultural norms, and so on, will not be any different from those of the adoptees' new families or the Scandinavians around them. Their appearance is the reason why they are often assumed to be immigrants or refugees. These are groups with which the adoptees themselves do not identify and that have low social status in the Scandinavian countries. It is not *their appearance in itself* that is the problem but rather the fact that their appearance sets them apart from their family, siblings, relatives, and friends. Their appearance is the visible marker that identifies them as being "different" and non-Scandinavian.

International adoptees are more accepting of their background than they are of their appearance. For some, their ideas about their cultural background are strongly linked to their thoughts about the adoption itself and their own biological family. They do not want to think too much about a past that no longer feels relevant to them. Several of them also refrain from raising any questions about this because they care about their parents and are afraid of hurting their feelings.

Attitudes toward Immigrants and Refugees

Young international adoptees have a varied, ambivalent, and complex attitude to both their own ethnic groups in Scandinavia and other immigrants. Most teenagers stated, in different ways and more or less covertly, that they wanted to distance themselves from immigrants and refugees (Brottveit, 1996, 1999; Sætersdal & Dalen, 1999, 2000). Such a distancing may be physical or psychological. They distanced themselves physically from immigrants in the school playground, on buses, and at social events in public places. The distancing could also be psychological. So, even though many had had immigrants in their class at school, very few had been friends with them.

Most of them rejected any communication of interest with immigrant groups. In this way, they also lost the opportunity for obtaining information on current conditions in their native country or on the country's religion, traditions, and customs, in which many of them otherwise showed an interest in other "nondangerous" contexts. Interviews with young adults adopted from Colombia, India, Korea, and Vietnam all confirm this distancing (Brottveit, 1999; Sætersdal & Dalen, 1999, 2000).

Follow-up studies of adult Vietnamese men and women who had been adopted and were now in their thirties showed that these had a more clarified attitude to their ethnicity as adults (Sætersdal & Dalen, 1999). The question of adoption, their biological family, and their attitude to immigrants and refugees no longer interested them in the same way. The problems that were so important during their teenage years were no longer problems or were lesser problems than they expected. They were now more interested in the present and the future.

Scandinavian Membership

The research carried out in all the Scandinavian countries shows that it is very important for internationally adopted teenagers to identify themselves as Danish, Swedish, or Norwegian (Brottveit, 1999; Irhammar, 1997;

Sætersdal & Dalen, 1999; Rørbech, 1989). In the following, we will talk about the concept of a "Scandinavian membership" that includes assertions of belonging with family, friends, boyfriends/girlfriends, and other primary social groups for the adoptees. The parents define their adopted children primarily on the basis of their own social class and status. They believe it is particularly important for those who "look like" immigrants to get an education. A high social status is a strategy for avoiding racism. The fear of being confused with immigrants, that racists will "make a mistake" and discriminate against the adopted children, is just as strong in the adopted themselves as in their parents. Such feelings are reflected in all the Scandinavian surveys of adults who were adopted as children.

It was also clear that the internationally adopted teenagers who identified themselves as being mainly Swedish, Norwegian, or Danish had fewer psychological problems and greater self-esteem than those who felt very different from their peer group as measured by interviews and on assessment scales (Botvar, 1999; Irhammar, 1997; Rørbech, 1989).

SEARCH FOR ORIGIN

A Swedish study focused especially on the international adopted children's search for their origin (Irhammar & Cederblad, 2000). In this study, a distinction was made between an *inner search* (thoughts about their biological family) and an *outer search* (a more active search for information about the biological family). The majority of adoptees (70%) in this study engage in some kind of inner search by thinking about their biological family, women significantly more often than men. This group was divided into four subgroups with respect to their interest in an outer search for their biological and/or ethnic origins. One group (30%) was interested in searching for both their biological and their ethnic origins, while another group of about the same size (29%) was not interested in their origins at all. A third group (31%) was interested only in biological but not in ethnic origins, and the last group (10%) was interested only in ethnic origin.

About half of the 70 percent of the adoptee who engaged in inner search had talked about this to their adoptive parents, and a further 14 percent had talked to someone outside the family. However, more than one-third had kept their thoughts to themselves. Most often, the adoptees showed interest in whom they resembled and whether they had siblings in their country of birth. They missed stories from the first period in their life. Irhammar interprets this as a search for a mirror in which to find themselves reflected. However, a small group (7%) was more intensively preoccupied by such thoughts. This group had a significantly lower degree of self-esteem compared to those who thought often or less often about their biological family. For this group, the inner search seemed to be less of a search for a mirror than a wish to escape from an unsatisfactory life situation.

More than half of those who showed an inner search for their biological family also wanted to try to get more information about the family. There were no statistical differences between women and men with respect to this outer, more active search. Adoptees who had grown up in families where the parents had encouraged them to voice their thoughts and feelings about their origin were more interested in these issues. Studies on search behavior in international literature demonstrate different conclusions as to whether the need to search is found mostly among adoptees with unsatisfactory adoptive experiences. However, the studies agree that the majority of searchers are females in young adulthood. There is a need for more research in this area to determine the psychological meaning of search behavior for international adoptees (see chapter 7 in this volume).

Coping Strategies

When they are young, internationally adopted children are relatively well protected against discrimination by their families. On the whole, their schools and local environment shield them because they are accepted and recognized as members of Scandinavian families. However, the protection during childhood disappears once the child becomes a teenager and has to face many situations alone. Strangers may not identify them as Scandinavians and may treat them as immigrants or refugees, with all the discriminatory attitudes that this involves.

Brottveit (1999) describes Korean and Colombian adoptees' attitudes to their own ethnicity as three different ways of relating to this: the *Norwegian*, the *double-ethnic*, and the *cosmopolitan*. The *Norwegian* is a person who insists on being Norwegian and often refuses to give special importance to his "roots." This kind of identity has to be *confirmed*. The *double-ethnic* identity describes a person who pays much attention to her background and the consequences of her exotic appearance. A person with this kind of "double-ethnic" identity can be said to build on an additional identity that must be *discovered*. The *cosmopolitan* identity describes a person who stresses neither his Norwegian nor his ethnic identity. Adoptees in this group show a kind of openness towards the world, and this identity has to be *created*. All three solutions are compatible with the adoptees having a good self-image and secure identity, including their view of their own appearance, which is crucial for being able to deal with external categorization when this conflicts with their own self-image.

Sætersdal & Dalen (1999) identified two types of strategies for coping that resulted in harmonious personal developments. The first type is characterized by an active exploration of the adoptees' adoptive status, ethnic identity, and biological backgrounds. This is a process of increasing awareness that results in the adopted person recognizing his or her situation in life as being internationally adopted. It can be described as "black is beautiful—and I am me." They also found another, more defensive and nonexploratory process that also seems to result in good psychological and social adaptation. Unlike the first type, this is characterized not by exploration and a process of increasing awareness but rather by a *denial* of the significance of the adoptees' own genetic and cultural background, a Norwegian reinterpretation of the concept of identity. In order for such an identity interpretation to succeed, those around them must recognize the international adoptees as Norwegian. One can look on such a defensive process as a sad compliance with a homogeneous society's pressure to assimilate.

This way of "solving" one's identity problems is often an effective strategy for coping during the teenage years, however, since it gives the adoptees a longed-for feeling of being included in the community and being like everyone else. As they grow into adulthood, the adoptees seem more able to take on board the complexities of a double-ethnic identity (Sætersdal & Dalen, 1999). The most important factor for internationally adopted teenagers and adults is for them to receive confirmation that they really belong, both as member of their nuclear and extended families and as a member of the society they have become a part of. There seems to be no "key" answer to how to arrive at a harmonious understanding of one's identity regarding who one is and how one wants to be defined by society. That is why the eternal existential question Who am I? has a deeper, more complicated meaning for this group than for many others.

The research on identity formation shows that international adoptees develop their identities in significantly different ways. This is in line with what Grotevant pointed out in his article from 1997. From his study on identity formation, he concludes that for some adoptees the process of constructing their identity is very difficult, while for others it is less problematic. He also makes a very important statement in saying that the act of struggling to construct a functional sense of identity is not in itself a sign of pathology.

INTERACTION IN ADOPTIVE FAMILIES

Forming a new family is a real challenge no matter how it is done. Any interaction in the new family must develop over a period of time, and the quality of this interaction is affected by several factors. In this chapter we will focus on the degree of similarity between child and parent in the adoptive family as well as the family's ability to deal with similarities and differences. Actually, this is a question of degree of flexibility in terms of family interaction and the approach to child rearing. In adoptive families where the limits of acceptable behavior are very restrictive and rigid, developing successful interaction is more of a challenge than in families where there is more tolerance and leniency for flexibility. In all families, perceived similarities and differences will affect interaction between parents and children, but this is perhaps an even more fundamental theme in families where children have been adopted from abroad because the differences in appearance are so obvious.

Similarity and difference is a theme frequently focused on in the literature on adoption (Dalen & Sætersdal, 1992; Grotevant & McRoy, 1988; Kirk, 1964, 1981, 1988; McRoy, Zurcher, Lauderdale, & Anderson, 1982; Raynor, 1980; Sachdev, 1989; Tizard & Phoenix, 1989). This is not surprising given how important it is for a biological family to find similarities in appearance as well as temperament, intelligence, manner, and behavior. This can, of course, be viewed in the light of the strong feelings associated with procreation, but similarity can also be viewed in relation to belonging and bonding with the family. Recognizing a part of yourself in your child will, naturally enough, strengthen the feeling of identification and closeness between children and parents.

Similarity as a Coping Strategy

Dalen and Sætersdal (1992) point out that emphasizing similarity can be a way of coping with the primary goal of increasing the possibility for mental and emotional attachment between adoptive parents and their child. It is important to discuss what similarity means in such a connection. For children adopted from abroad, recognition and identification of perceived similarity necessarily have to originate from something other than a biological basis. Dalen (1999) found in an interview study with young adoptees from India that they often expressed similarity with their adoptive parents. Actually, the results showed that the adoptees who really had a feeling of being similar to their adoptive parents in some ways felt more confident and were generally better adjusted. Differences and discrepancies between the child and the parents represent a constant reminder that the child is not the parents' biological child. Perceived similarity therefore becomes a coping strategy in a positive sense of the word and not a denial of the child's background. It is important to distinguish this strategy from Kirk's (1964) discussion on acceptance and rejecting of differences. Kirk strongly recommended that parents openly accept the differences between raising a biological and an adopted child. An atmosphere of acceptance would constitute the best climate for a healthy development of an adopted child. However, the term "perceived similarity" as a coping strategy can be combined with an overall acceptance of differences in the approach to raising the adopted child. It is important for the adopted child to share areas of interest with other members of the adoptive family. This can provide a chance of feeling similar by somewhat reducing the feeling of being different. Howell (1998) points out that some adoptive parents place a great deal of focus on the child's ethnicity with the best of intentions. She maintains that this can backfire and may in some cases strengthen a child's feeling of being different. The parents are actually overemphasizing the differences between the child and his adoptive family. This term has been elaborated from Kirk's discussion on differences on a continuum from acceptance to rejection. Brodzinsky (1987) introduced the term "insistence-of-difference" to describe how parents can emphasize the differences to such an extent that they become the major focus of the family. In the same way, Dalen and Sætersdal (1987) use the term "stressing of differences" in their study on identity formation and adoptive parents' attitude toward differences.

Belonging to the Family

In her study of young adoptees from India, Dalen (1999) described five different types of young adoptees. The *well-adjusted child* is a person who has adjusted very well into the adoptive family and has the feeling of being similar to the parents. The *creative child* has been very different from the adoptive family but still feels very well accepted by them. The *fighting child* has been very different from the adoptive family and has not been met with acceptance from them. The *ethnically different child* has had an earlier life in his or her country of origin before arriving in Norway and has felt throughout that the real roots are in India; in spite of this, the child has been met with acceptance in the adoptive family. The *satellite child* is a person who has lived in the periphery of the family life, although the adoptive family at the same time has represented a safe base.

Whether young family members feel that they belong to a family seems to be related to the degree of similarity, acceptance, and level of conflict. In her study, Dalen (1999) found that the degree of belonging is a function of the degree of acceptance in the family and the degree of perceived similarity between family members. Of the four types described here, Dalen found that the fighting child feels the least degree of belonging to the adoptive family. The child is living in a family where he or she experiences a great degree of difference and little acceptance in relation to his or her own individuality. This leads to a high degree of conflict in family interactions. A living situation like this can easily occasion the adoptive child to feel little sense of belonging to the adoptive family. The satellite child also experiences little sense of belonging, but his or her living situation is nonetheless somewhat different. The child has not experienced as many differences or discrepancies in the family, and the level of acceptance have been greater. This means that the level of conflict has not been as great as in the fighting child's family. All the same, the satellite child experiences only a limited sense of belonging, as symbolized in the description of this young person: "she has lived a life outside the family." The ethnically different child has a somewhat different situation. This child is initially vastly different from the family, but the family has a relatively high level of acceptance, and this has meant that the level of conflict has not been as great as for the preceding two other types of children. The sense of belonging is also considered to be greater than for the previous two types of children. The creative child has felt a great degree of difference right from the beginning. However, this child has experienced enough understanding and acceptance for the development of a unique individuality within family interaction. Finally, the well-adjusted child feels the strongest sense of belonging of all the five types since this young person has experienced a great degree of similarity to the family and also a great deal of acceptance and understanding.

This should mean that the most difficult constellation would be one in which parents and children are very different and where there is little acceptance or flexibility with regard to such differences in the family. Based on Dalen's research project, belonging is not only dependent on the degree of similarity; in fact, it is more dependent on the level of acceptance and accommodation in the family. For the young adopted person, this feeling of not belonging is very likely to have an unfortunate effect on his or her later adjustment. Irhammar (1997) points out that youth with an extreme interest in their ethnic background and with little self-confidence feel that they have less in common with their adoptive family. Those who experienced themselves as Swedes but could not find any similarities between themselves and their adoptive parents were more likely to show a higher interest in their ethnic origin. This can be interpreted as a sense of being different, which again can lead to a feeling of disharmony.

In families where the differences between children and their adoptive parents have been handled with flexibility, acceptance and warmth seem to lead to more optimal developmental opportunities for the adoptees. Maybe such a strategy on the part of the parents is what is considered as high quality in an adoption relationship. It seems to be especially important for bringing about a positive course of development (see chapter 9 in this volume).

OUTCOMES OF ADOPTION

Epidemiological studies carried out in Scandinavia up until 2000 have documented that the majority of international adoptees manage well in their new families and countries (Botvar, 1999; Cederblad et al., 1994; Irhammar & Cederblad, 2000; Rørbech, 1989). Around 70 to 80 percent of adopted children and young adults are growing up without any sign of major problems. These results are the same as those found in similar surveys carried out on Danish-, Swedish-, and Norwegian-born young people and in surveys that have directly compared international adoptees with young people in general (Botvar, 1999; Cederblad & Hook, 1986; Cederblad et al., 1994; Irhammar & Cederblad, 2000; Rørbech, 1989). The results from studies carried out in Scandinavia are quite similar to findings in international research, especially during early childhood adjustment (Bagley, 1993; Kim, Shin, & Carrey, 1999, Simon & Alstein, 1996; Verhulst, 2000a; Verhulst et al., 1990). International adoptees adapt well during their preschool and early school years.

That such a high percentage of the international adoptees manage so well must be seen as very positive and constitutes good feedback for the adoptive families, adoption agencies, and, not least, for the donor countries. When we take into account that many of the international adoptees have had a very difficult start in life, these results are even more gratifying and optimistic. It is possible to "heal" or "cure" previous wounds and injuries, and adoption seems to be a solution that provides new opportunities for many children. Adoption is a crucial turning point in a child's development and may lead to a better life for many people. Such radical change of living conditions may lead not only to physical but also to mental traumas being healed (see chapter 4 in this volume).

Despite the positive research results, we need to be cautious in presenting this area as being overly "rosy." The studies also show that 20 to 30 percent of the international adoptees do have some problems related to language, learning, identity, and ethnicity. We should also add that a small percentage of this group has really extensive emotional and social problems. The teenage years seem particularly demanding for many adoptees and their families. This is well documented in the international literature (Cederblad et al., 1994; Irhammar & Cederblad, 2000; Sætersdal & Dalen, 1999; Verhulst, 2000a; Verhulst et al., 1990).

The results differ more when it comes to health, well-being, and social adjustment during adolescence (Botvar, 1995; Cederblad et al., 1994; Irhammar & Cederblad, 2000; Rørbech, 1990; Verhulst, 2000a; Verhulst et al., 1990 and 2000). The mental health and social adjustment of internationally adopted children as adolescents and young adults has become an important issue in Scandinavia in recent years since many of them are now reaching adolescence in these countries.

A research team in Sweden has recently published a report on mental health disorders and social maladjustment in adolescence and young adulthood among international adoptees (Hjern et al., 2002). They argue that the inconsistent findings in previous studies could be accounted for by difficulties in obtaining large representative samples of adoptees and finding relevant groups for comparison. They have carried out a very large study based on a national cohort of international adoptees in Sweden and compared the mental health and social adjustment to Swedish-born siblings, a group of immigrant children, and a general population of Swedish-born residents.

The results from this study show that after adjustment for major sociodemographic confounders, international adoptees were more likely than Swedish-born children to die from suicide or attempted suicide; to be admitted for a psychiatric disorder, drug, or alcohol abuse; or to commit a crime. Siblings in adoptive homes had lower odd ratios for most outcomes than did adoptees. The results showed that adoptees and immigrant children had much the same odd ratios.

However, this study also confirms that most of the internationally adopted girls and boys did not have indications of mental health disorders or social maladjustment. The research team comments on this in the following manner: "Our results could also be seen as further evidence of resilience in children who start their early life in adverse circumstances" (Hjern et al., 2002, p. 447).

However, it is important to look more closely into the group of internationally adoptive families that have children with severe emotional and social problems. We have to interpret these findings to see why these difficulties exist and what to do about them. In doing this, we will consider the following areas: age of adoption, help-seeking pattern, interaction in the adoptive families, and experiences of social discrimination.

Age at adoption has in many research studies been considered a very important outcome variable. One seems to think that a child adopted at a young age (under one year) would have the best potential for healthy development. Some studies do in fact confirm this statement (Hoksbergen et al., 1987; Verhulst et al., 1990; chapter 6 in this volume). Other studies, however, have shown that age of adoption does not play such a crucial role in the child's development (Cederblad et al., 1999; Dalen, 1995, 2001; Kvifte-Andresen, 1992). Several factors have to be taken into consideration, such as sex, country of origin, and the child's general health and mental condition on arrival. The child's environmental conditions in the country of origin seem to be the most crucial factor to influence future development. Howe (1997) found in his study that it was the quality of the preplacement situation that was important rather than the age of placement in itself.

Help-seeking patterns in adoptive families seem to be different than in families with biological children. In interviews, adoptive parents clearly state that they feel they are under a great deal of pressure to cope with their own situation (Sætersdal & Dalen, 1999). The families try to sort things out on their own until it suddenly becomes too much for them once the child becomes a teenager. Perhaps they spend too much energy before and have none left once the typical teenage problems start. The parents shrink from seeking help for as long as possible. They have at one time been approved as parents and taken the initiative to bring a child from another part of the world to this country. They feel they have to master this situation, prefer- ably without bothering other people too much. Their problems have therefore been undercommunicated to the rest of the society, thus "veil- ing" the everyday lives of many adoptive families.

As described earlier, *interaction in adoptive families* varies a great deal. In the Swedish study, the biological children in the adoptive family had much lower odd ratios for mental health disorders and social adjustment compared to their adopted siblings. Many studies have shown that adop- tive parents are more competent than biological parents (Botvar, 1999; Dalen, 2000; Irhammar & Cederblad, 2000; Golombok, Cook, Bish, & Mur- ray, 1995). This means that we have to take a closer look at differences in patterns of interaction between adoptive parents and their adopted and biological children. In what ways do these patterns differ? In the Swedish study, the results documented a higher risk for social maladjustment in adoptive white-collar families than in blue-collar families. Similar find- ings have been found in other studies (Berry & Barth, 1990; Rosenthal, Schmidt, & Conner, 1988). As mentioned before, the results from several Scandinavian studies show that adoptive families are far more supportive of their children's school situation compared to parents of biological chil- dren (Dalen, 1995, 2001). Combined with the results from the Swedish study, one indication might be that the parents put too much pressure on their adoptive children. Difficulties in coping with high expectations of performance in school and other competitive arenas could explain the higher disruption rates of well-educated parents.

Social discrimination against foreigners has increased during the past 15 years in the Scandinavian countries. The immigration from the Third World began in these countries in the 1970s, about the same time as over- seas adoptions started. Today, all the Scandinavian countries have far more diverse populations, which also means that we have become famil- iar with the reactions of discrimination and racism. The results from the last Swedish study showed that international adoptees were more or less equal to immigrant children in their mental and social adjustment. The authors find these results surprising in view of the low socioeconomic positions held by many immigrant families. Discrimination and preju- dices against people with a non-Swedish appearance could be important in accounting for these similar odd ratios.

Concluding Remarks

When discussing the outcome of international adoptions in Scandi- navia, it is important to keep in mind that the concept of a successful adoption is a social as well as a psychological construct that varies from society to society and from family to family. The behavioral content of adjustment will differ, depending on the ruling ideologies and social values of the society and the subculture to which the families belong (see chapter 2 in this volume). "Success" is an ambiguous concept, and we must acknowledge the difficulties in interpreting it. How would biological parents answer questions about the outcome of their parenthood? How many of them would declare their parenthood a failure? Perhaps we should also ask what kind of standards we dared to set as an ideal for adoptive families: a life without problems, a life without shadows?

Today, quite a few of the international adoptees in Scandinavia have grown to young adulthood, and some of them have written about their own feelings of growing up in these countries (Follevåg, 2002; Tjønn, 2002; Trotzig, 1996). They often speak of being reminded of their special situation as "visible" adoptees compared to nonadopted young adults. Some feel uneasy when reading the literature and research on identity problems among adopted people. They feel that the link between adoption and identity has been dominated by a biological and psychological approach. The theories often result in a negative stigmatization of the adopted person as a less worthy human being. The young adoptees argue that as individuals they have to be responsible for their own life in spite of being separated from their biological parents early in life. Adoption must be viewed as a normal and natural situation, rather than like a pathological condition, that presents special challenges because of the children's background and origins. There is a danger of obscuring or denying the adopted person's right to develop complex and multiple identities as an individual.

IMPLICATIONS FOR RESEARCH AND PRACTICE

The research carried out in Scandinavia has disclosed a need for more knowledge about interactions in the adoptive families. The focus should be on the interaction between parents and child during the initial period in the new family. We need to prepare adoptive parents for accommodating the needs of the most vulnerable children and give them some guidance in how to interplay with them in a constructive manner. There is also a need to know more about how to strengthen the feeling of belonging in adoptive children who behave very differently from other members of the family. There has been a discussion in the Scandinavian countries about making compulsory the preparatory courses for parents who are planning to adopt. At the moment, Denmark is the only country that has practiced this. However, the experiences from these courses have shown that the content has to be adapted to the participants' individual position in the process of adoption. To manage this, the courses should have a professional leadership consisting of persons with both personal experiences related to adoption and training in clinical work with adoptive families. The research has also documented that adequate language acquisition is important for the adoptive children's further development, both intellectually and socially. We already know that the parents should be active in communication with the children in both verbal and nonverbal ways and have a special focus on how to stimulate the children's concept development. A good mastery of the new language is very important for learning in general and for later performance in school in particular. It is therefore very important that kindergartens and schools offer educational provisions for adopted children and their parents in these areas. Families having children with special needs should be offered programs for stimulation at an early age. However, we need to know more about the relationship between early childhood experiences, language development, and intellectual functioning in order to provide the best learning conditions for the adoptive children in school.

During the past five years, the Scandinavian countries have been more aware of the psychological problems that some of the internationally adopted children have as adolescents and young adults. Although this constitutes a relatively small group, it is important to pay more attention to their situation. Society should be more open for discussion about the psychological problems of young adoptees and their families. Until recently, the "sunshine" stories about international adoptions have dominated the media. Today, we are more aware of the families' need for more professional help in handling interactions within in the family. The young adult should also have more opportunities for receiving counseling and guidance. Furthermore, it is important to let international adoptees and their parents meet with other adoptive families in order to share common experiences. Meeting people with similar problems has been one of the best ways in helping adoptees and their families solve their problems.

Most of the results presented in this chapter can be generalized to countries outside Scandinavia. The way in which early trauma and deprivation can affect further development will differ within the group of internationally adopted children regardless of which country they arrive in. Knowledge about what the children have experienced before adoption is often limited. However, we may safely assume that the conditions for the child's development have not been the best. Many of them have spent their first year in institutions or orphanages. This may have serious adverse effects on the children, partly because of the absence of a close and continuous relationship with a caring adult. How these children are met in their new surroundings will be affected by the quality of the adoptive parents and what kind of professional help they are able to find when it is needed. These conditions will, of course, differ from one geographical region to another. The same will be the case when it comes to provisions for the children of preschool and school age. In the Scandinavian countries, the provisions for children with special needs are very well organized compared to many other countries.

When it comes to the outcomes related to identity formation, one should be more cautious in generalizing the results. Although being adopted is challenging wherever you grow up, the fact that the child looks different from the rest of the family will be affected by the social context in the receiving country. The results from the Scandinavian countries must be interpreted in the light of these countries' history and attitude toward immigrants and refugees.

In the research on identity formation, we should pay more attention to the young adoptees in the way they articulate their position in their new country. The research findings described in this chapter show that international adoptees develop their identities in significantly different ways compared to Scandinavian-born and immigrant teenagers. A person who has been adopted has had a more definite break in his or her life history than most of the immigrant and refugee youths. They have undertaken a long journey to a new culture and class, and they have no return ticket. Unlike immigrant and refugee children, they do not grow up in a bilingual environment in contact with their biological families. However, they must arrive at a harmonious understanding of their identity with regard to who they are and how they want society to define them. How they will manage to do this is to some degree related to how racism and discrimination will develop in the Scandinavian countries. If racism increases in the future, the international adoptees will be driven further into a marginal position, with all the psychological and social difficulties that such a position entails. Their position will be less problematic if Scandinavia develops into a more open, multicultural and multiethnic society. If that happens, international adoptees will be able to step forward with confidence as the people they truly are, people with roots and solidarity in two cultures.

Chapter 11

Methodological Issues in Using Large-Scale Survey Data for Adoption Research

Brent C. Miller, Xitao Fan, and Harold D. Grotevant

Many investigators have reported that adopted children and adolescents in the United States exhibit elevated levels of behavioral and psychological problems. Summary reviews of the research generally agree that, compared with nonadopted peers, adoptees have higher levels of externalizing behavior problems, are overrepresented in clinical populations, and are more likely to have learning and school difficulties (Brodzinsky, 1993; Haugaard, 1998; Ingersoll, 1997; Wierzbicki, 1993). Similar conclusions have been reached by researchers in other countries, including the United Kingdom (Howe, 1997) and the Netherlands (Stams, Juffer, Rispens, & Hoksbergen, 2000; Verhulst, Althaus, and Verluis-den Bieman, 1990; Versluis-den Bieman & Verhulst, 1995), and Sweden (Lindblad, Hjern, & Vinnerljung, 2003).

Explanations for differences between adoptees and the general population have tended to emphasize psychodynamic theories (especially attachment and loss), early environmental assaults and traumas (neglect and abuse), and biologic/genetic mechanisms (poor prenatal nutrition and exposure to alcohol/drugs and biological parents' transmission of heritable traits and conditions). Variations of these theoretical perspectives are discussed by Brodzinsky (1990), Ingersoll (1997), and Haugaard (1998). Studies of adjustment difficulties for children adopted internationally across racial lines have also focused on racial discrimination that such children experience, especially in racially homogeneous countries such as Sweden (Lindblad et al., 2003).

Still, there are substantial methodological challenges in conducting adoption research, leading Finley (1999) to argue that conclusive evidence is lacking to support the assertion that adoptees have elevated rates of psychopathology. Analyses do show that there is an adoptive parent referral bias, such that adopted children are more likely than their nonadopted peers to be referred for mental health treatment, controlling for their level of problems (Miller, Fan, Grotevant, Christensen, Coyl, van Dulmen, 2000; Warren, 1992). Debates about whether adopted children are at elevated risk for problems are partially centered on methodological issues.

Empirical research about adoption issues often has not met high standards of scientific rigor. Because adoption is such a rare event, most studies about adoptees and adoption issues are based on agency, clinical, or support group samples of adopted children. However, such samples are often small and usually are not representative of adoptees and adoptive families. Even when a clinical, support group, or agency-based sample is large (e.g., Benson, Sharma, and Roehlkepartain, 1994), selection bias may still be a serious issue. The major concern about using nonprobability samples of adopted persons in adoption research is their lack of representativeness and the potential sampling bias that might result from such samples (Miller, Fan, Grotevant, et al., 2000). Small, nonrepresentative samples could be one reason for the inconsistency of empirical adoption research findings.

An alternative approach for obtaining data to study adoption issues is to use large population-based surveys. There are two possible advantages in using large national databases ("archival data") for adoption-related research. The first is the large sample size that is typical of national survey databases. The second is the sampling representativeness that results from scientific sampling strategies. Most national data sets suitable for studying adoption in the United States are relatively new, as described and summarized by Feigelman, Bachrach, Chandra, and Wilson (1998). The National Longitudinal Study of Adolescent Health (Add Health) has unusual potential for adoption-related research because its large sample is representative of the U.S. population. It includes longitudinal data spanning from early adolescence into early adulthood, and it includes thousands of variables from several related data sets.

Large national surveys typically are not designed, however, for the purpose of studying adoption. As a result, the measurement of adoption status can be problematic because the questions asked about adoption may be indirect, ambiguous, and/or lacking in detail. Further, it usually is not possible to verify adoption status. This chapter illustrates some significant methodological challenges in using survey data for adoption research, and the Add Health data are used to illustrate these methodological issues. Although the analyses presented in this chapter are based on Add Health data, the adoption classification issues addressed pertain to the central concern of measuring "who is adopted" when using any archival data set.

SOME ISSUES IN USING SURVEY DATA FOR ADOPTION RESEARCH

The first difficulty in working with large-scale survey data in adoption research is inherent in the definition of adoption because of its subtle but importantly different meanings. Legally, adoption involves the official transfer of parental rights and responsibilities to adult(s) who are not a child's biological parents. In response to societal changes, adoption practice has changed dramatically in the past 30 years (Grotevant & McRoy, 1998). But it means a great deal that adopted children may vary in age from infants to adolescents when they are adopted. Further, they can differ in racial, ethnic, or national origin from their adoptive parents; they may or may not have been exposed to risks for long-term physical or mental disabilities; they may or may not know anything about their birth parents; and they may be adopted with or without siblings (Grotevant & Kohler, 1999). In addition, some adoptions occur within biological relationships when, following remarriage, a stepparent legally adopts the biological child of his or her new spouse. However, adopted stepchildren usually have some continuity in their living arrangements because they live with one biological parent. Within family lineages, nonparent relatives may formally or informally adopt nieces or nephews, siblings, or grandchildren. For all these reasons, adoption is more complex to conceptualize and measure than is often assumed (Brodzinsky & Pinderhughes, 2002; Brodzinsky, Smith, & Brodzinsky, 1998).

A second difficulty is related to the first, but it has to do with the specific questions asked in the survey. Before exploring substantive questions, researchers must first identify the adoptees in the sample (Miller et al., 2001). An affirmative answer to the simple question, "Are you adopted?" will lump together adoptees from many different living situations and backgrounds and may present serious difficulties to adoption researchers wanting a clearly defined sample (e.g., through including or excluding international or transracial adoptees).

A third difficulty is the uncertainty of adoption status in survey data. In samples recruited through agencies, private practice, support groups, or public service announcements, there is usually a high degree of certainty about the adoption status of the participants. In population-based survey data, however, adoption status is usually based on self-report. Especially when the survey participants are not adults, the validity of such self-reported adoption status can be uncertain. Invalid classification of adoptees and nonadoptees can distort the research findings about adoption adjustment (Fan et al., 2002).

PURPOSE

In this chapter, we use three related data sets to illustrate the challenges of classifying adolescents' adoption status in archival data. As will be shown, all data sources converged to identify most adopted individuals. However, a substantial number of cases were ambiguous with respect to adoption status, and classifying those cases as either adopted or non-adopted was problematic. Further, a group of adolescents who said they were adopted on a self-administered questionnaire appear to have provided false information both about their adoption status and about their responses to some psychosocial and behavioral outcome variables, thus causing considerable distortion in the comparison between adopted and nonadopted adolescents. Findings demonstrate that it is important to resolve adoption status ambiguities in archival data in order to avoid erroneous substantive conclusions. More specifically, we address the following objectives in this chapter:

1. To explain why discrepancies exist between alternative measures of adoption status in Add Health data and how such discrepancies could be resolved through triangulation of different data sources
2. To present evidence that erroneous classification of adoption status may cause distortion in substantive comparisons between adopted and nonadopted adolescents
3. To discuss general issues related to adoption status classification in archival data and make recommendations for future researchers gathering and analyzing data for adoption research

EXAMINING INCONSISTENCY IN ADOPTION STATUS CLASSIFICATION

Data and Sample

Add Health is a large data collection project designed to be nationally representative of adolescents in the United States that initially surveyed adolescents who were mostly between 12 and 17 years old. It was sponsored primarily by the National Institute of Child Health and Human Development, with cooperative funding from many U.S. federal agencies. The study was designed and implemented by the Carolina Population Center at the University of North Carolina at Chapel Hill. Add Health was designed to be a longitudinal data collection project that provides contextually sensitive information about the health status and health-related behaviors of adolescents as they grew to be adults. Three waves of Add Health data were completed and released by May 2003. Information about the availability of Add Health data is provided on Add Health's Web site at http://www.cpc.unc.edu/addhealth.

Add Health data initially were collected via self-report questionnaires from students in the school setting and subsequently by interviews completed with adolescents and parents at home. Thus, wave I Add Health data included three related data sets: data from the adolescents' self-administered in-school questionnaire (SAQ), data from the adolescents' in-home interview (wave I), and data from the parent questionnaire. Because of the three related data sets, Add Health data provide some unique opportunities to illustrate the methodological challenges of uncertain survey measurement of adolescents' adoption status and the potential effect such classification uncertainty has on adoption research findings. Like most population-based surveys, Add Health was not specifically designed to study adoption issues. As a result, the adoption-related questions in the wave I in-school SAQ and parent questionnaire were lacking in detail, and the questions about adoption in the wave I in-home interview were indirect, thus resulting in ambiguity.

A stratified cluster sampling design was used to obtain Add Health data. Details about the Add Health sampling design are provided by the National Longitudinal Study of Adolescent Health (http://www.cpc.unc.edu/ addhealth). For this study, data were analyzed from three linked data sets: the school survey SAQ of adolescents, wave I of the in-home interviews of adolescents, and the parent survey completed at home at the same time (1994–1995) as wave I interviews of adolescents.

The in-school SAQ was administered to students in grades 7 through 12, and the questionnaire included topics such as the social and demographic characteristics of respondents, risk behaviors, future expectations, personal feelings, health status, friendship, school extracurricular activities, and who lived in the household. More than 90,000 students completed the SAQ during school.

All students on school rosters were eligible to be selected for the core in-home interview sample; this sampling frame included some students who did not complete the SAQ (e.g., those who were absent from school at the time of SAQ administration). The core sample included 12,105 adolescents. Special oversamples were obtained for some ethnic groups, disabled adolescents, and sibling pairs with different degrees of genetic relatedness living in the same home and saturation samples of entire selected schools for network analysis. With the oversamples, the total sample size from wave I of in-home interview was 20,745. A parent (or custodial adult) of each adolescent interviewed in wave I was asked to complete an interviewer-assisted questionnaire. Parents also were asked about their relationship to the interviewed adolescent. Data were obtained from 17,670 parents (85% response rate), and the majority of the parent respondents (91%) were mothers (e.g., biological, step, and adoptive mothers).

Add Health focuses on the health issues of adolescents but not on adoption. As such, the wave I Add Health data sets have a limited number of questions related to adoption status and adoption-related issues. But the value of Add Health for adoption-related research is enhanced considerably by the multiple data sets. Although adoption status may be ambiguous in one data source, the multiple data sources provide a means of verifying the adoption status of the adolescents, thus overcoming a major potential shortcoming. For this chapter, we focus on data from the in-school SAQ, in-home interviews, and parent surveys to illustrate the challenges of using large-scale survey data in adoption research.

Measurement of Adoption Status

The measurement of adoption status was different in the Add Health data sets, and it is important to understand the potential problems associated with measuring adoption status in each of the three data sets.

In-School SAQ

Measurement of adoption status of an adolescent respondent was based on two questions in the school survey: question 25 asked, "Are you adopted?" (Yes, No), and question 26 asked, "Do you live with either of your biological parents?" (Yes, No). Respondents who answered "Yes" to the first question and "No" to the second question were classified as adoptees (excluding stepparent adoptions). This classification focused on self-identified adopted children who did not live with either biological parent, and it is consistent with the conceptual definition of adoption current in the field. The in-school SAQ measure of adoption status is summarized in the upper panel of Table 11.1.

In-Home Interview Data

Adoption status classification in Add Health wave I in-home interview data was not as straightforward as in the in-school SAQ. In the in-home interview, there were no direct questions about whether a respondent was adopted. Instead, the adoption status of adolescents can be *inferred* from who lived in the respondent's home. After asking the adolescent respondent to list the names of everyone who lived in their household, the interviewer asked the respondent, "What is [this person's] relationship to you?" If the adolescent answered that the person named was his or her "father," "mother's husband," "mother," or "father's wife," the interviewer showed the adolescent a card with definitions for six different

Table 11.1
Definitions of adoption status in three Add Health samples

Sample		Definitions	Number of cases
Adolescent in-school SAQ	1.	Adolescents answered "Yes" to "Are you adopted?" (question 25)	2,767
	2.	Adoptees answered "Yes" to question 25 above and "No" to "Do you live with either biological parent?" (question 26)[a]	1,583
Adolescent in-home interview	1.	Living with two adoptive parents	404
	2.	Living with adoptive mother, no father present	127
	3.	Living with adoptive father, no mother present	29
	4.	Total living with nonbiological adoptive parent(s)	560
Parent survey	1.	Parent respondent chose "adoptive mother" or "adoptive father" to answer question C1 "What is your relationship to (name of adolescent)?"	543
	2.	Total adoptive parents, after deleting those who answered "yes" to "Does the biological mother (C2) or father (C6B) live in this household?" (or for who bio parent data were missing)	514

[a] n = 1,583 because four cases who answered "no" to question 25 (and should have skipped question 26) answered by mistake.

types of parent–child relationships and asked the respondent to specify their exact parent–child relationship. The following are the verbatim definitions of "father" presented to adolescent respondents:

Biological father	He is the man who got your biological mother pregnant.
Stepfather	He is not your biological father, but he is (or has been) married to or living with your biological mother.
Adoptive father	He is not your biological father, and he is not married to or living with your biological parent, but he has legally adopted you.
Step/adoptive father	He is not your biological father, but he is (or has been) married to or living with your biological parent, and he has legally adopted you.
Foster father	He is not your biological father and is not married to or living with your biological parent, and he has not legally adopted you, but he cares for you at the request of an agency such as a department of social services.
Other	You think of him as your father, although he is not.

If a respondent specified both adoptive father and adoptive mother, or only adoptive father without mother (mother not living in the home), or only adoptive mother without father (father not living in the home), the respondent was classified as an adoptee. All others were classified as non-adoptees (e.g., adoptive father and biological mother). Adoption status results based on the wave I in-home interview measure of parent–child relationships are summarized in the center panel of Table 11.1.

Parent Interview Data

Parents usually are in a better position than children to give valid answers about children's adoption status both because they know the true biological or adoptive status of their children and because they generally understand the concepts of "adoption" and "biological parent" better than children. Even though some adoptive parents might not choose to identify themselves as such, in the absence of official adoption records, parents' report about the adoption status of a child probably would be considered the most accurate measure.

In the Add Health parent survey, parents were asked the question (question C1), "What is your relationship to [name of target adolescent]?" If parent respondents chose either "adoptive mother" or "adoptive father" from the alternatives, two questions followed. Question C2 asked, "Does [the adolescent's] biological mother live in this household?" (Yes, No), and the other (question C6B) asked, "Does [the adolescent's] biological father live in this household?" (Yes, No). If the parent respondent chose either "adoptive father" or "adoptive mother" for question C1, and answered "No" to both questions C2 and C6B, the adolescent was classified as adopted; otherwise, the adolescent was classified as nonadopted. The results based on the parent survey adoption definition are summarized in the bottom panel of Table 11.1.

The differences in defining adoption status in the three linked data sets (see Table 11.1) pose a challenge to investigators who want to use Add Health data for adoption research. But the information from different informants (adolescents, parents) in different settings (school, home) through different data collection modes (paper-and-pencil SAQ, interview) provide some unique opportunities for resolving the uncertainty in adoption status measurement in population-based archival data and for assessing the impact of adoption misclassification on adoption adjustment research. Miller et al. (2001) provided detailed analyses and findings in resolving adoption status measurement inconsistencies across the three Add Health data sets (in-school SAQ, wave I in-home interview, parent survey). In the following sections, we present the highlights of the findings as reported in Miller et al. (2001) to show how discrepant measures of adoption status across the three linked Add Health data sets were reconciled and what misleading results could be obtained by relying only on adolescents' self-reported adoption status.

Comparisons across Two Data Sets

In-School SAQ and In-Home Interview

Across the in-school SAQ and home interview data sets, there were 14,083 *linked* cases with nonmissing adoption status measures. Between these two data sets, 13,478 (95.7%) adolescents were consistently classified as nonadopted by their self-reports on both the in-school SAQ and their in-home interview. There were 446 (3.17%) adolescents consistently classified as adopted based on both data sets. On the other hand, there were 159 (1.13%) inconsistent cases where adolescents were classified as adopted in one but not in the other data set.

The overall consistency (nonadopted 95.7% and adopted 3.17%) is deceptive because in adoption research the concern is typically about the consistency of *adoption* cases. Out of the 14,083 cases who had nonmissing adoption status measures across the two data sets, 582 of them responded on the in-school SAQ that they were adopted and *not* living with a biological parent. It is somewhat surprising, therefore, that 136 of these (23.37%) were not classified as living with adoptive parent(s) in the home interview! Of these 136 cases, 107 cases gave directly contradictory answers about whether they lived with a biological parent. The remaining self-identified but inconsistent adoptees appear to have been living in more complex parent–child relationships rather than living only with adoptive parents. In addition, out of the 14,083 linked cases across the two data sets with nonmissing adoption measures, 469 adolescents reported in the in-home interview that they were living with adoptive parent(s), but 23 (4.9%) of them reported previously as being nonadopted in the in-school SAQ.

School SAQ and Parent Survey

Across the school SAQ and parent survey data sets, there were 12,834 *linked* cases with nonmissing data on questions assessing adoption status. Of these 12,834 cases, 12,239 (95.36%) were consistently classified as nonadopted, and 393 (3.06%) were consistently classified as being adopted in both data sets. On the other hand, there were 202 (1.57%) inconsistent cases where the adolescents were classified as adopted in one but not in the other data set.

Of the 202 inconsistent cases, 171 of them reported being adopted in the school SAQ, but were classified as nonadopted based on the parent survey. Of these 171 cases, parent data directly contradicted students' SAQ reports for 113 of them, making it reasonably certain (if parent responses are given greater credibility) that these 113 cases were not adopted. For the remaining 58 cases, however, parent survey data did not contradict students' SAQ reports because the parent survey respondents were adults other than biological or adoptive parents. There were also 31 adolescents who reported themselves as being nonadopted on the in-school SAQ but who were classified as adoptees based on parent reports. These are interesting cases. If parents' reports about adoption status of their children are considered more valid, it is possible that these adolescents might not know that they were adopted, or they deliberately chose not to disclose that they were adopted. Again, the seemingly overall small percentage of inconsistent cases is deceptive because the research concern is typically about the consistent classification of adoptees. Of the 564 self-reported adoptees on the in-school SAQ, 171 were contradicted by parent reports, making the inconsistency rate over 30 percent.

In-Home Interview and Parent Survey

There were 16,719 linked cases with nonmissing adoption status measures between the parent survey and the in-home interview data sets. Of these 16,719 cases, 16,184 (96.80%) responses for adolescents' nonadopted status were consistent, and 458 (2.74%) were consistently classified as adopted in both data sets. But there were 77 (.46%) inconsistent reports where adolescents were identified as adopted in one but not in the other data set.

Of the 77 inconsistent cases, 36 were classified as adopted based on adolescents' home living arrangements but were classified as nonadopted based on parent survey data. Of these 36 cases, parents' responses directly contradicted adolescents' reported home living arrangements for 21 cases, because the parent data showed that biological parent(s) were in the home. For the other 15 cases, parent data did not contradict adolescents' reported home living arrangements because respondents to the "parent survey" were neither biological nor adoptive parents. In this situation, the adoption status classification for adolescents based on parent data is unknown.

Again, it is interesting that there were 41 cases classified as adopted by parent survey data but not by the adolescents' reported home living arrangement. Of the 41 cases, 16 of the adolescents indicated that they were living with at least one biological parent, whereas the parents themselves reported that they were adoptive parents and that no biological parents lived in the home. This direct contradiction between parents and adolescents suggests that these adolescents are unwilling to acknowledge or might not know that they were adopted.

Reconciliation of Adoption Status Measures across Three Data Sources

Each of the two-way comparisons discussed in the previous sections provides insights about consistent and inconsistent classification of adoption status across two data sets at a time. A more conclusive approach would be to triangulate adoption status measures across all three sources of data. Table 11.2 shows how measures of adoption status were reconciled by identifying

30 groups, each based on a unique combination of adoption status as defined in the three data sets. As shown in column 2 ("Frequency") 793 individuals were identified as adopted in at least one of the three data sets, but only 370 individuals were identified as adopted by all three data sources (group 1).

Table 11.2
Reconciliation of adoption status definitions across three Add Health data sources

Group	Frequency	Data sources[a]			Adopted nonrelative	Not adopted	Don't know, unsure
		School	Home	Parent			
1	370	A[b]	A	A	370		
2	3	A	B	A	2		1
3	16	A	O	A	8		8
4	4	A	M	A	2		2
5	9	A	A	B			9
6	88	A	B	B		88	
7	1	A	O	B		1	
8	5	A	M	B			5
9	20	A	A	O	19		1
10	2	A	B	O		1	1
11	9	A	O	O	9		
12	37	A	M	O	11		26
13	47	A	A	M	47		
14	14	A	B	M		14	
15	3	A	O	M			3
16	18	A	M	M	10		8
17	13	N	A	A	13		
18	75	M	A	A	75		
19	2	N	A	B			2
20	1	M	A	B			1
21	1	N	A	O			1
22	3	M	A	O	3		
23	7	N	A	M	7		
24	12	M	A	M	12		
25	7	N	M	A	4		3
26	4	M	M	A	3		1
27	2	N	O	A	1		1
28	7	M	O	A	4		3
29	9	N	B	A	6		3
30	4	M	B	A	3		1
Totals	793				609	104	80

[a] Data sources are the SAQ completed by adolescents at *school*, the wave I interview of adolescents at *home*, and surveys of *parents* completed at the same time as adolescent home interviews.
[b] Adoption status definitions were adopted (A), nonadopted (N), or missing (M) for in-school SAQ data and nonadopted because living with biological parent (B) or other (O) nonadoptive parent in home and parent surveys.

To reconcile the discrepancies about adoption status across the three data sources, several general decision rules could be used:

1. If a case was identified as adopted in any data source, then that case was classified as an adoptee unless another data source contradicted that classification. For example, teens who said they were adopted at school were counted as adopted if other data sources were missing or inconclusive but not contradictory. Groups 11 and 24 are examples of this rule.

2. If a contradiction occurred between adolescent and parent data sources, parent data were generally considered more valid. For example, if teens were classified as adopted in both SAQ and home interview data sources but parents said they were biological, these teens were classified either as nonadopted (when home living arrangements do not contradict this classification, e.g., group 6) or as don't know/unsure when home living arrangements indicated considerable ambiguity (e.g., groups 5 and 8).

3. If only two contradictory adolescent data sources were available, the detailed home living arrangements were used as the primary information source for resolving the discrepancy, and the cases would be classified accordingly. Groups 14 (classified as nonadopted) and 23 (classified as adopted) are examples of this.

4. In any situation where there was some uncertainty, details of the home living arrangements reported by the adolescents during the in-home interview were carefully examined and used as supplemental information. Unless clearly and directly contradicted by parent survey responses, these home living arrangements were used to classify some cases. Groups 12 and 16 are examples of using the detailed analysis of home living arrangements for final categorization.

After carefully considering all the information from the three data sources, including case-by-case examination of home living arrangements of some selected adolescent respondents, a total of 609 cases were defined with reasonable certainty as adopted. On the other hand, 104 cases identified as adoptees in a single data source (almost all in the school SAQ responses) probably were *not* adopted. The adoption status of 80 cases is uncertain given the classification rules described previously. In the detailed case-by-case analysis of home living arrangements, some of the most confusing cases we encountered involved complicated relative/stepparent adoptions. Because relative/stepparent adoptions may be qualitatively different from nonrelative adoptions, this group was classified as "Don't Know/Unsure." The adoption status classification system presented in Table 11.2 is complicated and is the result of detailed detective work. It should be noted that the 609 adoptions in Table 11.2 are all nonrelative adoptions.

The largest numbers of adoption classification uncertainties across the data sources are included in groups 6, 13, and 18. The 88 cases under group 6 should *not* be defined as adopted because these 88 adolescents reported in the in-school SAQ that they were adopted, but during the in-home interview, they stated that they were living with biological parent(s), and their parents agreed. This is an interesting group of adolescent respondents, and later we will present analysis findings directly related to them. On the other hand, the 75 cases under group 18 should be defined as adopted because these 75 adolescents did not answer the in-school SAQ questions about adoption status, but in the in-home interview, they answered that they were living with adoptive parent(s), and their parents said they were adoptive parents and no biological parent lived in the home. The 47 cases under group 13 were classified as adoptees because the adolescents gave consistent answers in the in-school SAQ and later in the in-home interview that they were adopted, but these 47 cases had missing data on the parent survey.

POTENTIAL IMPACT OF MISCLASSIFICATION ON ADOPTION RESEARCH FINDINGS

The results presented here show that, in using archival data for adoption research, there are issues more complex than many researchers realize. Measuring adoption status can be problematic for many different reasons, such as the immaturity of young adolescent respondents, the deliberate efforts of some adolescents to hide or falsely claim adoption status, inconsistencies between the ways adoption status is reported across respondents, the mismatch between survey questions posed, and the complexity and fluidity of contemporary kinship relations. It was fortunate that multiple Add Health data sets allowed "triangulation" of information. What if this triangulation were not possible and only one data set, such as the Add Health in-school SAQ data, was relied on for adoption research? The following section explores some substantive consequences as a result of misclassification of adoption status.

Discrepancies in Substantive Findings across Two Add Health Data Sets

Using data from only the in-school SAQ data, Miller, Fan, Christensen, et al. (2000) showed that adopted and nonadopted adolescents exhibited differences in the magnitude of small to moderate effect sizes on a variety of behavioral and psychosocial outcome variables (e.g., school grades and school feelings, substance use, psychological well-being, physical health). Group differences were consistently in the direction favoring nonadopted adolescents, suggesting that adopted adolescents are at higher risk in almost all the substantive domains examined.

After the publication of Miller et al. (2000), a series of related analyses were pursued using the multiple data sets from Add Health, including similar comparisons between adoptees and nonadoptees using Add Health wave I in-home interview data. From the in-home interview data, a group of behavioral and psychological variables were constructed that were conceptually parallel to the in-school SAQ outcome measures used in Miller et al. (2000). It was surprising to find that the differences between the adoptee and nonadoptee groups on these Add Health wave I in-home interview outcome variables were noticeably smaller than those previously reported in Miller et al. (2000). Instead of differences ranging from small to medium effect size (standardized mean difference of .20 to .50) as observed in the SAQ data, the differences on the outcome variables in the in-home interview data between the adoptee and nonadoptee groups were much smaller (standardized mean difference of .00 to .20). Table 11.3 presents the effect sizes in the comparison between the adoptee and nonadoptee groups for the outcome variables in both the Add Health SAQ data (published in Miller et al., 2000) and the Add Health in-home interview data. The entries in Table 11.3 are effect sizes in the form of standardized mean differences between the adoptee and nonadoptee groups.

From Table 11.3, it is obvious that the observed differences indicating that the adopted group has higher levels of psychosocial and behavioral problems in the Add Health in-school SAQ data (first column, mean absolute effect size .31) were not replicated in the wave I in-home interview data (second column, mean absolute effect size .08). If the substantive differences between the two groups (i.e., adoptee and nonadoptee groups) are real, analysis of the two data sets should have produced more similar results despite the differences between the two data sets (e.g., sample size differences, differences in operationalization of outcome variables, differences in defining adoption status, and so on). The lack of consistent findings as shown in Table 11.3 prompted closer scrutiny of the data to discover what might have contributed to the observed inconsistencies.

Impact of Erroneous Adoption Classification on Substantive Findings

We explored several alternatives for analyzing the observed inconsistent findings across the two Add Health data sets as shown in Table 11.3. The most relevant conjecture was that mischievous or dishonest responses from a relatively small group of adolescents in the in-school SAQ might have been responsible for the observed discrepancy in the results (Fan et al., 2002). This hypothesis was formulated because we noticed that a group of adolescents identified themselves as being "adopted" in the in-school SAQ but later stated in the in-home interview that they were living with biological parents. This contradiction raised the possibility that some nonadopted adolescents might have been mischievous/dishonest in identifying themselves as "adopted" in their paper-and-pencil SAQ completed at the school setting. This "jokester" group, as we nicknamed them, of non-

Table 11.3
Adopted/nonadopted group differences (effect size) in two Add Health data sets

	Effect size (ES)	
Outcome variables	SAQ [a]	In home interview [b]
School grades +	-0.17	-0.18
School troubles	0.14	0.14
Positive school feelings +	-0.27	0.02
Skipping school	0.42	0.08
Smoking	0.31	-0.02
Drinking	0.34	-0.05
Drunk	0.42	-0.06
Self-esteem +	-0.29	0.00
Fighting	0.34	0.06
Lie to parents		-0.07
Academic clubs +	0.24	
Extracurricular clubs +	0.08	
Emotional distress	0.40	
Future hope +	-0.45	
Health problems	0.32	
Physical problems	0.56	
Sickness	0.26	
Suspension / expulsion		0.13
Drug use		0.05
Suicide		0.08
Depression		0.16
Emotional upheaval		0.08
Hopelessness		0.03
Family closeness +		-0.10
Closeness to others +		-0.09
Theft		0.02
Mean of absolute ES	0.31	0.08

+ Outcome variables on which a higher value is desirable.

[a] This column of effect sizes on SAQ outcome variables is reproduced from table 2 in Miller, Fan, Christensen, et al. (2000). See the original article for details about the analysis and construction of the SAQ outcome variables.

[b] This column of effect sizes are from the in-home interview outcome variables. The sample sizes for the adopted and nonadopted groups are $N_{adopted} = 514$ and $N_{nonadopted} = 17,241$, respectively, and were reduced to a certain extent because of missing values on the sample weight variables. The actual sample size for a particular outcome variable comparison may be lower because of missing data. For details about the construction of these outcome variables, see Miller, Fan, Grotevant, et al. (2000).

adopted adolescents who falsely identified themselves as being "adopted" may also have answered the behavioral and psychosocial outcome variables mischievously or dishonestly, thus distorting the differences between adopted and nonadopted groups in the in-school SAQ data.

To empirically verify this conjecture, three adoption status groups were created, based on the "triangulation" results summarized in Table 11.2. First, a group of "true" adoptees ($n = 370$; group 1 in Table 11.2) was identified whose status of being adopted was confirmed in all three data sources (self-reports in the in-school SAQ survey, living arrangement in the in-home interview, and adoptive parent report), so it is quite certain that this group of adolescents truly were adoptees. In this true adoptee group, male (51%) and female (49%) proportions were approximately equal, and the gender classification based on self-reports in the in-school SAQ and on the interviewer classification in the in-home interview was perfectly consistent for all members in this group. Although other adolescents might be adoptees, to avoid any degree of uncertainty in this comparison analysis between adopted and nonadopted groups, we used this group of 370 as true adoptees.

Second, a group of adolescents (group 6, $n = 88$) were identified who, very likely, had mischievously or dishonestly identified themselves as adopted in the in-school SAQ when in fact they were not adopted. This group was singled out because in the later face-to-face in-home interview, these adolescents reported that they were living with their biological parent(s), and the respondents to the parent survey reported that they were the biological parents of these adolescents. This group of jokester adolescents appeared to have fooled around with the adoption identification questions in the in-school SAQ. In addition to their contradictory adoption status, these 88 jokesters also showed considerable inconsistencies in gender classification between the self-reported gender status in the in-school SAQ and the interviewer-observed gender status in the in-home interview. Based on their self-reports in the in-school SAQ, 68 percent of them were males, and 32 percent of them were females. During the face-to-face interview, however, the interviewers classified 81 percent of them as males and 19 percent of them as females. More specifically, among the self-reported "female" respondents to the in-school SAQ ($n = 27$), more than one-third of them ($n = 10$) were later classified as males by the interviewers during the in-home interview. In addition to these 88 cases, there might be others who are also jokesters with regard to adoption identification, but the degree of certainty is not as high as this group of 88. To minimize uncertainty, only these 88 cases were used in the following comparison analysis as the group of Add Health jokester adoptees.

Finally, a comparison group of adolescents who were *not* identified as adoptees in *any* of the three data sources (the in-school SAQ, the in-home interview, and the parent survey) were identified as true nonadoptees ($n =$

14,662). Although some others might also be nonadoptees, the degree of certainty is not as high. To minimize uncertainty, only this triangulated group was used as true nonadoptees in the following comparison analysis.

The results of the comparison analyses based on these three groups (true adoptees, nonadoptees, and jokester adoptees) suggest that the jokesters may have considerably inflated the differences reported in our previous comparisons, based only on in-school SAQ, of the adoptee and

Table 11.4
Detecting the effect of "jokesters" in SAQ data: Effect sizes between (variously defined) adoptee and nonadoptee groups

Self Administered Questionnaire (SAQ)	All adoptees vs. non-adoptees	True adoptees vs. non-adoptees	Jokester adoptees vs. non-adoptees
Outcome variables	$N_{adopted}$ 458 $N_{nonadopted}$ 14,662	$N_{adopted}$ 370 $N_{nonadopted}$ 14,662	$N_{jokesters}$ 88 $N_{nonadopted}$ 14,662
School grades +	-.13	-.11	-.24
Academic clubs +	.21	.04	.95
Extracurricular clubs +	.11	.09	.19
School troubles	.01	-.10	.53
Positive school feelings +	-.13	.05	.94
Skipping school	.36	.02	1.97
Smoking	.21	.05	.94
Drinking	.24	-.03	1.45
Drunk	.28	-.02	1.68
Self-esteem +	-.18	-.01	-.97
Emotional distress	.28	.12	1.02
Future hope +	-.23	-.01	-.97
Health problems	.24	.06	1.08
Physical problems	.31	.02	1.73
Sickness	.13	-.08	1.15
Fighting	.28	.04	1.36
Lie to	.33	.22	.84
Mean of absolute ES	.21	.06	1.09

+ Positive variables on which a higher value is desirable.
Note: The column entries are effect sizes in the form of the standardized mean difference between adopted and nonadopted groups. Classification for the groups ("true" adoptees, "jokester" adoptees, and nonadoptees) is based on triangulation from three data sources as described in the chapter. The sample sizes for the adopted and nonadopted groups presented in the table are the maximum sample sizes for the groups in this analysis. The actual sample sizes for a particular outcome variable comparison may be lower because of missing data. Because only selected groups were used, the sampling weight was not applied in these analyses.

nonadoptee groups (Miller et al., 2000). Table 11.4 presents the analysis results involving these three groups.

When the jokester adoptees were included in the adoptee group, the differences between adoptees and nonadoptees (column 1 effect sizes; mean absolute effect size across all the variables: 0.21) were similar but somewhat smaller than those reported in Miller et al. (2000) and reproduced in Table 11.3 (mean absolute effect size across all the variables: 0.31). However, when the jokester adoptees were removed from the adoptee group (column 2 effect sizes), the differences between the true adoptee and nonadoptee groups became very small (mean absolute effect size across all variables: 0.06) and were similar to those observed for the in-home interview data (see column 2 in Table 11.3; mean absolute effect size across all variables: 0.06).

Most revealing is that, when only the jokester adoptees ($n = 88$) were compared with the nonadoptees (Table 11.4, column 3), the jokester group showed extreme differences from the nonadoptees (mean absolute effect size across all variables: 1.09), with the majority of the effect sizes substantially larger than 0.8, the criterion typically considered as representing a large effect in social and behavioral sciences (Cohen, 1988). These findings suggest that the differences between adoptees and nonadoptees were substantially exaggerated by including the group of jokesters. Based on these results, it appears that the jokester group's extreme responses on the in-school SAQ considerably inflated the differences previously reported (Miller et al., 2000) in the comparison between adopted and nonadopted groups.

Theoretically, a jokester effect could occur in either direction; that is, nonadoptees mischievously identify themselves as adoptees, and true adoptees deliberately identify themselves as nonadoptees. However, the jokester effect is more problematic for the former group (nonadoptees identifying themselves as "adoptees") than for the latter. This is because adoption is such a rare event, constituting only about 3 percent of the U.S. population (Center for Adoption Research and Policy, 1997). Because the true adoptee group will usually be small, even in a large representative sample, a small group of jokesters is able to seriously distort the results for the small adoptee group. For the Add Health data sets analyzed in this chapter, out of the 646 self-identified adoptees in the in-school SAQ sample who were included in the in-home interview sample, it is reasonably certain that 88 of them were jokesters (Table 11.2, group 6) who mischievously identified themselves as adoptees when in fact they were not. Compared with the size of the true adoptee group, this jokester group was large enough to distort the comparison between the adoptee and nonadoptee groups.

On the other hand, the nonadoptee group is typically large, and a similar number of true adoptees who knowingly misidentified themselves as nonadoptees would not cause any noticeable distortion in the findings. For example, in the Add Health in-school SAQ and in-home interview data sets, only about two dozen adolescents self-identified themselves as nonadoptees, but their parents later indicated that they were adoptees (e.g., groups 17, 25, 29 in Table 11.2). Even if this small group provided exaggerated responses on the behavioral and psychosocial outcome variables, the group was so small compared to the nonadoptee group (n = 14,662 true nonadoptees who were participants in both the in-school SAQ and the in-home interview) that their responses could not have substantially altered the results comparing the adoptee and nonadoptee groups.

IMPLICATIONS FOR ADOPTION RESEARCH USING LARGE SAMPLE SURVEY DATA

This study has implications beyond Add Health; it can be viewed as a case study of how investigators could analyze secondary data in order to classify adoption subgroups. Researchers using archival data to examine variables related to adoption status are cautioned to consider the complexities of measuring adoption status. Some of the ways in which adoptees might be misclassified are illustrated by the inconsistencies presented previously. In the following sections, we discuss some general approaches and issues in adoption status measurement in archival data and provide some guidelines for future survey data collection with regard to adoption.

Different Approaches for Adoption Status Measurement

The Add Health in-school SAQ contained the fewest and most direct questions for determining adoption status (two direct questions to adolescent respondents), but it was also the crudest in terms of not being able to distinguish between parents who might have been "foster," "step," or "other." In addition to the general problems that are common to all self-report data (e.g., response carelessness, dishonesty), there are potential problems in measuring adoption status this way. First, the investigator must be able to specify the meaning of "adoption" for his or her research question. If extended family relative adoptions (e.g., grandparents or uncles and aunts) are to be included, there must be a way of identifying the appropriate subsample within the data set. Second, there is the issue of "secrecy" associated with U.S. adoptions; adoption status is not concealed from most adolescent adoptees in the United States, but there may be some adoptees who were not told that they were adopted. Because measurement of adoption status in the in-school SAQ data relied solely on adolescents' self-report, their adoption classification may underestimate the true proportion of adoptees by classifying as "not adopted" some unknown number of adoptees who did not know or did not disclose that they were adopted.

Another potential problem of only using children's responses to define their adoption status is related to the respondent's maturity and understanding. Young respondents may not fully understand the survey terminology of "adoption" and/or "biological parents." On the other hand, some adolescents who clearly understand the meaning of adoption might report themselves as being adopted just for fun or as a joke. As a result, not all in-school SAQ responses about adoption questions will accurately reflect adolescents' true adoption status. In fact, the largest group of reporting inconsistencies (Table 11.2, group 6, $n = 88$) were adolescents who said they were adopted on the in-school SAQ but recanted when interviewed at home to say that they were living with biological parents and their parents agreed.

In the Add Health wave 1 in-home interview, the measurement of adoption status relied on the inference from the home living arrangement of adolescents, but it was the most complicated, indirect, and confusing way to measure adoption status. Some potential problems exist that may undermine the integrity of this inference about the adoption status of an adolescent. First, an adopted adolescent might not be living with his or her adoptive parent(s) (e.g., in aunt's or grandma's home, group home, or somewhere else). In this situation, the adopted respondent would not have listed the name(s) of his or her adoptive parent(s) at all because they were not coresiding. As a result, the adoptee should be classified as either adopted but living with nonrelatives (e.g., living in group home or by self) or adopted but living with nonparent relatives (e.g., living with aunt or grandma). If the classification of adoption status depended on having adoptive parent(s) living in the household at the time of the home interview, nonparental living arrangements of adoptees could cause underestimation of adopted children.

Another potential problem is related to the definitions for different types of parent–child relationships. Because it is somewhat challenging even for mature adults to understand the different parent–child relationships (see the Add Health in-home interview definitions for these relationships under the previous section "Measurement of Adoption Status"), it would be easy for adolescents to be confused, thus making an incorrect choice about their parent–child relationship and causing misclassification of their adoption status.

Parent responses about adolescent's adoption status would generally be considered valid. In the Add Health parent survey, the parent or guardian was asked to define their parent–child relationship (and their spouse's relationship) with the target adolescent. The respondent was asked, "What is your relationship to [name]?" If the respondent selected "adoptive mother" or "adoptive father" from the options provided, follow-up questions asked, "Does [name's] biological mother live in this household?" and "Does [name's] biological father live in this household?" It appears that, if the respondent is the parent, this line of questioning provides reasonably valid responses concerning the adoption status of the target adolescent. But the adoption classification based on these questions would be crude at the best because it would be impossible to distinguish different types of adoption (e.g., relative adoption vs. nonrelative adoption) without follow-up questions.

Suggestions for Future Researchers Gathering Data for Adoption Research

Future survey-based adoption research must address several issues. First, because the concept of adoption is quite broad and applies to a number different circumstances (e.g., international adoption, transracial adoption, infant adoption, adoption from foster care, stepparent adoption, kinship adoption), surveys need to be able to distinguish among these subgroups. Adoption researchers must be clear about the inclusion and exclusion criteria they use for defining who is adopted for the particular study they are conducting. For some research questions, an investigator might want to exclude children adopted internationally; for others, a researcher might want to include children adopted by stepparents. Questions in the data must be sufficiently detailed to permit investigators to make such distinctions.

Second, a single general adoption question does not allow for triangulation or verification of adoption status. If a survey simply asked, "Are you adopted?" or "Is your child adopted?" with no follow-up questions, the analyses we have reported in this chapter suggest that a substantial amount of misclassification could result.

Third, future survey research that employs more than one method of assessing adoption status (e.g., self-report questionnaires, interviews) and/or multiple respondents should be designed to maximize consistency and correct classification given the researchers' definitions of adoption. One obvious way to accomplish this is to ensure that the questions regarding adoption status are consistent for each assessment and for each respondent. If other family or household members are included in the data collection process, it would be important to ask them if the target adolescents (i.e., the adolescents who completed the other measures for the study) were adopted. A follow-up question that would help in determining the accuracy of adolescents' self-report would be to ask parent respondents if the target adolescent is aware of his or her adoption status. As we suggested earlier, asking about a household member's relation to the target adolescent may lead to an omission of information regarding that child's adoption status, particularly if the child is not living with parents or the adult respondent household member is not a parent or parent figure for the youth involved in the study. Asking about an adolescent's adoption status is a more direct means of identifying adoptees and non-adoptees than adoption classification based on relationships of adults and children who coreside.

CONCLUSIONS

In this chapter, three related Add Health data sets were used to illustrate the challenges of classifying adolescent respondents' adoption status in large-scale surveys. Discrepancies exist between alternative measures of adoption status in different Add Health data sets, and such discrepancies can be resolved through triangulation of different data sources. Further, evidence was presented that erroneous classification of adoption status can cause substantial distortions in substantive findings in the comparison between adopted and nonadopted adolescents.

The issues and findings presented in this chapter provide insights about the degree of influence that different measurement strategies can exert on the findings in the comparison between adopted and nonadopted adolescents. Different measurement contexts and procedures can substantially affect the magnitude of differences between adoptee and nonadoptee groups. It is possible that inconsistent findings in substantive comparisons between adopted and nonadopted adolescents might be caused by these and other methodological variations.

These analyses are also a reminder that investigators should be cautious when interpreting the effect of adoption on adolescent adjustment and well-being based on a single set of findings. The results presented here provide evidence that, at least in the school setting, some teens do not pro-vide valid answers regarding their adoption status and, more important, that there is a relationship between falsely claiming to be adopted and giving extreme answers about adolescent problem behaviors. Even in a large, nationally representative sample like the Add Health in-school SAQ, mea-surement problems can distort the results and, in the case presented here, exaggerate the negative effects of adoption.

Previously, adoption research studies relied primarily on agency and clinical adoptee samples as well as samples recruited from adoption sup-port groups. For such samples, there is typically a high degree of certainty regarding adoption status of the participants. Some researchers began using large-scale data sets to avoid problems inherent with nonprobabil-ity samples, such as small sample size and sample nonrepresentativeness. There are, however, advantages and disadvantages associated with each approach, and the strength of one approach appears to be the weakness of the other. It is important for adoption researchers to keep these method-ological strengths and weaknesses in mind while interpreting adoption research findings from different studies. For example, studies with more valid measures of adoption status (e.g., agency or clinical samples of adoptees) are likely to suffer from sample selection bias, and this methodological problem will affect the results to an unknown extent. Similarly, studies based only on samples of volunteer adoptive families will probably underestimate the negative effects of adoption because adoptive parents may be less likely to participate in such a study if their family is having problems related to adoption. On the other hand, studies based on large-scale archival data may suffer from problems like those described in this chapter, where measurement is less precise. These issues impose some limitations on conclusions about the effect of adoption on child/adolescent adjustment and reinforce the caution that each investigation must be considered in light of its research methodology.

ACKNOWLEDGMENTS

This chapter is an integration of several related published articles in which all three authors of this chapter were involved. These articles are cited in the chapter where appropriate and listed in the References section of this book. We gratefully acknowledge the support provided by grant HD36479 from the National Institute of Child Health and Human Development, to Brent C. Miller, P.I. Send correspondence to Brent C. Miller, Vice President for Research, Utah State University, 1450 Old Mail Hill, Logan, UT 84322-1450 (E-mail: brent.miller@USU.edu).

This research uses data from Add Health, a program project designed by J. Richard Udry, Peter S. Bearman, and Kathleen Mullan Harris, and funded by a grant P01-HD31921 from the National Institute of Child Health and Human Development, with cooperative funding from 17 other agencies. Special acknowledgment is due Ronald R. Rindfuss and Barbara Entwisle for assistance in the original design. Persons interested in obtaining data files from Add Health should contact Add Health, Carolina Population Center, 123 W. Franklin Street, Chapel Hill, NC 27516-2524 (http://www.cpc.unc.edu/addhealth/contract.html).

Chapter 12

Recent Changes and Future Directions for Adoption Research

Jesús Palacios and David M. Brodzinsky

Like many forms of nontraditional family life, adoption has gained increased visibility in the past few decades in both North America and Europe. However, the nature of adoption has changed quite dramatically over the years and currently is represented quite differently in different parts of the world. Although domestic infant adoption continues to be quite prevalent in the United States and Canada and to some extent in Great Britain, a growing percentage of adoptions throughout most Western countries involve children from the foster care and residential care systems as well as children adopted internationally, often from countries experiencing civil strife, poverty, or other social conditions that make it difficult for biological parents to raise their youngsters. In fact, in many parts of Europe (e.g., Sweden, Norway, Holland, Denmark, Spain, Italy), international adoptions constitute the majority of new adoption placements (see chapters 2 and 10 in this volume). Thus, although adoption has become increasingly visible throughout Western societies, the nature of adoptive family life often is quite different from one country to another as well as from one adoptive family to another within any specific country.

The exact number of adoptions occurring each year is difficult to estimate. In many countries, adoption statistics are not available, and those that are often have been found to be incomplete and unreliable. Nevertheless, at the beginning of the twenty-first century, it can be estimated that between 120,000 and 150,000 children are adopted each year by nonbiological relatives in North America and Europe (http://www.acf.hhs.gov, www.dfes.gov.uk, http://www.cic.gc.ca, http://www.racinesdenfance.org, http://www.destatis.de, http://www.commissioneadozioni.it, http:// www.mtas.es, http://www.ssb.no, http://www.doh.ie, http://www. adopte.ch). Moreover, when we consider that adoption by biological relatives and stepparents, often called kinship adoption, represents yet another and in some countries such as the United States (Stolley, 1993), a more common form of adoption, it is clear that this type of nontraditional family life is not only growing but also diversifying. The visibility of adoption in contemporary society also can be seen in the increasing number of adoption-related organizations, associations, and agencies whose activities and services focus exclusively on this population as well as by the growing number of Internet sites focusing on the needs of adoption triad members and the adoption professional community.

Paralleling the increased visibility of adoption in most Western societies is the increased visibility of adoption in professional service fields. Not only has there been an increase in the number of agencies facilitating adoption placements in many countries, but in the past few decades there has been an increased focus on professional interventions for members of the adoption triad during both preadoption and postadoption periods. As adoption has grown and become more complex, there has emerged an increasing concern about the psychological needs of adopted individuals, adoptive parents, and biological parents. As a result, social service and mental health professionals have begun to focus more on improved professional training in this area and on the development of better support and intervention services for adoption triad members.

Research scientists also have found in adoption a complex phenomenon to be studied, not only to understand the unique dynamics of the adoption experience but also because the study of adoptive families allows investigators to shed light on important scientific questions related to human development, such as the relative contribution of genetics versus environment in the behavior and development of the child, the impact of early adverse social experiences on the development of the child, and the identification of individual and systemic factors that foster resiliency in "atrisk" children. The visibility and interest in adoption among these investigators is attested to by the growing number of scientific books on adoption, the rise of empirical studies on adoption in referred journals, and the relatively recent development of a journal focused exclusively on the study of adoption: *Adoption Quarterly*.

It was in the context of the growing visibility of adoption throughout North America and Europe that we embarked on this edited volume. The contributions of the authors in this book attest to the complexity of adoption—as a form of family life, as a social service practice, and as a topic of research interest. In this final chapter, we would like to draw together some lessons learned from the various contributors as well as the broader psychological literature on this topic, highlighting some of the recent changes occurring in adoption research as well as pointing out areas for future empirical study. We also address the issue of translating research into sound adoption policy and practice.

CHANGES IN ADOPTION RESEARCH

From Descriptive Studies to Theory-Driven Research

The vast majority of adoption research over the past half century has been descriptive in nature, highlighting psychological outcomes for adopted children and the nature of adoptive family life. This trend is consistent with any new area of inquiry, where description always precedes explanation. More recently, however, we have witnessed a significant increase in theory-driven research as empirical efforts have shifted toward understanding the basis for adjustment patterns in adopted children, adoptive parents, and the adoptive family as a whole.

A diverse array of theories have been brought to bear on questions related to adoption adjustment, including genetic theory (Cadoret, 1990), prenatal and postnatal neurobiological risk theory (chapter 3 in this volume), risk and resilience theory (chapter 4 in this volume), psychodynamic theory (Brinich, 1990; Nickman, 1985), attachment theory (Johnson & Fein, 1991; chapter 5 in this volume), social role theory (Kirk, 1964, 1981), family systems theory (Reitz & Watson, 1992), family life cycle theory (Brodzinsky, 1987; Brodzinsky & Pinderhughes, 2002; Brodzinsky, Schechter, & Henig, 1992; Hajal & Rosenberg, 1991), cognitive-developmental theory (Brodzinsky, Schechter, & Brodzinsky, 1986; Brodzinsky, Singer, & Braff, 1984), stress and coping theory (Brodzinsky, 1990, 1993; Smith & Brodzinsky, 1994, 2002), and communication theory (Wrobel, Kohler, Grotevant, & McRoy, 2003; chapter 7 in this volume). Each of these perspectives has offered valuable insights into individual, interpersonal, and/or systemic perspectives on adoption and furthered our understanding of adjustment issues in adopted children and adoptive parents and, in some cases, biological parents. In short, the emergence of theory-driven adoption research represents a significant advance over earlier descriptive studies of adoption adjustment. Yet because each of these theories has focused only on selected aspects of the adoption experience, they typically have failed to capture the true complexity of adoption adjustment.

As the practice of adoption has become more diverse, the nature of adoptive family life also has become more varied. Understanding contemporary adoption as a developing, multisystemic experience necessitates a more complex representation than most theoretical models have provided to date. Thus, although we strongly support the shift toward increased theory-driven research in the adoption field, we also urge investigators to broaden their theoretical models to provide a more complete understanding of adoption dynamics (see, e.g., Barth & Berry, 1988; Berry, 1989–1990; Brodzinsky, 1990, 1993; Brodzinsky & Pinderhughes, 2002; McRoy, Grotevant, & Zurcher, 1988; chapter 1 in this volume).

From Looking at Outcomes to Looking at Family and Systemic Processes

A related change in adoption research is one involving a shift from focusing on outcomes in adopted children and their families to one focusing on family and systemic processes (see chapters 6 to 10 in this volume). Historically, most research in this area has been very child centered and specifically focused on the extent and nature of psychological risk associated with adoptive status. Although this research validated the increased psychosocial and academic problems manifested by adopted children, it did little to foster an understanding of the bases for these problems or for the range of normal behavior in the vast majority of these youngsters. Furthermore, it also shed little light on the nature of adoptive family dynamics or on the dynamics within the adoptive kinship system. In contrast, recent theory-driven research has focused more on exploring family and systemic processes that serve as risk and protective factors in the adjustment of adoption triad members. For example, there is a growing body of research focusing on adoption communication, both within the adoptive family (Wrobel, Kohler, et al., 2003; chapters 7 to 9 in this volume) and between the adoptive and biological families (Grotevant, Ross, Marchel, & McRoy, 1999; chapter 8 in this volume), as a factor mediating patterns of adoption adjustment. This type of research is providing valuable insights into the way in which adoptees, adoptive parents, and biological parents cope with adoption-related tasks across the family life cycle, which in turn has significant practical implications for parents and professionals. It also is shifting the research from a person-oriented focus to a systems-oriented focus, which is consistent with looking at adoption in a more complex and realistic manner. However, there remains a host of important questions that, as yet, have been inadequately addressed concerning the role of adoption-specific family dynamics, as well as more general family dynamics and systemic dynamics, in the adjustment of adopted children and their parents. For example, does the timing and manner of adoption revelation influence children's adjustment? What type of information do adoptive parents find most difficult to share with their children, and does the nature of this "sensitive" information influence children's attitudes about adoption and/or their birth heritage? How does the role of infertility and other experiences with loss impact on the adoptive parents' ability to manage adoption-specific parenting tasks? What is the best way for adoptive parents to facilitate appropriate attachments with those children who have experienced early neglect, abuse, and/or the deprivations of orphanage life? Under what conditions do children benefit from contact with their birth family, and when is it best to shield them from such contact? As researchers continue to shift their focus of attention from documenting the risk associated with adoption to questions concerning the role of family and systemic processes in adoption adjustment, we will be in a better position to provide the type of pre- and postadoption services that will reduce the risk of placement disruption and/or dissolution as well as increase the sense of satisfaction and emotional well-being among all members of the adoption triad.

From a Psychopathological to a Resilience and Developmental Perspective

As a nonnormative form of family life, adoption has been viewed by researchers and clinicians primarily as a source of problems in the adjustment of the child. In fact, as noted previously, the vast majority of early research on adoption focused on the increased risk of adopted children for psychological, social, and academic problems (for reviews of this research, see Brodzinsky, Smith, & Brodzinsky, 1998; Wierzbicki, 1993).

The initial pathologizing of adoption was supported by several factors. First, when adoption research began in the 1950s and 1960s, it still was a relatively invisible form of family life in Western societies and lacked validation for the "normalcy" of adoptive parent–child relationships. Second, most of the early descriptions of adoptive family life emerged from clinical case studies emphasizing adjustment difficulties in these families. Third, initial empirical studies did validate significant differences between adopted and nonadopted children in a host of adjustment areas. Finally, early adoption research and practice was influenced by psychoanalytic theory (e.g., Blum, 1983; Deutsch, 1945; Schechter, 1970; Toussieng, 1962), which emphasized a risk perspective as opposed to viewing adoption as a potential solution to a host of societal problems. The pathologizing of adoption ultimately culminated in the now repudiated concept of the "adopted child syndrome" (Kirschner, 1980, 1990; Smith, 2001).

As family life in Western societies has become more diverse in the past few decades, there has been a noticeable shift in the attitudes of many people toward members of nonnormative families. To live in a nontraditional family no longer is equated automatically with being deficient or problematic. In fact, there is a growing acceptance and validation of family diversity (Lamb, 1999). This is clearly seen in the area of adoption, where recent survey research in the United States has found that the vast majority of individuals hold positive attitudes about adoptive family life (Evan B. Donaldson Adoption Institute, 2002b). In short, although adoption is not a traditional family type, it is certainly a normal type of family.

There also has been a shift in the professional adoption community from viewing adoption as a problem to one in which increasingly it is seen as a potential solution for problems confronting children (Brodzinsky & Pinderhughes, 2002; Hoksbergen, 1999). Although most current studies have confirmed the increased adjustment difficulties of adopted children compared to nonadopted children, this research also has emphasized that the differences between the groups in adjustment patterns typically are relatively small (Haugaard, 1998) and, more important, that the vast majority of adoptees are well within the normal range of adjustment (see Brodzinsky & Pinderhughes, 2002; Brodzinsky et al., 1998). In addition, there has been a new focus in contemporary adoption research on understanding those resilience factors protecting children from early biological and social adversity (see chapter 4 and 10 in this volume) as well as understanding the variability in psychosocial functioning and developmental trajectories among adopted children and their families. This shift in adoption research has brought about a more balanced view of the adoption experience and its impact on children and their parents.

From Small-Scale Studies to Large-Scale Studies

Historically, most adoption research utilized relatively small, convenience samples. In some cases, these samples involved clinical patients; in others, they were children from community settings (Brodzinsky et al., 1998). In both cases, however, the use of small, convenience samples raised questions about possible sampling bias, the representativeness of the research subjects in relation to the broader population of adoptees, and the generalizability of the findings derived from the studies (Miller, Fan, Grotevant, et al., 2000; chapter 11 in this volume).

Recently, a number of investigators have utilized an alternative approach for collecting data on adoption adjustment—large population-based surveys (Burrow, Tubman, & Finley, 2004; Feigelman, Bachrach, Chandra, & Wilson, 1998; Miller, Fan, Grotevant, et al., 2000). As Miller et al. (chapter 11 in this volume) note, there are two advantages with using this approach, both of which are inherent to national database surveys. Specifically, the sample is likely to be both larger and, because of the use of scientific sampling techniques, more representative than would be found in typical, small-scale adoption research studies. Despite these advantages, Miller et al (chapter 11 in this volume) also point out certain drawbacks to this research strategy. First, national database surveys such as the National Longitudinal Study of Adolescent Health (Add Health), which has been used by adoption researchers in the United States, typically are not designed for the purpose of collecting information specifically about adoption. Consequently, questions of interest to adoption researchers are seldom included in these surveys with the exception of those items related to general adjustment outcomes (e.g., level of school attainment, academic performance, involvement with the mental health community, and so on). Second, and more important, it is often difficult to discern who is adopted and who is not from these surveys or the specific nature of the person's adoption (Miller et al., 2001; chapter 11 in this volume). The ambiguity of this information increases the risk of misclassifying survey participants as well as grouping together adoptees who come from quite different backgrounds (e.g., those who were placed as infants vs. those placed at an older age, those who were placed domestically vs. those placed from another country, those who were placed in-racially vs. those who were not, those who have had contact with birth family members vs. those who have not, and so on). As Fan et al. (2002) and Miller et al. (chapter 11 in this volume) have shown, misclassification of survey participants can lead to distortion of research findings related to adjustment issues.

It is clear that the utilization of large-scale survey research data in the area of adoption is a complicated matter involving both benefits and drawbacks. We believe, however, that careful use of this research methodology (see the suggestions offered by Miller et al., chapter 11 in this volume) can help adoption professionals gain a better understanding of how adoptive family status impacts on children and their parents, especially when combined with data derived from other methodologies, including the use of meta-analytic techniques for assessing general patterns of research findings (Bimmel, Juffer, van Ijzendoorn, & Bakermans-Kranenburg, 2003; Wierzbicki, 1993). The usefulness of national survey research data would be enhanced, however, if future surveys were designed with items more specific to adoption issues.

From Cross-Sectional to Longitudinal Studies

Like in most areas of child development and family research, the majority of adoption researchers have utilized cross-sectional designs in exploring adjustment issues among adoption triad members. The rationale for this approach is simple—it is relatively inexpensive and efficient in terms of data collection. Unfortunately, cross-sectional designs limit what can be said about developmental trajectories and processes as well as the impact of early experiences (e.g., prenatal exposure to illicit substances, multiple foster placements, neglect, abuse, and so on) on later patterns of adaptation.

Fortunately, a growing number of studies in adoption, in both North America and Europe, have utilized longitudinal designs, following the same children and/or families for varying periods of time (Bohman & Sigvardsson, 1990; Braungart-Rieker, Rende, Plomin, DeFries, & Fulker, 1995; Brooks & Barth, 1999; Coon, Carey, Corley, & Fulker, 1992; Lambert

& Streather, 1980; Maughan & Pickles, 1990; Stein & Hoopes, 1985; chapters 4, 5, 6, and 8 in this volume). These research efforts, as well as others, have provided invaluable information on developmental issues in adoption adjustment. Although expensive and requiring extraordinary commitment by the researchers, longitudinal studies provide us with the best opportunities for understanding the true complexity of the adoption experience within the context of the developing person, the evolving family, and the changing ecology within which family members live.

Examining the Impact of Openness in Adoption

For most of the twentieth century, adoption was a closed and confidential practice. Adoption agencies prohibited contact between the adoptive and biological families and provided adoptive parents with minimal information about the child's history. Furthermore, there was little preparation of adoptive parents for handling children's questions about adoption. In fact, adoptive parents often were encouraged to minimize adoption issues in discussions with their child and to integrate the child into their family in such a way as to mirror the biological family (see chapter 2 in this volume). In the late 1970s and 1980s, however, a small group of adoption professionals, as well as members of the adoption triad, began to advocate for greater openness in adoption (Sorosky, Baran, & Pannor, 1978). Over the past few decades, the efforts of these individuals (and others) have had a tremendous impact on the way adoption is practiced both in North American and in many parts of Europe.

Adoption today is moving decidedly toward increased openness. More and more adoptive parents and birth parents are meeting, exchanging identifying information, and, in some cases, arranging for ongoing contact following the child's placement. Recognition of the right and need of adoptees to access information about their origins has prompted adoption agencies to collect more detailed information about the birth family and to share it with adoptive parents at the time of placement. It also has resulted in increased efforts by adult adoptees to challenge existing laws that sealed their original birth certificates at the time of placement. In addition, openness in adoption is being manifested in a growing recognition of the importance of facilitating clear, honest, and emotionally sensitive communication between adoptive parents and their children (Wrobel, Kohler, et al., 2003; chapters 6 to 9 in this volume).

As the practice of adoption has become more open, adoption researchers have begun to explore the impact of this change on adoption triad members (Grotevant & McRoy, 1998; chapters 7 and 8 in this volume). Although critics of open adoption have warned that this practice will have grave consequences for all members of the adoption triad (Kraft, Palombo, Mitchell, Woods, & Schmidt, 1985a, 1985b; Kraft, Palombo, Woods, Schmidt, & Tucker,

1985), existing research has not supported these fears. In fact, the bulk of the data on open adoption suggest that there are significantly more benefits than drawbacks for adoptive parents and birth parents as well as for adopted children (for reviews of this research, see Brodzinsky et al., 1998; Grotevant & McRoy, 1998; Rushton, 2004; chapter 8 in this volume).

Research also has supported the benefits of open adoption communication both between adoptive parents and their children and between adoptive and birth family members as a factor in the adjustment of adoptees (Wrobel, Kohler, et al., 2003; chapters 7 and 8 in this volume). In fact, Brodzinsky (2004; chapter 7 in this volume) has suggested that openness in communication may have greater predictive power in terms of children's psychological adjustment than the extent of structural openness existing between the adoptive and biological families.

The practice of open adoption still is relatively new and, in fact, is in its infancy in many parts of Europe. Empirical efforts to examine variations in adoption practice in relation to adoption outcome also are relatively new, with only a few research teams displaying a systematic approach to investigating this issue. As a result, many questions remain about the impact of openness on adoption triad members. What factors determine why some individuals chose a closed, confidential adoption and others a more open adoption? Are there developmental differences related to the impact of openness on children? What factors predict different patterns of adoption communication in families? How do children communicate about adoption with siblings, extended family, peers, and others? How do adoptive and biological families negotiate the extent of contact and communication with one another over the years, and how do changing levels of openness impact on the adopted child? What are some of the cross-cultural factors associated with the practice of open adoption? Do adoption triad members experience open adoption similarly across cultures and countries? These are but a few of the issues related to open adoption that have yet to be explored or about which we still have too little information.

FUTURE DIRECTIONS FOR ADOPTION RESEARCH

The past few decades have witnessed a tremendous growth of interest in the impact of adoption on children and families. We expect this interest to continue, especially as adoption broadens in its complexity, becomes more accepted as a nontraditional but normal type of family, and offers researchers opportunities to examine interesting and theoretically relevant developmental issues. To further our understanding of adoption and render research more relevant to practice issues, a number of suggestions are offered.

First, as noted previously, adoption research needs to be well grounded in theory that reflects the diversity of contemporary adoptive family life and the complexity of current adoption practice. We also need to move away from theoretical models focusing exclusively on the psychopathology of adoption to those also seeking to understand positive adaptation in adopted children and their families. As Brooks et al. (chapter 1 in this volume) note, the "resilience paradigm" is well suited for this purpose, especially because of its emphasis on examining developmental trajectories in response to different patterns of early and later experience.

Second, there needs to be greater focus on biological factors underlying the adjustment of adopted children and the way in which environment can enhance children's potentials and offset their vulnerabilities. Gunnar and Kertes (chapter 3 in this volume), for example, discuss various prenatal experiences (e.g., malnutrition, exposure to alcohol and drugs, deficiencies in micronutrients, and heightened maternal stress) as well as perinatal and postnatal experiences (e.g., premature birth, inadequate nutrition, intestinal parasites, infectious disease, inadequate sensory and social stimulation, and exposure to chronic stress and other trauma experiences) that increase the risk of developing neurobehavioral problems for many adopted children, especially those youngsters adopted internationally or from foster care. These findings suggest the need for a more thorough assessment of these youngsters at the time of adoption and for better planning for postplacement interventions. Successful interventions aimed at ameliorating adverse prenatal and early postnatal experiences, however, require a more thorough awareness of brain plasticity and the effects of environmental factors on the structure and functioning of the neural system than currently exits. Yet there is reason to be hopeful regarding the long-term outcome for many of these adopted children. For example, although research suggests that adopted children who experience early institutional life (chapter 4 in this volume) or who are exposed prenatally to drugs and alcohol (Barth & Brooks, 2000) are at increased risk for a variety of cognitive and socioemotional problems, it has also been found that early placement in a warm, loving, and stable adoptive family can often prevent or offset the adverse impact of these experiences. Given the rise in international adoptions in Western societies as well as the rise in foster care adoptions in North America and parts of Europe, it is critical that future research focus greater attention on the role of early risk factors.

We also need more longitudinal studies in this area. Although a number of long-term studies already have been conducted, most were designed with a focus only on the relative outcome of adopted children compared to various nonadopted groups of children. Prospective studies of the adoptive family system and the adoptive kinship system need to be conducted (see chapter 8 in this volume) in order to understand the role of early adoption experiences—on the individual, familial, and systemic levels—for later patterns of development. Particular attention needs to be given to the adoptee's transition from adolescence to young adulthood, an especially neglected developmental phase in the adoption literature (Rushton, 2004).

It has been argued that the meaning of adoption is socially constructed (Leon, 2002; Miall, 1996; chapter 2 in this volume) and that the way in which adoption triad members adjust to their unique experiences can be understood only in the specific historical and cultural context in which they live. We share this view, as do many other adoption theorists and researchers. Yet despite the fact that adoption is practiced throughout Western society as well as in many Eastern societies, there have been few attempts to explore the social representation of adoption across cultures or the way in which culture impacts on adoption practice and adjustment outcomes. For example, how do societal attitudes and values about out-of-wedlock pregnancy, single parenthood, and adoption impact on the decision of a young woman to place her child for adoption? Is the experience of adoption-related loss influenced by societal values regarding the importance of biological family connections? Are the experiences and adjustment outcomes of transracially placed adoptees who grow up in a racially, ethnically, and cultural diverse country such as the United States different from those who grow up in countries with a more homogeneous population such as Sweden, Norway, Spain, or Italy? These are interesting and theoretically relevant questions about which we have few answers. It is our hope that future researchers will begin to explore these and related questions concerning the cultural context of adoption. The creation of this book represents an initial effort at fostering transnational communication among adoption researchers.

Another area deserving of more attention is the impact of preadoption and postadoption services on adoption triad members. There is no question that as adoption practice has become increasingly complex, birth parents, adoptive parents, and adopted children have been offered a wider range of adoption services than they were in the past (Brooks, Allen & Barth, 2002; chapter 1 in this volume). Most of these services, however, are provided prior to adoption finalization. It is well recognized in the adoption field that adequate postadoption services do not exist, yet are critical for the well-being of adoption triad members (Barth & Miller, 2001; Howard & Smith, 2000). In addition, as Brooks et al. (2002) have reported, the specific adoption services needed, as well as client utilization and satisfaction with the services, vary by type of adoption, that is, public agency, private agency, or independent adoption. There is a significant need for research on the availability, utilization, and efficacy of postadoption services. Although efforts are being made to increase the level of postadoption services, we simply do not know which services are most effective in promoting long-term psychological well-being for adoption triad members.

Finally, we need to think more seriously about the practice and policy implications of adoption research. Achieving this goal will require greater cross-discipline collaboration than has existed in the past as well as greater collaboration between researchers and clinicians. Adoption, by its very nature, has attracted the interest of researchers from many disciplines, including social welfare, psychology, psychiatry, sociology, medicine, anthropology, and demography. Too often, however, these researchers have worked in isolation from one another and have been uninformed about the empirical work outside their respective disciplines. In addition, there has been relatively little communication and collaboration between researchers and clinicians in this field. Yet the need for developing and testing effective preadoption and postadoption services is best achieved through this type of professional collaboration. In developing their research models, we strongly urge our colleagues to incorporate the insights gained from disciplines beyond their own field as well as from clinicians who seek to put into practice the lessons learned from the day-to-day experience with adoption triad members.

SUMMARY AND CONCLUSIONS

If there is a single theme that runs through this book, it is that the practice of adoption and the nature of adoptive family life have undergone some remarkable changes over the past few decades. Although social scientists have begun to explore the impact of many of these changes on the adjustment of adoption triad members, research generally has not kept up with the pace of these changes, nor, until recently, has it reflected the complexity of the changes. Fortunately, we appear to be entering a new wave of adoption research, one that is being guided by more sophisticated adoption theory and methodology as well as a more pronounced focus on the connection between research, policy, and practice. We are heartened by this trend and hope that the current volume not only supports and reinforces the efforts of our research colleagues but also fosters greater interest in cross-fertilization among researchers from different parts of the world.

Finally, we also are encouraged by the efforts of our colleagues who see in adoption a fruitful arena in which to study central issues concerning human development and family life. The natural experiments offered by the study of adopted children and their families have allowed a growing number of researchers to explore the role of individual and cumulative risks experienced early in life and the ameliorating influence of subsequent protective factors on the long-term adjustment of children (Barth & Brooks, 2000; O'Connor, Rutter, Beckett, et al., 2000; chapters 3 and 4 in this volume). We hope the insights gained from this type of research will be incorporated into more effective postplacement services so as to improve the lives of the many thousands of children who experience early biological and social adversity.

References

Abidin, R.R. (1995). *Parenting stress index* (3rd ed.). Odessa, FL: Psychological Assessment Resources, Inc.

Accornero, V.H., Morrow, C.E., Bandstra, E.S., Johnson, A.L., & Anthony, J.C. (2002). Behavioral outcome of preschoolers exposed prenatally to cocaine: Role of maternal behavioral health. *Journal of Pediatric Psychology, 27,* 259–269.

Achenbach, T. M. (1991). *Manual for the CBCL/4–18 and 1991 Profile.* Burlington: University of Vermont Press.

Achenbach, T. M., & Edelbrock, C. (1983). *Manual for the Child Behavior Checklist and Revised Child Behavior Profile.* Burlington: University of Vermont Press.

Achenbach, T.M., & Edelbrock, C. (1987). *Manual for the Youth Self-Report and Profile.* Burlington: University of Vermont, Department of Psychiatry.

Ainsworth, M., Blehar, M., Waters, E., & Wall, S. (1978). *Patterns of attachment: A psychological study of the Strange Situation.* Hillsdale, NJ: Lawrence Erlbaum Associates.

Altstein, H., & Simon, R. J. (Eds.). (1991). *Intercountry adoption: A multinational perspective.* New York: Praeger.

American Psychiatric Association. (1994). *Diagnostic and statistical manual of mental disorders* (4th ed.). Washington, DC: Author.

Ames, E.W. (1997). *The development of Romanian orphanage children adopted to Canada.* Final report to Human Resources Development Canada.

Anderson, J.W., Johnstone, B.M., & Remley, D.T. (1999). Breast-feeding and cognitive development: A meta-analysis. *American Journal of Clinical Nutrition 70,* 525–535.

Andrews, H., Goldberg, D., Wellen, N., Pittman, B., & Struening, E. (1995). Prediction of special-education placement from birth certificate data. *American Journal of Preventive Medicine, 11,* 55–61.

Andujo, E. (1988). Ethnic identity of transethnically adopted Hispanic adolescents. *Social Work, 33,* 531–535.

Antonovsky, A. (1979). *Health, stress and coping.* San Francisco: Jossey-Bass.

Antonovsky, A. (1989). *Unravelling the mystery of health: How people manage stress and stay well.* San Francisco: Jossey-Bass.

Aronson, M., Kyllerman, M., Sabel, K., Sandin, B., & Alegard, R. (1985). Children of alcoholic mothers: Developmental, perceptual and behavioral characteristics as compared to matched controls. *Acta Psychiatrica Scandinavica, 74,* 27–35.

Bachrach, C. A., Stolley, K. S., & London, K. A. (1992). Relinquishment of premarital births: Evidence from national survey data. *Family Planning Perspectives, 24,* 27–38.

Bagley, C. (1993). *International and transracial adoptions: A mental health perspective.* Avebury: Aldershot.

Bagley, C., Young, L., & Scully, A. (1993). Transracial adoption in Britain: A follow-up study, with policy considerations. *Child Welfare, 72,* 285–299.

Baran, A., & Pannor, R. (1993). Perspectives on open adoption. *The Future of Children, 11,* 119–124.

Barker, D.J. (1997). Fetal nutrition and cardiovascular disease in later life. *British Medical Bulletin, 53,* 96–108.

Barnes, H. L., & Olson, D. H. (1985). Parent-adolescent communication and the circumplex model. *Child Development, 56,* 438–447.

Baron, R.M., & Kenny, D.A. (1986). The moderator-mediator variable distinction in social psychological research: Conceptual, strategic, and statistical considerations. *Journal of Personality and Social Psychology, 51,* 1173–1182.

Barth, R.P. (1994). Adoption research: Building blocks for the next decade. *Child Welfare, 73,* 625–638.

Barth, R. P. (2002). Outcomes of adoption and what they tell us about designing adoption services. *Adoption Quarterly, 6,* 45–60.

Barth, R.P., & Berry, M. (1988). *Adoption and disruption: Rates, risks and resources.* New York: Aldine de Gruyter.

Barth, R.P., & Berry, M. (1991). Preventing adoption disruption. *Prevention in Human Services, 9,* 205–222.

Barth, R.P., & Brooks, D. (1997). A longitudinal study of family structure, family size, and adoption outcomes. *Adoption Quarterly, 1,* 29–56.

Barth, R. P., & Brooks, D. (2000). Outcomes of drug-exposed children eight years post adoption. In R.P. Barth, M. Freundlich, & D. Brodzinsky (Eds.), *Adoption and prenatal alcohol and drug exposure: Research, policy and practice* (pp. 23–58). Washington, DC: Child Welfare League of America.

Barth, R. P., Brooks, D., & Iyer, S. (1995). *California adoptions: Current demographic profiles and projections through the end of the century.* Berkeley: University of California, Child Welfare Research Center.

Barth, R.P., Gibbs, D., & Siebenaler, K. (2001). *Assessing the field of post-adoption services: Family needs, program models, and evaluation issues* (U.S. DHHS Contract No. 100-99-0006). Research Triangle Park, NC: RTI International. Available: http://aspe.os.dhhs.gov/hsp/post-adoption01

Barth, R.P., & Miller, J. (2001). Building effective post-adoption services: What are the empirical foundations? *Family Relations, 49,* 447–455.

Barth, R.P., & Needell, B. (1996). Outcomes for drug-exposed children four years after adoption. *Children and Youth Services Review, 18,* 37–56.

Bateson, P., & Martin, P. (1999). *Design for a life: How behaviour develops.* London: Jonathan Cape.

Becker, H. A., & Hermkens, P. L. J. (1993). Introduction: Generations between market and solidarity. In H. A. Becker & P. L. J. Hermkens, *Solidarity of generations* (pp. 17–46). Amsterdam: Thesis Publishers.

Becker, H. C., Randall, C. L., Salo, A. L., Saulnier, J. L., & Weathersby, R. T. (1994). Animal research: Charting the course for FAS. *Alcohol Health & Research World, 18,* 10–16.

Benson, P. L., Sharma, A. R., & Roehlkepartain, E. C. (1994). *Growing up adopted: A portrait of adolescents and their families.* Minneapolis: Search Institute.

Berge, J. M., Mendenhall, T. J., Wrobel, G. M., Grotevant, H. D., & McRoy, R.G. (in press). Adolescents' feelings about openness in adoption: Implications for adoption agencies. *Child Welfare.*

Berntsen, M., & Eigeland, S. (1987). *Utenlandsadopterte barn og overgang til nytt språk* [International adopted children and their transition to a new language]. Oslo: University of Oslo, Department of Special Needs Education.

Berry, M. (1989–1990). Stress and coping among older adoptive families. *Social Work and Social Sciences Review, 1,* 71–93.

Berry, M. (1990). Preparing and supporting special needs adoptive families: A review of the literature. *Child and Adolescent Social Work Journal, 7,* 403–418.

Berry, M. (1991). The practice of open adoption: Findings from a study of 1,396 families. *Children and Youth Services Review, 13,* 379–395.

Berry, M., & Barth, R. (1990). A study of disrupted adoptive placements of adolescents. *Child Welfare, 69,* 209–225.

Berry, M., Cavazos Dylla, D., Barth, R. P., & Needell, B. (1998). The role of open adoption in the adjustment of adopted children and their families. *Children and Youth Services Review, 20,* 151–171.

Bimmel, N., Juffer, F., van Ijzendoorn, M. H., & Bakermans-Kranenburg, M. J. (2003). Problem behavior of internationally adopted adolescents: A review and meta-analysis. *Harvard Review of Psychiatry, 11,* 64–77.

Black, J. E., & Greenough, W. T. (1986). Induction of pattern in neural structure by experience: Implications for cognitive development. In B. Rogoff (Ed.), *Advances in developmental psychology* (Vol. 4, pp. 1–50). Hillsdale, NJ: Lawrence Erlbaum Associates.

Blotcky, M. J., Looney, J. G., & Grace, K. D. (1982). Treatment of the adopted adolescent: Involvement of the biologic mother. *Journal of the American Academy of Child Psychiatry, 21,* 281–285.

Blum, H. P. (1983). Adoptive parents: Generative conflict and generational continuity. *Psychoanalytic Study of the Child, 38,* 141–163.

Bock, G. R., & Whelan J. (1991). The childhood environment and adult disease. *Ciba Foundation Symposium, 156.* Chichester: Wiley.

Bogenschneider, K. (2002). *Family policy matters: How policymaking affects families and what professionals can do.* Mahwah, NJ: Lawrence Erlbaum Associates.

Bohman, M., & Sigvardsson, S. (1990). Outcome in adoption: Lessons from longitudinal studies. In D. M. Brodzinsky & M. D. Schecter (Eds.), *The psychology of adoption* (pp. 93–106). New York: Oxford University Press.

Borders, L. D., Black, L. K., & Pasley, B. K. (1998). Are adopted children and their parents at greater risk for negative outcomes? *Family Relations, 47,* 237–241.

Borders, L. D., Penny, J. M., & Portnoy, F. (2000). Adult adoptees and their friends: Current functioning and psychological well-being. *Family Relations, 49,* 407–418.

Boston, M., & Lush, D. (1993). Can child psychotherapists predict and assess their own work? A research note. *ACPP Review and Newsletter, 15,* 112–119.

Botvar, P. K. (1995). *Når øst møter vest... En undersøkelse blant adopterte fra Korea, India og Thailand* [When East meets West... A study among adoptees from Korea, India and Thailand]. Oslo: Diaconia College Center.

Botvar, P. K. (1999). *Meget er forskjellig, men det er utenpå: Unge adoptertes levekår og livsforhold* [We are different on the outside, but not on the inside: Young adoptees' lifestyles and conditions]. Oslo: Diaconia College Center.

Bowlby, J. (1969). *Attachment and loss: Attachment* (Vol. 1). New York: Basic Books.

Bowlby, J. (1973). *Attachment and loss: Separation* (Vol. 2). New York: Basic Books.

Bowlby, J., Ainsworth, M. D. S., Boston, M., & Rosenbluth, D. (1956). The effects of mother-child separation: A follow-up study. *British Journal of Medical Psychology, 49,* 211–247.

Bradley, R. H. (2002). Environment and parenting. In M. Bornstein (Ed.), *Handbook of parenting: Vol. 2, Biology and ecology of parenting* (2nd ed., pp. 281–314). Hillsdale, NJ: Lawrence Erlbaum Associates.

Bramanti, D., & Rosnati, R. (1998). *Il patto adottivo: L'adozione internazionale di fronte alla sfida dell'adolescenza* [The adoptive pact: Intercountry adoption in front of the adolescent challenge]. Milan: Franco Angeli.

Brand, A. E., & Brinich, P. M. (1999). Behavior problems and mental health contacts in adopted, foster, and nonadopted children. *Journal of Child Psychology and Psychiatry, 40,* 1221–1229.

Braungart-Rieker, J., Rende, R. D., Plomin, R., DeFries, J. C., & Fulker, D. W. (1995). Genetic mediation of longitudinal associations between family environment and childhood behavior problems. *Development and Psychopathology, 7,* 233–245.

Bray, J., Maxwell, S. E., & Cole, D. (1995). Multivariate statistics for family psychology research. *Journal of Family Psychology, 9,* 144–160.

Bremner, J. D. (1999). Does stress damage the brain? *Biological Psychiatry, 45,* 797–805.

Bretherton, I. (1985). Attachment theory: Retrospect and prospect. In I. Bretherton & E. Waters (Eds.), Growing points of attachment theory and research. *Monographs of the Society for Research in Child Development,50*(1–2, Serial No. 209).

Bretherton, I., & Oppenheim, D. (2003). The MacArthur Story Stem Battery: Development, administration, reliability, validity and reflections about meaning. In R. N. Emde, D. P. Wolf, & D. Oppenheim (Eds.), *Revealing the inner worlds of young children: The MacArthur Story Stem Battery and parent-child narratives* (pp. 55–80). New York: Oxford University Press.

Bretherton, I., Ridgeway, D., & Cassidy, J. (1990). Assessing internal working models of the attachment relationship: An attachment story completion task for 3-year-olds. In M. T. Greenberg, D. Cicchetti, & E. M. Cummings (Eds.), *Attachment in the preschool years* (pp. 273–308). London: University of Chicago Press.

Brinich, P. M. (1990). Adoption from the inside out: A psychoanalytic perspective. In D. Brodzinsky & M. Schechter (Eds.), *The psychology of adoption* (pp. 42–61). New York: Oxford University Press.

Brodzinsky, A. B. (1992). *The relation of learned helplessness, social support, and avoidance to grief and depression in women who have placed an infant for adoption.* Unpublished doctoral dissertation, New York University.

Brodzinsky, D. M. (1984). New perspectives on adoption revelation. *Adoption and Fostering, 8,* 27–32.

Brodzinsky, D. M. (1987). Adjustment to adoption: A psychosocial perspective. *Clinical Psychology Review, 7,* 25–47.

Brodzinsky, D. M. (1990). A stress and coping model of adoption adjustment. In D. M. Brodzinsky & M. D. Schechter (Eds.), *The psychology of adoption* (pp. 3–24). New York: Oxford University Press.

Brodzinsky, D. M. (1993). Long-term outcome in adoption. *The Future of Children, 11,* 153–166.

Brodzinsky, D. M. (2004). *Family structural openness and communication openness as predictors in the adjustment in adopted children.* Paper presented at the 18th biennial meeting of the International Society for the Study of Behavioral Development, Ghent, Belgium.

Brodzinsky, D. M., & Brodzinsky, A. B. (1991). The impact of family structure on the adjustment of adopted children. *Child Welfare, 71,* 69–76.

Brodzinsky, D. M., Elias, M. J., Steiger, C., Simon, J., Gill, M., & Hitt, J. C. (1992). Coping Scale for Children and Youth: Scale development and validation. *Journal of Applied Developmental Psychology, 13,* 195–214.

Brodzinsky, D. M., Patterson, C. J., & Vaziri, M. (2003). Adoption agency perspectives on lesbian and gay prospective parents: A national study. *Adoption Quarterly, 5,* 5–23.

Brodzinsky, D. M., & Pinderhughes, E. E. (2002). Parenting and child development in adoptive families. In M. H. Bornstein (Ed.), *Handbook of parenting: Vol. 1. Children and parenting* (pp. 279–311). Mahwah, NJ: Lawrence Erlbaum Associates.

Brodzinsky, D. M., & Schechter, M. D. (Eds.). (1990). *The psychology of adoption.* New York: Oxford University Press.

Brodzinsky, D. M., Schechter, D. E., Braff, A. M., & Singer, L. M. (1984). Psychological and academic adjustment in adopted children. *Journal of Consulting and Clinical Psychology, 52,* 582–590.

Brodzinsky, D. M., Schechter, D., & Brodzinsky, A. B. (1986). Children's knowledge of adoption: Developmental changes and implications for adjustment. In R. Ashmore & D. Brodzinsky (Eds.), *Thinking about the family: Views of parents and children* (pp. 205–232). Hillsdale, NJ: Lawrence Erlbaum Associates.

Brodzinsky, D. M., Schechter, M. D., & Henig, R. M. (1992). *Being adopted: The lifelong search for self.* New York: Doubleday.

Brodzinsky, D. M., Singer, L. M., & Braff, A. M. (1984). Children's understanding of adoption. *Child Development, 55,* 869–878.

Brodzinsky, D. M., Smith, D. W., & Brodzinsky, A. B. (1998). *Children's adjustment to adoption: Developmental and clinical issues.* Thousand Oaks, CA: Sage.

Brodzinsky, D. M., & Steiger, C. (1991). Prevalence of adoptees among special education populations. *Journal of Learning Disabilities, 24,* 484–489.

Bronfenbrenner, U. (1992). Ecological systems theory. In R. Vasta (Ed.), *Six theories of child development* (pp. 187–249). Philadelphia: Kingsley.

Bronfenbrenner, U., & Morris, P. A. (1998). The ecology of developmental processes. In W. Damon (Series Ed.) & R. M. Lerner (Vol. Ed.), *Handbook of child psychology: Vol. 1. Theoretical models of human development* (5th ed., pp. 993–1028). New York: Wiley.

Brooks, D. (2004).*Psychosocial outcomes for adult transracial and inracial adoptees: Similarities and differences within and across groups.* Manuscript submitted for publication.

Brooks, D. (in press). The impact of transracial placement on racial affiliations and identifications: Self-reported experiences of adult African American, Asian and Caucasian adoptees. *Children and Youth Services Review.*

Brooks, D., Allen, J., & Barth, R. P. (2002). Adoption service use, helpfulness, and need: A comparison of public and private agency and independent adoptive families. *Children and Youth Services Review, 24,* 213–238.

Brooks, D., & Barth, R. P. (1998). Characteristics and outcomes of drug-exposed and non drug-exposed children in kinship and non-relative foster care. *Children and Youth Services Review, 20,* 475–501.

Brooks, D., & Barth, R. P. (1999). Adjustment outcomes of adult transracial and inracial adoptees: Effects of race, gender, adoptive family structure, and placement history. *American Journal of Orthopsychiatry, 69,* 87–102.

Brooks, D., Barth, R. P., Bussiere, A., & Patterson, G. (1999). Adoption and race: Implementing the Multiethnic Placement Act of 1994 and the Interethnic Adoption provisions. *Social Work, 44,* 167–178.

Brooks, D., & Goldberg, S. (2001). Gay and lesbian adoptive and foster care placements: Can they meet the needs of waiting children? *Social Work, 46*(2), 147–157.

Brooks, D., James, S., & Barth, R. P. (2002). Preferred characteristics of children in need of adoption: Is there a demand for available foster children? *Social Service Review, 76,* 575–602.

Brooks, D., Wind, L. H., & Barth, R. P. (2005). Parents' knowledge of their adopted children's special needs: Its role in adoption preparation, expectations and satisfaction? Manuscript submitted for publication.

Brottveit, Å. (1996). "Rasimen" og de utenlandsadopterte. Norsk nyrasisme og kulturforståelse, belyst ved utenlandsadopsjon ["Racism" and international adoptees in Norway]. *Norsk antropologisk tidsskrift, 2,* 132–148.

Brottveit, Å. (1999). *"Jeg ville ikke skille meg ut"—Identitetsutvikling, ekstern kategorisering og etnisk identitet hos adopterte fra Colombia og Korea* ["I didn't want to look different—The identity development, external categorization and ethnic identity of adoptees from Colombia and Korea]. Oslo: Diaconia College Center.

Buchsbaum, H. K., Toth, S., Clyman, R. B., Cicchetti, D., & Emde, R. N. (1992). The use of a narrative story stem technique with maltreated children: Implications for theory and practice. *Development and Psychopathology, 4,* 603–625.

Burrow, A. L., Tubman, J. G., & Finley, G. E. (2004). Adolescent adjustment in a nationally collected sample: Identifying group differences by adoption status, adoption subtype, developmental stage and gender. *Journal of Adolescence, 27,* 267–282.

Bussiere, A. (1998). The development of adoption law. *Adoption Quarterly, 1,* 3–25.

Butz, A. M., Pulsifer, M., Marano N., Belcher, H., Lears, M. K., & Royall, R. (2001). Effectiveness of a home intervention for perceived child behavioral problems and parenting stress in children with in utero drug exposure. *Archives of Pediatric and Adolescent Medicine, 155,* 1029–1037.

Byrd, A. D. (1988). The case for confidential adoption. *Public Welfare, 46,* 20–23.

Cadoret, R. J. (1990). Biologic perspectives of adoptee adjustment. In D. Brodzinsky & M. Schechter (Eds.), *The psychology of adoption* (pp. 25–41). New York: Oxford University Press.

Caldji, C., Tannenbaum, B., Sharma, S., Francis, D., Plotsky, P. M., & Meaney, M. J. (1998). Maternal care during infancy regulates the development of neural systems mediating the expression of fearfulness in the rat. *Proceedings of the National Academy of Sciences USA, 95,* 5335–5340.

Carlson, M., & Earls, F. (1997). Psychological and neuroendocrinological sequelae of early social deprivation in institutionalized children in Romania. *Annals of the New York Academy of Sciences, 807,* 419–428.

Carlson, V., Cicchetti, D., Barnett, D., & Braunwald, K. (1989). Disorganised/disoriented attachment relationships in maltreated infants. *Developmental Psychology, 25,* 525–531.

Carp, E. W. (1998). *Family matters: Secrecy and disclosure in the history of adoptions.* Cambridge, MA: Harvard University Press.

Carrà, E., & Marta, E. (1995). *Adolescenza e relazioni familiari* [Adolescence and family relations]. Milan: Franco Angeli.

Carrion, V. G., Weems, C. F., Eliez, S., Patwardhan, A., Brown, W., Ray, R. D., et al. (2001). Attenuation of frontal asymmetry in pediatric posttraumatic stress disorder. *Biological Psychiatry, 50,* 943–951.

Carrion, V. G., Weems, C. F., Ray, R. D., Glaser, B., Hessl, D., & Reiss, A. L. (2002). Diurnal salivary cortisol in pediatric posttraumatic stress disorder. *Biological Psychiatry, 51,* 575–582.

Carter, E. A., & McGoldrick, M. (Eds.). (1980). *The family life cycle.* New York: Gardner Press.

Carver, J. D. (2003). Advances in nutritional modifications of infant formulas. *American Journal of Clinical Nutrition, 77*(6), 1550S–1554S.

Caspi, A., McClay, J., Moffitt, T. E., Mill, J., Martin, J., Craig, I. W., et al. (2002). Role of genotype in the cycle of violence in maltreated children. *Science, 297,* 851–854.

Caspi, A., Sugden, K., Moffitt, T. E., Taylor, A., Craig, I. W., Harrington, H. L., et al. (2003). Influence of life stress on depression: Moderation by a polymorphism in the 5-HTT gene. *Science, 301,* 386–389.

Cassidy, J., & Shaver, P. R. (1999). *Handbook of attachment: Theory, research and clinical applications.* New York: Guilford Press.

Castle, J., Groothues, C. D., Bredenkamp, D., Beckett, C., O'Connor, T., Rutter, M., et al. (1999). Effects of qualities of early institutional care on cognitive attainment. *American Journal of Orthopsychiatry, 69,* 424–437.

C.B.S. (2003). *Jaarcijfers Geboorte, Maandstatistiek Bevolking* [Year figures, birth month statistics of the population]. Utrecht: Author.

Cederblad, M. (1981). Utlänska adoptivbarns psykiska anpassning [The psychological adjustment of intercountry adoptees]. *Läkatidningen, 78*(9), 816–819.

Cederblad, M. (1982). *Utländska adoptivbarn som kommit till Sverige efter tre års ålder: Anpassningsprocessen under det förste året i familjen* [International adoptees who have been adopted to Sweden after the age of three years: The adaptation process during the first year in the family]. Stockholm: Statens Nämnd for Internatonallea Adotivfrågor.

Cederblad, M. (1989). *Utlandsfödda adoptivbarn—Anpassningsproblem i tonåren* [International adoptees—Adaptation problems during teenage years]. Lund: University of Lund, Department of Child and Adolescent Psychiatry.

Cederblad, M. (1991). Utlandsfödda adoptivbarn: Hög ålder vid adoptionen största risken för att utveckla anpassningsproblem i tonåren [International adopted children: High adoption age gives high risk for developing mental problems in teenage years]. *Läkartidningen, 88,* 1084–1085.

Cederblad, M., & Hook, B. (1986). Vart sjätte barn har psykiska störninger [One child in six has mental problems]. *Läkartidningen, 83,* 953–959.

Cederblad, M., Hook, B., Irhammar, M., & Mercke, A. M. (1999). Mental health in international adoptees as teenagers and young adults: An epidemiological study. *Journal of Child Psychology and Psychiatry, 40,* 239–248.

Cederblad, M., Rhammer, M., Mercke A. M. & Norlander, S. (1994). *Identitet och anpassning hos utlandsfödda adopterade [Identity and adaptation of foreign adoptees].* Forskning om barn och familj nr 4. Institutionen for barn- och ungdomspsykiatri, Universitetet i Lund. [Research on children and the Family. no.4. Department of child and adolescent psychiatry. University of Lund, Sweden.]

Center for Adoption Research and Policy. (1997). Available: http://www. ummed.edu/main/purpose.htm

Chapman, D., Dorner, P., Silber, K., & Winterberg, T. (1986). Meeting the needs of the adoption triangle through open adoption: The birthmother. *Child and Adolescent Social Work, 3,* 203–213.

Chapman, D., Dorner, P., Silber, K., & Winterberg, T. (1987a). Meeting the needs of the adoption triangle through open adoption: The adoptee. *Child and Adolescent Social Work, 4,* 78–91.

Chapman, D., Dorner, P., Silber, K., & Winterberg, T. (1987b). Meeting the needs of the adoption triangle through open adoption: The adoptive parent. *Child and Adolescent Social Work, 4,* 3–12.

Chasnoff, I.J., Anson, A., Hatcher, R., Stenson, H., Iaukea, K., & Randolph, L. (1998). Prenatal exposure to cocaine and other drugs. *Annals of the New York Academy of Sciences, 846,* 314–328.

Chisholm, K. (1998). A three-year follow-up of attachment and indiscriminate friendliness in children adopted from Romanian orphanages. *Child Development, 69,* 1092–1106.

Chisholm, K., Carter, M.C., Ames, E.W., & Morison, S.J. (1995). Attachment security and indiscriminately friendly behavior in children adopted from Romanian orphanages. *Developmental Psychopathology, 7,* 283–294.

Christian, C. L., McRoy, R. G., Grotevant, H. D., & Bryant, C. M. (1997). Grief resolution of birthmothers in confidential, time-limited mediated, ongoing mediated, and fully disclosed adoptions. *Adoption Quarterly, 1,* 35–58.

Chugani, H.T., Behen, M.E., Muzik, O., Juhasz, C., Nagy, F., & Chugani, D. C. (2001). Local brain functional activity following early deprivation: A study of postinstitutionalized Romanian orphans. *Neuroimage, 14,* 1290–1301.

Cicchetti, D. (1996). Child maltreatment: Implications for developmental theory and research. *Human Development, 39,* 18–39.

Cicchetti, D., & Rogosch, F. A. (2001). Diverse patterns of neuroendocrine activity in maltreated children. *Development and Psychopathology, 31,* 677–693.

Cocozzelli, C. (1989). Predicting the decision of biological mothers to retain or relinquish their babies for adoption: Implication for open placement. *Child Welfare, 68,* 33–44.

Cohen, J. (1988). *Statistical power analysis for the behavioral sciences* (2nd ed.). Hillsdale, NJ: Lawrence Erlbaum Associates.

Cohen, N., Coyne, J., & Duvall, J. (1996). Parents' sense of "entitlement" in adoptive and nonadoptive families. *Family Process, 35,* 441–456.

Cohen, N. J. (2002). Adoption. In M. Rutter & E. Taylor (Eds.), *Child and adolescent psychiatry* (4th ed., pp. 373–381). Malden, MA: Blackwell.

Cole, E. S., & Donley, K. S. (1990). History, values, and placement policy issues. In D. M. Brodzinsky & M. D. Schechter (Eds.), *The psychology of adoption* (pp. 273–294). New York: Oxford University Press.

Collishaw, S., Maughan, B., & Pickles, A. (1998). Infant adoptions: Psychosocial outcomes in adulthood. *Social Psychiatry and Psychiatric Epidemiology, 33,* 57–65.

Committee Blok. (2004). *Bruggen bouwen: Eindrapport* [Building bridges: Final report]. The Hague: SDU Uitgevers.

Connor, J. R. (1994). Iron acquisition and expression of iron regulatory proteins in the developing brain: Manipulation by ethanol exposure, iron deprivation, and cellular dysfunction. *Developmental Neuroscience, 16,* 233–247.

Coon, H., Carey, G., Corley, R., & Fulker, D. (1992). Identifying children in the Colorado Adoption Project at risk for conduct disorder. *Journal of the American Academy of Child and Adolescent Psychiatry, 31,* 503–511.

Crittenden, P. M. (1988). Relationships at risk. In J. Belsky & T. Nezworski (Eds.), *Clinical Implications of Attachment* (pp. 136–174). Hillsdale, NJ: Lawrence Erlbaum Associates.

Crittenden, P. M. (1992). Quality of attachment in the preschool years. *Developmental Psychopathology, 4,* 209–243.

Crittenden, P. M. (1994). Peering into the black box: An exploratory treatise on the development of self in young children. In D. Cicchetti & S. Toth (Eds.), *Rochester Symposium on Developmental Psychopathology: Vol. 5. The self and its disorders* (pp. 79–148). Rochester, NY: University of Rochester Press.

Curtis, W. J., & Nelson, C. A. (2003). Toward building a better brain: Neurobehavioral outcomes, mechanisms, and processes of environmental enrichment. In S. S. Luthar (Ed.), *Resilience and vulnerability: Adaptation in the context of childhood adversities* (pp. 463–488). Cambridge: Cambridge University Press.

Dalen, M. (1988, November). *Intercountry adopted children: Under-achievers at school?* Paper presented at the International Conference on Adoption, Melbourne, Australia.

Dalen, M. (1995). Learning difficulties among inter-country adopted children. *Nordisk pedagogikk, 15,* 195–208.

Dalen, M. (1999). Interaction in adoptive families. In A. Rygvold, M. Dalen, & B. Sætersdal (Eds.), *Mine—yours—ours and their: Adoption, changing kinship and family patterns* (pp. 82–100). Oslo: University of Oslo.

Dalen, M. (2001). School performances among internationally adopted children in Norway. *Adoption Quarterly, 5,* 39–58.

Dalen, M. (2002). Adoptivfamilien år 2000: Hvem er de, hvordan lever de og hvilke utfordringer står de overfor [Adoptive families in the year 2000: Who are they, how do they live and what kind of challenges will they meet?]. In I. Söderlind (Ed.), *Uppväxt, familjeformer och barns bästa* [Growing up, family patterns for the best of the child] (pp. 61–76). Stockholm: Institutet for Framtidsstudier.

Dalen, M., & Rygvold, A. L. (1999). *Hvordan går det på skolen? En analyse av utenlandsadopterte elevers skolekompetanse* [How are they doing at school? A study of international adoptees' school performances]. Oslo: University of Oslo, Department of Special Needs Education.

Dalen, M., & Sætersdal, B. (1987). Transracial adoption in Norway. *Adoption and Fostering, 4,* 41–47.

Dalen, M., & Sætersdal, B. (1992). *Utenlandsadopterte barn i Norge: Tilpasning—Opplæring—Identitetsutvikling* [International adopted children in Norway: Adaptation—learning—identity]. Unpublished doctoral dissertation, University of Oslo.

Dalen, M., & Sætersdal, B. (1999). Utenlandsadoptert ungdom—En ny kulturell kategori? [International adoptees—A new cultural category?]. In A. M. Jensen, E. Backe-Hansen, H. Bache-Wiig, & K. Heggen (Eds.), *Oppvekst I barnets århundre* [Growing up in the century of the child] (pp. 268–281). Oslo: Ad Notam, Gyldendal.

Daly, K. (1988). Reshaped parenthood identity: The transition to adoptive parenthood. *Journal of Contemporary Ethnography, 17,* 40–66.

Daly, K. (1989). Infertility resolution and adoption readiness. *Families in Society: Journal of Contemporary Human Services, 71,* 483–492.

Daly, K. J., & Sobol, M. P. (1994). Public and private adoption: A comparison of service and accessibility. *Family Relations, 43,* 86–93.

D'Atena, P., & Ardone, R. G. (1991). Rappresentazione familiare e comunicazione: Contributo empirico su famiglie con adolescenti [Family representation and communication: A study on families with adolescents]. *Terapia familiare, 35,* 37–48.

De Bellis, M. D., Keshavan, M. S., Clark, D. B., Casey, B. J., Giedd, J. B., Boring, A. M., et al. (1999). Developmental traumatology, Part 2: Brain development. *Biological Psychiatry, 45,* 1271–1284.

de Geer, B. (1992). *Internationally adopted children in communication: A developmental study.* Unpublished doctoral dissertation, Lund University.

de Haan, M., Bauer, P. J., Georgieff, M. K., & Nelson, C. A. (2000). Explicit memory in low-risk infants aged 19 months born between 27 and 42 weeks of gestation. *Developmental Medicine & Child Neurology, 42,* 304–312.

Derogatis, L. R. (1993). *Brief Symptom Inventory: Administration, scoring, and procedures manual.* Minneapolis: National Computer Systems.

Deutsch, D. K., Swanson, J. M., Bruell, J. H., Cantawell, D. P., Weinberg, F., & Baren, M. (1982). Overrepresentation of adoptees in children with the attention deficit disorder. *Behavior Genetics, 12,* 231–238.

Deutsch, H. (1945). *The psychology of women: A psychoanalytic interpretation* (Vol. 2). New York: Grune & Stratton.

Dobbing, J., & Smart L. L. (1974). Vulnerability of developing brain and behaviour. *British Medical Bulletin, 30,* 164–168.

Drewett, R., Wolke, D., Asefa, M., Kaba, M., & Tessema, F. (2001). Malnutrition and mental development: Is there a sensitive period? A nested case-control study. *Journal of Child Psychology and Psychiatry 42,* 181–187.

Dunbar, N. (2003). *Typologies of adolescent adoptive identity: The influence of family context and relationships.* Unpublished doctoral dissertation, University of Minnesota, St. Paul.

Dunbar, N., & Grotevant, H. D. (2004). Adoption narratives: The construction of adoptive identity during adolescence. In M.W. Pratt & B.H. Fiese (Eds.), *Family stories and the life course: Across time and generations* (pp. 135–161). Mahwah, NJ: Lawrence Erlbaum Associates.

Dunbar, N., van Dulmen, M. H. M., Ayers-Lopez, S., Berge, J. M., Christian, C., Fitzgerald, N., et al. (2000, November). *Openness changes in adoptive kinship network connections.* Paper presented at the meeting of the National Council on Family Relations, Minneapolis.

Duyme, M., Arseneault, L., & Dumaret, A-C. (2004). Environmental influences on intellectual abilities in childhood: Findings from a longitudinal adoption study. In P. L. Chase-Lansdale, K. Kiernan, & R. Friedman (Eds.), *Human development across lives and generations: The potential for change* (pp. 278–292). New York: Cambridge University Press.

Duyme, M., Dumaret, A.-C., & Tomkiewicz, S. (1999). How can we boost IQs of "dull children"? A late adoption study. *Proceedings of the National Academy of Sciences, 96,* 8790–8794.

Dyer-Friedman, J., Glaser, B., Hessl, D., Johnston, C., Huffman, L. C., Taylor, A., et al. (2002). Genetic and environmental influences on the cognitive outcomes of children with fragile X syndrome. *Journal of the American Academy of Child and Adolescent Psychiatry, 41,* 237–244.

Egmond van, G. (1987). *Bodemloos bestaan: Problemen met adoptiekinderen* [Bottomless existence: Problems with adoptive children]. Baarn: Ambo.

Elbert, T., Pantev, C., Weinbruch, C., Rockstroh, B., & Taub E. (1995). Increased cortical representation of the fingers of the left hand in string players. *Science, 270,* 305–307.

Emde, R. N., Wolf, D. P., & Oppenheim, D. (Eds.). (2003). *Revealing the inner worlds of young children: The MacArthur Story Stem Battery and parent-child narratives.* New York: Oxford University Press.

Epstein, N. B., Baldwin, L. M., & Bishop, D. (1983). The McMaster Family Assessment Device. *Journal of Marital and Family Therapy, 9,* 171–180.

Erikson, E. H. (1968). *Identity: Youth and crisis.* New York: Norton.

Erikson, E. H. (1982). *The life cycle completed: A review.* New York: Norton .

Eriksson, P. S., Perfilieva, E., Bjork-Eriksson, T., Alborn, A. M., Nordborg, C., Peterson, D. A., et al. (1998). Neurogenesis in the adult human hippocampus. *Nature Medicine, 4,* 1313–1317.

Eth, S., & Pynoos, R. S. (1985). Developmental perspectives on psychic trauma in childhood. In C. R. Figley (Ed.), *Trauma and its wake: The study and treatment of post-traumatic stress disorder* (pp. 36–52). New York: Brunner/Mazel.

Etter, J. (1993). Levels of cooperation and satisfaction in 56 open adoptions. *Child Welfare, 72,* 257–267.

Evan B. Donaldson Adoption Institute. (1997). *Benchmark adoption survey: First public opinion survey on American attitudes toward adoption.* New York: Author.

Evan B. Donaldson Adoption Institute. (2002a). *International adoption facts.* New York: Author.

Evan B. Donaldson Adoption Institute. (2002b). *National adoption attitudes survey.* New York: Author.

Evan B. Donaldson Adoption Institute. (2002c). *Overview of adoption in the United States.* New York: Author.

Fan, X., Miller, B. C., Christensen, M., Bayley, B., Park, K. E., Grotevant, H. D., et al. (2002). Questionnaire and interview inconsistencies exaggerated differences between adopted and non-adopted adolescents in a national sample. *Adoption Quarterly, 6,* 7–27.

Fanshell, D. (1972). *Far from the reservation: The transracial adoption of American Indian children.* Metuchen, NJ: Scarecrow Press.

Fava Vizziello, G., Antonioli, M., Bartoli, S., Volpe, B., & Zancato, P. (1996). Genitorialità biologica e adottiva: Analogie e differenze dei percorsi rappresentativi [Biological and adoptive parenthood: Analogies and differences in the representational courses]. *Consultorio Familiare, 3,* 35–55.

Feast, J., & Howe, D. (2003). Talking and telling. In A. Douglas & T. Philpot (Eds.), *Adoption: Changing families, changing times* (pp. 139–146). London: Routledge.

Federici, R. (2003). *Help for the hopeless child: A guide for families with special discussion for assessing and treating the post-institutionalized child.* Washington: Federici and Associates.

Federici, R. (2003, October). *Neuropsychological and psychoeducational evaluation of the post-institutionalized child.* Paper presented at the 1st Annual Conference for International Adoptees from Eastern Europe, Arlington, VA.

Feigelman, W. (1997). Adopted adults: Comparisons with persons raised in conventional families. *Marriage and Family Review, 25,* 199–223.

Feigelman, W., Bachrach, C. A., Chandra, A., & Wilson, J. (1998). Using archival data sets to study adoption-related questions. *Adoption Quarterly, 2,* 79–88.

Feigelman, W., & Silverman, A. R. (1983). *Chosen children: New patterns of adoptive relationships.* New York: Praeger.

Fergusson, D. M., Lynskey, M., & Horwood, L. J. (1995). The adolescent outcomes of adoption: A 16-year longitudinal study. *Journal of Child Psychology and Psychiatry, 36,* 597–615.

Fernández, M., & Fuentes, M. J. (2001). Variables infantiles de riesgo en el proceso de adaptación de niños/as de adopciones especiales [Children's risk variables in special needs adoption process of adaptation]. *Infancia y Aprendizaje, 24,* 341–359.

Fernandez-Teruel, A., Escorihuela, R. M., Castellano, B., Gonzalez, B., & Tobena, A. (1997). Neonatal handling and environmental enrichment effects on emotionality, novelty/reward seeking, and age-related cognitive and hippocampal impairments: Focus on the Roman rat lines. *Behavior Genetics, 27,* 513–526.

Festinger, T. (1986). *Necessary risk: Adoption disruption.* New York: Child Welfare League of America.

Fields, J., & Casper, L. M. (2001). *America's families and living arrangements: March 2000.* (Current Population Reports No. P20–537). Washington, DC: U.S. Bureau of the Census.

Finley, G. E. (1999). Children of adoptive families. In W. K. Herman & T. H. Ollendick (Eds.), *Developmental issues in the clinical treatment of children* (pp. 358–370). Needham Heights, MA: Allyn & Bacon.

Fisher, L., Ames, E. W., Chisholm, K., & Savoie, L. (1997). Problems reported by parents of Romanian orphans adopted to British Columbia. *International Journal of Behavioral Development, 20,* 67–82.

Follevåg, G. (2002). *Adoptert identitet* [Adoptive identity]. Oslo: Spartacus Forlag.

Francis, D., Diorio, J., Liu, D., & Meaney, M. J. (1999). Nongenomic transmission across generations of maternal behavior and stress responses in the rat. *Science, 286,* 1155–1158.

Frasch, K., Brooks, D., & Barth, R. P. (2000). Openness and contact in adoptions by foster families: An eight-year follow-up. *Family Relations, 49,* 435–446.

Fraser, M. (Ed.). (2004). *Risk and resilience in childhood: An ecological perspective* (2nd ed.). Washington, DC: NASW Press.

Fravel, D. L., McRoy, R. G., & Grotevant, H. D. (2000). Birthmother perceptions of the psychologically present adopted child: Adoption openness and boundary ambiguity. *Family Relations, 49,* 425–433.

Frederickson, C., & Danscher, G. (1990). Zinc-containing neurons in hippocampus and related CNS structures. *Progress in Brain Research, 83,* 71–84.

Freundlich, M. (2002). Adoption research: An assessment of empirical contributions to the advancement of adoption practice. *Journal of Social Distress and the Homeless, 11,* 143–166.

Friedlander, M. L. (1999). Ethnic identity development of internationally adopted children and adolescents: Implications for family therapists. *Journal of Marital and Family Therapy, 25,* 43–60.

Garbarino, J. (1992). *Children and families in the social environment* (2nd ed.). New York: Aldine.

Gardell, I. (1979). *Internationella adoptioner* [International adoptions]. Stockholm: Allmänna Barnhuset.

Garmezy, N. (1987). Stress, competence, and development. *American Journal of Orthopsychiatry, 57,* 159–174.

Geerars, H. C., & Hoksbergen, R. A. C. (1991). Uithuisplaatsing van adoptiekinderen, meningen van ouders, hulpverleners en geadopteerden [Out-of-home placement of adoptive children: Opinions of parents, caretakers and adoptees]. In R. A. C. Hoksbergen & H. Walenkamp (Eds.), *Kind van andere ouders, theorie en praktijk van adoptie* [Child from other parents, theory and practice of adoption] (pp. 98–113). Houten/Antwerpen: Bohn Stafleu van Loghum.

General Accounting Office. (1994). *Foster care: Parental drug abuse has alarming impact.* Washington, DC: Author.

Georgieff, M. K., & Rao, R. (2001). The role of nutrition in cognitive development. In C. A. Nelson & M. Luciana (Eds.), *Handbook of cognitive developmental neuroscience* (pp. 491–504). Cambridge, MA: MIT Press.

Gianino, A., & Tronick, E. Z. (1987). The mutual regulation model: The infant's self and interactive regulation and coping and defensive capacities. In T. Field, P. McCabe, & N. Schneiderman (Eds.), *Stress and coping* (pp. 47–68). Hillsdale, NJ: Lawrence Erlbaum Associates.

Gindis, B. (1999). Language-related issues for international adoptees and adoptive families. In T. Tepper, L. Hannon, & D. Sandstrom (Eds.), *International adoption: Challenges and opportunities* (pp. 98–108). Meadow Lands, PA: Parents Network for the Postinstitutionalized Child.

Gioia, G. A. (2003, October). *Executive dysfunction in children and its impact on education.* Paper presented at the 1st Annual Conference for International Adoptees from Eastern Europe, Arlington, VA.

Glidden, L.M. (1991). Adopted children with developmental disabilities: Post-placement family functioning. *Children and Youth Services Review, 13,* 363–377.

Glidden, L.M. (1992). Chosen ones: Adopted children with disabilities. In T. Thompson & S.C. Hupp (Eds.), *Saving children at risk: Poverty and disabilities* (pp. 116–140). Newbury Park, CA: Sage.

Glidden, L.M. (2000). Adopting children with development disabilities: A long-term perspective. *Family Relations, 49,* 397–405.

Glidden, L. M., & Johnson, V. E. (1999). Twelve years later: Adjustment in families who adopted children with developmental disabilities. *Mental Retardation, 37,* 16–24.

Godbout, J. T. (1992). *L'esprit du don* [The gift's spirit]. Paris: La Découverte.

Goerge, R., Howard, E., Yu, D., & Radomsky, S. (1997). *Adoption, disruption, and displacement in the child welfare system: 1976–1994.* Chicago: Chapin Hall Center for Children.

Goldberg, D., & Wolkind, S. N. (1992). Patterns of psychiatric disorder in adopted girls: A research note. *Journal of Child Psychology and Psychiatry, 33,* 935–940.

Golombok, S., Cook, R., Bish, A., & Murray, C. (1995). Families created by the new reproductive technologies: Quality of parenting and social and emotional development of the children. *Child Development, 66,* 285–298.

Goodman, R. (1997). The Strengths and Difficulties Questionnaire: A research note. *Journal of Child Psychology and Psychiatry, 35,* 581–586.

Gottfried, A. E., Gottfried, A. W., & Bathurst, K. (2002). Maternal and dual-earner employment status and parenting. In M. Bornstein (Ed.), *Handbook of parenting: Vol. 2. Biology and ecology of parenting* (2nd ed., pp. 207–230). Hillsdale, NJ: Lawrence Erlbaum Associates.

Gozzoli, C., & Tamanza, G. (1998). *Il Family Life Space* [The family life space], Milan: Franco Angeli.

Grantham-McGregor, S. (1987). Field studies in early nutrition and later achievement. In J. Dobbing (Ed.), *Early nutrition and later achievement* (pp. 128–153). London: Academic Press.

Greco, O., Ranieri S., & Rosnati, R. (2003). *Il percorso della famiglia adottiva: Strumenti per l'ascolto e l'accompagnamento* [The route of adoptive family: Instruments for listening and accompanying]. Milan: Unicopli.

Greco, O., & Rosnati, R. (1998). Alla ricerca di un patto adottivo [Searching an adoptive pact]. In D. Bramanti & R. Rosnati (Eds.), *Il patto adottivo: L'adozione internazionale di fronte alla sfida dell'adolescenz*a [The adoptive pact: Intercountry adoption in front of the adolescent challenge] (pp. 172–208). Milan: Franco Angeli.

Green, J., Stanley, C., Smith, V., & Goldwyn, R. (2000). A new method of evaluating attachment representations in young school age children: The Manchester Child Attachment Story Task. *Attachment and Human Development, 2* ,48–70.

Greene, A. L., & Grimsley, M. D. (1990). Age and gender differences in adolescents' preferences for parental advice: Mum's the word. *Journal of Adolescence Research, 5,* 396–413.

Greenough, W.T. (1987). Experience effects on the developing and the mature brain: Dendritic branching and synaptogenesis. In *Prenatal development: A psychobiological perspective* (pp. 195–221). New York: Academic Press.

Greenough, W.T., Black, J.E., & Wallace, C.S. (1987). Experience and brain development. *Child Development, 58*, 539–559.

Greenough, W. T., & Chang, F. L. (1988). Plasticity of synapse structure and pattern in the cerebral cortex. In A. Peters & E. G. Jones (Eds.), *Cerebral cortex: Development and maturation of cerebral cortex* (Vol. 7, pp. 391–440). New York: Plenum.

Gritter, J. L. (1997). *The spirit of open adoption*. Washington, DC: Child Welfare League of America.

Groark, C.J., McCall, R.B., Muhamedrahimov, R., Nikoforova, N., & Palmov, O. (2000). The effects of improving caregiving on early development. Retrieved May 5, 2003, from http://www.pitt.edu/~ocdweb/policy21.htm.

Groothues, C., Beckett, C., & O'Connor, T. (1998). The outcome of adoptions from Romania. *Adoption and Fostering, 22*, 30–39.

Grossman, A.W., Churchill, J.D., Bates, K.K., Kleim, J.A., & Greenough, W.T. (2002). A brain adaptation view of plasticity: Is synaptic plasticity an overly limited concept? In M.A. Hofman, G.J. Boer, A.J.G.D. Holtmaat, E.J.W. van Someren, J. Verhagen, & D.F. Swaab (Eds.), *Progress in brain research* (Vol. 138, pp. 91–108). Amsterdam: Elsevier.

Grossman, A. W., Churchill, J.D., McKinney, B. C., Kodish, I. M, Otte, S. L., & Greenough, W.T. (2003). Experience effects on brain development: Possible contributions to psychopathology. *Journal of Child Psychology and Psychiatry, 44*, 3–63.

Grotevant, H.D. (1993). The integrative nature of identity: Bringing the soloists to sing in the choir. In J. Kroger (Ed.), *Discussions on ego identity* (pp. 121–146). Hillsdale, NJ: Lawrence Erlbaum Associates.

Grotevant, H. D. (1997). Coming to terms with adoption: The construction of identity from adolescence into adulthood. *Adoption Quarterly, 1*, 3–27.

Grotevant, H. D. (1998). Adolescent development in family contexts. In W. Damon (Series Ed.) & N. Eisenberg (Vol. Ed.), *Handbook of child psychology: Vol. 3. Social, emotional, and personality development* (5th ed., pp. 1097–1149). New York: Wiley.

Grotevant, H. D., Dunbar, N., Kohler, J. K., & Esau, A. L. (2000). Adoptive identity: How contexts within and beyond the family shape developmental pathways. *Family Relations, 49*, 379–387.

Grotevant, H. D., & Kohler, J. K. (1999). Adoptive families. In M. Lamb (Ed.), *Nontraditional families: Parenting and child development* (2nd ed., pp. 161–190). Mahwah, NJ: Lawrence Erlbaum Associates.

Grotevant, H., & McRoy, R. (1988). Emotionally disturbed adolescents: Early patterns of family adoptions. *Family Process, 27*, 439–457.

Grotevant, H. D., & McRoy, R. G. (1997). The Minnesota/Texas Openness in Adoption Research Project: Evolving policies and practices and their implications for development and relationships. *Applied Developmental Science, 1*, 166–184.

Grotevant, H. D., & McRoy, R. (1998). *Openness in adoption: Exploring family connections*. Thousand Oaks, CA: Sage.

Grotevant, H. D., McRoy, R. G., Elde, C., & Fravel, D. L. (1994). Adoptive family system dynamics: Variations by level of openness in the adoption. *Family Process, 33*, 125–146.

Grotevant, H. D., McRoy, R. G., & van Dulmen, M. H. (1998). The adoptive kinship network: Putting the perspectives together. In H. D. Grotevant & R. G. McRoy, *Openness in adoption: Exploring family connections* (pp. 173–194). Thousand Oaks, CA: Sage.

Grotevant, H. D., Ross, N. M., Marchel, M. A., & McRoy, R. G. (1999). Adaptive behavior in adopted children: Predictors from early risk, collaboration in relationships within the adoptive kinship network, and openness arrangements. *Journal of Adolescent Research, 14*, 231–247.

Grotevant, H. D., Wrobel, G. M., van Dulmen, M. H., & McRoy, R. G. (2001). The emergence of psychosocial engagement in adopted adolescents: The family as context over time. *Journal of Adolescent Research, 16*, 469–490.

Grow, L. J., & Shapiro, D. (1974). *Black children—white parents: A study of transracial adoption*. Washington, DC: Child Welfare League of America.

Groze, V. K., & Rosenthal, J. A. (1991). Single parents and their adopted children: A psychosocial analysis. *Families in Society: The Journal of Contemporary Human Services, 72*, 67–77.

Gunnar, M., Bruce, J., & Grotevant, H. D. (2000). International adoption of institutionally reared children: Research and policy. *Development and Psychopathology, 12*, 677–693.

Gunnar, M., Grotevant, H. D., & Johnson, D. (2002). *Preliminary report of the Minnesota International Adoption Survey*. Minneapolis: University of Minnesota.

Gunnar, M., & Kertes, D. (2003, April). Early risk factors and development of internationally adopted children: Can we generalize from the Romanian case? In T. G. O'Connor & M. Rutter (Chairs), *Psychological and biological evidence concerning the role of early experiences in development*. Symposium conducted at the biennial meeting of the Society for Research in Child Development, Tampa, FL.

Gunnar, M., Morison, S. J., Chisholm, K., & Schuder, M. (2001). Salivary cortisol levels in children adopted from Romanian orphanages. *Development and Psychopathology, 13*, 611–628.

Gunnar, M. R. (2000). Early adversity and the development of stress reactivity and regulation. In C. A. Nelson (Ed.), *The effects of adversity on neurobehavioral development: The Minnesota Symposia on Child Psychology* (Vol. 31, pp. 163–200). New York: Lawrence Erlbaum Associates.

Gunnarby, A., Hofvander, Y., Sjölin, S., & Sundelin, C. (1982). Utländska adoptivbarns hälsotilstand och anpassning till svenska förhållanden [International adoptees' health and adaptation to Swedish conditions]. *Läkartidningen, 79*, 1697–1705.

Hack, M., Klein, N. K., & Taylor, H. G. (1995). Long-term developmental outcomes of low birth weight infants. *The Future of Children, 5*, 176–196.

Hajal, F., & Rosenberg, E. G. (1991). The family life cycle in adoptive families. *American Journal of Orthopsychiatry, 61*, 78–85.

Halldèn, G. (1981). *Adoption i ett konflikt- och utvecklingsperspektiv* [Adoption in a conflict- and developmental perspective]. Unpublished doctoral dissertation, Stockholm University.

Harter, S. (1980). *The pictorial of perceived competence and acceptance for young children preschool/kindergarten form*. Denver: University of Denver.

Harter, S. (1985). *What I am like: Self-perception profile for children*. Denver: University of Denver.

Haugaard, J. J. (1998). Is adoption a risk factor for the development of adjustment problems? *Clinical Psychology Review, 18*, 47–69.

Hebb, D. O. (1947). The effects of early experiences on problem solving at maturity. *American Psychologist, 2*, 737–745.

Heim, C., & Nemeroff, C. B. (2001). The role of childhood trauma in the neurobiology of mood and anxiety disorders: Preclinical and clinical studies. *Biological Psychiatry, 49*, 1023–1039.

Helsen, M., Vollebergh, W., & Meeus, W. (2000). Social support from parents and friends and emotional problems in adolescence. *Journal of Youth and Adolescence, 29*, 319–335.

Hene, B. (1987). *De utländska adoptivbarnen och deras språkutveckling* [International adoptees and their language development] (Sprins rapport: 36). Göteborg: University of Göteborg, Institutionen for Lingvistik.

Hene, B. (1988). *Proficiency in a new native language: On investigating the proficiency in Swedish of intercountry adoptees between 10 and 12 years of age* (Paper No. 4). Göteborg: University of Göteborg, Institutionen for Lingvistik.

Henney, S., McRoy, R. G., Ayers-Lopez, S., & Grotevant, H. D. (2003). The impact of openness on adoption agency practices: A longitudinal perspective. *Adoption Quarterly, 6*, 31—51.

Henney, S. M., Onken, S. J., McRoy, R. G., & Grotevant, H. D. (1998). Changing agency practices toward openness in adoption. *Adoption Quarterly, 1*, 45–76.

Henry, C., Kabbaj, M., Simon, H., LeMoal, M., & Maccari, S. (1994). Prenatal stress increases the hypothalamic-pituitary-adrenal axis response in young and adult rats. *Journal of Neuroendocrinology 6*, 341–345.

Hessl, D., Dyer-Friedman, J., Glaser, B., Wisbeck, J., Barajas, G., Taylor, A., et al. (2001). The influence of environmental and genetic factors on behavior problems and autistic symptoms in boys and girls with fragile X syndrome. *Pediatrics, 108*, 88.

Hetherington, E. M., & Stanley-Hagan, M. (2002). Parenting in divorced and remarried families. In M. Bornstein (Ed.), *Handbook of parenting: Vol. 3. Being and becoming a parent* (2nd ed., pp. 287–316). Hillsdale, NJ: Lawrence Erlbaum Associates.

Hjern, A., Lindblad, F., & Vinnerljung B. (2002). Suicide, psychiatric illness, and social maladjustment in intercountry adoptees in Sweden: A cohort study. *Lancet, 360*, 443–448.

Hobbs, J. R., & Davis, J. A. (1967). Serum gamma-G-globulin levels and gestational age in premature babies. *Lancet, 19*, 223–227.

Hodges, J. (1990) The relationship to self and objects in early maternal deprivation and adoption. *Journal of Child Psychotherapy, 16*, 53–73.

Hodges, J. (2003). Adoption and fostering. In D. H. Skuse (Ed.), *Child psychology and psychiatry: An introduction* (pp. 177–181). Abingdon: Medicine Publishing Company.

Hodges, J., & Steele, M. (2000). Effects of abuse on attachment representations: Narrative assessments of abused children. *Journal of Child Psychotherapy, 26,* 433–455.

Hodges, J., Steele, M., Hillman, S., & Henderson, K. (2002). *Coding manual for LP story stem narrative responses: GOS/AFC /Coram study.* Unpublished manuscript, Anna Freud Centre, London.

Hodges, J., Steele, M., Hillman, S., & Henderson, K. (2003). Mental representations and defenses in severely maltreated children: A story stem battery and rating system for clinical assessment and research applications. In R. N. Emde, D. P. Wolf, & D. Oppenheim (Eds.), *Revealing the inner worlds of young children: The MacArthur Story Stem Battery and parent-child narratives* (pp. 240–267). New York: Oxford University Press.

Hodges, J., Steele, M., Hillman, S., Henderson, K., & Kaniuk, J. (2003). Changes in attachment representations over the first year of adoptive placement: Narratives of maltreated children. *Journal of Clinical Child Psychology and Psychiatry, 8,* 351–367.

Hodges, J., & Tizard, B. (1989a). IQ and behavioural adjustment of ex-institutional adolescents. *Journal of Child Psychology and Psychiatry, 30,* 53–75.

Hodges, J., & Tizard, B. (1989b). Social and family relationships of ex-institutional adolescents. *Journal of Child Psychology and Psychiatry, 30,* 77–97.

Hogg, C., Rutter, M., & Richman, N. (1997). Emotional and behavioural problems in children. In I. Sclare (Ed.), *Child psychology portfolio.* Windsor, ON: NFER-Nelson.

Hoksbergen, R. A. C. (1991). Intercountry adoption coming of age in the Netherlands. In H. Altstein & R. Simon (Eds.), *Intercountry adoption: A multinational perspective* (pp. 141–158). New York: Praeger.

Hoksbergen, R. A. C. (1999). The importance of adoption for nurturing and enhancing the emotional and intellectual potential of children. *Adoption Quarterly, 3,* 29–42.

Hoksbergen, R. A. C. (2000). Changes in attitudes in three generations of adoptive parents: 1950–2000. In P. Selman (Ed.), *Intercountry adoption: Developments, trends and perspectives* (pp. 86–102). London: British Agencies for Adoption and Fostering.

Hoksbergen, R. A. C. (2001). *Vijftig jaar adoptie in Nederland: Een historisch-statistische beschouwing.* [Fifty years of adoption in the Netherlands: A historical-statistical consideration]. Utrecht: Department of Adoption.

Hoksbergen, R. A. C., Juffer, F., & Waardenburg, B. C. (1987). *Adopted children at home and at school.* Lisse: Swets & Zeitlinger.

Hoksbergen, R. A. C., Spaan, J. J. T. M., & Waardenburg, B. C. (1988). *Bittere Ervaringen: Uithuisplaatsing van buitenlandse adoptiekinderen* [Bitter experiences: Placement in residential care of foreign adoptees]. Amsterdam: Swets & Zeitlinger.

Hoksbergen, R., ter Laak, J., van Dijkum, C., Rijk, K., & Stoutjesdijk, F. (2003). Attention deficit, hyperactivity disorders in adopted Romanian children living in the Netherlands. *Adoption Quarterly, 6,* 59–73.

Holahan, C. J., & Moos, R. H. (1991). Life stressors personal and social resources and depression: A 4-year structural model. *Journal of Abnormal Psychology, 100,* 31–38.

Holahan, C. J., Valentiner, D. P., & Moos, R. H. (1994). Parental support and psychological adjustment during the transition to young adulthood in a college sample. *Journal of Family Psychology, 2,* 215–223.

Holfvander, Y. (1978). Kliniska fynd vid hälskontroll av adoptivbarn [Clinical findings made during health checkups on children adopted from developing countries]. *Läkartidningen, 75,* 4674–4675.

Hostetter, M., & Johnson, D. E. (1990). International adoption: An introduction for physicians [comment]. *American Journal of Diseases of Children, 144,* 523–524.

Howard, J. A., & Smith, S. L. (2000). *The needs of adopted youth: A study of Illinois adoption assistance families.* Washington, DC: Child Welfare League of America.

Howe, D. (1997). Parent-reported problems in 211 adopted children: some risk and protective factors. *Journal of Child Psychology and Psychiatry, 38,* 401–411.

Howe, D. (1998). *Patterns of adoption: Nature, nurture and psychosocial development.* Oxford: Blackwell.

Howe, D., & Feast, J. (2000). *Adoption, search and reunion: The long term experience of adopted adults.* London: The Children's Society.

Howell, S. (1998). *Is blood thicker than water? Some issues derived from transnational adoption in Norway* (Intern rapport IMA). Oslo: University of Oslo.

Howell, S. (1999). Biologizing and de-biologizing kinship: The case of transnational adoption Norway. In A. Rygvold, M. Dalen, & B. Sætersdal (Eds.), *Mine—yours—ours and their. Adoption, changing kinship and family patterns* (pp. 32–51). Oslo: University of Oslo

Howell, S. (2001). "En vanlig familie": Utenlandsadopsjon i Norge, et stadig voksende fenomen ["An ordinary family": International adoptions in Norway, a growing phenomenon]. In S. Howell & M. Melhus (Eds.), *Blod—lykkere enn vann?* [Is blood thicker than water?] (pp. 73–98). Oslo: Fagbokforlaget.

Hubel, D. H., Wiesel, T. N., & Le Vay, S. (1977). Plasticity of ocular dominance columns in monkey striate cortex. *Philosophical Transactions of the Royal Society of London Series B Biological Sciences, 278,* 377–409.

Hueber, E. S. (1991). Initial development of the Student's Satisfaction Scale. *School Psychology International, 12,* 2321–2340.

Hughes, B. (1995). Openness and contact in adoption: A child-centered perspective. *British Journal of Social Work, 25,* 729–747.

Huttenlocher, P. R. (2002). *Neural plasticity: The effects of environment on the development of the cerebral cortex.* Cambridge, MA: Harvard University Press.

Iafrate, R., & Rosnati, R. (1998). La percezione della genitorialità e della filiazione adottive: uno strumento di misurazione [The perception of adoptive parenthood and filiation: A measurement instrument]. *Età evolutiva, 59,* 3–10.

Igumnov, S., & Drozdovitch, V. (2000). The intellectual development, mental and behavioural disorders in children from Belarus exposed in utero following the Chernobyl accident. *European Psychiatry, 15,* 244–253.

Ingersoll, B. D. (1997). Psychiatric disorders among adopted children: A review and commentary. *Adoption Quarterly, 1,* 57–74.

Irhammar, M. (1997). *Att uttforska sitt ursprung: Identitetsformande under adolescensen hos utlandsfödda adopterade* [Exploring one's origins: International adoptees' identity formation during adolescence]. Unpublished doctoral dissertation, University of Lund.

Irhammar, M., & Cederblad, M. (2000). Outcome of intercountry adoption in Sweden. In P. Selman (Ed.), *Intercountry adoption: Developments, trends and perspectives* (pp. 143–163). London: British Agencies for Adoption and Fostering.

James, S. S. (2002). *Foster care placement change and mental health service use.* Unpublished doctoral dissertation, University of Southern California.

Jenista, J. A. (Ed.). (2000a). Medical issues in international adoption [Special issue]. *Pediatric Annals, 29.*

Jenista, J. A. (2000b). Preadoption review of medical records. *Pediatric Annals, 29,* 212–215.

Johansson, S. (1976). *Tjänstledighet och föräldrapenning för adoptivföräldrar* [Vacation and costs for adoptive parents]. Sundbyberg: Adoption Center.

Johnson, D. E. (2000a). Long-term medical issues in international adoptees. *Pediatric Annals, 29,* 234–241.

Johnson, D. E. (2000b). Medical and developmental sequelae of early childhood institutionalization in Eastern European adoptees. In C. A. Nelson (Ed,), *The Minnesota Symposia on Child Psychology: Vol. 31. The effects of early adversity on neurobehavioral development* (pp. 113–162). New York: Lawrence Erlbaum Associates.

Johnson, F., & Fein, E. (1991). The concept of attachment: Applications to adoption. *Child and Youth Services Review, 13,* 397–412.

Kadushin, A., & Seidl, F. (1971). Adoption failure—A social work post-mortem. *Social Work, 16,* 32–37.

Kaler, S. R., & Freeman, B. J. (1994). Analysis of environmental deprivation: Cognitive and social development in Romanian orphans. *Journal of Child Psychology and Psychiatry, 35,* 769–781.

Kaye, K. (1990). Acknowledgment or rejection of differences? In D. Brodzinsky & M. Schechter (Eds.), *The psychology of adoption* (pp. 121–143). New York: Oxford University Press.

Kaye, K., & Warren, S. (1988). Discourse about adoption in adoptive families. *Journal of Family Psychology, 1,* 406–433.

Kegan, R. (1982). *The evolving self: Problem and process in human development.* Cambridge, MA: Harvard University Press.

Kennard, M. (1942). Cortical reorganization of motor function. *Archives of Neurology, 48,* 227–240.

Kenny, D. A. (1994). *Interpersonal perception: a social relations analysis.* New York: Guilford Press.

Kenny, D. A., & Judd, C. M. (1986). Consequences of violating the independence assumption in analysis of variance. *Psychological Bulletin, 99,* 422–431.

Kenny, T., Baldwin, R., & Mackie, J. B., (1967). Incidence of minimal brain injury in adopted children. *Child Welfare, 46,* 24–29.

Kertes, D. A., & Madsen, N. (2003, April). *Salivary cortisol levels and behavioral adjustment in post-institutionalized children.* Poster presented at the biennial meeting of the Society for Research in Child Development, Tampa, FL.

Killingsworth-Rini, C., Dunkel-Schetter, C., Wadhwa, P. D., & Sandman, C. A. (1999). Psychological adaptation and birth outcomes: the role of personal resources, stress and sociocultural context during pregnancy. *Health Psychology, 18,* 333–345.

Kim, W. J., Shin, Y. J. & Carrey, M. P. (1999). Comparison of Korean-American adoptees and biological children of their adoptive parents: A pilot study. *Child Psychiatry and Human Development, 29,* 221–228.

King, J. A., Mandansky, D., King, S., Fletcher, K., & Brewer, J. (2001). Early sexual abuse and low cortisol. *Psychiatry & Clinical Neurosciences, 55,* 71–74.

Kirk, H. D. (1964). *Shared fate: A theory and method of adoptive relationships.* New York: Free Press.

Kirk, H. D. (1981). *Adoptive kinship: A modern institution in need of reform.* Toronto: Butterworths.

Kirk, D. H. (1988). *The collected adoption papers.* Washington, DC: Ben-Simon Publications.

Kirschner, D. (1980). *The adopted child syndrome: A study of some characteristics of disturbed adopted children* (Report of the South Shore Institute of Advanced Studies). New York: Merrick.

Kirschner, D. (1990). The adopted child syndrome: Considerations for psychotherapy. *Psychotherapy in Private Practice, 8,* 93–100.

Kittson, R. I I. (1968). *Orphan voyage.* New York: Vantage Press.

Klinger, E. (1998). The search for meaning in evolutionary perspective and its clinical implications. In P. T. F. Wong & P. S. Fry (Eds.), *The human quest for meaning: A handbook of psychological research and clinical applications* (pp. 27–50). Mahwah, NJ: Lawrence Erlbaum Associates.

Kofman, O. (2002). The role of prenatal stress in the etiology of developmental behavioural disorders. *Neuroscience & Biobehavioral Reviews, 26,* 457–470.

Kohler, J. K., Grotevant, H. D., & McRoy, R. G. (2002). Adopted adolescents' preoccupation with adoption: The impact on adoptive family relationships. *Journal of Marriage and the Family, 64,* 93–104.

Kolb, B. (1995). *Brain plasticity and behavior.* Mahwah, NJ: Lawrence Erlbaum Associates.

Kolb, B., & Elliot, W. (1987). Recovery from early cortical damage in rats II: Effects of experience on anatomy and behavior following frontal lesions at 1 or 5 days of age. *Behavior and Brain Research, 26,* 47–56.

Kolb, B., & Gibb, R. (2001). Early brain injury, plasticity and behavior. In C. A. Nelson & M. Luciana (Eds.), *Handbook of cognitive developmental neuroscience* (pp. 175–190). Cambridge, MA: MIT Press.

Kotsopoulos, S., Coté, A., Joseph, L., Pentland, N., Staurakaki, C., Sheahan, P., & Oke, L. (1988). Psychiatric disorders in adopted children: A controlled study. *American Journal of Orthopsychiatry, 58,* 608–610.

Kotsopoulos, S., Walker, S., Copping, W., Coté, A., & Stavrakaki, C. (1993). A psychiatric follow-up study of adoptees. *Canadian Journal of Psychiatry, 38,* 391–396.

Kraft, A., Palumbo, J., Mitchell, D., Woods, P., & Schmidt, A. (1985a). Some theoretical considerations on confidential adoptions. Part 2: The adoptive parent. *Child and Adolescent Social Work, 2,* 69–82.

Kraft, A., Palumbo, J., Mitchell, D., Woods, P., & Schmidt, A. (1985b). Some theoretical considerations on confidential adoptions. Part 1: The birth mother. *Child and Adolescent Social Work, 2,* 13–21.

Kraft, A., Palumbo, J., Woods, P., Schmidt, A., & Tucker, N. (1985). Some theoretical considerations on confidential adoptions. Part 3: The adopted child. *Child and Adolescent Social Work, 2,* 139–153.

Kramer, L., & Houston, D. (1998). Supporting families as they adopt children with special needs. *Family Relations, 47*, 423–432.

Kreppner, J. M., O'Connor, T. G., Rutter, M., & the E. R. A. Research Team. (2001). Can inattention/overactivity be an institutional deprivation syndrome? *Journal of Abnormal Child Psychology, 29*, 513–528.

Kuhl, P. K. (1994). Learning and representation in speech and language. *Current Opinion in Neurobiology, 4*, 812–822.

Kuhl, P. K., Andruski, J. E., Chistovich, I. A., Chistovich, L. A., Kozhevnikova, E. V., Ryskina, V. L., et al. (1997). Cross-language analysis of phonetic units in language addressed to infants. *Science, 277*, 684–686.

Kuhl, W. (1985). *Wenn fremdländisch adoptivkinder erwachsen werden* [When adopted children of foreign origin grow up]. Osnabrück: Terre des Hommes.

Kvifte-Andresen, I. L. (1992). Behavioral and school adjustment of 12–13 year old internationally adopted children in Norway. *Journal of Child Psychology and Psychiatry, 33*, 427–439.

Ladner, J. (1977). *Mixed families: Adopting across racial boundaries.* New York: Anchor Press.

Lahti, J. (1982). A follow-up study of foster children in permanent placements. *Social Service Review, 56*, 556–71.

Lamb, M. E. (Ed.). (1999). *Parenting and child development in nontraditional families.* Mahwah, NJ: Lawrence Erlbaum Associates.

Lambert, L., & Streather, J. (1980). *Children in changing families: A study of adoption and illegitimacy.* London: Macmillan.

Lanz, M., Iafrate, R., Rosnati, R., & Scabini, E. (1999). Parent-child communication and adolescents' self-esteem in separated, inter-country adoptive and intact-nonadoptive families. *Journal of Adolescence, 22*, 785–794.

Lanz, M., & Rosnati, R. (1995). La comunicazione familiare: uno studio sulle famiglie con adolescenti [Family communication: A study on families with adolescents]. *Ricerche di psicologia, 19*, 81–98.

Lanz, M., & Rosnati, R. (2002). *Metodologia della ricerca sulla famiglia* [Methodology of research on family]. Milan: LED.

Larque, E., Dammelmair, H., & Koletzko, B. (2002). Perinatal supply and metabolism of long-chain polyunsaturated fatty acids: Importance for the early development of the nervous system. *Annals of the New York Academy of Sciences, 967*, 299–310.

Lemaire, V., Koehl, M., Le Moal, M., & Abrous, D. M. (2000). Prenatal stress produces learning deficits associated with an inhibition of neurogenesis in the hippocampus. *Proceedings of the National Academy of Sciences, 97*, 11032–11037.

Leon, I. G. (2002). Adoption losses: Naturally occurring or socially constructed? *Child Development, 73*, 652–663.

LeVay, S., Wiesel, T. N., & Hubel, D. H. (1980). The development of ocular dominance columns in normal and visually deprived monkeys. *Journal of Comparative Neurology, 191*, 1–51.

LeVine, E. S., & Sallee, A. L. (1990). Critical phases among adoptees and their families: Implications for therapy. *Child and Adolescent Social Work, 7*, 217–232.

Levy-Shiff, R., Goldschmidt, I., & Har-Even, D. (1991). Transition to parenthood in adoptive families. *Developmental Psychology, 27*, 131–140.

Levy-Shiff, R., Zoran, N., & Shulman, S. (1997). International and domestic adoption: Child, parents and family adjustment. *International Journal of Behavioural Development, 20,* 109–129.

Lieblum, S. (Ed.). (1997). *Infertility: Psychological issues and counseling strategies.* New York: Wiley.

Lightburne, A., & Pine, B. A. (1996). Supporting and enhancing the adoption of children with developmental disabilities. *Children and Youth Services Review, 18,* 139–162.

Lindblad, F., Hjern, A., & Vinnerljung, B. (2003). Intercountry adopted children as young adults: A Swedish cohort study. *American Journal of Orthopsychiatry, 73,* 190–202.

Livingston Smith, S., & Howard, J. A. (1999). *Promoting successful adoptions: Practice with troubled families.* Thousand Oaks, CA: Sage.

Loehlin, L. C., Willerman, L., & Horn, J. M. (1982). Personality resemblances between unwed mothers and their adopted-away offspring. *Journal of Personality and Social Psychology, 42,* 1089–1099.

Logan F., Morral, P., & Chambers, H. (1998). Identification of risk factors for psychological disturbance in adopted children. *Child Abuse Review, 7,* 154–164.

Lyngstøl, S. (1994). *Utenlandsadopterte 5-åringers språk: En kartlegging av språklig nivå* [International adopted 5-year-old children's language: A survey of language abilities]. Oslo: University of Oslo, Institutt for Spesialpedagogikk.

Maccari, S., Plazza, P., Kabbaj, M., Barbazanges, A., Simon, H., & Le Moal, M. (1994). Adoption reverses the long-term impairments in glucocorticoid feedback induced by prenatal stress. *Journal of Neuroscience, 15,* 110–116.

MacFie, J., Toth, S. L., Rogosch, F. A., Robinson, J., Emde, R. N., & Cicchetti, D. (1999). Effect of maltreatment on preschoolers' narrative representations of responses to relieve distress and of role reversal. *Developmental Psychology, 35,* 460–465.

Mackie, A. J. (1985). Families with adopted adolescents. *Journal of Adolescence, 5,* 167–178.

Maguire, E. A., Gadian, D. G., Johnsrude, I. S., Good, C. D., Ashburner, J., Frackowiak, R. S., et al. (2000). Navigation-related structural change in the hippocampi of taxi drivers. *Proceedings of the National Academy of Sciences USA, 97,* 4398–4403.

Main, M., & Cassidy, J. (1988). Categories of response to reunion with the parent at age 6: Predictable from infant attachment classifications and stable over a 1-month period. *Developmental Psychology, 24,* 1–12.

Main, M., Kaplan, N., & Cassidy, J. (1985). Security in infancy, childhood, and adulthood: A move to the level of representation. In I. Bretherton & E. Waters (Eds.), Growing points in attachment theory and research. *Monographs of the Society for Research in Child Development, 50*(1–2, Serial No. 209).

Mainemer, H., Gilman, L. C., & Ames, E. W. (1998). Parenting stress in families adopting children from Romanian orphanages. *Journal of Family Issues, 19,* 164–180.

Mannheim, K. (1928). Das problem der generationen [The problem of generations]. *Kölner Vierteljahreshefte für Soziologie, 8,* 157–185.

Mansvelt, H. F. M. (1967). *Adoptief-ouders aan het woord* [Adoptive parents speak out]. Alphen a.d. Rijn: Samson.

Marcovitch, S., Goldberg, S., Gold, A., Washington, J., Wasson, C., Krekewitch, K., et al. (1998). Determinants of behavioural problems in Romanian children adopted in Ontario. *International Journal of Behavoiral Development, 20,* 17–31.

Marcus, C. (1981). *Who is my mother? Birth parents, adoptive parents and adoptees talk about living with adoption and the search for lost family.* Toronto: Gage Publishing.

Mason, S. J., & Gleeson, J. P. (1999). Adoption and subsidized guardianship as permanency options in kinship foster care: Barriers and facilitating conditions. In J. P. Gleeson & C. Finney Hairston (Eds.), *Kinship care: Improving practice through research* (pp. 85–114). Washington, DC: Child Welfare League of America.

Masten, A. S., & Reed, M.-G. (2002). Resilience in development. In C. R. Snyder & S. J. Lopez (Eds.), *The handbook of positive psychology* (pp. 74–88). London: Oxford University Press.

Maugham, B., & Pickles, A. (1990). Adopted and illegitimate children growing up. In L. Robins & M. Rutter (Eds.), *Straight and devious pathways from childhood to adulthood* (pp. 36–61). New York: Cambridge University Press.

Maza, P. L. (1999). Recent data on the number of adoptions of foster children. *Adoptions Quarterly, 3,* 71–81.

McAdams, D. P. (1987). A life-story model of identity. In R. Hogan & W. Jones (Eds.), *Perspectives in personality* (Vol. 2, pp. 15–50). Greenwich, CT: JAI Press.

McAdams, D. P. (1993). *The stories we live by: Personal myths and the making of the self.* New York: Morrow.

McAdams, D. P. (2001). The psychology of life stories. *Review of General Psychology, 5,* 100–122.

McCarton, C. M., Wallace, I. F., Divon, M., & Vaughan, H. G., Jr. (1996). Cognitive and neurologic development of the premature, small for gestational age infant through age 6: Comparison by birth weight and gestational age. *Pediatrics, 98,* 1167–1178.

McCrone, E., Egeland, B., Kalkoske, M., & Carlson, E. (1994). Relations between early maltreatment and mental representations of relationships assessed with projective storytelling in middle childhood. *Development and Psychopathology, 6,* 99–120.

McDonald, T. P., Lieberman, A., Partridge, S., & Hornby, H. (1991). Assessing the role of agency services in reducing adoption disruptions. *Children and Youth Services Review, 13,* 425–438.

McEwen, B. (1999). The effects of stress on structural and functional plasticity in the hippocampus. In D. S. Charney, E. J. Nestler, & B. S. Bunney (Eds.), *Neurobiology of mental illness* (pp. 475–493). New York: Oxford University Press.

McEwen, B., & Lasley, E. N. (2002). *The end of stress.* Washington, DC: Joseph Henry Press.

McGuinness, T. M, McGuinness, J. P., & Dyer, J. G. (2000). Risk and protective factors in children adopted from the former Soviet Union. *Journal of Pediatric Health Care, 14,* 109–116.

McMahon, S. D., Grant, K. E., Compas, B., Thurm, A. E., & Ey, S. (2003). Stress and psychopathology in children and adolescents: Is there evidence of specificity? *Journal of Child Psychology and Psychiatry, 44,* 107–133.

McMorris, F. A., & Dubois-Dalcq, M. (1988). Insulin-like growth factor I promotes cell proliferation and oligodendroglial commitment in rat glial progenitor cells developing in vitro. *Journal of Neuroscience Research, 21,* 199–209.

McNichol, T., & Tash, C. (2001). AOD use and child development. *Child Welfare, 53,* 239–256.

McRoy, R. G. (1999). *Special needs adoptions: Practice issues.* New York: Taylor & Francis.

McRoy, R. G., Ayers-Lopez, S., Henney, S. M., Christian, C., & Gossman, G. (2001). *Adoption openness: Longitudinal birthmother outcomes.* Austin, TX: University of Texas Center for Social Work Research.

McRoy, R. G., Grotevant, H. D., & White, K. L. (1988). *Openness in adoption: New practices, new issues.* New York: Praeger.

McRoy, R. G., Grotevant, H. D., & Zurcher, L. A. (1988). *Emotional disturbance in adopted adolescents: Origins and development.* New York: Praeger.

McRoy, R., Zurcher, L. A., Lauderdale, M. L., & Anderson, R. E. (1982). Self-esteem and racial identity in transracial and inracial adoptees. *Social Work, 27,* 522–526.

Melosh, B. (2002). *Strangers and kin: The American way of adoption.* Cambridge, MA: Harvard University Press.

Meltzer, H., Corbin, T., Gatward, R., Goodman, R., & Ford, T. (2003). *The mental health of young people looked after by local authorities in England: Summary report.* London: Office for National Statistics, Her Majesty's Stationery Office.

Mendenhall, T. J., Berge, J. M., Wrobel, G. M., Grotevant, H. D., & McRoy, R. G. (2004). Adolescents' satisfaction with contact in adoption. *Child and Adolescent Social Work Journal, 21,* 175–190.

Miall, C. E. (1996). The social construction of adoption: Clinical and community perspectives. *Family Relations, 45,* 309–317.

Miller, B. C., Bayley, B. K., Christensen, M., Fan, X., Coyl, D., Grotevant, H. D., et al. (2001). Who is adopted? Measuring adoption status using national survey data. *Adoption Quarterly, 5,* 23–44.

Miller, B. C., Fan, X., Christensen, M., Grotevant, H. D., & van Dulmen, M. (2000). Comparisons of adopted and nonadopted adolescents in a large, nationally representative sample. *Child Development, 71,* 1458–1473.

Miller, B. C., Fan, X., Grotevant, H. D., Christensen, M., Coyle, D., & van Dulmen, M. (2000). Adopted adolescents' overrepresentation in mental health counseling: Adoptee's problems or parents' lower threshold for referral? *Journal of the American Academy of Child & Adolescent Psychiatry, 39,* 1504–1511.

Minde, K. (2003). Assessment and treatment of attachment disorders. *Current Opinion in Psychiatry 16,* 377–381.

Minister of Justice. (2003). *Statistische gegevens betreffende de opneming in gezinnen in Nederland van buitenlandse adoptiekinderen in de jaren 1998–2002* [Statistics concerning foreign adoption in the Netherlands]. The Hague: Author.

Mishler, E. G. (1999). *Storylines: Craft artists' narratives of identity.* Cambridge, MA: Harvard University Press.

Mitchell, K. T. (2001). Fetal alcohol syndrome and other alcohol related birth defects: Identification and implications. *The Nadd Bulletin, 4,* 11–14.

Mitchell, M. A., & Jenista, J. A. (1997). Health care of internationally adopted children part 1: Before and at arrival into the adoptive home. *Journal of Pediatric Health Care, 11,* 51–60.

Moe, V. (2002). Foster-placed and adopted children exposed in utero to opiates and other substances: Prediction and outcome at four and a half years. *Journal of Developmental and Behavioral Pediatrics, 23,* 330–339.

Moe, V., & Slinning, K. (2001). Children prenatally exposed to substances: Gender-related differences in outcome from infancy to three years of age. *Infant Mental Health Journal, 22,* 334–350.

Morgane, P. J., Austin-LaFrance, R., Bronzino, J., Tonkiss, J., & Galler, J. R. (1992). Malnutrition and the developing central nervous system. In R. L. Isaacson & K. F. Jensen, (Eds.), *Malnutrition and hazard assessment: Vol. 1. The vulnerable brain and environmental risks* (pp. 3–44). New York: Plenum Press.

Morgane, P. J. Mokler, D. J., & Galler, J. R. (2002). Effects of prenatal protein malnutrition on the hippocampal formation. *Neuroscience & Biobehavioral Reviews, 26,* 471–483.

Morison, S. J., Ames, E. W., & Chisholm, K. (1995). The development of children adopted from Romanian orphanages. *Merrill-Palmer Quarterly, 41,* 411–430.

Mulder, E. J. H., de Medina, P. G. R., Huizink, A. C., Van den Bergh, B. R. H., Buitelaar, J. K., & Visser, G. H. A. (2002). Prenatal maternal stress: Effects on pregnancy and the (unborn) child. *Early Human Development, 70,* 3–14.

Murphy, J. M., Jellinek, M., Quinn, D., Smith, G., Poitrast, F.G., & Goshko, M. (1991). Substance abuse and serious child maltreatment: Prevalence, risk, and outcome in a court sample. *Child Abuse & Neglect, 15,* 197–211.

National Adoption Information Clearinghouse. (2001). Immigrant visas issued to orphans coming to U.S. Available: http://www.calib.com/naic/pubs/s_number.cfm

Neil, E. (2003). Understanding other people's perspectives: Tasks for adopters in open adoption. *Adoption Quarterly, 6,* 3–30.

Neil, E. & Howe, D. (Eds.) (2004). *Contact in adoption and permanent foster care.* London: British Association for Adoption and Fostering.

Nelson, K. A. (1985). *On the frontier of adoption: A study of special-needs adoptive families.* Washington, DC: Child Welfare League of America.

Nickman, S. L. (1985). Losses in adoption: The need for dialogue. *Psychoanalytic Study of the Child, 40,* 365–398.

Nishijima, M. (1986). Somatomedin-C as a fetal growth promoting factor and amino acid composition of cord blood in Japanese neonates. *Journal of Perinatological Medicine, 14,* 163–166.

Noller, P. (1995). Parent-adolescent relationships. In M. A. Fitzpatrick & A. L. Vangelisti (Eds.), *Explaining family interactions* (pp. 77–111). London: Sage.

Noller, P., & Callan, V. (1990). Adolescents' perceptions of the nature of their communication with parents. *Journal of Youth and Adolescence, 19,* 349–362.

Nulman, I., Rovet, J., Altmann, D., Bradley, C., Einarson, T., & Koren, G. (1994). Neurodevelopment of adopted children exposed in utero to cocaine. *Canadian Medical Association Journal, 151,* 1591–1597.

Nyagu, A. I., Loganovsky, K. N., & Loganovskaja, T. K. (1998). Psychophysiologic after effects of prenatal irradiation. *International Journal of Psychophysiology, 30*, 303–311.

O'Brien, P. M., Wheeler, T., & Barker, D. J. (1999). *Fetal programming: Influences on development and disease in later life.* London: RCOG Press.

O'Connor, T., Bredenkamp, D., Rutter, M., & the E.R.A. Research Team. (1999). Attachment disturbances and disorders in children exposed to early severe deprivation. *Infant Mental Health Journal, 20*, 10–29.

O'Connor, T., Heron, J., Golding, J., Glover, V., & the ALSPAC Study Team. (2003). Maternal antenatal anxiety and behavioural/emotional problems in children: A test of a programming hypothesis. *Journal of Child Psychology and Psychiatry, 44*, 1025–1036..

O'Connor, T. G., Marvin, R. S., Rutter, M., Olrick, J. T., Britner, P. A., & the E.R.A. Research Team. (2003). Child-parent attachment following early institutional deprivation. *Developmental Psychopathology, 15*, 19–38.

O'Connor, T., Rutter, M., Beckett, C., Keaveney, L., Kreppner, J. M., & the E.R.A. Research Team (2000). The effects of global severe privation on cognitive competence: Extension and longitudinal follow-up. *Child Development, 71*, 376–390.

O'Connor, T., Rutter, M., & the E.R.A. Research Team. (2000). Attachment disorder behavior following early severe deprivation: Extension and longitudinal follow-up. *Journal of the American Academy of Child and Adolescent Psychiatry 39*, 703–712.

Olson, D. H. (1993). Circumplex model of marital and family systems: Assessing family functioning. In F. Walsh (Ed.), *Normal family processes* (pp. 104–137). New York: Guilford Press.

Olson, D. H., McCubbin, H. I., Barnes, H., Larsen, A., Muxen, M., & Wilson, M. (1982). *Family inventories in family social science.* Minneapolis: University of Minnesota Press.

Olson, H. C., Streissguth, A. P., Sampson, P. D., Barr, H. M., Bookstein, F. L., & Thiede, K. (1997). Association of prenatal alcohol exposure with behavioral and learning problems in early adolescence. *Journal of the American Academy of Child and Adolescent Psychiatry, 36*, 1187–1194.

Oppenheim, D., Emde, R. N., & Warren, S. (1997). Children's narrative representations of mothers: Their development and associations with child and mother adaptation. *Child Development, 68*, 127–138.

Oppenheim, E., & Bussiere, A. (1996). Adoption: Where do relatives stand? *Child Welfare, 75*, 471–488.

Pagliaro, A. M., & Pagliaro, L. A. (1997). Teratogenic effects of in utero exposure to alcohol and other abusable psychotropics. In M. M. Haack (Ed.), *Drug dependent mothers and their children: Issues in public policy and public health* (pp. 215–235). New York: Springer Publishing.

Palacios, J. (1998). Familias adoptivas [Adoptive families]. In M. J. Rodrigo & J. Palacios (Eds.), *Familia y desarrollo humano* [Family and human development] (pp. 353–371). Madrid: Alianza.

Palacios, J., Amorós, P., Fuertes, J., León, E., Sánchez-Sandoval, Y., & Fuentes, N. (1999). *Programa de Formación para la Adopción* [A training program for adoptive parents]. Seville: Junta de Andalucía, Consejería de Asuntos Sociales.

Palacios, J., & Sánchez-Sandoval, Y. (1999, August). *Adoptive families and adoptive children in southern Spain.* Paper presented at the International Conference on Adoption Research, Minneapolis.

Palacios, J., Sánchez-Sandoval, Y., & Sánchez-Espinosa, E. M. (1997). *La adopción en Andalucía* [Adoption in Andalusia]. Seville: Junta de Andalucía, Consejería de Asuntos Sociales, Dirección General de Atención al Niño.

Parke, R. D. (2002). Fathers and families. In M. Bornstein (Ed.), *Handbook of parenting: Vol. 3. Being and becoming a parent* (2nd ed., pp. 27–74). Hillsdale, NJ: Lawrence Erlbaum Associates.

Partridge, S., Hornby, H., & McDonald, T. (1986). *Learning from adoption disruption: Insights for practice.* Portland: University of Southern Maine.

Patterson, C. J. (2002). Lesbian and gay parenthood. In M. Bornstein (Ed.), *Handbook of parenting: Vol. 3. Being and becoming a parent* (2nd ed., pp. 317–338). Hillsdale, NJ: Lawrence Erlbaum Associates.

Patton, J. M. (1954). *The adopted break silence.* Acton, CA: Life History Study Center.

Pecora, P. J., Whittaker, J. K., Maluccio, A. N., & Barth, R. P. (2000). *The child welfare challenge: Policy, practice, and research* (2nd ed.). New York: Aldine de Gruyter.

Perry, Y. V. (2002). *Assisted reproductive technology through a family policy lens: Some lessons from adoption policy. Report of the National Council on Family Relations, 47,* F1–F4.

Perry, Y. V. (2003, November). *The ties that matter: Towards a reconceptualization of adoptive kinship.* Paper presented at the Theory Construction and Research Methodology Workshop, National Council on Family Relations, Vancouver.

Peters, B. R., Atkins, M. S., & McKay, M. M. (1999). Adopted children's behavior problems: A review of five explanatory models. *Clinical Psychology Review, 19,* 297–328.

Phillips, R. (1988). Post-adoption services: The views of adopters. *Adoption and Fostering, 12,* 4, 24–29.

Pinderhughes, E. E. (1996). Toward understanding family readjustment following older child adoptions: The interplay between theory generation and empirical research. *Children and Youth Services Review, 18,* 115–138.

PIU (Performance and Innovation Unit). (2000). *Prime minister's review of adoption.* Available: http://www.number-10.gov.uk/su/adoption

Priel, B., Melamed-Hass, S., Besser, A., & Kantor B. (2000), Adjustment among adopted children: The role of maternal reflectiveness. *Family Relations, 48,* 389–396.

Proos, L. (1992). *Growth and development: Indian children adopted in Sweden* (Dissertation Thesis, No. 363). Uppsala: University of Uppsala.

Pruzan, V. (1977). *Født i utlandet—Adoptert i Danmark* [Born abroad—Adopted to Denmark] (Rapport 77). Copenhagen: Socialforskningsinstituttet.

Purves, D., & Lichtman, J. W. (1985). *Principles of neural development.* Sunderland, MA: Sinauer Associates.

Quinton, D., Rushton, A., Dance, C., & Mayes, D. (1998). *Joining new families: A study of adoption and fostering in middle childhood.* Chichester: Wiley.

Rathbun, C., McLaughlin, H., Bennet, C., & Garland, J. A. (1965). Later adjustment of children following radical separation from family and culture. *American Journal of Orthopsychiatry 35,* 604–609.

Raynor, L. (1970). *Adoption of non-white children: The experience of a British adoption project.* London: George Allen & Unwin.

Raynor, L. (1980). *The adopted child comes of age.* London: George Allen & Unwin.

Reitz, M., & Watson, K. W. (1992). *Adoption and the family system.* London: Guilford Press.

Rice, D., & Barone, S. (2000). Critical periods of vulnerability for the developing nervous system: Evidence from humans and animal models. *Environmental Health Perspectives, 108,* 511–533.

Ridley, M. (2003). *Nature via Nurture: Genes, experience and what makes us human.* London: Fourth Estate.

Rørbech, M. (1989). *Mit land er Danmark* [My country is Denmark] (Rapport 14). Copenhagen: Socialforskningsinstituttet.

Rosenberg, E. B. (1992). *The adoption life cycle: The children and their families through the years.* New York: Free Press.

Rosenberg, K. and Groze, V. (1997). The Impact of secrecy and denial in adoption: Practice and treatment issues. *Families and Society, 78,* 522–530.

Rosenberg, M. (1965). *Society and the adolescent self-image.* Princeton, NJ: Princeton University Press.

Rosenfeld, A. A., Pilowsky, D. J., Fine, P., Thorpe, M., Fein, E., Simms, M. D., et al. (1997). Foster care: An update. *The American Academy of Child and Adolescent Psychiatry, 36,* 448–457.

Rosenthal, J. A. (1993). Outcomes of adoption of children with special needs. *The Future of Children, 3,* 77–88.

Rosenthal, J. A., & Groze, V. K. (1992). *Special needs adoption: A study of intact families.* New York: Praeger.

Rosenthal, J., Schmidt, D., & Conner, J. (1988). Predictors of special needs adoption: An exploratory study. *Children and Youth Services Review, 10,* 101–117.

Rosnati, R. (1998). Relazioni familiari e rischio psicosociale dell'adolescente adottato [Family relations and adoptive adolescents' psychosocial risk]. In D. Bramanti & R. Rosnati (Eds.), *Il patto adottivo: L'adozione internazionale di fronte alla sfida dell'adolescenza* [The adoptive pact: Intercountry adoption in front of the adolescent challenge]. (pp. 161–171). Milan: Franco Angeli.

Rosnati R., & Bazzani, G. (2005). *La percezione della genitorialità adottiva: Una ricerca empirica su coppie con figli in età scolare* [The perception of adoptive parenthood: An empirical research on couples with school-year children]. Unpublished manuscript.

Rosnati, R., & Iafrate, R. (1997). Adozione internazionale: Relazioni familiari e percezione della genitorialità e della filiazione adottive [International adoption: Family relationships and the perception of adoptive parenthood and filiation]. *Rassegna di Psicologia, 3,* 9–24.

Rosnati, R., & Marta, E. (1997). Parent-child relationships as protective factors for preventing adolescent's psycho-social risk in adoptive and non-adoptive families. *Journal of Adolescence, 20,* 617–631.

Ross, N. M. (1995). *Adoptive family processes that predict adopted child behavior and self-esteem.* Unpublished master's thesis, University of Minnesota.

Rowe, J. (1959). *Yours by choice: A guide for adoptive parents.* London: Routledge & Kegan Paul.

Roy, P., Rutter, M., & Pickles, A. (2000). Institutional care: Risk from family back-ground or pattern of rearing? *Journal of Child Psychology and Psychiatry 41*, 139–149.

Roy, P., Rutter, M., & Pickles, A. (2004). Institutional care: Associations between overactivity and a lack of selectivity in social relationships. *Journal of Child Psychology and Psychiatry, 45*, 866–873..

Rushton, A. (2004). A scoping and scanning review of research on the adoption of children placed from public care. *Clinical Child Psychology and Psychiatry, 9*, 89–106.

Rushton, A., Treseder, J., & Quinton, D. (1995). An eight year prospective study of older boys placed in permanent substitute families. *Journal of Child Psychology and Psychiatry, 36*, 687–695.

Rutter, M. (1981). *Maternal deprivation reassessed*. New York: Penguin Books.

Rutter, M. (1998). Practitioner review: Routes from research to clinical practice in child psychiatry: Retrospect and prospect. *Journal of Child Psychology and Psychiatry, 39*, 805–816.

Rutter, M. (1999). The Emanuel Miller Memorial Lecture 1998: Autism: Two-way interplay between research and clinical work. *Journal of Child Psychology and Psychiatry, 40*, 169–188.

Rutter, M. (2000a). Psychosocial influences: Critiques, findings, and research needs. *Developmental Psychopathology, 12*(3), 375–405.

Rutter, M. (2000b). Resilience reconsidered: Conceptual considerations, empirical findings, and policy implications. In J. P.Shonkoff & S.J. Meisels (Eds.), *Handbook of early childhood intervention* (2nd ed., pp. 651–682). New York: Cambridge University Press.

Rutter, M. (2002). Nature, nurture, and development: From evangelism through science toward policy and practice. *Child Development, 73*, 1–21.

Rutter, M. (2003a). Genetic influences on risk and protection: Implications for understanding resilience. In S. Luthar (Ed.), *Resilience and vulnerability: Adaptation in the context of childhood adversities* (pp. 489–509). New York: Cambridge University Press.

Rutter, M. (in press a). The psychological effects of institutional rearing. In P. Marshall & N. Fox (Eds.), *The development of social engagement*. New York: Oxford University Press.

Rutter, M. (in press b). The promotion of resilience in the face of adversity. In J. Dunn & A. Clarke-Stewart (Eds.), *The Jacobs Foundation Conference 2003: In what ways do families matter in young people's development?* New York: Cambridge University Press.

Rutter, M., Andersen-Wood, L., Beckett, C., Bredenkamp, D., Castle, J., Groothues, C., et al. (1999). Quasi-autistic patterns following severe early global privation. *Journal of Child Psychology and Psychiatry, 40*, 537–549.

Rutter, M., Bolton, P., Harrington, R., Le Couteur, A., Macdonald, H., & Simonoff, E. (1990). Genetic factors in child psychiatric disorders. I. A review of research strategies. *Journal of Child Psychology and Psychiatry, 3*, 3–37.

Rutter, M., & the E.R.A. Research Team. (1998). Developmental catch-up, and deficit, following adoption after severe global early privation. *Journal of Child Psychology and Psychiatry, 39*, 465–476.

Rutter, M., Kreppner, J., O'Connor, T. G., & the E.R.A. Research Team. (2001). Specificity and heterogeneity in children's responses to profound institutional deprivation. *British Journal of Psychiatry, 179,* 97–103.

Rutter, M., O'Connor, T., Beckett, C., Castle, J., Croft, C., Dunn, J., et al. (2000). Recovery and deficit following profound early deprivation. In P. Selman (Ed.), *Intercountry adoption: Developments, trends and perspectives* (pp. 107–125). London: British Association for Adoption and Fostering.

Rutter, M., O'Connor, T., & the E.R.A. Research Team. (2004). Are there biological programming effects for psychological development: Findings from a study of Romanian adoptees. *Developmental Psychology, 40,* 81–94.

Rutter, M., Pickles, A., Murray, R., & Eaves, L. (2001). Testing hypotheses on specific environmental causal effects on behavior. *Psychological Bulletin, 127,* 291–324.

Rutter, M., & Silberg, J. (2002). Gene-environment interplay in relation to emotional and behavioral disturbance. *Annual Review of Psychology, 53,* 463–490.

Rutter, M., Silberg, J., O'Connor, T., & Simonoff, E. (1999). Genetics and child psychiatry: I. Advances in quantitative and molecular genetics. *Journal of Child Psychology and Psychiatry, 40,* 3–18.

Rutter, M., Tizard, J., & Whitmore, K. (Eds.). (1970). *Education, health and behaviour.* London: Longman.

Rygvold, A. L. (1999). Better or worse? Intercountry adopted children's language. In A. L. Rygvold, M. Dalen, & B. Sætersdal (Eds.), *Mine—yours—ours and their: Adoption, changing kinship and family patterns* (pp. 221–229). Oslo: University of Oslo.

Sachdev, P. (1989). *Unlocking the adoption files.* Lexington, MA: Lexington Books.

Sackett, G. P. (1965). Effects of rearing conditions upon the behavior of rhesus monkeys (*Macaca mulatta*). *Child Development, 36,* 855–868.

Sætersdal, B., & Dalen, M. (1991). Norway: Intercountry adoptions in a homogeneous country. In H. Alstein & R. J. Simon (Eds.), *Intercountry adoption: A multinational perspective* (pp. 83–107). New York: Praeger.

Sætersdal, B., & Dalen, M. (1999). *Hvem er jeg? Adopsjon, idenitet og etnisitet* [Who am I? Adoption, identity and ethnicity]. Oslo: Akribe Forlag.

Sætersdal, B., & Dalen, M. (2000). Identity formation in a homogeneous country. In P. Selman (Ed.), *Intercountry adoption* (pp. 164–178). London: British Agencies for Adoption and Fostering.

Salm, A. K., Pavelko, M., Krouse, E. M., Webster, W., Kraszpulski, M ., & Birkle, D. L. (2004). Lateral amygclaloid nucleus expansion in adult rats is associated with exposure to prenatal stress. *Developmental Brain Research, 148,* 159–236.

Sameroff, A. J., Seifer, R., Zax, M., Barocas, R., & Greenspan, S. (1992). Social-environmental risk and early competence. In C. Chiland & J. G. Young (Eds.), *New approaches to mental health from birth to adolescence* (Vol. 9, pp. 269–280). New Haven, CT: Yale University Press.

Sanchez, M. M., Hearn, E. F., Do, D., Rilling, J. K., & Herndon, J. G. (1998). Differential rearing affects corpus callosum size and cognitive function of rhesus monkeys. *Brain Research, 812,* 38–49.

Sanchez, M. M., Ladd, C. O., & Plotsky, P. M. (2001). Early adverse experience as a developmental risk factor for later psychopathology: Evidence from rodent and primate models. *Development and Psychopathology, 13,* 419–450.

Sanchez, M. M., Winslow, J., Plotsky, P., & McCormack, K. (2002, February). *Effects of early maltreatment and relationship disruption on rhesus daytime diurnal cortisol rhythms.* Paper presented at the meeting of the NIMH Early Experience, Stress, and Prevention Science Network, Emory University, Atlanta, GA.

Saneto, R. P., Low, K. G., Melner, M., H., & de Vellis, J. (1988). Insulin/insulin-like growth factor I and other epigenetic modulators of myelin basic protein expression in isolated oligodendrocyte progenitor cells. *Journal of Neuroscience Research, 21,* 210–219.

Sar, B. K. (2000). Preparation for adoptive parenthood with a special-needs child: Role of agency preparation tasks. *Adoption Quarterly, 3,* 63–80.

Scabini, E., & Cigoli, V. (1992). *The Parent-Adolescent Support Scale.* Unpublished manuscript.

Scabini, E., & Cigoli, V. (2000). *Il famigliare: Legami, simboli e transizioni* [The familiar: Bonds, symbols and transitions]. Milan: Raffaello Cortina.

Scabini, E., & Iafrate, R. (2003). *Psicologia dei legami familiari* [Psychology of family bonds]. Bologna: Il Mulino.

Schaefer, E. S., Edgerton, M. D., & Aaronson, M. (1978). *Classroom Behavior Inventory.* Princeton, NJ: Educational Testing Services.

Schaerlakens, A., & Dondeyne, N. (1985). Taalaanpassing bij buitenlandse adoptiekinderen [Language adaptation in foreign adopted children]. *Kind en adolescent, 6,* 201–218.

Schechter, M. D. (1970). About adoptive parents. In E. J. Anthony & T. Benedek (Eds.), *Parenthood: Its psychology and psychopathology* (pp. 85–105). Boston: Little, Brown.

Scheeringa, M. S., Zeanah, C. H., Drell, M. J., & Larrieu, J. A. (1995). Two approaches to the diagnosis of posttraumatic stress disorder in infancy and early childhood. *Journal of the American Academy of Child and Adolescent Psychiatry, 34,* 191–200.

Schelsky, H. (1957). *Die skeptische generation, eine soziologie der deutschen Jugend* [The sceptic generation, a sociology of the German youth]. Düsseldorf: Ullstein.

Schjelderup-Mathiesen, K., & Nytrøhaug, L. (1977). *Vietnambarn i Norge* [Children from Vietnam in Norway]. Oslo: Grøndahl.

Schneider, M. L., & Moore, C. F. (2000). Effects of prenatal stress on development: A nonhuman primate model. In C. A. Nelson (Ed.), *The effects of early adversity on neurobehavioral development: The Minnesota Symposia on Child Psychology* (Vol. 31, pp. 202–244). Mahwah, NJ: Lawrence Erlbaum Associates.

Schneider, M. L., Roughton, E. C., Koehler, A. J., & Lubach, G. R. (1999). Growth and development following prenatal stress exposure in primates: An examination of ontogenetic vulnerability. *Child Development, 70,* 263–274.

Schneider, S. (1995). Adoption and ordinal position. *Adoption and Fostering, 19,* 21–23.

Schwartz, A. E. (2002). Societal value and the funding of kinship care. *Social Service Review, 76,* 430–459.

Seifer, R., Sameroff, A. J., Baldwin, C. P., & Baldwin, A. (1992). Child and family factors that ameliorate risk between 4 years and 13 years of age. *Journal of the American Academy of Child and Adolescent Psychiatry, 31,* 893–903.

Selman, P. (Ed.). (2000). *Intercountry adoption: Developments, trends and perspectives.* London: British Agencies for Adoption and Fostering.

Shapiro, V. B., Shapiro, J. R., & Paret, I. H. (2001). *Complex adoption and assisted reproductive technology: A developmental approach to clinical practice.* New York: Guilford Press.

Sharma, A. R., McGue, M. K., & Benson, P. L. (1998). The psychological adjustment of United States adopted adolescents and their nonadopted siblings. *Child Development, 69,* 791–802.

Sheras, P. L., Abidin, R. R., & Konold, T. R. (1998). *Stress Index for Parents of Adolescents.* Odessa, FL: Psychological Assessment Resources, Inc.

Shireman, J. F., & Johnson, P. R. (1986). A longitudinal study of black adoptions: Single parent, transracial, and traditional. *Social Work, 31,* 172–176.

Siegel, D. H. (1993). Open adoption of infants: Adoptive parents' perceptions of advantages and disadvantages. *Social Work, 38,* 15–23.

Silber, K., & Dorner, P. M. (1990). *Children of open adoption.* San Antonio, TX: Corona Press.

Silver, L. B., (1989). Frequency of adoption in children and adolescents with learning disabilities. *Journal of Learning Disabilities, 22,* 325–328.

Silverstein, D. R., & Demick, J. (1994). Toward an organizational-relational model of open adoption. *Family Process, 33,* 111–124.

Simmel, C. (2001). *The effects of early maltreatment and foster care history on adopted foster youths' psychosocial functioning.* Unpublished doctoral dissertation, University of California, Berkeley.

Simmel, C., Brooks, D., Barth, R. P., & Hinshaw, S. P. (2001). Externalizing symptomatology among adoptive youth: Prevalence, pre-adoption risk factors, and eight year outcomes. *Journal of Abnormal Child Psychology, 29,* 57–70.

Simmons, B., Allphin, S., & Barth, R. (2000). The changing face of public adoption practice. *Adoption Quarterly, 3,* 43–62.

Simon, R., & Alstein, H. (1996). The case for transracial adoption. *Children and Youth Services Review, 18,* 5–22.

Simon, R. J., Altstein, H., & Melli, M. S. (1994). *The case for transracial adoption.* Washington, DC: American University Press.

Slap, G., Goodman, E., & Huang, B. (2001). Adoption as a risk factor for attempted suicide during adolescence. *Pediatrics, 108*(2), e30. Retrieved August 13, 2001, from http://www.pediatrics.org/ cgi/content/full/108/2/e30

Smith, D. W., & Brodzinsky, D. M. (1994). Stress and coping in adopted children. *Journal of Clinical Child Psychology, 23,* 91–99.

Smith, D. W., & Brodzinsky, D.M. (2002). Coping with birthparent loss in adopted children. *Journal of Child Psychology and Psychiatry, 43,* 213–223.

Smith, J. (2001). The adopted child syndrome: A methodological perspective. *Families in Society, 82,* 491–497.

Smith, S. L., & Howard, J. A. (1999). *Promoting successful adoptions: Practice with troubled families.* Thousand Oaks, CA: Sage.

Smolowe, J. (1994). Babies for export. *Time, 144*(8), 64–65.

Snarey, J. (1993). *How fathers care for the next generation.* Cambridge, MA: Harvard University Press.

Sobol, M. P., & Cardiff, J. (1983). A socio-psychological investigation of adult adoptees' search for birth parents. *Family Relations, 32,* 477–483.

Sobol, M. P., Delaney, S., & Earn, B. M. (1994). Adoptees' portrayal of the development of family structure. *Journal of Youth and Adolescence, 32,* 385–401.

Sociaal en Cultureel Planbureau. (2003). *Rapportage Minderheden 2003: Onderwijs, Arbeid en Sociaal-Culturele Integratie* [Report Minorities 2003: Education, labor, and social-cultural integration]. The Hague: Author.

Sokoloff, B. (1993). Antecedents of American adoption. *The Future of Children, 3,* 17–25.

Solomon, J., & George, C. (1999). The place of disorganisation in attachment theory: Linking classic observations with contemporary findings. In J. Solomon & C. George (Eds.), *Attachment disorganisation* (pp. 3–32). New York: Guilford Press.

Sorosky, A. D., Baran, A., & Pannor, R. (1978). *The adoption triangle.* New York: Doubleday.

Staat, M. A. (2002). Infections disease issues in internationally adopted children. *Pediatric and Infectious Disease Journal, 21,* 257–258.

Stacey, J. (2002). Gay and lesbian families: Queer like us. In M. A. Mason, A. Skolnick, & S. D. Sugarman (Eds.), *All our families* (2nd ed., pp. 144–169). New York: Oxford University Press.

Stams, G. J. M., Juffer, M., Rispens, J., & Hoksbergen, R. (2000). The development and adjustment of 7-year-old children adopted in infancy. *Journal of Psychology and Psychiatry, 414,* 1025–1037.

Steele, M., Hodges, J., Kaniuk, J., Hillman, S., & Henderson, K. (2003). Attachment representation and adoption—Associations between maternal states of mind and emotion narratives in previously maltreated children. *Journal of Child Psychotherapy, 29,* 187–205.

Stein, L. M., & Hoopes, J. L. (1985). *Identity formation in the adopted adolescent.* New York: Child Welfare League of America.

Steinberg, G., & Hall, B. (2000). *Insider transracial adoption.* Indianapolis: Perspective Press.

Stern, D. N. (1985). *The interpersonal world of the infant.* New York: Basic Books.

Stolley, K. D. (1993). Statistics on adoption in the United States. *The Future of Children: Adoption, 3,* 26–42.

Stonequist, E. V. (1935). The problem of marginal man. *American Journal of Sociology, 7,* 12.

Streissguth, A. P., & Conner, P. D. (2001). Fetal alcohol syndrome and other effects of prenatal alcohol: Developmental cognitive neuroscience implications. In C. A. Nelson & M. Luciana (Eds.), *Handbook of cognitive developmental neuroscience* (pp. 505–518). Cambridge, MA: MIT Press.

Streissguth, A. P., & Kanter, J. (1997). *The challenge of fetal alcohol syndrome: Overcoming secondary disabilities.* Seattle: University of Washington Press.

Streissguth, A. P., Sampson, P. D., Olson, H. C., Bookstein, F. L., Barr, H. M., Scott, M., et al. (1994). Maternal drinking during pregnancy: Attention and short-term memory in 14-year-old offspring—A longitudinal prospective study. *Alcoholism, Clinical and Experimental Research, 18,* 202–218.

Strupp, B. J., & Levitsky, D. A. (1995). Enduring cognitive effects of early malnutrition: A theoretical reappraisal. *Journal of Nutrition, 125*(Suppl. 8), 2221S–2232S.

Sykes, M. R. (2001). Adoption with contact: A study of adoptive parents and the impact of continuing contact with families or origin. *Journal of Family Therapy, 23,* 296–316.

Taneja, V., Sriram, S., Beri, R. S., Sreenivas, V., Aggarwal, R., Kaur, R., et al. (2002). "Not by bread alone": Impact of a structured 90-minute play session on development of children in an orphanage. *Child: Care, Health & Development*, *28*, 95–100.

Tessem, H. (1998) *Utenlandsfødte barn på skolens arena* [International adopted children at school]. Oslo: University of Oslo, Pedagogisk Forskningsinstitutt.

Testa, M. F. (2002). Subsidized guardianship: Testing an idea whose time has finally come. *Social Work Research*, *26*, 145–158.

Te Velde, E. R. (1991). *Zwanger worden in de 21ste eeuw: Steeds later, steeds Kunstmatiger* [Becoming pregnant in the 21st century: Increasingly later, increasingly more artificial]. (Inaugural lecture). Utrecht.

Tizard, B. (1977). *Adoption: A second chance*. London: Open Books.

Tizard, B., & Phoenix, A. (1989). Black identity and transracial adoption. *New Community*, *15*, 427–437.

Tjønn, B. (2002). *Eg kom for å elske* [I came to be loved]. Oslo: Det Norske Samlaget.

Toth, S. L., Cicchetti, D., MacFie, J., Maughan, A., & VanMeenen, K. (2000). Narrative representations of caregivers and self in maltreated pre-schoolers. *Attachment and Human Development*, *29*, 271–305.

Tottenham, N., Eigsti, I., Davidson, M. C., Watts, R., Altemus, M., Aronson, J., et al. (2003, March). *Hippocampal and amygdala development following institutionalization and subsequent adoption*. Poster presented at NYAS Roots of Mental Illness in Children Conference, New York.

Toussieng, P. W. (1962). Thoughts regarding the etiology of psychological difficulties in adopted children. *Child Welfare*, *41*, 59–65.

Triseliotis, J. (1973). *In search of origins*. London: Routledge & Kegan Paul.

Triseliotis, J. (2000). Identity formation and the adopted person revisited. In A. Treacher & I. Katz (Eds.), *The dynamics of adoption* (pp. 81–97). London: Jessica Kingsley Publishers.

Triseliotis, J., Shireman, J., & Hundleby, M. (1997). *Adoption theory, policy and practice*. London: Cassell.

Trotzig, A. (1996): *Blod är tjockare än vatten* [Blood is thicker than water]. Stockholm: Bonniers.

UNICEF. (2001). Progress since the World Summit for Children: Antenatal care. Retrieved May 3, 2003, from http://www.childinfo.org/eddb/antenatal/index2.htm

U.S. Department of Health and Human Services. (2000, June). *Report to Congress on kinship foster care*. Washington, DC: Author.

U.S. Department of Health and Human Services, Children's Bureau. (2002). *Adoption and foster care analysis and reporting system*. Washington, DC: Author.

U.S. Department of Health and Human Services, Children's Bureau. (2003). *Adoption and foster care analysis and reporting system*. Washington, DC: Author.

U.S. Department of State, Office of Children's Issues. (n.d.). Retrieved May 3, 2003, from http://travel.state.gov/children's_issues.html

Vaid, R. R., Yee, B. K., Shalev, U., Rawlins, J. N., Weiner, I., Feldon, J., et al. (1997). Neonatal handling and in utero prenatal stress reduce the density of NADPH-diaphorase-reactive neurons in the fascia dentata and Ammon's horn of rats. *Journal of Neuroscience*, *17*, 5599–5609.

Varnis, S. L. (2001). Regulating the global adoption of children. *Society*, *38*, 2, 39–46.

Verhulst, F.C. (2000a). The development of internationally adopted children. In P. Selman (Ed.), *Intercountry adoption: Developments, trends and perspectives* (pp. 126–142). London: British Agencies for Adoption and Fostering.

Verhulst, F.C. (2000b). Internationally adopted children: The Dutch longitudinal adoption study. *Adoption Quarterly, 4*, 27–44.

Verhulst, F. C., Althaus, M., & Versluis-den Bieman, H. (1990). Problem behaviour in international adoptees *Journal of American Academy of Child and Adolescent Psychiatry, 29*, 94–103.

Verhulst, F. C., Althaus, M., & Versluis-den Bieman, H. J.M. (1992). Damaging backgrounds: Later adjustment of international adoptees. *Journal of the American Academy of Child and Adolescent Psychiatry, 31*, 518–524.

Verhulst, F. C., & Versluis-den Bieman, H. J. (1989). *Buitenlandse adoptiekinderen: Vaardigheden en probleemgedrag* [Foreign adoptive children: Capacities and problem behavior]. Assen: Van Gorcum.

Verrier, N. N. (1993). *The primal wound: Understanding the adopted child.* Baltimore: Gateway Press.

Versluis-den Bieman, H. J. M., & Verhulst, F. C. (1995). Self-reported and parent reported problems in adolescent international adoptees. *Journal of Child Psychology and Psychiatry, 36*, 411–428.

Viljoen, D. L., Carr, L. G., Foroud, T.M., Brooke, L., Ramsay, M., & Li, T. K. (2001). Alcohol dehydrogenase-2*2 allele is associated with decreased prevalence of fetal alcohol syndrome in the mixed-ancestry population of the Western Cape Province, South Africa. *Alcoholism, Clinical and Experimental Research, 25*, 1719–1722.

Volpe, J. J. (2001). *Neurobiology of the newborn* (4th ed.). Philadelphia: W. B. Saunders.

Vroegh, K. S. (1992). *Transracial adoption: How it is 17 years later.* Chicago: Chicago Child Care Society.

Wadhwa, P. D., Sandman, C. A., & Garite, T. J. (2001). The neurobiology of stress in human pregnancy: Implications for prematurity and development of the fetal central nervous system. *Progress in Brain Research, 133*, 131–142.

Warren, S. (2003). Narratives in risk and clinical populations. In R. N. Emde, D. P. Wolf, & D. Oppenheim (Eds.), *Revealing the inner worlds of young children: The MacArthur Story Stem Battery and parent-child narratives* (pp. 222–239). New York: Oxford University Press.

Warren, S. B. (1992). Lower threshold for referral for psychiatric treatment for adopted adolescents. *Journal of the American Academy of Child & Adolescent Psychiatry, 31*, 512–527.

Wegar, K. (1997). *Adoption, identity, and kinship: The debate over sealed birth records.* New Haven, CT: Yale University Press.

Weinraub, M., Horvath, D. L., & Gringlas, M. B. (2002). Single parenthood. In M. Bornstein (Ed.), *Handbook of parenting: Vol. 3. Being and becoming a parent* (2nd ed., pp. 109–140). Hillsdale, NJ: Lawrence Erlbaum Associates.

Weyer, M. (1979). *Die adoption fremdländischer kinder* [The adoption of foreign children]. Stuttgart: Quell Verlag.

Wieder, H. (1977). On being told of adoption. *Psychoanalytic Quarterly, 46*, 1–22.

Wiener, S. G., & Levine, S. (1978). Perinatal malnutrition and early handling: Interactive effects on the development of the pituitary-adrenal system. *Developmental Psychobiology, 11*, 335–352.

Wierzbicki, M. (1993). Psychological adjustment of adoptees: A meta-analysis. *Journal of Clinical Child Psychology, 22*, 447–454.

Wills, T. A., & Clearly, S. T. (1996). How are social support effects mediated? A test with parental support and adolescent substance use. *Journal of Personality and Social Psychology, 71*, 952–973.

Wilson, S. L. (2004). A current review of adoption research: Exploring individual differences in adjustment. *Children and Youth Services Review, 26*, 687–696.

Wind, L. (2003). *Exploration of the relationships between child and family characteristics, pre-adoptive risk history, and adoption services utilization.* Unpublished doctoral dissertation, Boston College.

Windle, M. (1992). A longitudinal study of stress buffering for adolescent problem behaviours. *Developmental Psychology, 28*, 522–530.

Woolgar, M. (1999). Projective doll play methodologies for preschool children. *Child Psychology and Psychiatry Review, 4*, 126–134.

Wrobel, G. M., Ayers-Lopez, S., Grotevant, H. D., McRoy, R. G., & Friedrick, M. (1996). Openness in adoption and the level of child participation. *Child Development, 67*, 2358–2374.

Wrobel, G. M., Grotevant, H. D., Berge, J. M., Mendenhall, T. J., & McRoy, R. G. (2003). Contact in adoption: The experience of adoptive families in the USA. *Adoption and Fostering, 27*, 57–67.

Wrobel, G. M., Grotevant, H. D., & McRoy, R. G. (2004). Adolescent search for birthparents: Who moves forward? *Journal of Adolescent Research, 19*, 132–151.

Wrobel, G. M., Kohler, J. K., Grotevant, H. D., & McRoy, R. G. (1999, November). *The family adoption communication model (FAC): Identifying pathways of adoption-related communication.* Paper presented at the 29th Annual Theory Construction and Research Methodology Workshop of the National Council on Family Relations, Irvine, CA.

Wrobel, G. M., Kohler, J. K., Grotevant, H. D., & McRoy, R. G. (2003). The family adoption communication model (FAC): Identifying pathways of adoption-related communication. *Adoption Quarterly, 7*, 53–84.

Wrobel, G. M., Kohler, J. K., Grotevant, H. D., & McRoy, R. G. (1998). Factors related to patterns of information exchange between adoptive parents and children in mediated adoptions. *Journal of Applied Developmental Psychology, 19*, 641–657.

Wulczyn, F. (2002). *Adoption dynamics: The impact of the Adoption and Safe Families Act.* Chicago: Chapin Hall Center for Children.

Youniss, J., & Ketterlinus, R. (1987). Communication and connectedness in mother- and father-adolescent relationships. *Journal of Youth and Adolescence, 16*, 265–280.

Youniss, J., & Smollar, J. (1985). *Adolescent relations with mothers, fathers, and friends.* Chicago: University of Chicago Press.

Zill, N. (1990, June). *Some national comparisons of adopted and nonadopted children.* Exhibits for a paper presented at the Adoption Research Workshop, National Institute for Child Health and Human Development, Washington, DC.

Author Index

Aaronson, M., 124
Abidin, R. R., 136
Abrous, D. M., 54
Accornero, V. H., 88
Achenbach, T. M., 122, 160, 176, 178
Ainsworth, M, 18, 112, 193
Allen, J., 2, 267
Allphin, S., 8
Althaus, M., 3, 38, 57, 216, 233
Altstein, H., 12, 36, 226
American Psychiatric Association, 57
Ames, E. W., 77–79, 136
Anderson, J. W., 87
Anderson, R. E., 14, 223
Andrews, H., 8
Andujo, E., 14
Anthony, J. C., 88
Antonioli, M., 199
Antonovsky, A., 209
Ardone, R. G., 200
Areseneault, L., 72
Aronson, M., 70
Asefa, M., 87
Atkins, M. S., 21, 168
Austin-LaFrance, R., 53
Ayers-Lopez, S., 148, 168, 174

Bachrach, C. A., 34, 234, 262
Bagley, C., 12, 14, 226

Bakermans-Kranenburg, M. J., 4, 119, 263
Baldwin, A., 21
Baldwin, C. P., 21
Baldwin, L. M., 176
Bandstra, E. S., 88
Baran, A., 30, 145, 147, 189, 264
Barker, D. J., 86
Barnes, H. L., 160, 200, 202
Barnett, D., 100
Barocas, R., 214
Baron, R. M., 72
Barone, S., 84
Barth, R. P., 1–4, 6–11, 13–15, 17–19, 21, 23, 24, 38, 61, 70, 97, 137, 148, 154, 228, 260, 263, 266–68
Bartoli, S., 199
Bates, K. K., 85
Bateson, P., 86
Bathurst, K., 151
Bauer, P. J., 55
Bazzani, G., 195
Becker, H. A., 27, 34, 39
Becker, H. C., 52
Beckett, C., 52, 82, 137, 268
Bennet, C., 36
Benson, P. L., 118, 234
Berge, J. M., 148, 173, 174, 176
Berntsen, M., 215, 216

Berry, M., 7, 9, 23, 38, 97, 148, 165, 228, 260
Besser, A., 190
Bimmel, N., 4, 8, 119, 263
Birkle, D. L., 54
Bish, A., 228
Bishop, D., 176
Black, J. E., 85, 86
Black, L. K., 119, 199
Blehar, M., 112, 193
Blotcky, M. J., 15
Blum, H. P., 18, 261
Bock, G. R., 86
Bogenschneider, K., 184
Bohman, M., 7, 263
Borders, L. D., 119, 137, 141, 199
Boston, M., 18, 114
Botvar, P. K., 211, 220, 225, 226, 228
Bowlby, J., 18, 56, 57, 96, 193
Bradley, R. H., 151
Braff, A. M., 20, 118, 126, 176, 217, 259
Bramanti, D., 191
Brand, A. E., 21, 189, 204
Braungart-Rieker, J., 263
Braunwald, K., 100
Bray, J., 201
Bredenkamp, D., 81
Bremner, J. D., 86
Bretherton, I., 96, 99, 101, 103, 109, 113
Brewer, J., 60
Brinich, P. M., 21, 161, 189, 204, 259
Brodzinsky, A. B., 19, 20, 32, 96, 129, 147, 148, 161, 189, 235, 259, 261
Brodzinsky, D. M., 5, 9, 16, 18–20, 23, 30, 32, 38, 96, 98, 118, 123, 126, 129–31, 133–35, 137, 140, 143, 145, 147, 152, 154, 156–59, 161, 162, 164, 165, 176, 189–91, 197, 199, 204, 206–8, 217, 224, 233, 235, 257, 259–62, 264
Bronfenbrenner, U., 157, 162, 170
Bronzino, J., 53
Brooks, D., 1, 2, 4, 8, 11, 13–17, 20, 23, 24, 137, 154, 263, 266–68
Brottveit, A., 211, 218, 219, 221
Bruce, J., 168
Bryant, C. M., 169
Buchsbaum, H. K., 99

Burrow, A. L., 262
Bussiere, A., 13, 17, 32
Butz, A. M., 88
Byrd, A. D., 147

Cadoret, R. J., 259
Caldji, C., 86
Callan, V., 198
Cardiff, J., 159
Carey, G., 263
Carlson, E., 99, 100
Carlson, M., 59
Carp, E. W., 167
Carra, E., 198, 205
Carrey, M. P., 226
Carrion, V. G., 57, 59
Carter, E. A., 19
Carter, M. C., 77
Carver, J. D., 55
Casper, L. M., 1
Caspi, A., 91
Cassidy, J., 99, 100, 104, 193
Castellano, B., 51
Castle, J., 80
Cavazos Dylla, D., 148
Cederblad, M., 36, 75, 189, 211, 220, 225–28
Center for Adoption Research and Policy, 250
Chambers, H., 204
Chandra, A., 234, 262
Chang, F. L., 86
Chapman, D., 147
Chasnoff, I. J., 85
Chisholm, K., 59, 77, 78
Christensen, M., 4, 5, 21, 118, 119, 234, 245, 247
Christian, C. L., 169, 170, 174
Chugani, D. C., 59
Churchhill, J. D., 85
Cicchetti, D., 18, 60, 99, 100
Cigoli, V., 189, 191, 194, 202
Clearly, S. T., 200
Clyman, R. B., 99
Cocozzelli, C., 147
Cohen, J., 250
Cohen, N. J., 67, 90, 196
Cole, E. S., 32, 146

Cole, D., 201
Collishaw, S., 3, 8
Compas, B., 81
Conner, J. R., 55, 228
Conner, P. D., 53
Cook, R., 228
Coon, H., 263
Copping, W., 118
Corbin, T., 95
Corley, R., 263
Cote, A., 118
Coyl, D., 234
Coyne, J., 196
Crittenden, P. M., 79, 96, 97, 102
Curtis, W. J., 84

Dalen, M., 11, 152, 211, 212, 214–28
Daly, K., 20, 152
Dammelmair, H., 55
Dance, C., 98, 122
Danscher, G., 54
D'Atena, P., 200
Davis, J. A., 55
DeBellis, M. D., 57
DeFries, J. C., 263
De Geer B., 211, 215, 216
De Haan, M., 55
Delaney, S., 159, 199
Demick, J., 147
Derogatis, L. R., 178
Deutsch, D. K., 18
Deutsch, H., 261
De Vellis, J., 57
Diorio, J., 85
Divon, M., 52
Do, D., 57
Dobbing, J., 87
Dondeyne, N., 12
Donley, K. S., 32, 146
Dorner, P. M., 147
Drell, M. J., 57
Drewett, R., 87
Drozdovitch, V., 85
Dubois-Dalcq, M., 57
Dumaret, A. C., 72
Dunbar, N., 150, 170, 173–75, 178–80
Dunkel-Schetter, C., 52
Duvall, J., 196

Duyme, M., 72, 73, 89, 90
Dyer, J. G., 214
Dyer-Friedman, J., 87

Earls, F., 59
Earn, B. M., 159, 199
Eaves, L., 68
Edelbrock, C., 160, 178
Edgerton, M. D., 124
Egeland, B., 99
Eigeland, S., 215, 216
Elbert, T., 86
Elde, C., 15
Elias, M. J., 123
Elliot, W., 51
Emde, R. N., 99, 103
English and Romanian Adoptees
    Research Team, 52, 80–82, 122
Epstein, N. B., 176
Erikson, E. H., 179, 195
Eriksson, P. S., 48
Esau, A. L., 150, 178
Escorihuela, R. M., 51
Eth, S., 107
Etter, J., 15
Evan B. Donaldson Adoption Insti-
    tute, 1, 2, 6, 184, 261
Ey, S., 81

Fan, X., 4, 5, 21, 118, 119, 233–35,
    245–47, 262, 263
Fanshell, D., 14, 17
Fava Vizziello, G., 199
Feast, J., 126, 158, 159
Federici, R., 41, 216, 217
Feigelman, W., 8, 12–14, 36, 234, 262
Fein, E., 259
Fergusson, D. M., 118
Fernandez, M., 137
Fernandez-Teruel, A., 44
Festinger, T., 9
Fields, J., 1
Finley, G. E., 234, 262
Fisher, L., 77
Fletcher, K., 60
Follevag, G., 229
Ford, T., 95
Francis, D., 85

Frasch, K., 15, 154, 166
Fraser, M., 21
Fravel, D. L., 15, 169, 170
Frederickson, C., 54
Freeman, B. J., 80
Freundlich, M., 41
Friedlander, M. L., 12
Friedrick, M., 129, 148
Fuentes, M. J., 137
Fulker, D. W., 263

Galler, J. R., 53
Garbarino, J., 21
Gardell, I., 11, 12, 36, 211, 212, 216
Garite, T. J., 54
Garland, J. A., 36
Garmezy, N., 214
Gatward, R., 95
Geerars, H. C., 32
General Accounting Office, 11
George, C., 106
Georgieff, M. K., 52, 53, 55, 57
Gianino, A., 56
Gibb, R., 50, 51
Gibbs, D., 24
Gilman, L. C., 136
Gindis, B., 216
Gioia, G. A., 216
Gleeson, J. P., 18
Glidden, L. M., 20, 21, 137
Godbout, J. T., 190
Goerge, R., 9
Goldberg, D., 8, 118
Goldberg S., 16
Goldschmidt, I., 136
Goldwyn, R., 110
Golombok, S., 228
Gonzalez, B., 51
Goodman, E., 4
Goodman, R., 95, 108
Gossman, G., 174
Gottfried, A. E., 151
Gottfried, A. W., 151
Gozzoli, C., 192
Grace, K. D., 15
Grant, K. E., 81
Grantham-McGregor, S., 87
Greco, O., 190, 192–94, 196, 199, 207

Green J., 109
Greene, A. L., 198
Greenough, W. T., 51, 85, 86
Greenspan, S., 214
Grimsley, M. D., 198
Gringlas, M. B., 151
Gritter, J. L., 147, 149
Groark, C. J., 62
Groothues, C., 137
Grossman, A. W., 84, 85, 87
Grotevant, H. D., 4, 15, 21, 37, 57, 129, 130, 145–50, 152–58, 161–63, 167–73, 175–82, 184, 198, 217, 218, 223, 233–35, 247, 259, 260, 262, 264, 265
Grow, L. J., 14
Groze, V. K., 9, 126, 137, 140
Gunnar, M. R., 47, 57–59, 65, 168, 266
Gunnarby, A., 12, 212

Hack, M., 52
Hajal, F., 19, 157, 259
Hall, B., 14
Hallden, G., 211, 212
Har-Even, D., 136
Harter, S., 124, 160
Haugaard, J. J., 4, 5, 20, 21, 168, 184, 233, 262
Hearn, E. F., 57
Hebb, D. O., 49
Heim, C., 59
Helsen, M., 200
Henderson, K., 99, 103, 109
Hene, B., 11, 211, 215
Henig, R. M., 30, 152, 154, 157, 259
Henney, S., 145, 146, 165, 168–70, 174
Henry, C., 85
Hermkens, P. L., 27, 34, 39
Herndon, J. G., 57
Heron, J., 85
Hessl, D., 87
Hetherington, E. M., 151
Hillman, S., 99, 103, 109
Hinshaw, S. P., 8
Hjern, A., 3, 4, 17, 211, 226, 227, 233
Hobbs, J. R., 55
Hodges, J., 56, 76, 77, 88, 93, 96, 98–100, 103, 107, 109, 111, 113, 120, 122

Hofvander, Y., 12, 211, 212
Hogg, C., 122
Hoksbergen, R.A.C., 27, 32, 36–39,
    146, 203, 216, 217, 227, 233, 262
Holahan, C. J., 200
Hook, B., 189, 211, 226
Hoopes, J. L., 158, 264
Horn, J. M., 18
Hornby, H., 9, 20
Horvath, D. L., 151
Horwood, L. J., 118
Hostetter, M., 63
Houston, D., 20
Howard, E., 9
Howard, J. A., 8, 96, 97, 168, 184, 267
Howe, D., 100, 113, 117, 126, 140, 158,
    159, 166, 189, 204, 227, 233
Howell, S., 211, 224
Huang, B., 4
Hubel, D. H., 85
Hueber, E. S., 124
Hughes, B., 145–47
Hundleby, M., 3, 158
Huttenlocher, P. R., 84

Iafrate, R., 189, 194, 197, 198, 202, 206
Igumnov, S., 85
Ingersoll, B. D., 168, 233
Irhammar, M., 75, 189, 211, 219, 220,
    225, 226, 228
Iyer, S., 2

James, S., 13
James, S. S., 9
Jenista, J. A., 52, 63
Johansson, S,. 39
Johnson, A. L., 88
Johnson, D. E., 20, 47, 56, 57, 63, 80
Johnson, F., 259
Johnson, P. R., 14
Johnstone, B. M., 87
Judd, C. M., 201
Juffer, F., 4, 37, 119, 203, 216, 233, 263

Kaba, M., 87
Kabbaj, M., 85
Kadushin, A., 9
Kaler, S. R., 80

Kalkoske, M., 99
Kaniuk, J., 99, 103, 109
Kanter, J., 84, 87
Kantor, B., 190
Kaplan, N., 100
Kaye, K., 158
Kegan, R., 178
Kennard, M., 49
Kenny, D. A., 72, 201, 217
Kertes, D. A., 47, 58, 60, 75, 266
Ketterlinus, R., 198
Killingsworth-Rini, C., 52
Kim, W. J., 226
King, J. A., 60
King, S., 60
Kirk, H. D., 15, 27–29, 31, 33, 37, 42,
    133, 152, 156–59, 161, 191, 223, 259
Kirschner, D., 261
Kittson, R. H., 35
Kleim, J. A., 85
Klein, N. K., 52
Klinger, E., 178
Koehl, M., 54
Koehler, A. J., 85
Kofman, O., 54
Kohler, J. K., 129, 130, 148, 152, 159,
    163, 176, 178, 180, 181, 184, 235, 259,
    260, 264, 265
Kolb, B., 50, 51
Koletzko, B., 55
Konold, T. R., 136
Kotsopoulos, S., 118
Kraft, A., 15, 147, 264
Kramer, L., 20
Kraszpulski, M., 54
Kreppner, J. M., 52, 81
Krouse, E. M., 54
Kuhl, P. K., 86
Kuhl, W., 12, 38
Kvifte-Andresen, I. L., 216, 217, 227

Ladd, C. O., 59
Ladner, J., 14
Lahti, J., 7
Lamb, M. E., 261
Lambert, L., 263
Lanz, M., 198, 200, 201, 205
Larque, E., 55

Larrieu, J. A., 57
Lasley, E. N., 86
Lauderdale, M. L., 14, 223
Lemaire, V., 54
LeMoal, M., 54, 85
Leon, E., 283
Leon, I. G., 130, 131, 139, 140, 266
LeVay, S., 85
LeVine, E. S., 25
Levitsky, D. A., 52
Levy-Shiff, R., 136, 199
Lichtman, J. W., 48
Lieberman, A., 20
Lieblum, S., 41, 43
Lightburne, A., 20
Lindblad, F., 3, 211, 233
Liu, D., 85
Livingston Smith, S., 96, 97
Loehlin, L. C., 18
Logan, F., 204
Loganovskaja, T. K., 85
Loganovsky, K. N., 85
London, K. A., 34
Looney, J. G., 15
Low, K. G., 57
Lubach, G. R., 85
Lush, D., 114
Lyngstol, S., 215
Lynskey, M., 118

Maccari, S., 54, 85
MacFie, J., 99
Mackie, A. J., 198
Madsen, N., 60
Maguire, E. A., 86
Main, M., 100, 104
Mainemer, H., 136, 137
Maluccio, A. N., 17
Mandansky, D., 60
Mannheim, K., 27
Mansvelt, H.F.M., 33
Marchel, M. A., 21, 149, 170, 260
Marcovitch, S., 189, 203, 204
Marcus, C., 32
Marta, E., 190, 198, 200, 205, 207
Martin P., 86
Marvin, R. S., 81, 83
Mason, S. J., 18

Masten, A. S., 58
Maughan, A., 99
Maughan, B., 3, 264
Maxwell, S. E., 201
Mayes, D., 98, 122
Maza, P. L., 5
McAdams, D. P., 179
McCall, R. B., 62
McCarton, C. M., 52
McCormack, K., 60
McCrone, E., 99
McDonald, T. P., 9, 20
McEwen, B., 86
McGoldrick, M., 19
McGue, M. K., 118
McGuinness, J. P., 214
McGuinness, T. M., 214, 216, 217
McKay, M. M., 21, 168
McLaughlin, H., 36
McMahon, S. D., 81
McMorris, F. A., 57
McNichol, T., 11
McRoy, R. G., 14, 15, 21, 37, 129, 130,
    145–49, 152, 154–56, 158, 161–63,
    167–74, 176, 177, 180, 191, 217, 223,
    235, 259, 260, 264, 265
Meaney, M. J., 85
Meeus, W., 200
Melamed-Hass, S., 190
Melli, M. S., 12
Melner, M. H., 57
Melosh, B., 185
Meltzer, H., 95
Mendenhall, T. J., 148, 155, 173, 174,
    176
Mercke, A. M., 75, 189, 211
Miall, C. E., 267
Miller, B. C., 4, 5, 21, 118, 119, 233–35,
    240, 245–47, 250, 255, 262, 263
Miller, J., 23, 267
Minde, K., 90
Minister of Justice, 41
Mishler, E. G., 179
Mitchell, D., 15, 147, 264
Mitchell, K. T., 217
Mitchell, M. A., 63
Moe, V., 70, 71
Mokler, D. J., 53

Moore, C. F., 54, 85
Moos, R. H., 200
Morgane, P. J., 53
Morison, S. J., 59, 77, 78
Morral, P., 204
Morris P. A., 170
Morrow, C. E., 88
Muhamedrahimov, R., 62
Mulder, E.J.H., 7
Murphy, J. M., 11
Murray, C., 228
Murray, R., 68

National Adoption Information
   Clearinghouse, 6
Needell, B., 11, 70, 148
Neil, E., 166, 168
Nelson, C. A., 55, 84
Nelson, K. A., 7, 137
Nemeroff, C. B., 59
Nickman, S., 38, 152, 259
Nikoforova, N., 62
Nishijima, M., 53
Noller, P., 198, 200, 205
Nulman, I., 69
Nyagu, A. I., 85
Nytrohaug, L., 212

O'Brien, P. M., 86
O'Connor, T. G., 52, 68, 80–83, 85, 86,
   89, 90, 122, 137, 268
Olson, D. H., 160, 200, 202
Olson, H. C., 84
Onken, S. J., 145, 168
Oppenheim, D., 17, 99, 101, 103, 108,
   113

Pagliaro, A. M., 7
Pagliaro, L. A., 7
Palacios, J., 117, 121, 137, 143, 257
Palmov, O., 62
Palumbo, J., 15, 147, 264
Pannor, R., 30, 145, 147, 189, 264
Pantev, C., 86
Paret, I. H., 185
Parke, R. D., 151
Partridge, S., 9, 20, 23
Pasley, B. K., 119, 199

Patterson, C. J., 16, 151
Patterson, G., 13
Patton, J. M., 31
Pavelko, M., 54
Pecora, P. J., 17
Penny, J. M., 137
Perry, Y. V., 167, 185
Peters, B. R., 21, 168, 184
Phillips, R., 20
Phoenix, A., 223
Pickles, A., 3, 68, 77, 81, 264
Pinderhughes, E. E., 9, 10, 19, 23, 126,
   135, 137, 143, 151, 152, 154, 158, 164,
   165, 189, 190, 208, 235, 257, 260, 262
Pine, B. A., 20
Pittman, B., 8
PIU, 93–96
Plomin, R., 263
Plotsky, P. M., 59, 60
Portnoy, F., 137
Priel, B., 190
Proos, L., 212
Pruzan, V., 211
Purves, D., 48
Pynoos, R. S., 107

Quinton, D., 98, 99, 105, 116, 122, 140

Radomsky, S., 9
Randall, C. L., 52
Ranieri, S., 192, 196
Rao, R., 52, 53, 55
Rathbun, C., 36
Raynor, L., 36, 126, 223
Reed, M. G., 58
Reitz, M., 33, 158, 161, 259
Remley, D. T., 87
Rende, R. D., 263
Rice, D., 84
Richman, N., 122
Ridgeway, D., 99
Ridley, M., 87
Rijk, K., 217
Rilling, J. K., 57
Rispens, J., 212, 233
Rockstroh, B., 86
Roehlkepartain, E. C., 234
Rogosch, F. A., 60

Rorbech, M., 220, 225, 226
Rosenberg, E. G., 19, 259
Rosenberg, K., 126, 140, 157
Rosenberg, M., 124
Rosenbluth, D., 18
Rosenfeld, A. A., 7, 8, 11
Rosenthal, J. A., 9, 137, 228
Rosnati, R., 187, 190–98, 200–202, 205–7
Ross, N. M., 21, 149, 170, 177, 260
Roughton, E. C., 85
Rowe, J., 31
Roy, P., 77, 88, 217
Rushton, A., 98, 99, 122, 141, 265, 267
Rutter, M., 47, 52, 56, 58, 67, 68, 77, 80–83, 86, 87, 89–91, 99, 122, 131, 139, 214, 216, 217, 268
Rygvold, A. L., 211, 215–17

Sachdev, P., 223
Sackett, G. P., 86
Saetersdal, D., 211, 212, 214, 216, 218–24, 226, 227
Sallee, A. L., 25
Salm, A. K., 54
Salo, A. L., 52
Sameroff, A. J., 21, 214
Sanchez, M. M., 57, 59, 60
Sanchez-Espinosa, E. M., 121
Sánchez-Sandoval, Y., 117, 121
Sandman, C. A., 52, 54
Saneto, R. P., 57
Sar, B. K., 23
Saulnier, J. L., 52
Savoie, L., 77
Scabini, E., 189, 191, 194, 198, 202
Schaefer, E. S., 124
Schaerlakens, A., 12
Schechter, D. E., 20, 118, 152, 154, 157, 162, 217
Schechter, M. D., 30, 33, 38, 190, 197, 199, 206, 207, 259, 261
Scheeringa, M. S., 57
Schelsky, H., 27
Schjelderup-Mathiesen, K., 212
Schmidt, A., 15, 147, 264
Schmidt, D., 228
Schneider, M. L., 32, 54, 85

Schuder, M., 59
Schwartz, A. E., 17, 18
Scully, A., 12
Seidl, F., 9
Seifer, R., 21, 214
Selman, P., 34, 35, 41, 67
Shapiro, D., 14, 185
Shapiro, V. B., 185
Sharma, A. R., 118, 119, 234
Shaver, P. R., 193
Sheras, P. L., 136
Shin, Y. J., 226
Shireman, J., 3, 14, 158
Shulman, S., 199
Siebenaler, K., 24
Siegel, D. H., 148
Sigvardsson, S., 7, 263
Silber, K., 147
Silberg, J., 68, 82, 87, 91
Silver, L. B., 217
Silverman, A. R., 12–14, 36
Simmel, C., 1, 8, 9
Simmons, B., 8
Simon, H., 85
Simon, R. J., 12, 14, 36, 226
Simonoff, E., 68
Singer, L. M., 20, 118, 126, 131, 157, 162, 176, 217, 259
Sjolin, S., 12, 212
Slap, G., 4, 8
Slinning, K., 70, 71
Smart, L. L., 87
Smith, D. W., 19, 32, 96, 129, 147, 161, 189, 235, 259, 261
Smith, J., 261
Smith, S. L., 8, 168, 184, 267
Smith, V., 109
Smollar, J., 205
Smolowe, J., 1
Snarey, J., 195
Sobol, M. P., 20, 159, 199
Sokoloff, B., 33, 145
Solomon, J., 106
Sorosky, A. D., 30, 31, 145, 146, 189, 263
Spaan, J.J.T.M., 38
Staat, M. A., 7
Stacey, J., 2

Stams, G.J.M., 203, 233
Stanley, C., 109
Stanley-Hagan, M., 151
Stavrakaki, C., 118
Steele, M., 93, 99, 100, 103, 109, 111, 116
Steiger, C., 118
Stein, L. M., 158, 264
Steinberg, G., 14
Stern, D. N., 96
Stolley, K. S., 1, 5, 34, 258
Stonequist, E., V. 12
Stoutjesdijk, F., 217
Streather, J., 263
Streissguth, A. P., 53, 84, 87
Struening, E., 8
Strupp, B. J., 52
Sundelin, C., 2, 212
Sykes, M. R., 2, 3, 145–47

Tamanza, G., 192
Taneja, V., 62
Tash, C., 11
Taub, E., 86
Taylor, H. G., 52
ter Laak, J., 27, 217
Tessem, H., 217
Tessema, F., 87
Testa, M. F., 18
Te Velde, E. R., 41, 43
Thurm, A. E., 81
Tizard, B., 31, 56, 76, 77, 88, 98, 113, 120, 122, 137, 223
Tjonn, B., 229
Tobena, A., 51
Tomkiewicz, S., 72
Tonkiss, J., 53
Toth, S. L., 99, 111
Tottenham, N., 60
Toussieng, P. W., 261
Treseder, J., 98
Triseliotis, J., 3, 11, 12, 126, 139, 140, 158
Tronick, E. Z., 56
Trotzig, A., 229
Tubman, J. G., 262
Tucker, N., 147, 264

UNICEF, 52, 62
U. S. Department of Health and Human Services, 5, 6, 9, 10, 17
U. S. Department of State, 47

Vaid, R. R., 54
Valentiner, D. P., 200
van Dijkum, C., 217
van Dulmen, M.H.M., 4, 149, 176, 177, 234
van Egmond, G., 38
van Ijzendoorn, M. H., 4, 119, 263
van Meenen, K., 99
Varnis, S. L., 3
Vaughan, H. G., Jr., 52
Vaziri, M., 16
Verhulst, F. C., 3, 36, 38, 57, 74, 118, 139, 216, 217, 226, 227, 233
Verluis-den Bieman, H., 3, 36, 38, 57, 216, 233
Verrier, N. N., 30
Viljoen, D. L., 87
Vinnerljung, B., 3, 211, 233
Vollebergh, W., 200
Volpe, B., 199
Volpe, J. J., 55
Vroegh, K. S., 14

Waardenburg, B. C., 37, 216
Wadhwa, P. D., 52, 54
Walker, S., 118
Wall, S., 112, 193
Wallace, C. S., 85
Wallace, I. F., 52
Warren, S., 99, 100, 158
Warren, S. B., 20, 234
Waters, E., 112, 193
Watson, K. W., 33, 158, 161, 259
Weathersby, R. T., 52
Webster, W., 54
Wegar, K., 145, 146
Weinbruch, C., 86
Weinraub, M., 151
Wellen, N., 8
Weyer, M., 36
Wheeler, T., 86
Whelan, J., 86
White, K. L., 172

Whitmore, K., 122
Whittaker, J. K., 17
Wieder, H., 33
Wierzbicki, M., 20, 233, 261, 263
Wiesel, T. N., 85
Willerman, L., 18
Wills, T. A., 200
Wilson, J., 234, 262
Wilson, S. L., 122, 130
Wind, L., 1, 6, 7, 21
Windle, M., 200
Winslow, J., 60
Winterberg, T., 147
Wolf, D. P., 103
Wolke, D., 87
Wolkind, S. N., 118
Woods, P., 15, 147, 264

Woolgar, M., 102
Wrobel, G. M., 129, 148, 149, 152,
    154–58, 161, 162, 173, 176, 177, 183,
    259, 260, 264, 265
Wulczyn, F., 6, 13

Young, L., 12
Youniss, J., 198, 205
Yu, D., 9

Zancato, P., 199
Zax, M., 214
Zeanah, C. H., 57
Zill, N., 10
Zoran, N., 199
Zurcher, L. A., 14, 129, 223, 260

Subject Index

Adopted children. *See also* Foster care adoptions, International adoption, Open adoption; Special needs adoption
  academic performance, 3, 100, 119, 124, 142, 233, 245, 249, 261
  adjustment of, 10, 27, 29, 140, 146–47, 151, 155, 157–60, 162, 164, 166, 168, 177–78, 209, 249–50, 260, 262–63, 265
  age at placement, 3, 9–10, 58, 113, 119, 125, 134, 138–39, 160, 171, 189, 203
  externalizing problems, 8, 38–39, 98, 119, 177, 200, 233, 249
  genetic issues, 21–22, 31, 40, 67–68, 72–73, 87, 91, 196, 218, 222, 233, 258
  hyperactivity, 8, 39, 52, 70, 81, 95, 98, 119, 122–23, 125, 131–32, 142, 217
  identity issues, 42, 126, 131, 137, 147, 154, 158, 164, 169, 174, 178–80, 198
  internalizing problems, 8, 52, 177, 200, 249
  peer relationships, 12, 52, 76–77, 79, 98, 108–9, 114, 203, 219–20
  physical development and health, 3, 11, 40, 50–58, 63, 245
  preplacement issues, 3, 10–11, 40, 47, 49, 119, 132, 204, 214, 217, 266
  satisfaction, 124–25, 130, 138, 159–60, 162, 174, 261
  search for origins, 28, 31, 148, 154, 157, 159, 163, 166, 169, 174, 176–77, 184, 218, 220–22
  self-esteem, 12, 13, 99, 118, 120–21, 122, 124, 140, 147, 159–60, 164, 200, 203, 206, 217, 220
  understanding of adoption, 18, 129–31, 148, 154, 197, 249
Adoption disruption, 9, 10, 23–24, 98, 143, 228
Adoption from care. *See* Institutional care; Foster care adoptions
Adoption kinship system, 168–69, 173, 176, 178, 180, 183, 185, 266
Adoption legislation, 2, 120, 167, 183–85, 187, 208
Adoption professionals, 3, 29, 158, 184, 208, 258
  attitudes and beliefs, 37, 63, 90, 262
Adoption services and support, 3, 5, 20–24, 64, 96, 141, 194–95, 230, 258, 261

post-adoption, 23, 33, 64, 116, 142,
    165, 182–84, 208–9, 266, 267–68
pre-placement, 23, 38, 40, 42, 115,
    128, 142, 163, 165, 182–84, 208,
    229
Adoption statistics, 1, 5–6, 9, 11, 34,
    250, 257. *See also* International
    adoptions
Adoption theory
    attachment theory, 96–97, 193, 259
    biological theory, 48–58, 259
    ecological theory, 157, 162, 170
    family life cycle theory, 19, 157,
        191, 259
    psychodynamic theory, 161, 233,
        259, 261
    risk and resilience theory, 18–19,
        67–68, 259
    stress and coping theory, 161, 189
Adoption triangle. *See* Adoption kin-
    ship system
Adoptive families
    challenges of, 4, 19, 24, 28, 126,
        142–43, 164, 189–90
    family structure, 2, 5–6, 22, 132, 151
    life cycle, 5, 10, 14, 19, 21, 133, 143,
        154, 157, 161, 190, 260
Adoptive parents
    acknowledgment/rejection of
        differences, 28, 30–31, 32–33,
        37–38, 42–43, 118, 121, 133–35,
        137–38, 143, 156–57, 159, 177,
        191–92, 208, 223
    attitudes of, 30, 133–34, 149, 153,
        155, 158
    expectations, 9–10, 23, 38, 40, 63,
        89–90, 97–98, 115, 143, 149, 153,
        189–91, 193, 217
    generations of, 27–43, 128
    infertility, 31–32, 41, 43, 152, 156,
        171, 189, 260
    motivation for adoption, 28, 37–38,
        121, 170
    rearing styles, 9, 116, 132–33, 136,
        138, 140–41, 151, 194, 222, 225
    satisfaction with adoption, 3, 24,
        118, 121, 137–38, 143, 147, 155,
        161, 267

socioeconomic status (SES) and
    educational level, 5, 24, 71–73,
    79, 83, 132, 136, 141, 171, 220,
    228
    stress, 28, 38, 118, 135–37, 161, 227
Attachment and adoption
    age of placement, 10, 109
    implications for research and inter-
        vention, 113–16, 260
    internal working models, 96–97,
        101, 193
    narrative assessment, 97, 99, 101–4,
        114
    patterns of, 100, 105–7, 109–11
    problems and disturbances, 56,
        108–9, 147

Behavior genetics, 68, 91, 258
Biological parents, 28, 31, 146
    adjustment of, 20, 33, 39, 147–48,
        169, 174
    child relinquishment, 32–34,
        164–65, 208
    open adoption, 33, 171, 173,
        175–76, 182

Child maltreatment, 94, 132, 153, 164
    attachment patterns, 96, 100,
        109–11
    cognitive development, 52, 59,
        72–73, 89
    posttraumatic stress disorder
        (PTSD), 57, 98
Communication, 29, 33, 121, 126–29,
    142–43, 146–47, 151–52, 155,
    158–66, 197, 200, 205, 208, 230,
    260
Cultural and historic context of adop-
    tion, 29–30, 34–36, 42–43, 139,
    146, 167, 170, 188, 195, 218–20,
    228, 231, 235, 257, 261, 265,
    267

Foster care adoptions, 5–8, 39–40,
    93–94, 165–66, 257, 266

Gay/lesbian adoptions, 2, 13, 16–17,
    32

Gender differences, 5, 8–9, 18, 72, 74,
     123, 131–32, 136–38, 177, 180,
     195, 198–9, 201, 203, 205,
     220–221, 248

Hague Convention, 3, 40, 187

Individual differences, 83, 88–89, 91,
     113–14, 153, 161, 163, 170,
     180–81, 183, 191–93, 216
Institutional care
   adjustment outcomes, 58, 76–77,
     95, 122, 124, 138, 230, 266
   length of care, 75, 78–79, 81–83, 88,
     123, 136
   nutritional problems, 11, 36, 49,
     52–53, 80, 83–84, 86, 89, 88–89,
     212, 266
International adoption
   age at adoption, 74, 80–81, 83, 216,
     227
   attachment issues, 79, 81, 83, 89–90,
     213, 223
   identity issues, 12–13, 212, 214, 218,
     221–22, 224, 226, 231
   intelligence development, 47, 52,
     58, 78, 80–82, 88, 230
   language development, 11, 215–16,
     226, 229–30
   outcomes, 3–4, 11–12, 36–37, 59,
     74–77, 79, 212, 214, 216, 220, 225,
     231, 233, 266
   statistics, 1, 6, 35, 41, 47, 187–88,
     211

Loss, adopted children experiences of,
     18, 29–30, 130–31, 139–40, 142,
     147, 156, 218, 267

Methodological issues, 5, 20–22, 69,
     91, 120, 233–55, 262, 263

longitudinal designs, 8, 19–20, 22,
     84–87, 104, 117, 121–22, 169–71,
     207, 214, 236, 263–64, 266

Neurobiological development, 48–58,
     58–64, 84, 259, 266

Open adoption, 13, 15, 167–86, 260, 264
   attachment issues, 15, 177
   definition of, 15, 147, 149–51, 168
   outcomes, 147–48, 177–81, 265
   types of, 15, 149, 168, 172–73, 175
Openness, 37, 128, 145–66, 200,
     264–265

Practice issues, 22–25, 91–92, 114–16,
     141–43, 163–66, 183–84, 208–9,
     229–31, 267–68
Preadoption experiences, 3, 9–11, 18,
     21, 51–53, 56–58, 74, 88, 94, 99,
     104, 120, 212, 214
Prenatal drug exposure, 18, 39, 52–53,
     69–72, 84–85, 164, 217, 233, 266

Residential care. See Institutional care
Resilience and recovery, 18, 24,
     226–27, 258, 261–62, 266
   in adoption, 58, 64, 68, 89–90, 140,
     207, 212, 214, 230
   protective factors, 42, 91, 198–99,
     207, 209, 214–15, 260
Risk in adoption, 18, 21, 24, 39, 184,
     206, 260, 266

Sibling adoption, 6–7, 13, 104, 121,
     136–38, 172, 228, 235
Special needs adoption, 6–7, 9, 40, 42,
     94, 99, 121, 132, 136, 168

Transracial adoption, 2, 13–15, 20,
     35–36, 267

About the Contributors

Richard P. Barth, MSW, PhD, is a Frank A. Daniels Distinguished Professor in the School of Social Work at the University of North Carolina. He is coauthor of *Adoption and Disruption* and coeditor of *Adoption and Prenatal Drug Exposure.* He is a recipient of the Presidential Award for Excellence in Research from the National Association of Social Workers and has published extensively in the areas of adoption, foster care, and child welfare.

David M. Brodzinsky, PhD, is a professor of developmental and clinical psychology at Rutgers University. His research and practice interests focus on adoption and foster care, stress and coping in children, nontraditional family life, and the interface of mental health and the law. He is the author or coeditor of four other books on the psychology of adoption. He also directs the Rutgers Foster Care Counseling Program.

Devon Brooks, MSW, PhD, is an assistant professor and director of the Institute on Urban and International Families in the School of Social Work at the University of Southern California. His research and practice interests revolve around adoption, child maltreatment prevention and treatment, and child welfare services, policy, and outcomes. He is coauthor of several book chapters on these issues and has published widely in peer-reviewed journals.

Monica Dalen, PhD, is a professor in the Department of Specialty Needs Education, University of Oslo, Norway. Her research focuses primarily on international adoption, with a special interest in early attachment, ethnic identity, academic performance and language development. Currently, she is conducting a longitudinal study on the development of children adopted from China. She has published widely on adoption in books, book chapters, and peer-reviewed journal articles.

Xitao Fan, PhD, is a professor of quantitative methods in the Curry School of Education, University of Virginia. His research focuses on applications of multivariate methods in research and on measurement validity and reliability issues. He is the author of three books and about 50 articles and chapters.

Harold D. Grotevant, PhD, is a Distinguished University Teaching Professor of Family Social Science at the University of Minnesota. His research focuses on parent–adolescent relationships, especially in adoptive families, and on identity development in adolescents and young adults. His work has resulted in over 100 articles as well as several books, including *Openness in Adoption: Connecting Families of Birth and Adoption* (with Ruth McRoy, 1998).

Megan R. Gunnar, PhD, is a Distinguished McKnight Professor of Child Development at the Institute of Child Development, University of Minnesota. In over 100 publications, she has documented the powerful role of close relationships in regulating stress biology in young children. She directs the Minnesota International Adoption Project, which focuses on assessing the development of postinstitutionalized children.

Kay Henderson is a research officer, research coordinator for M.Sc. students, and course tutor for the diploma in the practice of psychoanalytic developmental psychology at the Anna Freud Centre. Her research interests lie in the areas of parenting skills and adoption.

Saul Hillman is a research officer and research coordinator for the M.Sc. in psychoanalytic developmental psychology at the Anna Freud Centre and carries out training and development in the use of narrative stem techniques.

Jill Hodges, PhD, is a consultant and child and adolescent psychotherapist in the Department of Psychological Medicine at Great Ormond Street Hospital for Sick Children and Honorary Senior Lecturer in the Brain and Behavioural Sciences Unit of the Institute of Child Health, London. She has long-standing research and clinical interests in adoption, attachment, and the sequelae of adverse childhood experiences.

René Hoksbergen, PhD, is Emeritus Professor of Psychology at the Utrecht University, the Netherlands, and guest professor at the Institute of Psychology, Pune, India. With long-standing research interests and clinical practice in adoption, child abuse, and treatment, he has published widely on these topics in books and articles in peer-reviewed journals.

Since 1998, he has conducted longitudinal research on children adopted from Romania.

Jeanne Kaniuk is the head of the Coram Adoption and "Permanent Families Service," one of the United Kingdom's leading adoption agencies. The service places and supports children with complex needs who are looked after by local authorities and provides ongoing support to their adoptive families.

Darlene A. Kertes is a National Science Foundation Fellow at the Institute of Child Development, University of Minnesota. She has published several articles relating children's experiences to stress hormone levels. Her research focuses on how qualities of early care shape neurophysiological and behavioral development in typically developing and postinstitutionalized children.

Jan ter Laak, PhD, is an assistant professor of developmental psychology at the University of Utrecht, the Netherlands. He is member of the Dutch Psychological Association, Section Assessment and Section Child and Youth. His research interest is in assessment, personality, and adoption. He is the author of a handbook on assessment and has published several articles on assessment and personality.

Ruth G. McRoy, PhD, is a Ruby Lee Piester Centennial Professor in Services to Children and Families and is the associate dean for research and director of the Center for Social Work Research, University of Texas at Austin. She has written extensively on adoption. Recent books include *Openness in Adoption: Exploring Family Connections* (with H. Grotevant, 1998) and *Special Needs Adoptions: Practice Issues* (1999).

Brent C. Miller, PhD, is vice president for research and professor of Family and Human Development at Utah State University. His research has focused on adolescent sexual behavior and pregnancy and the adjustment of adopted children. He is the author of several books and over 100 articles and chapters.

Jesús Palacios, PhD, is a professor of developmental psychology at the University of Seville, Spain. He has conducted research on both domestic and international adoption in Spain, published books and articles on foster care and adoption, and coauthored a preadoption training program for prospective adopters as well as a book for adoptive parents (*Adelante con la adopción* [Ahead with Adoption]).

Yvette V. Perry is a PhD student, Department of Family Social Science, University of Minnesota. She has served as a research assistant on the Minnesota-Texas Adoption Research Project (MTARP).

Rosa Rosnati, PhD, is an associate professor of social psychology at the Catholic University of Milan, Italy. In her work at the Center of Family Studies and Research, she is involved in research projects and training programs on adoptive families. She published *The Adoptive Pact* (with D. Bramanti, 1998) and is author of many contributions in scientific journals.

Michael Rutter, MD, is a professor of developmental psychopathology, Institute of Psychiatry, Kings College, London. He set up the MRC Child Psychiatry Research Unit (1984) and the Social, Genetic, Developmental Psychiatry Centre (1994). His research areas include the genetics of autism, the effects of early severe deprivation on Romanian orphans, and the interplay between genetic and psychosocial risk factors. He is the author of 40 books (including *Maternal Deprivation Reassessed*), 400 chapters, and journal articles.

Yolanda Sánchez-Sandoval, PhD, is an associate professor of developmental psychology at the University of Seville, Spain. For her PhD dissertation, she conducted longitudinal research on adoption outcomes. Also involved in research on intercountry adoption, she has coauthored a training program for prospective adopters and a book for adoptive parents (*Adelante con la adopción* [Ahead with Adoption]).

Cassandra Simmel, MSW, PhD, is an assistant professor in the School of Social Work at Rutgers University. She conducts research in the areas of child maltreatment, child welfare services, and child and youth mental health and has published several chapters and articles on these topics.

Miriam Steele, PhD, was, when this research was done, lecturer and director of the M.Sc. in psychoanalytic developmental psychology, University College and the Anna Freud Centre, London. She is now associate professor at the New School University, New York. She has researched and published extensively on the intergenerational transmission of attachment and clinical and psychotherapeutic aspects of attachment theory.

Leslie Wind, MS.W, PhD, is an assistant professor at the Boston College Graduate School of Social Work. She has worked as a clinical social worker, administrator, and trainer in outpatient and inpatient settings. Among her areas of interest are child abuse, trauma, and adoption.